Caldwell and Company

CALDWELL AND COMPANY

A Southern Financial Empire

By John Berry McFerrin

Vanderbilt University Press

To the memory of
my Mother and Father

INTRODUCTION

THE THIRTY YEARS since the publication of this book—even more, the forty years since Caldwell and Company reached the pinnacle of its power—have included some of the most momentous events in this country's history. Everyone recognizes this, and it is unnecessary to document or elaborate on this statement. Among the more pervasive developments, undoubtedly, has been the change in economic conditions and in economic magnitudes. The failure today of a firm controlling a half billion or so dollars of assets would be significant. It is unlikely, however, that such an event would shake—perhaps "paralyze" is a better word—an entire state, much less an entire region. Generally prosperous conditions would help absorb the shock, and a half billion dollars is now about two days' spending by the military. By present standards, therefore, the Caldwell episode may appear insignificant.

I am convinced that it was not insignificant when it occurred nor when I was first writing about it. I am persuaded, if not convinced, that it is important now. I believe this is true, not merely because of its being a unique event in the business and economic history of the South, but also because important lessons may be learned from this tragedy. I think these lessons are applicable to the present and are likely to be applicable to the future, given the frailty of human beings.

There has been an almost complete turnover of business leadership since the heyday of Rogers Caldwell. These new leaders have largely been spared the scourge of a real depression, and one may hope that they and their successors will continue to be. I have sufficient confidence in the effectiveness of economic controls to think this will be the case for a good many years. Other types of catastrophes seem more likely to overtake us. Yet some knowledge of what occurred during this period before comprehensive Federal regulation of the securities industry by the Securities and Exchange Commission, the separation of commercial and investment banking, and the dominance of the commercial banking system by federal agencies may serve to make these present curbs on freedom of enterprise more palatable. More important, such knowledge should produce a more willing acceptance of the proposition that, despite many individual exceptions, business must be conducted on the basis of mutual trust. Failure to do so is not always as calamitous as the Caldwell debacle, but a dramatic case such as this may help emphasize the importance of this view.

If a subtitle were being selected for this book now, it would probably be "A Pioneer Conglomerate." In a very real sense, this is what Caldwell and Company was. The term "conglomerate" is more appropriate than the more restrictive term "congeneric," which is now frequently applied to financial organizations. If Caldwell and Company had limited its acquisitions to banks and insurance companies and its activities to investment banking and the establishment of an investment company, it could properly be placed in the latter category. I would argue, however, that the acquisition of control of a professional baseball team, to say nothing of newspapers and a wide range of industrial enterprises, clearly justifies calling it a conglomerate. Its chief difference from present-day conglomerates is that most of these, at least the more visible ones, are publicly held. Caldwell and Company was not. Six months before its demise, as the text spells out, it merged by a stock swap with a publicly-held corporation, BancoKentucky Company. Caldwell and Company had expected to sell a part of this stock to raise money. Had this been successful, there would have been even this final characteristic of the present-day conglomerate. The similarities do not end with the diversity of types of controlled companies. The shifting of funds from one company to another, the use of the new acquisition to make the whole look better, the apparent hope, if not conviction, that the upward movement of stock prices would offset any overoptimistic outlay made for an acquired company, all of which were so destructively characteristic of the operations of Caldwell and Company, are not without parallel in the modern conglomerate. In this sense at least, Caldwell and Company was thirty-five years ahead of its time. It may be that the managers of some of the present-day conglomerates will be aided by some knowledge of a pioneer in their field.

The development and crash of Caldwell and Company happened long enough ago to make it enticing to attempt to evaluate its long-run impact on the region it purported to serve. "We Bank on the South" was not without its implications. I do not believe that my over-all assessment has particularly changed during the passage of these years. The firm unquestionably aided, during its years of operation, in attracting capital to the region. Some of the capital goods, both private and public, financed by the company are still in use. It is impossible to say how much and by what rate economic development would have been delayed had these improvements not occurred when they did. Clearly the surge of new real capital into the South during and in the years following World War II was not materially influenced by the presence or absence of capital attracted by Caldwell and Company. Viewed in this way, the longer-run contributions of this firm to the development of the region seem relatively unimportant. Its constructive effects have been largely swamped by subsequent growth. Yet the improvements were important at the time. The South had been starved for capital for many decades. The activities of Caldwell and Company, while not curing this condition, clearly helped alleviate it. One specific favorable effect clearly related to the company's activities is the existence of several strong investment banking houses, some based in Nashville, some in other Southern cities, which, when the securities markets revived, were able to take advantage of the vacuum left by the Caldwell collapse. I am still of the opinion, however—and I emphasize that it is only an opinion—that the losses suffered through the collapse of the Caldwell empire more than wiped out any long-run economic contribution, and its net impact on Southern economic development was unquestionably adverse.

It is also appealing, after this thirty-year interval, to reassess the moral implications of the operation. I made some brief comments about this in the conclusion of the book. My judgment on this point has not mellowed. Were I rewriting this section now, I am sure my comments concerning the ethics of what was done and not done, both during the operations of the business and the legal actions following the crash, would be more severe. These men were not uninformed, inexperienced neophytes. The violations of trust agreements were present and were reported for several years by auditors and employees. Personal surety bonds to cover public deposits in the Bank of Tennessee were signed by individuals whose ability to meet the obligations of the bonds depended entirely upon the Bank's continuing to operate. With the failure of the Bank, the worth of the sureties vanished. I do not believe these and like matters can be expurgated under the shibboleth of "the losses occurred because of the Great Depression." These are personal judgments, however, and I am not inclined to push the point further.

II

I would like to emphasize that this is not a revision of the original book. It is simply a reprinting, and some of the material will obviously seem dated. No mention is made of regulatory agencies which would be intervening in the activities of the firm if it were operating today because they did not then exist. Amounts which appeared large, particularly salaries, at the time the book was written are now modest. Even the volume of business and the amounts of profits and losses are not now particularly impressive. The political alignments in Tennessee which are discussed briefly and in a doubtless oversimplified manner even for that earlier period are so different from the present situation as to be hardly recognizable. On this latter point, it should be mentioned that William D. Miller's biography of Ed Crump, *Mr. Crump of Memphis* (Baton Rouge: Louisiana State University Press, 1964), has a much more complete account of the facts regarding Crump's insistence that Scott Fitzhugh resign as Speaker of the Tennessee Senate in 1931 than is found in my book. There are numerous other such examples, but I hope that the reader will place himself in the 1939 period.

I do want to develop some of the matters, particularly legal actions, that were still pending in 1939, and, to this degree, update the book. The most significant of these from the standpoint of the Caldwell story were the efforts of the State of Tennessee to collect on the surety bond which Rogers Caldwell had signed covering the State's deposit in the Bank of Tennessee. The State obtained a judgment of some $4,354,000 against Mr. Caldwell in 1938. The activities on the part of Mr. Caldwell, Caldwell and Company, and the Bank of Tennessee that gave rise to this judgment are related in some detail in the book. The final reference to this is made in Chapter XIX, where it is noted that as of 1939 the State had accomplished little more than establishing the amount of the claim and having it reduced to a judgment. As indicated at that point, the most visible asset which Rogers Caldwell had that could presumably be attached as partial payment was his home, Brentwood House. I use the word "presumably" advisedly for, again as developed in the book, the house was paid for by the Bank of Tennessee and carried as an asset on the books of this bank for some three years but was actually located on land owned by James E. Caldwell, Rogers's father. This asset was removed from the books of the Bank at the time of the merger with Banco-Kentucky Company when Rogers Caldwell's indebtedness to his firm was canceled by a dividend of $1,200,000 payable to him alone.

The litigation by which the State finally gained possession of Brentwood was long and involved. The correctness of the first adjective, "long," is attested to by the fact that Caldwell and Company failed in 1930; the State's judgment was established in 1938; the Caldwells actually vacated the house in 1957! Even an admittedly sketchy account of what happened should show that the process was involved.

The issue was basically very simple. The father owned the land on which the son's house was built. The house was paid for by the son's Bank of Tennessee. The father conveyed the property to the son in a spendthrift trust legalized by an 1832 Tennessee statute which permitted property to be placed in such trusts, free from claims of any creditors of the beneficiary. The deed of trust was dated in September 1930 but was not actually registered until some twelve days after the Bank of Tennessee failed.

The State engaged in a two-pronged thrust to obtain Brentwood. ("Thrust" may be too strong a word for a campaign that took twenty-seven years.) One approach was legislative, the other by court action. The legislative attempt was a failure. The Tennessee Legislature in 1943 modified the old 1832 spendthrift trust statute to enable the State to proceed against property in such trusts where the State was a creditor of the beneficiary of the trust. Moreover, this modification was made retroactive. By this time, two additional trusts had been created by the senior Caldwells for the benefit of Rogers Caldwell, one in December 1937 and the other a year later. The State took action under the law to obtain all of the property in the three trusts, including, of course, Brentwood. The Supreme Court of Tennessee, from this layman's point of view quite rightly, would have none of it, at least insofar as the retroactive part of the statute was concerned (181 Tennessee 74). This approach, therefore, did not work.

This put the State back where it was in 1938 when the judgment against Rogers Caldwell was first established. It apparently had no claim against the land, but what about the house on the land for the construction of which the Bank of Tennessee had paid out, if one is to be precise, $350,133.80? Did the State have a claim for this amount? The Tennessee Court of Appeals in November 1944 settled this issue in favor of the State in an opinion that contained rather harsh language concerning the whole situation. The Supreme Court of Tennessee denied certiorari, thus leaving the issue as settled by the Court of Appeals. The decision in the Appeals Court (28 Tennessee Appeals 388) seems worth considering in somewhat more detail. I would even suggest that it supports the general conclusions I have drawn earlier regarding the ethical standards of the Caldwell operation.

The legitimacy of the spendthrift trust insofar as the land owned by James E. Caldwell was not questioned. This was protected from Rogers Caldwell's creditors. But the $350,000 paid out by Rogers Caldwell's Bank of Tennessee was another matter. The State maintained that, to the extent that Rogers Caldwell had, through his Bank of Tennessee, made a contribution to the trust, he had provided a trust for his own benefit, and that he could not under the law withhold his property from his creditors in this way. The Court agreed, saying that the transfer by Rogers Caldwell of $350,000 "of his own money into the trust property was a fraudulent conveyance, without regard to his actual intent, since its inevitable effect was to hinder and delay his creditors, existing and subsequent." Continuing, the decision stated that in this case

there are a number of other circumstances or "badges of fraud" evidencing an intent to hinder, delay, or defraud creditors. There was a secret agreement between father and son that the father would give the son this land in a trust beyond the reach of the son's creditors; the son was engaged in a hazardous business; the money was taken secretly and illegally out of the Bank to make the improvements on the land; this taking was concealed by false records showing the improvements as an asset of the bank; the secrecy and deception was [sic] carried on three years; when it was discovered that the improvements were not on the Bank's land, the improvements and the Bank's land [adjacent to the Brentwood property] were transferred through Caldwell and Company to Mr. Caldwell; the deed conveying this land [to Rogers Caldwell] was dated back to April 15 but was not recorded till August 4, 1930; the securities of Caldwell and Company were written up nearly $3,000,000 to pay for the improvements and the Bank's land and to clear Mr. Caldwell's enormous overdraft with his company; and the deed of the father giving the son the land in a spendthrift trust free from the son's creditors seems to have been made a few days before, but was not recorded until a few days after, the failure of Mr. Caldwell's companies.

These badges of fraud called for an explanation and put upon him the burden not only of showing he was solvent and in a position to transfer the $350,133.80 without injury to his creditors, but also of showing the entire good faith of the transaction. We think he [Rogers Caldwell] has failed to carry this burden.

The Court then proceeded to give the State a lien of $350,133.80 against the land and the authority to sell the land, if necessary, to enforce the lien.

This is the last recorded decision that I have been able to locate regarding the acquisition of Brentwood by the State of Tennessee. It was not the last action, however. In October 1948, the Brentwood property was put up for public auction to satisfy the State and the Federal government's liens against it. The State bought the property for $150,000, simply applying this to its claim against Rogers Caldwell, and paid the federal government $56,000 in a compromise settlement to remove its claim from the property. At the same time, the State allowed the Caldwells to continue to occupy the house. They were charged a monthly rental of $250. It was not until June 1957, however, that the State required the Caldwells to move out (Nashville *Tennessean,* June 16, 1957). Before they moved, the State sanctioned an auction of the remaining Caldwell horses and livestock and a part of the contents of the house. Under an agreement with the State, the Caldwells were allowed to keep half of the proceeds, about

$40,000 (*Tennessean,* November 3, 1963). A short time later, it was revealed that while the Caldwells had occupied the property for 110 months following the acquisition of its title by the State in 1948, they had paid rent for only 84 months. An additional judgment of $4,000 was, therefore, levied against Mr. Caldwell (*Tennessean,* May 9, 1959).

When the Caldwells moved, the State indicated that the place would be sold. The state property administrator estimated that the property was then worth between $125,000 and $150,000 and noted that the house was badly in need of repair. The State of Tennessee, however, retained possession of the property and established there the Ellington Agricultural Center. In some conversations with George Barker of the Nashville *Tennessean* in 1963, on which I comment later at greater length, Mr. Caldwell discussed the taking of Brentwood. "They had to pass some new laws to do it, but they finally succeeded. They thought they would resell it, but they couldn't—the title is still clouded by a lot of legal uncertainties, that's why they decided to just go ahead and use it." (*Tennessean,* November 3, 1963.) This statement of Mr. Caldwell probably sums up the situation about as succinctly as possible.

In addition to the contest over Brentwood, there were a number of other lawsuits that were still pending when this book was originally published. I am not aware of any further criminal actions, and I am virtually sure there were none. Some of the civil suits were of some notoriety and importance. In a footnote on page 228, reference is made to the suit by Knox County, Tennessee, against Fourth and First Banks, Inc., *et al.* (the *et al.* in this case covers five other Caldwell affiliated companies, the receivers of Caldwell and Company, nine individuals as well as certain trustees) to recover a loss of more than $560,000 which it had sustained on its deposit of $735,000 in the Bank of Tennessee when the Bank failed. The Bank was obligated to cover the deposit with securities pledged with the trust department of Fourth and First National Bank. When the Bank of Tennessee failed, the collateral which Fourth and First held to secure the deposit consisted of 25,000 shares of BancoKentucky and 25,000 shares of Shares in the South, Incorporated. The latter were eventually paid off at $7 a share, but the Banco stock was worthless. Knox County sued to recover, claiming that Fourth and First National Bank had been derelict in its duty as trustee in accepting this paper, that a conspiracy had existed between the leading figures of the various institutions involved, and that the County had been a victim of this conspiracy. The suit was filed in 1932. In fact, the first document relating to Caldwell and Company that I ever saw was the original bill in this case. After developing a comprehensive and voluminous record, supported by all possibly relevant exhibits, the suit was heard in the Chancery Court of Davidson County and was dismissed. On appeal to the Tennessee Court of Appeals, the decision in the lower court was sustained. Finally, however, the case reached the Tennessee Supreme Court which, in a decision handed down on October 14, 1944, held that the Fourth and First National Bank had violated the trust agreement in that this collateral would not have been accepted if the trustee had used reasonable and appropriate care (181 Tennessee 569). The conspiracy theory, though, got nowhere. It was denied both in the Chancery Court and in the Court of Appeals, and the Supreme Court did not go further into the matter. Actually because so much of the record in the case had been developed to establish the existence of a conspiracy, the Supreme Court assessed one third of the costs against Knox County. It also made the rather cogent statement that "the case should have been disposed of finally within three or four years." It actually took twelve years from the time it was originally filed.

There were several damage suits in Kentucky still pending in 1939, all arising from the failure of National Bank of Kentucky. One of these cases, referred to in Chapter XIX, *Atherton* v. *Anderson,* concerned the liability of the directors of the National Bank of Kentucky for certain loans which they had approved and which the receiver of the bank regarded as unlawful. In the final decision in this case, which was in the Sixth Circuit Court after the United States Supreme Court had remanded the case for rehearing, losses from loans to three borrowers, none connected with Caldwell and Company, were assessed against the directors. In the original suit, the receiver had sought recovery from the directors on losses sustained on thirteen major loans (99 Federal [2d] 883).

The more noteworthy cases in Kentucky, however, centered around the question of the incidence of double liability on the stock of the National Bank of Kentucky. In 1930, when the Bank failed, the Federal statutes governing national banks imposed on stockholders of such banks personal liability equivalent to the par value of the stock they owned in the event the assets of a failed bank were not sufficient when liquidated to pay off the depositors in full. With the establishment of the Federal Deposit Insurance Corporation, this double liability on national bank stocks, and on stocks of most state banks as well, was dropped, but in 1930 it was on the statute books. When National Bank of Kentucky failed, the receiver was unable to pay the depositors in full, so he proceeded against his stockholders. As developed in Chapter XIII, virtually all of the stock of this Bank was held by BancoKentucky Company. Anderson, the receiver of National Bank of Kentucky, filed an action against Laurent, the receiver of BancoKentucky, for payment of an amount equal to the par value of National Bank of Kentucky stock held by Banco. This action was successful, at least from a legal standpoint, for a judgment of approximately $3,750,000 was entered against Banco. Since only slightly more than $90,000 of this amount could be paid by Banco, financially the action was not a success. (*Laurent* v. *Anderson,* 70 Federal [2d] 819.)

Having established his right to the payment of the assessment on the stock, but having found Banco's treasury largely bare, the receiver of National Bank of Kentucky brought action against the *stockholders* of Banco for the assessment. The case, *Anderson* v. *Abbott,* eventually produced what must be regarded as a landmark decision by the U.S. Supreme Court on the question of the degree of protection from personal liability which the corporate form actually affords. "Piercing the corporate veil" is the phrase the legal profession bandies about.

The position taken by the receiver, Anderson, was that Banco was really just a subterfuge that had been interjected between the stockholders of National Bank of Kentucky and the Bank, that the stockholders of Banco were really stockholders of the Bank, and that they should be held personally responsible for the liability on the stock, since Banco itself was unable to pay. It should, at this point, be noted that Banco stock was held by individuals who had received their Banco stock in exchange for their participation certificates in the trust owning the stock of the bank and the stock of Louisville Trust Company, and also by individuals who had bought Banco stock for cash. Actually, Banco had raised $9,000,000 in cash through the sale of its stock, albeit some $6,000,000 of these sales was financed by the Bank. Anderson had no success in the lower courts. In March 1940, the District Court held that "they are not stockholders of the Bank if Banco was an operating company and not merely a holding company." After citing Banco's activities, the Court satisfied itself that Banco did not fall into the latter category. "Banco was established for its avowed purposes, with no thought, on the part of any of its organizers, of avoiding double liability on their bank stocks, hence the stockholders of Banco were not liable." The decision contained one sentence at least the second part of which is not likely to be questioned. "They were suffering not so much from fear of impending disaster, but from a Napoleonic complex not uncommon to the times." (*Anderson* v. *Abbott,* 32 Federal Supplement 328.)

Some two years later, in March 1942, the Sixth Circuit Court of Appeals upheld the lower court, again relying heavily upon the activities other than the acquisition of National Bank of Kentucky in which Banco had engaged. (*Anderson* v. *Abbott,* 127 Federal [2d] 696.) At the beginning of his decision, the Judge rather wearily stated: "This court must again travel the tangled trail of ramifications resultant from the failure of the National Bank of Kentucky."

When the case reached the United States Supreme Court, the script changed. The decision came in March 1944, almost fourteen years after the Bank had failed and long after Congress had removed double liability from national bank stocks. Justice Douglas wrote the majority opinion; Justice Jackson the minority opinion, and the Court divided five to four. But the majority opinion levied an assessment against the stockholders of Banco, both those who had received their stock through exchange and those who had bought it outright for cash. The position taken by Justice Douglas is perhaps best epitomized by the following: "When after the sale, he [the stockholder] retains through his transferee an investment position in the bank, including control, he cannot escape the statutory liability if his transferee does not have resources commensurate with the risks of those holdings. The law has been edging toward that result." This decision seemed to have pushed it the rest of the way. Continuing, he added, "The device used here can be so readily utilized in circumvention of the statutory policy of double liability that the stockholders of the holding company rather than the depositors of the subsidiary banks must take the risk of the financial success of the undertaking." He thus removed the insulation from personal liability from claims of creditors normally afforded by the corporate form. He emphasized that to do otherwise would result in using the corporate form to contravene public policy. "It has often been held that the interposition of a corporation will not be allowed to defeat a legislative policy, whether that was the aim or only the result of the arrangement." (*Anderson* v. *Abbott,* 321 United States 349.) Subsequently, the lower courts, in conformity with this decision, determined the assessments to be levied against the Banco stockholders.

One final episode seems noteworthy. On page 243, it is mentioned that in 1937 Rogers Caldwell and his father, James E. Caldwell, had acquired control of Apex Oil Corporation, and I wrote that, thus, one of the less-important industrial corporations which Caldwell and Company had financed was being used as a vehicle for Rogers Caldwell to attempt a business and financial comeback. Meredith Caldwell, a brother, was also a participant in this venture. It was not successful. By 1940 it was in bankruptcy, and in 1947 the Tennessee Supreme Court took a rather jaundiced view of the whole undertaking (*Dale* v. *Thomas H. Temple Company, et al.,* 186 Tennessee 69).

Briefly, according to the court decision, this is what happened. In 1937, Edward Potter Jr., the dominant figure in the Commerce Union

Bank of Nashville, sold the control of Apex to a corporation set up by the Caldwells for this purpose. The price of the stock was $285,000. Potter accepted some Fourth and First Banks, Inc., stock for the downpayment and took promissory notes of $225,000 for the balance. Potter paid $1 per share for the last 28,333 shares which he purchased from his bank's Commerce Union Company some two weeks before he sold it to the Caldwells for $2.81¼ per share. Soon the payments on the notes were in arrears, but this was worked out. There were the usual multilevels of corporations—the Court referred to at least some of them as dummy—and there was the characteristic shifting of funds from one corporation to another. As early as 1939, some two years after the Caldwells took over, a minority stockholder asked for a receivership. This was denied, partly at least because of the position taken by Potter, who assured the Court that no such action was justified. A year later, however, another minority stockholder was successful. The receiver brought suit against the Caldwells, several of their companies, and Potter and his associates, claiming conspiracy, fraud, and unjust enrichment. In general, the Tennessee Supreme Court sustained the stockholder's position. The Court agreed that a conspiracy did indeed exist, that there had been acts which bore the "badge of fraud," and that there had been unjust enrichment. A mention of two of the items producing judgments against the defendants will suffice. One was that the funds the Caldwells were using to pay Potter for his stock were actually being taken from Apex Oil Corporation. Thus, we get again the pattern characteristic of so many of the Caldwell and Company acquisitions; namely, the funds of the acquired firm being used to finance the transference of its ownership. The second item was the recovery of salaries paid to Rogers, James E., and Meredith Caldwell amounting to more than $65,000. In levying this judgment, the Court had some rather harsh words for the defendants: "The Courts below have concurred in finding that the only service the Caldwells rendered Apex was the wrecking of that corporation by misappropriation of its corporate assets for their personal benefit. Therefore ... they were not entitled to salaries." It is not clear from the record just how active Rogers Caldwell was in this operation. He generally did not assume any titles, though he was a director of at least one of the corporations. If the amounts of the salaries for each of the Caldwells are any criterion by which to judge his degree of activity, he was the head man. The amount of the salary of each of the three Caldwells as stated in the decision was as follows: James E., $12,056; Meredith, $16,401; and Rogers, $36,915. By the date of this decision, 1947, James E. Caldwell had died. Rogers was, of course, still living in Brentwood.

III

When Mr. and Mrs. Rogers Caldwell moved from Brentwood they occupied an antebellum house in Franklin, Tennessee, until they died; Mr. Caldwell in October 1968 and Mrs. Caldwell some seven years earlier. Luke Lea, the major figure associated with Caldwell, died in 1945. While Mr. Caldwell had a wide circle of friends whom he saw frequently, he apparently generally shunned publicity. In 1963, however, he granted a series of interviews to George Barker, a reporter and feature writer on the Nashville *Tennessean*. Barker then wrote a three-part series on Caldwell for the Sunday magazine supplement of the *Tennessean* (October 20, 27, November 3, 1963). In this series Barker reported several statements of Caldwell on which I would like to comment.

One is the statement, which Barker notes was made with "surprising candor," that he, Caldwell, could have had the appointment to the U.S. Senate when Tennessee Senator Lawrence D. Tyson died in office in September 1929. According to the Caldwell statement, as reported by Barker, Governor Horton offered the seat to Luke Lea who turned it down publicly. "Then Lea came to me and said, 'Caldwell, how would *you* like to go to the Senate?' I told him I didn't want to go. I was making too much money. I finally arranged it for William E. Brock, the Chattanooga candy-maker, to finish Tyson's term. Of course, we elected Cordell Hull at the next regular election." I did not hear this story when I was doing my original research. It illustrates further the political power of Lea and Caldwell during the Horton administration. The phrase "we elected Cordell Hull" is also interesting. Hull, in his memoirs (page 135), noted the strong opposition he received from both Luke Lea and Ed Crump in his 1930 race for the Senate. He also related that he defeated Luke Lea's renomination for the Senate in 1915.

Caldwell's concern with and influence on political affairs is also indicated by his admission that Caldwell and Company and the Bank of Tennessee "should have collapsed a week before they did. But it was the end of October 1930, and we were afraid of what effect the bank closing would have on Governor Horton's re-election. We held out. We stayed open until the day after Horton was elected."

Mr. Caldwell was also reported to have stated that "the millions that were lost were Caldwell and Company millions. Outside a few small bills, I didn't owe anybody anything, not personally." This is a rather fascinating point of view. Limiting the discussion simply to the surety bonds covering the deposits of the State of Tennessee in the Bank of Tennessee, Rogers Caldwell personally signed those bonds. The State obtained a judgment against him personally for more than $4,000,000. In order to prevent the statute of limitations from voiding the judgment, it was renewed in 1949 and again in 1959. At the latter date, the amount of the State's claim against Mr. Caldwell had grown, through accrual of interest, to more than $11,000,000 (*Tennessean,* May 9, 1959). I have not calculated the exact amount by which the claim increased between 1959 and the date of Caldwell's death in 1968, but it would by that time have been approaching $20,000,000. Mr. Caldwell assumed personal responsibility for the debts of his corporation by signing the surety bonds. I find it difficult not to regard this as a personal debt.

The final point in the interviews with Mr. Barker on which I want to comment is more personal. Barker notes the publication of my book and then adds, quoting Caldwell, "The young man never came to see me. He was writing from the depths of the Depression and everything looked its worst. Political critics of the Horton administration helped the writer interpret certain things." The fact that Mr. Caldwell had said that I did not come to see him was repeated in his obituary in the *Tennessean* (October 10, 1968). This is simply not the case. I shall be the first to admit that my conversations with Mr. Caldwell added little—nothing, in fact—to my knowledge of his company. Actually, however, I spoke with him three times. First, I met him briefly in the spring of 1935 before I began my research; the final meeting, also very brief, was some two years later when he was involved in the operations of Apex Oil Corporation. Had these been the only two visits, I would have to accept his statement as true, at least in spirit. But the other time I saw him—my second visit— was quite different. While I was engaged in the original research in Nashville in the summer of 1935, Mr. T. G. Donovan, whose help in the original undertaking is acknowledged, but perhaps not sufficiently, in the preface of the book, thought that I should see Brentwood House. He regarded himself as sufficiently intimate with Mr. Caldwell to suggest that he and I be invited out there some evening for dinner. The gracious invitation was extended and on the appointed day we presented ourselves there and were very courteously and pleasantly welcomed by Mr. and Mrs. Caldwell. They showed me the house, or at least part of it, and the stables, which were then largely depleted, and served me an excellent meal. I remember being particularly impressed by the dessert. I also remember the beauty of the sunset from the great hall. But my efforts to turn the conversation to the affairs of Caldwell and Company were entirely futile. I remember well on our way home Mr. Donovan's remarking to the effect that if he had been head of the largest and most powerful financial enterprise in the South and knew that it was being studied he would certainly have had at least one story or anecdote to relate. I must say that Mr.

Caldwell was much freer with his conversation with Mr. Barker than he was with me. In fairness to him, however, when he talked with Barker, the legal actions in which he was involved were settled. This was far from the case when I was there. But "the young man" did go to see him. I wrote a letter to the *Tennessean* about this. While I received a reply, my letter was not to my knowledge published.

Mr. Caldwell's statement that "critics of the Horton administration helped the writer interpret certain things" is a judgmental rather than a factual statement. I don't really recall any such help, but perhaps without my realizing it I was influenced by individuals having this point of view. I would note, however, that the only two real blastings I received on the book were, one, from a reviewer who regarded Caldwell and Lea as scoundrels or worse and upbraided me roundly because I had not pictured them as such; and, the other, from a member of Ed Crump's family who thought I had maligned Mr. Crump. I am not suggesting that these were the only criticisms I received; far from it, but, again, these were the only real castigations.

* * * *

I hope the reader will forgive me for the obviously personal stand-point from which I have written this introduction to this new printing. Perhaps I can plead that I have followed the affairs of the company even in its "after life" for so many years that I have a personal as well as an intellectual interest in it. It is a privilege to be able again to acknowledge the help of the individuals named in the original preface. I have lost touch with most of them. Some have died. I am still indebted to them all in varying degrees. I will mention by name again only one, Neville McFerrin, who has been and continues to be my main source of help in all undertakings.

Gainesville, Florida
July 1969

JOHN B. McFERRIN

PREFACE

THE SOUTH has received much advice and some help from outside sources in its efforts to solve its numerous economic problems. Not infrequently, however, there appears a Southerner with ideas concerning the solution of these problems which he is able to put into effect, sometimes without and sometimes with considerable profit to himself. One such Southerner was Rogers Caldwell of Nashville, Tennessee, who in 1917 established Caldwell and Company to help Southern municipalities in the sale of their bonds. Soon his house was aiding in the financing of Southern industry and was attempting to strengthen several Southern banks and insurance companies, all of these fields of endeavor being taken over primarily to increase the profits and power of Caldwell and Company. As these new fields were entered, the practices the company indulged in, unfortunately, became dangerously unsound and in some cases clearly illegal. When its crash occurred in 1930, it had so pervaded the financial structure of the South that the losses sustained by this event more than wiped out any contribution the company and its founder had made to the financing of Southern enterprise. It does not necessarily follow that, because the attempts of one Southerner to cope with the South's problems met with disastrous results, their solution should be left to outsiders. Rather, it means that constructive operations which turn into exploitation, whether they originate from within or without, can result in no improvement in the economic well-being of the region.

The purpose of this book is to portray against the background of Southern economic development during the 1920's the history of an enterprise whose remarkably rapid growth and tragic collapse constitute a unique episode in Southern finance.

In attempting to achieve this purpose, I have had aid from numerous individuals. Above all, I am indebted to two men: Mr. Timothy Graham Donovan, former secretary of Caldwell and Company, who was in charge of the offices of the receivers of Caldwell and Company during the period I was in Nashville conducting the basic research for this book; and Professor John B. Woosley, Director of Research in the Department of Economics at the University of North Carolina. Mr. Donovan gave me access to many essential records, related incidents not found in corporate records, and directed me to valuable sources other than those in his office. Professor Woosley has given unsparingly of his time and thought to assist me in the organization and writing of the book through all of its various stages. To these two men I desire to express sincere thanks.

Messrs. J. D. Carter and Frank D. Marr, both former vice presidents of Caldwell and Company, and Mr. V. H. Kennedy, former auditor of the company, graciously furnished information to me in interviews. Others who have been particularly helpful in the obtaining of data, the aid of each of whom I desire to acknowledge, include Mr. Marion Wasson, Arkansas Bank Commissioner; Mr. R. T. Bugg, Tennessee Bank Examiner; Mrs. Finis V. Gold, Deputy Clerk of the Tennessee Supreme Court; Miss Margaret Hall, formerly a member of the staff of the law library of the University of North Carolina; and the following attorneys: Messrs. K. T. McConnico, J. V. Conner, John G. Heyburn, William H. Crutcher, Jr., J. Merrick Moore, and F. E. Hagler. Professors E. M. Bernstein, M. S. Heath, and R. J. M. Hobbs of the University of North Carolina and Professor R. B. Eutsler of the University of Florida have each read all or substantial parts of the manuscript and made helpful suggestions. The *Southern Economic Journal* has permitted me to include material I have previously published under the title of "The Kentucky Rock Asphalt Company."

I am more than grateful to my wife, Neville North McFerrin, for assuming much of the drudgery involved in the preparation of the manuscript and for her wholehearted support of the project.

While thus deeply indebted, I wish to assume full responsibility for errors of fact or interpretation. The study necessarily encompasses much that is controversial and more that is personal and partisan. I can but hope that I have maintained that degree of objectivity essential to sound judgment.

J. B. M.

Gainesville, Florida
December, 1938

CONTENTS

CALDWELL AND COMPANY

CHAPTER I

THE FOUNDING OF CALDWELL AND COMPANY

A NEWLY established Southern municipal bond house in the fall of 1917 was faced by at least two considerable obstacles to success. The more important and general obstacle, one that confronted bond houses all over the country, was the effect on the bond market of the entrance of the United States into the World War. To finance the war, the United States government appeared as the prime borrower in the capital markets for the first time in many years and to a large extent attracted the funds of those investors who normally bought municipal bonds. The superior safety and marketability of the Federal issues, coupled with the spur of patriotism that was freely and vigorously employed, assured the successful sale of these issues, regardless of what the effect might be on other types of bonds.

Facing competition of this kind, municipalities were forced to offer their bonds to yield a rate decidedly higher than Federal bonds or not sell them at all. Market values of the outstanding obligations fell and continued to do so as the financial requirements of the Federal Government grew larger. It was not until 1918 that the Capital Issues Committee of the War Finance Corporation was set up, but the feeling throughout the country that issues other than war loans should be postponed, coupled with the fact that if municipalities sold their bonds they must yield higher rates, was sufficient to reduce appreciably the demand on the money markets made by municipal issues. The successful sale of $2,000,000,000 of Liberty bonds at 3.5 per cent in June, 1917, and of $3,808,766,150 at 4 per cent in October of the same year is indicative of the willingness of the market to absorb these bonds and to let other issues have what money was left.[1]

Another obstacle to the success of a Southern municipal bond house was more local in character. It was that municipal bonds of the South were not regarded with unreserved approval in the bond markets of the country. The stigma attached to such bonds, due to a rather long history of defaulted issues, remained a sufficiently potent influence to make them relatively unattractive to investors. Municipal bond defaults in the

---

[1] *State and Municipal Compendium* (supplement to *Commercial and Financial Chronicle*), CVI (May, 1918), 5-8.

South began at least as early as 1839 when Mobile, Alabama, defaulted its bonds and the practice reached its peak after the Civil War as a result of carpetbag administrations in most of the Southern states. It was primarily the experience during this latter period that resulted in the generally lower standing of Southern issues.[2]

With the bond market overshadowed by Government financing and Southern bonds even in normal times considered inferior to bonds of most other sections of the country, the time seemed hardly appropriate for establishing a Southern municipal bond house. But such were the conditions when, in 1917, Rogers Clarke Caldwell, at the age of twenty-seven, launched Caldwell and Company in Nashville, Tennessee, to deal in Southern municipal bonds. In the space of thirteen years this firm became the largest investment banking house the South had ever had.

There were two factors, other than the personality of the founder, that augured well for the business. The first was the position of Nashville as a security market. Security trading in Nashville dated at least from 1857, when the security house of Thomas S. Marr was established. This house and its direct successor, the firm of Goulding Marr and Brother, owned by two sons of Thomas S. Marr, still continued in the security business there in 1917. Trading in securities had long been the chief interest of investors and speculators in the town. Whereas in certain Southern cities speculation in cotton was the dominant trading interest and in others real estate operations were most prominent, securities have received primary attention in Nashville. This has taken the form of trading in stocks and bonds listed on the New York and other exchanges as well as in local securities. Stocks of certain Nashville banks, and securities of railroads with their chief offices in Nashville, of the local street railways, of the old Cumberland Telephone and Telegraph Company, and of some local industrial firms had at various times been quite actively exchanged. Also a substantial part of the bonds of Tennessee municipalities, as well as those from neighboring states, was handled through Nashville each year. Due to this traditional interest in securities, Nashville appears to have been the logical place for establishing an investment banking house.[3]

The second favorable factor was the name Caldwell, which, while not the oldest name in Nashville business and financial circles, was certainly one of the best known. In 1870, at the age of sixteen, James E. Caldwell had come to Nashville, where he obtained employment in a wholesale

---

[2] Albert M. Hillhouse, *Municipal Bonds: A Century of Experience*, p. 42. Publication facts of general works are given in the Bibliography.

[3] This information has been obtained from conversation with individuals engaged in this earlier security business.

grocery house.[4] Finding it difficult one day to fill an order for millet seed, he proceeded on his own account to buy up the entire supply in the city, thereby cornering the local market. The next day he sold his seed for twice the price he had paid. The profit he made from this venture enabled him to start "shaving" notes. His activities from that time on were many and varied but nearly always profitable. In 1876 he went into the insurance business in which he remained active for many years. In 1883 he became interested in the Cumberland Telephone and Telegraph Company. Later he sold his interest in this company and in 1887 built the Glendale Street railway line in Nashville, which he sold in 1889 and again purchased a large block of stock in the telephone company. The following year he became president of the company, holding this office until 1913 when he became chairman of the board of directors, an office he held until 1925.

Meanwhile, Mr. Caldwell had also become interested in the Fourth National Bank of Nashville. Some eight years after coming to the city he had become a director of this bank and by 1912 was its dominant figure and largest stockholder. A merger of this institution with the First National Bank was inaugurated in 1912 and successfully carried through by Mr. Caldwell, after which he assumed the presidency and became the active head of the institution, the Fourth and First National Bank.

In 1910 one of Mr. Caldwell's younger sons, Rogers Caldwell, after two years of study at Vanderbilt University, wanted to enter business and his father gave him the desired opportunity by admitting him to his insurance company, a firm operated as James E. Caldwell and Son. The company wrote all types of insurance and Rogers Caldwell became primarily interested in selling surety bonds.[5] When counties and towns sold bonds for a construction project, he would get in touch with the various parties involved and write the contractor's surety bond. In this way he became acquainted with a large number of officials in near-by Tennessee communities, who at times requested him to attempt to secure bids for the bonds the municipalities intended to offer. His experience in doing this gave rise to the idea that a Southern house could be organized to deal profitably in Southern municipal bonds. This idea no doubt grew as

[4] Facts concerning the life of James E. Caldwell are taken from his autobiography, *Recollections of a Life Time.*

[5] Two sources have been available concerning these events in the life of Rogers Caldwell which led to the formation of Caldwell and Company; namely, T. H. Alexander, "A Rich Man's Son Earns His Own Success," in *The New South,* 1 (March, 1927), 23 ff.; and "Bill of Exceptions," v, 1-20, in the case *State of Tennessee* v. *Rogers Caldwell,* Davidson Criminal Law No. 14, in the Supreme Court of Tennessee, December Term, 1931. Cited hereafter as "Caldwell Bill of Exceptions."

Caldwell became more active in handling this type of business, and his experience with one issue for which he had presented a bid for a Chicago bank caused him to determine definitely to establish a Southern municipal bond house of his own.

Hickman County, Tennessee, offered in May, 1915, an issue of bonds and Rogers Caldwell was asked to get a bid for them. He succeeded in obtaining an offer from the Harris Trust and Savings Bank of Chicago and on the date of the sale, May 7, went to the county seat, Centerville, to follow up the bid. While he was there he received a telegram from the Chicago house withdrawing the offer. The sinking of the "Lusitania" the previous day had so upset the security markets that the bank felt it could not afford to make the commitment.

The experience made a decided impression on Caldwell. It revealed to him how sensitive the bond business of the South was to external forces. To him it appeared that whenever money tightened for any cause the South was the first to feel the stringency. He was impressed in this instance, as well as by his former experiences, with the great possibilities for profit in the handling of Southern municipal bonds because of the restricted number of bidders. Caldwell has stated that on his trip back to Nashville, after he had been forced to withdraw the bid of the Chicago firm for the Hickman County bonds, he resolved to establish a Southern municipal bond house.

For some two years Rogers Caldwell was content to carry on his bond business on a small scale through his father's insurance firm, James E. Caldwell and Son. No commitments were made for bonds in the name of the company but Rogers Caldwell earned small commissions by obtaining buyers for various issues. Under this arrangement the danger of being unable to secure a buyer for a given issue remained and, since James E. Caldwell did not want to add a bond department to his business and Rogers Caldwell wanted a business of his own, an entirely distinct organization, Caldwell and Company, was established in September, 1917.

A charter was obtained from the state of Tennessee on September 26, 1917, creating Caldwell and Company "a body politic and corporate for the purpose of dealing in, buying and selling securities, stocks and bonds" and authorizing a capital stock of $100,000. This capital was divided into 1,000 shares, with a par value of $100 each, all of which was owned by Rogers Caldwell, although directors' qualifying shares were issued to Dandridge Caldwell, Meredith Caldwell, and C. W. Caldwell, all brothers of Rogers, and to L. J. Trousdale, a relative by marriage. These men, together with Rogers Caldwell, constituted the original incorporators and directors of Caldwell and Company.[6]

The first meeting of the stockholders was held on October 23, 1917, at which time the directors were elected and the by-laws of the company adopted. In addition to the customary provisions, one section of the by-laws provided that "no officer or employee shall be retained in the service of the corporation whose expenditures seem to be profligate or to exceed his known income, or who is not sober and of good moral character." On the same date the first meeting of the directors was held and officers were elected. Rogers Caldwell became president and treasurer and Dandridge Caldwell, vice president. Colonel Harvey C. Alexander, who had been a bond buyer for a number of years and had agreed to work for the new company, was chosen as secretary.[7]

Most new corporations having only common stock are supplied with funds with which to begin their operations either from contributions of the incorporators in exchange for stock or from the sale of stock to the public. But such was not the case with this company. The entire capital stock of $100,000 was issued to Rogers Caldwell and his account with the corporation was charged with that amount. Thus the company began operations with capital stock of $100,000 and accounts receivable of the same amount. When the company bought its first issue of bonds from Robertson County, Tennessee, the bonds were hypothecated with the Fourth and First National Bank to cover a loan to pay for the issue, the loan being repaid out of the proceeds of the sale of the bonds.[8]

The first offices of the company were at 205 Third Avenue, near Union Street, in the financial section of Nashville.[9] The offices were small but sufficient at first for the volume of business and the personnel. Rogers Caldwell was the only director active in the business. He, together with Colonel Alexander, who devoted his entire time to buying bonds, and two clerical assistants composed the company's entire personnel.[10]

The fever of expansion began to show itself at a very early date in the company's life. In the early part of 1918 Goulding Marr and Brother was purchased by Caldwell and Company for a "nominal" amount.[11] Goulding Marr desired to retire from business and arranged for the sale

---

[6] "Minute Book of the Stockholders' and Directors' Meetings of Caldwell and Company." Cited hereafter as "Caldwell Minute Book."   [7] *Ibid.*

[8] Statement to the writer by T. G. Donovan, former secretary of Caldwell and Company.

[9] "Caldwell Minute Book."

[10] "Development of Caldwell and Company," a mimeographed pamphlet (undated) compiled by Caldwell and Company.

[11] "Nominal" is the word used by Rogers Caldwell in relating this transaction.—"Caldwell Bill of Exceptions," v, 15.

of the company. In the transaction Caldwell and Company obtained the services of Frank D. Marr, made him vice president, and placed him in charge of local sales. His long connection with the security business in Nashville and vicinity made him of great value to the new company. Also, Caldwell and Company obtained the banking house which had been occupied by the Marr firm, a much more desirable location than the offices occupied at first.

With Caldwell and Company's business increasing, additions to the personnel had to be made from time to time. A few months after the Marr firm was purchased, another bookkeeper was needed. James De-Witt Carter, a young draft teller at the Fourth and First National Bank who had made quite a favorable impression on Rogers Caldwell, was employed for this position at a salary of $175 a month and immediately became very active in the business.[12] The company's first branch office was established in the early part of 1919 in St. Louis. Edward J. Heitzeberg, who was then active in the investment banking business, was placed in charge of the branch.[13] Its operations were at first quite small but this office in St. Louis furnished the company early in its life with connections in a city where later some of its largest transactions were to take place.[14]

A final step taken by the promoters of the business during its earlier years of operation was the establishment in 1919 of the Bank of Tennessee, which was completely owned and controlled by Caldwell and Company. From the beginning, Caldwell and Company had bought bonds under depository agreements. These agreements provided that proceeds from the sale of bonds should be left on deposit with banks acceptable to Caldwell and Company until the funds were needed to pay for actual construction on the projects being financed.[15] In many cases deposits were left directly with Caldwell and Company. It was thought, though, that it would appear better if the funds were deposited with a bank. Yet Caldwell and Company needed these deposits as working capital if the business was to continue to expand. The solution of the problem lay in the establishment of the Bank of Tennessee.

The bank was chartered under the laws of Tennessee and had a capital of $200,000 and a capital surplus of $50,000. It occupied the same offices and had the same personnel as Caldwell and Company. Its existence as an institution separate and distinct from Caldwell and Company was in no way advertised to the general public, and it is no doubt true that

[12] *Ibid.*, pp. 18-20.
[13] "Development of Caldwell and Company."
[14] See particularly Chapter VII, *infra.*
[15] For further discussion of these depository agreements see Chapter II, *infra.*

relatively few people except those individuals who had business connections with the bank knew it existed. There were no signs on the building notifying the public of the location of the Bank of Tennessee, no tellers' windows, always little cash on hand, and usually little in its depositories. At no time did it attempt to secure deposits of individuals and its customers were limited to those municipalities, and later business corporations, which Caldwell and Company financed. Funds which were left on deposit with the bank were, from all practical considerations, on deposit with Caldwell and Company. The extremely important rôle of the bank in the company's development is revealed in its later history.

Very early in its existence the promoters of Caldwell and Company prepared for a period of rapid expansion. Prestige in the financial community was enhanced by the name of the firm and by the purchase of the old Marr house. Funds for operating the business were more readily obtained because of the establishment of the Bank of Tennessee. The men who were to help Rogers Caldwell with the executive direction of the business, namely, Carter and Heitzeberg, had already been brought into the company. These two men, as well as Rogers Caldwell, were young, aggressive, and ambitious; and all of them were determined to make a success both of the company and of themselves. The stage was set for the very rapid growth of the company.

Chapter II

MUNICIPAL BOND OPERATIONS

The obstacles in the municipal bond market which confronted Caldwell and Company when it began operations did not long continue.[1] With the issuance of the Victory Loan in 1919 the Federal Government ceased to dominate the bond market, thus giving state and local governments more favorable conditions for floating their issues. Then, too, the South at the end of the World War was about to go through a period of extremely rapid development, a fact which was of tremendous importance to Caldwell and Company not only in the development of its municipal bond business but also in all of its other activities.

The war and high prices brought a degree of prosperity to the South greater than any experienced since pre-Civil-War days. Cotton prices soared, tobacco production and manufacture strikingly increased, while expanding building activity stimulated notably the region's lumber industry. Although the break in prices in 1920 was a very serious blow, recovery was rapid and the South came back with renewed vigor. Construction in the region showed a remarkable growth. The volume of contracts awarded increased from $330,000,000 in 1921 to $894,000,000 in 1925, to $891,000,000 in 1926, and, during the three-year period, 1927-1929, varied between $775,000,000 and $800,000,000.[2]

The Florida land boom was an intensified sector of a movement which was felt in the entire region, but, just as Florida was swept to dizzier heights than any other state, so did the collapse of its boom leave it more completely flattened. Other states were affected by that collapse but for the South as a whole the results were not quite so devastating. From 1927 to 1930, however, the drop in the prices of agricultural commodities, particularly cotton, was making itself felt and business activity which had reached new highs began to level off and later to decline markedly. But from the close of the war to 1927, and in some respects to 1929, Caldwell and Company operated under ideal conditions for successful expansion.

[1] See Chapter I, supra.

[2] Taken from the *Manufacturers Record* for years mentioned. The data concerning the growth of industry in the South have largely been obtained from this publication. The South as defined by this publication and the *State and Municipal Compendium* includes the following states: Delaware, Maryland, Virginia, West Virginia, North Carolina, South Carolina, Georgia, Florida, Alabama, Mississippi, Tennessee, Kentucky, Arkansas, Louisiana, Texas, and Oklahoma.

A glance at the developments in the municipal bond market, particularly with regard to the South, will provide the necessary background for dealing with Caldwell and Company's operations in this field. In 1918, the year following the company's incorporation, the large borrowings of the Federal Government, together with the work of the Capital Issues Committee, reduced the volume of new municipal bonds to $296,000,000, the smallest amount issued in the United States since 1907. The decline in the volume of municipal issues in 1918 was general but the relative decline in the South was not as great as in the rest of the country. Total issues in the South amounted to approximately $75,000,000, or 25 per cent of the total for the entire country, a record percentage up to that time.[3] The explanation of this lies largely in the fact that the Capital Issues Committee apportioned issues on the basis of relative need, and the necessity for public improvements in the South was more pressing, but the effect of the existence of a Democratic administration must not be overlooked.

The withdrawal of the Federal Government from the market and the lifting of the restrictions of the Capital Issues Committee allowed the volume of new municipal issues to increase to $692,000,000 in 1919 and $683,000,000 the following year. In 1921 the billion-dollar level was surpassed for the first time, with over $1,200,000,000 of municipal bonds issued. This was a boom year for investment banking houses dealing in municipal bonds. Many investment houses which previously had done little or nothing in the municipal field found this the most active branch of their business, while the distinctly municipal bond houses had difficulty in obtaining sufficient issues to meet the ever increasing demand of investors.[4] The billion-dollar level of new municipal issues was maintained from 1921 through 1930, reaching $1,400,000,000 in 1925, $1,510,-000,000 in 1927, and varying between $1,415,000,000 and $1,487,000,000 in the following three years.[5]

While the volume of municipal bonds in the country as a whole was maintaining an exceedingly high level down through 1930, the percentage of this volume from the South changed materially during the period. The record high of 25 per cent of the total in 1918 was surpassed in 1919 with 32 per cent, while during the next seven years the South accounted for between 20 and 25 per cent of the total. In 1926 this increased to 27.5 per cent and in 1927, to 30 per cent. Thereafter the percentage declined, first to 25 per cent and then to 20 per cent in 1929 and 1930.[6]

[3] *State and Municipal Compendium*, cviii (June, 1919), 3-6.
[4] *Ibid.*, cxiv (June, 1922), 3-7.
[5] *Ibid.* for years mentioned.   [6] Compiled from *ibid.*

The generally increasing percentage of new municipal issues coming from the South until 1927 was due to the small previous expenditures of the region, to a greater percentage increase in the hard-surfaced roads in the South than in the country as a whole,[7] and to the South's comparatively more rapid urbanization.[8]   Finally, the Florida land boom was affecting the total by 1925, the new bonds from that state having increased from $38,000,000 in 1924 to $95,000,000 in 1925, $135,000,000 in 1926, and $105,000,000 in 1927.[9]

The decline in the percentage of bonds from the South after 1927 can be attributed to three conditions. First, the South after 1927 was issuing an amount of new municipal bonds more in line with its population and income, the latter amounting to approximately 20 per cent of the national income,[10] while the population of the section was approximately 24 per cent of the country's total in 1930. Second, the decline in agricultural prices, particularly in the price of cotton, was cutting Southern income and appreciably retarding municipal expenditures. Third, and perhaps more important, the collapse of the Florida land boom dried up the source of a substantial part of new Southern municipal issues, bonds from this state falling from $32,000,000 in 1928 to $13,000,000 in 1929 and $3,500,000 in 1930.

The increasing volume of bonds from the South that were sold during the twenties should indicate an improved position for these bonds. This is substantiated by the reduced differential in coupon rates between Southern bonds and those from the whole country. Thus, in 1923, 18.8 per cent of all new issues were sold with coupon rates of between 4 and 4.25 per cent, yet only 2.8 per cent of Southern issues could be sold at rates that low. On the other hand, while 19.1 per cent of all bonds had coupon rates of above 5 per cent, 34.8 per cent of Southern bonds were in this group. By 1929 the coupon differential was reduced to such an extent that, while issues with coupon rates of 4 and 4.25 per cent accounted for 16.8 per cent of the total for the nation and 6.7 per cent of the total from the South, issues with coupon rates above 5 per cent accounted for 19.6 per cent of the total for the nation and 21.5 per cent of the issues from the South. In spite of the fact that the regional differential existed throughout the period and more Southern issues were sold at the higher rates than at the lower, nevertheless the spread between rates on bonds

[7] B. U. Ratchford, "Public Debts in the South," in *Southern Economic Journal,* II (January, 1936), 21.

[8] W. J. Matherly, "The Urban Development of the South," in *ibid.,* I (February, 1935), 19.

[9] *State and Municipal Compendium* for years mentioned.

[10] M. Leven, *et al., America's Capacity to Consume,* p. 172.

from this section and from the country as a whole had definitely narrowed by 1929.[11]

Caldwell and Company's operations in the municipal bond field were at first closely restricted to a few Southern states.[12] Issues from Tennessee accounted for most of the business for several years. Expansion into other states soon followed, however, and by 1925 the company was well established in Alabama, Louisiana, and Florida. During the next five years these states continued to contribute a large volume of bonds to the company's total purchases, yet at the same time its activities were extended into almost all of the remaining Southern states. Greatest gains were made in North Carolina, South Carolina, Kentucky, Mississippi, and Texas. This growth in area is indicative of the expanding size and importance of the company.

During the first few years Caldwell and Company's operations in the municipal bond field were relatively simple. Colonel Alexander, as buyer for the house, chose the issues for which he would offer bids and kept in touch with the officials of the various issuing communities. This necessitated his being away from Nashville a great part of the time. As long as the volume of business handled was small, this raised no particular problems. At the home office Mr. Caldwell and his assistants managed the few details necessary and also handled sales, which at first were largely made to institutional buyers. As the company expanded its operations in municipal bonds over the entire South, other bond buyers were added and, while Alexander continued as head of these road buyers, someone at the Nashville office was needed to co-ordinate their efforts. For this job, Mr. Heitzeberg was brought in from the St. Louis office and made vice president in charge of buying.[13]

In offering bids for municipal bonds, Caldwell and Company almost always specified the condition that funds payable to the community from the purchase of its bonds should be deposited with banks chosen by Caldwell and Company. The desire to secure control of these funds more easily, led to the establishment of the Bank of Tennessee.[14] The

[11] Data compiled from *State and Municipal Compendium*. Conclusions are based on comparisons of the percentage of new issues sold at all coupon rates in the United States and the South from 1915 through 1930.

[12] Complete lists of the municipal bonds purchased by Caldwell and Company have not been available. This discussion is based upon a sample of issues bought by the company compiled from *Manufacturers Record*, 1918-1930, and "Report of Lee Douglas and Rutledge Smith, Receivers of Caldwell and Company" (hereafter cited as "Report of Receivers of Caldwell and Company"), Part I, in the action *Fred Dean, et al. v. Caldwell and Company* (hereafter cited as *Dean v. Caldwell*), No. 434 in Equity, United States District Court at Nashville. See Appendix A for summary.

[13] "Caldwell Bill of Exceptions," IV, 87-89.

[14] See Chapter I, *supra*.

bids further specified that the funds should be drawn out only when needed to pay for actual construction on the project being financed by the bonds. In the meantime Caldwell and Company controlled the funds, a fact which helped the company in one of two ways. If the funds were actually needed in the company's operations, they would be deposited in the Bank of Tennessee or directly with Caldwell and Company and used as the company saw fit. If they were not needed they could be deposited in some bank that would pay interest to Caldwell and Company for the deposit. Rogers Caldwell claimed that by using such a system the house could offer the bonds to the public at a somewhat lower price and thus aid in the development of a market for Southern bonds in general. He also claimed that, in offering bonds of small Southern communities to Eastern buyers, sale could be facilitated if the funds were on deposit with the Bank of Tennessee rather than in some local bank with capital of $10,000 to $25,000.[15]

To Caldwell and Company, however, the important feature of the depository agreement was the vast amount of funds made available by its use. From the standpoint of the development of the banking house, the importance of the depository agreement cannot be overemphasized. The scanty data that exist indicate that the company's municipal bond business alone had become highly unprofitable at least by 1928, probably much earlier. In 1928-1929 approximately $21,000,000 of municipal bonds were sold by the company on which the gross profit amounted to only $47,000. From this amount $152,000 had to be deducted to adjust inventory to market and $99,000 to write off worthless securities, leaving a total loss sustained on its municipal bond business of $204,000, before making any provision for expenses of selling, buying, or administration.[16]

In spite of such losses the company attempted to expand its municipal bond operations as much as possible to obtain the much needed funds furnished by the deposits, paying relatively high premiums for the majority of the issues it bought. Funds from municipal deposits increased from $1,500,000 on December 31, 1918, to over $5,000,000 on December 31, 1924. Six months later, as a result of a deposit obtained from the purchase of a $7,000,000 issue of the state of Alabama, the amount had jumped to $12,300,000. At no time during the next five years was the volume of state and municipal deposits quite so large, remaining in the neighborhood of $10,000,000.[17] The importance of these deposits is seen even more clearly when it is pointed out that they furnished between 50

[15] "Caldwell Bill of Exceptions," v, 117-20.
[16] "Audit Report of Caldwell and Company," June 30, 1929.
[17] *Ibid.*, as of dates mentioned.

and 70 per cent of the funds of the company between 1918 and 1926 and between 30 and 45 per cent the following three years.[18]

A rather suggestive side light on the company's policies is furnished by the manner in which funds of Louisiana municipalities were obtained. The Louisiana law required the deposit of municipal funds in banks of that state. This would have effectively prevented the purchase of bonds under the usual depository agreement had not a method of evading it been devised. This involved getting friendly Louisiana banks to receive the deposits and then redeposit the funds with Caldwell and Company which carried the funds in the name of the bank but earmarked for the particular municipal depositor. The Rapides Bank and Trust Company of Alexandria was one of the most frequent depositors of this type.[19]

The deposit of the proceeds of the sale of municipal issues with the Bank of Tennessee or with Caldwell and Company did not give unrestricted use of these funds to the investment house. In practically all cases trust agreements were executed covering the deposits. These provided that while funds were on deposit they would be secured by collateral, pledged with a trustee, sufficient to cover the deposit. Frequently Caldwell and Company served as trustee for deposits in the Bank of Tennessee, and the Bank of Tennessee was trustee for deposits with Caldwell and Company. Also the Fourth and First National Bank, headed by Rogers Caldwell's father, acted as trustee on numerous trust agreements.

The system worked out by Caldwell and Company to pay for issues purchased involved little more than operations between itself and the Bank of Tennessee. Caldwell and Company would purchase an issue of municipal securities and pledge them with the Bank of Tennessee as collateral for funds borrowed to pay for the issue. Then this borrowed credit would be deposited in the bank for the issuing municipality and the bank would pledge the bonds with Caldwell and Company, as trustee, to secure the deposit. The sale of the bonds to the public would furnish the actual funds needed to meet the withdrawals by the municipality. If the sale of bonds had synchronized exactly with the drawing down of funds, little actual cash would have been needed in the operation of the business, but since this was not the case a minimum cash margin had to be maintained.

The amount of cash needed, however, was reduced by the privilege of substituting collateral on the trust agreements. When these agreements would be first made, usually the actual bonds, the purchase of

[18] Compiled from *ibid.*
[19] Statement to the writer by V. H. Kennedy, former auditor of Caldwell and Company.

which resulted in the trust agreement, would be pledged, but these bonds could always be replaced by other collateral. When the company first made use of these trust agreements, substitutions could be made only with other municipal bonds. As long as this was the case Caldwell and Company's municipal bond business was not furnishing funds to carry on other parts of its operations. As it widened the scope of its business, however, it became imperative to use the funds in more speculative ventures. Hence, other types of substitution provisions would, whenever possible, be inserted in the trust agreements.

In some cases Caldwell and Company would get the depositor to accept as security a personal bond signed by the officers of the company,[20] but for most deposits securities had to be pledged. Under some of these agreements only municipal bonds or certificates of deposits in banks with a capital and surplus of at least $1,500,000 could be substituted for the original collateral, and written permission for the substitution obtained from the depositor and the trustee. Others provided for substitution of municipal bonds or other securities satisfactory to depositor and trustee. The most lenient substitution privileges specified the pledging of "other collateral satisfactory to the trustee."[21]

The looseness of this last type of provision is emphasized when it is borne in mind that Caldwell and Company and the Bank of Tennessee were each acting as trustee for deposits with the other. Such a contract gave Caldwell and Company all the latitude which was necessary or desired and it was used on all agreements when the depositor did not insist upon more rigid provisions. The practice of the company, under the lax type of agreement, was to secure the deposit first with municipal bonds and then to substitute almost immediately collateral composed exclusively of its general run of first mortgage and industrial bonds and its various stock issues.[22]

During the last five years of Caldwell and Company's operations, 1926 through 1930, it handled over 1,000 trust agreements with an average active list of about 150.[23] As early as 1926 the auditors of the company at the annual audit began pointing out irregularities in these trusts, only one trust being reported out of line at that time. In 1927 the auditors pointed out that in a number of instances the collateral pledged was less than the amount required, while in a few cases the opposite condition

[20] "Caldwell Bill of Exceptions," IV, 104.
[21] From a copy of memorandum from E. A. Goodloe to Rogers Caldwell, October 24, 1930.
[22] From a copy of memorandum from E. A. Goodloe to J. D. Carter and E. J. Heitzeberg, June 20, 1929.
[23] "Caldwell Bill of Exceptions," III, 75-76.

existed. They also mentioned ten trusts covering deposits of approximately $875,000 on which substitution of collateral had been made without the proper notices to the depositors having been given. By 1928 the condition had become aggravated. There were two deposits totaling $321,000 secured by only $76,000 of collateral, and substitutions had been made on nine agreements covering deposits of $1,548,000 where no notices had been given to the depositors as required. No improvement had been made by June 30, 1929, when it was reported that $1,332,000 of collateral was pledged on deposits totaling $1,626,800 and that $1,684,000 of deposits were secured by collateral which had been pledged without giving proper notices to depositors.[24]

The earlier trust violations probably grew out of the general laxness with which the business was conducted[25] and the inadequacy of trust records kept by the company. Later, however, trust violations arose primarily because of the company's need for funds. Municipal bonds that could be sold with relative ease were taken from trusts, and securities for which there was little demand would be substituted.[26] Thus it is evident that the company's expansion into the more speculative security fields which began with the first mortgage real estate bonds in 1923[27] resulted in placing the safety of its municipal depositors in a precarious condition, to say nothing of making those responsible for the situation criminally liable for breach of trust.

Closely allied to, but much more speculative than, its strictly municipal bond business was the drainage district bond business engaged in by Caldwell and Company. In a sense these bonds might be classed as municipals but the almost universal defaults among this type of bond warrant a separate treatment of them. The drainage bond established itself in American finance during the early twentieth century. Although not confined to the Mississippi Valley it was in that section that most of them originated, due to the estimated 25,000,000 acres of land there which would make exceptionally good farm land if properly drained.[28]

Caldwell and Company's activity in this field was limited almost completely to drainage districts which were located in counties touching the Mississippi River or drained by the small streams that flow directly into it. The formation of drainage districts in Tennessee was based on a law passed in 1909 vesting power in the county courts to create these districts.[29] If after proper investigation the court decided it was feasible to

---

[24] "Audit Report of Caldwell and Company" for years mentioned.
[25] See Chapter v, *infra*.
[26] "Caldwell Bill of Exceptions," iv, 100.   [27] See Chapter iii, *infra*.
[28] W. E. Lagerquist, *Investment Analysis*, p. 541.
[29] *Public Acts of Tennessee*, 1909, Chapter 185.

construct a ditch, a drainage ditch district would be created with the power to construct and finance the ditch. Taxes to cover the cost of the project were prorated according to the benefits accruing to the particular plots of land drained. If the cost of the project was greater than the amount of tax that could well be levied in a single year, the drainage district had the right to issue bonds, to be retired with taxes collected the following years. Most of the districts issued bonds and a relatively large amount of these securities were sold during the early twenties.

Caldwell and Company was active in the underwriting of drainage district bonds from shortly after its establishment until 1923. During this period it underwrote approximately forty issues from West Tennessee districts, selling some $4,000,000 of these bonds.[30] The issues ranged in size from as low as $7,000 up to several hundred thousand dollars, while all bore coupon rates of 6 per cent. Debt service on the issues ran as high as $1.66 per acre in one district and was well over $1.00 in all except one, thus necessitating excessively high taxes.[31]

The operations in this field came rather early in the life of Caldwell and Company and were an important feature in the company's early growth. The bonds were all bought under depository agreements, which provided funds for the company in the same way the more conservative municipal issues did, and in general their high coupon rates, together with their exemption from Federal income taxes, enabled the company for a while to dispose of these bonds advantageously. This situation was later reversed when property owners stopped paying drainage taxes. Some of the ditches constructed proved to be highly beneficial while others were complete failures. But all were constructed at high costs and before many years property owners began to cease paying the excessively high taxes and one after another the districts defaulted on their bonds until by 1929 every such issue underwritten by Caldwell and Company was in default.[32]

When these defaults came, Caldwell and Company had no less than $385,000 of these bonds[33] which it had either not sold to the public or had bought back to protect itself with the investing public. Thus when in 1927 a bill was presented in the Tennessee legislature providing for the assumption and refunding of all drainage district bonds by the State,[34] it was heartily approved, if not sponsored, by Caldwell and Company.

[30] Memorandum from files of Receivers of Caldwell and Company.

[31] From data compiled from "Report of Receivers of Caldwell and Company," Part I, pp. 241-61.

[32] Memorandum in files of Receivers of Caldwell and Company.

[33] "Audit Report of Caldwell and Company," June 30, 1929.

[34] Senate Journal, State of Tennessee, 1927.

The passage of the bill would not only have benefited the company directly by making the bonds it owned worth par, but would have saved the investment of a large number of individuals who would doubtless have been more willing to continue to purchase securities from Caldwell and Company. Fortunately for the financial condition of the State, the bill failed to pass, and by the end of 1929 the company had had to write off as worthless the drainage district bonds it held.

The activity of Caldwell and Company in this field is typical of the company's policy during its entire history. Here was a speculative type of municipal bond that it was able to sell and it spared no efforts in marketing it. Conceivably the company could not forecast the breakdown of the drainage tax system. But the fact that every issue it underwrote defaulted is evidence that ably supports the view that the company was not adequately protecting the interests of its clients nor its own reputation as a sound investment analyst.

CHAPTER III

REAL ESTATE BOND OPERATIONS

ALTHOUGH it might justifiably be claimed that the company was remaining within the bounds of the municipal field when it underwrote and distributed drainage district bonds, Caldwell and Company was certainly leaving that field in which it was primarily established to operate when it began dealing in real estate mortgage bonds. This phase of the business dates from 1923 when a real estate mortgage bond department was created and four issues of these bonds were underwritten.[1] Caldwell and Company's entrance into the real estate bond field synchronized with the increased use of this type of bond to finance a very large volume of construction all over the country. Although the real estate mortgage bond had been used for a number of years to finance construction, the volume offered to the public in 1919 has been estimated to have been only $50,000,000, while by 1923 it had grown to $500,000,000 and by 1925 to $1,000,000,000.[2]

Having had little experience with this type of business prior to the World War, the average investment banker was being confronted with problems he proved little able to solve. Attempts were made by the Investment Bankers Association of America to set up sound policies with regard to valuation, percentage of loan to valuation, type and term of loan, representations in the descriptive circular, and other matters. As a result of these efforts the association in its 1923 convention adopted a report of its committee on real estate securities setting up definite standards in this field of investment banking. This report recommended that appraisals of property be made by independent local appraisers and that the circular offering the issue specify by whom the appraisal was made and the separate values given the land, buildings, and equipment. Loans should be set at approximately 50 per cent of the value of the property with 60 per cent as the maximum, the remainder of the funds to be raised by the sale of preferred or common stock of the corporation operating the building, for it was thought that the first mortgage loan should not perform the function of junior financing or assume the risks of operation

---

[1] "Development of Caldwell and Company."

[2] *Proceedings of the Fourteenth Annual Convention of the Investment Bankers Association of America,* 1925, p. 81.

and management. Finally, the report urged that all essential facts concerning the issue be clearly stated in the circular; that there be no evasion or silence on points which might lead the investor to the wrong conclusion.[3] In spite of the adoption of this report, the rapid expansion of the volume of offerings of real estate securities gave rise to serious doubts in the minds of some thinking investors and bankers as to the soundness of the real estate bond. The business was not infrequently being undertaken by houses irrespective of their resources or experience. Salutory regulation either by public authority or established canons of business practice was often lacking.[4]

In addition to the fact that many investment bankers were not very well equipped to carry on operations in the real estate bond field, there were other factors making for weaknesses in the real estate bond of the twenties. Bonds were being issued on the basis of the appraised value of the property with little thought given to its earning power. If these appraisals had corresponded to the salable values which experienced buyers of real estate would place upon the properties, they would have been of real use in the choice of real estate bonds. But unfortunately they were frequently artificial valuations, to which the appraisers were willing to attach their names for a fee and whose only function was to deceive the investor as to the equity behind the bond. Further, where estimated earnings were used in the offering of bonds, they were usually based upon abnormally high rentals and complete occupancy of the building. Finally, the real estate bonds issued in the twenties were on buildings constructed at high costs, the sharp drop of which in the thirties reduced the replacement cost of many buildings below the amount of bonds outstanding.[5]

The inevitable collapse of the real estate bond was making itself felt as early as 1928 when there were $36,229,000 of real estate bonds in default. By 1929 this amount had grown to $59,755,000 and by 1933 had reached the staggering sum of $995,017,000.[6]

Caldwell and Company had been operating only five years when it entered the real estate mortgage bond field and hence its ability to cope with the problems involved was uncertain and its policies were exceedingly questionable. Appraisal of the land was usually made by some outside party whose name might or might not be given on the circular.

[3] *Proceedings of the Twelfth Annual Convention of the Investment Bankers Association of America*, 1923, pp. 246-53.

[4] *Proceedings of the Fourteenth Annual Convention of the Investment Bankers Association of America*, 1925, pp. 82-83.

[5] B. Graham and D. L. Dodd, *Security Analysis*, pp. 116-17.

[6] *Ibid.*, p. 647.

Valuations of the buildings were usually based on construction costs. The amount of the bonds usually approximated 60 per cent of these given valuations; but the authenticity of the valuations must be accepted hesitatingly. The circulars offering the bonds contained a maximum of cuts and descriptive material with a minimum of investment data essential to the prospective buyer.

Appropriately enough, the first issue of real estate bonds offered by Caldwell and Company was on the Harry Nichol Building in Nashville which, when it was completed in 1923, became the home office of the company. The issue of $400,000, 7 per cent bonds was secured by a first mortgage on the building and was carried as an obligation of Caldwell and Company on its balance sheet. The actual cost of the building is doubtful, figures ranging from less than the amount of the bond issue up to $489,191.[7] Even using the largest figure, the bond ratio amounted to 80 per cent.

Caldwell and Company underwrote sixty-eight issues of first mortgage real estate bonds totaling $25,487,500. Hotels and apartments were most important, accounting for seventeen issues and $10,482,500 of bonds. The other issues were distributed primarily among churches, hospitals, colleges, office buildings, garages, theatres, and lodges. The properties were located in all of the Southern states, while two hotels in Illinois were financed. There was a decided prevalence of high coupon rates, twenty-three issues having rates of 7 per cent; fourteen of 6.5 per cent; and twenty-two of 6 per cent.[8] Finally, the spread between the purchase price and offering price of the issues should be noted. For most issues the company paid 90 and offered them to the public at 100, while occasionally as high as 92 would be paid.[9] All issues were bought with the provision that funds thus obtained by the issuing company should be deposited by Caldwell and Company in banks of its choice until they were actually needed in meeting construction expenses.

The handling of the bonds under such circumstances placed the company in a position to make a large gross profit on this phase of its business and it is no doubt true that some of the issues were very remunerative. On the other hand some issues were difficult to move and at nearly all times the company had in its inventory a relatively large vol-

[7] V. H. Kennedy, auditor of the company in 1929 and 1930, stated to the writer that the building cost less than the amount of the bond issue. A report in the files of the receivers of the company gives the above figure. The audit report of December 31, 1923, gives $456,514.

[8] Compiled from a memorandum in the files of the Receivers of Caldwell and Company. A complete list of real estate bonds originated and underwritten by Caldwell and Company is given in Appendix B.

[9] Statement of T. G. Donovan to the writer.

ume of bonds of this type. On the whole, though, from the standpoint of Caldwell and Company, the real estate mortgage bond business constituted a very satisfactory part of its business until 1929.

By that year the defaults that were beginning to become all too prevalent in real estate bonds as a whole did not leave Caldwell and Company's issues unaffected. The first Caldwell issue to default was that of the Wolford Hotel in Danville, Illinois. To meet this situation, early in 1929 a reorganization was arranged and Caldwell and Company guaranteed the bonds to the amount of $425,000.[10] As other issues began defaulting it was quite impracticable for the company to continue this policy of guaranteeing the issues and no more were handled in this way. By October, 1929, companies which had issued $5,292,000, or 20 per cent of the real estate bonds underwritten by Caldwell and Company, were in arrears on either interest or sinking fund payments or both. These issues included those of the Associated Motor Terminals of St. Louis; the Bankhead Hotel in Birmingham; the Lookout Mountain Hotel on Lookout Mountain, just outside of Chattanooga; the Hotel Prichard of Huntington, West Virginia; the Broadview Hotel in East St. Louis; and the National Memphis Garage.[11]

Two of these issues illustrate the poor security upon which many of the bonds underwritten by Caldwell and Company were based. The Lookout Mountain Hotel was constructed on a rather out-of-the-way location on Lookout Mountain, in competition with another resort hotel on the mountain which was much more strategically located. The new hotel was to be very exclusive, appealing to a limited clientele. It opened in June, 1928, to the music of Paul Whiteman's orchestra but thereafter remained quite dead. It operated only a few months each year and failed to open between 1931 and the summer of 1936. The result was of course extremely heavy losses for the bondholders. The National Memphis Garage was located near one of the largest free parking areas in any city in the South. It set its prices, originally, higher than the general level in the city and attempted to attract customers by its uniformed attendants, its unique floor arrangement, and officious but none too efficient service. The free parking area constituted too much competition for it and, although it has operated continuously, at no time has it earned enough to make the bonds on the building attractive even from a speculative standpoint.

Caldwell and Company attempted to improve its real estate bond

[10] "Caldwell Minute Book," Meeting of the Board of Directors, April 17, 1929.

[11] List appended to a letter from L. B. Stevens, manager of the real estate mortgage bond department, to Rogers Caldwell, E. J. Heitzeberg, and J. D. Carter, October 18, 1929.

operations by reorganizing that department of its business late in 1929 and placing one of its minor officials, L. B. Stevens, in charge. Stevens had some rather definite ideas as to how the department should be conducted and in a letter to the executives of the company on October 18, 1929, he said in part:

It appears to me that a matter of great importance is the outlining of an efficient and effective policy of procedure on loans in arrears. In the past we have been somewhat reluctant to face a troublesome situation and give the time and attention required to cope with it successfully. This has been due largely to the lack of available time on the part of our officers together with the failure of this department to handle such matters aggressively. In my opinion it is very essential that we face this situation squarely and conclude it as rapidly as possible and I am sure that such a policy will inspire our bondholders with confidence rather than a lack of it. I realize the effect on sales of the formation of protective committees and will therefore avoid such procedure when possible to do so.

I also feel that a certain percentage of trouble may be avoided in the future through taking preventative measures and giving necessary attention at the proper time. General conditions in the various parts of the country will change from time to time and we shall probably always be faced with a certain amount of slow collections. Preventative measures should be taken whenever it is first apparent that an issue may get into difficulty. These may take the form of segregation of income, change in management, sale of property, or entire reorganization. The greater part of our difficulties have resulted not from lack of security or potential earning power of various projects, but from poor management, financing, and organization on the part of the owning companies. There are of course a few instances where the underlying security has been overestimated. [A mild admission of a glaringly apparent fact.]

A real opportunity presents itself at this time to revise and revamp the operating practices of this department and to expand our former ideas of investigation and study so that future loans will be better risks. In approving or making loans you gentlemen depend to a degree upon the reports of investigations and study conducted by individual members of the buying organization. I feel that the information which reaches you should be the summary of the best thoughts and ideas of respective members of each interested department of the organization.

Stevens advocated the formation of a holding company to buy in those properties which were already in difficulty and which would have to be sold at foreclosure sales, thus adding the operation of hotels, office buildings, etc., to the wide variety of enterprises which the company was directing at the time. The holding company was, of course, to manage the properties for the best interest of bondholders. Perhaps because such a policy, namely, managing companies for the best interest of the bondholders, by 1929 ceased to have much weight in the operation of Caldwell and Company and certainly because the company did not at that time have the funds necessary for carrying through the proposal, the holding company was not set up. Nor did Stevens have much opportunity to test his ideas as to the management of the department, particularly with respect to more rigid investigation, for the only construction financed after September, 1929, was a store building in Nashville occupied by Montgomery Ward and Company. This gave rise to an issue of $200,000, 6.5 per cent first mortgage bonds dated April 1, 1930, which were never offered to the public.

The real estate mortgage bond department of Caldwell and Company enjoyed its greatest success during the six-year period, 1923 to 1928. It was during this time that the bulk of the issues was underwritten and the difficulties that arose were at a minimum. It was in no sense the outstanding department of the company, the volume of issues handled not approaching the volume of municipal bonds and being smaller than the volume of other corporation securities underwritten by the company. But this part of the business was of great importance in introducing the executives of the company to the problems involved in corporate financing and served as a stepping stone from municipal bonds to industrial securities.

CHAPTER IV

INITIAL INVESTMENTS IN FINANCIAL
INSTITUTIONS

LESS THAN a year after Caldwell and Company was chartered it made a substantial investment of a permanent nature in the stock of the Fourth and First National Bank of Nashville which was followed in the period between 1918 and 1925 by the purchase of the controlling interest in two life insurance companies, the Cotton States Life Insurance Company and the North American National Life Insurance Company. All of these investments provided the company with sources of greatly needed funds and outlets for some of its securities.

THE FOURTH AND FIRST NATIONAL BANK

The Fourth and First National Bank, as has been mentioned, arose from a merger of the First National Bank and the Fourth National Bank of Nashville. The two banks at that time already had a long history. The First National Bank, chartered in 1863, was the one-hundred-and-fiftieth national bank organized in the United States. Chartered after Nashville had been taken by Federal troops, one of its chief functions was to act as a depository and paymaster for United States soldiers. Three years later, in 1866, the Fourth National Bank of Nashville was chartered. These banks served the city and surrounding territory satisfactorily until 1893. In the depression of that year the Fourth National Bank was the only one in the city that did not suspend operations, a fact which naturally enhanced its position in banking circles.[1]

James E. Caldwell was elected to the board of directors of the Fourth National Bank in 1878. His profitable business ventures enabled him to expand his interests in this bank and to become its largest stockholder. He was also a large stockholder in the First National Bank and, when the president of this latter institution resigned to accept a position in St. Louis, Mr. Caldwell was asked by the directors of the two banks to merge them and take over the presidency of the new bank. This was accomplished on July 1, 1912,[2] when the bank began operations with total

---

[1] Typewritten memorandum concerning history of these two banks, compiled by the Fourth and First National Bank. Not dated.

[2] Caldwell, *op. cit.*, p. 90.

assets of $14,500,000 and deposits of $8,700,000. By 1920 these two figures had grown to $38,000,000 and $13,000,000 respectively.[3]

It seems only natural that by virtue of family ties Rogers Caldwell would look to this bank as a source of funds for his new business. But to strengthen these ties he invested a part of the early profits of his firm in the stock of the bank and was elected to its board of directors. At the close of 1918 Caldwell and Company had stock in the Fourth and First National Bank totaling $100,282, an amount which had increased to $445,566 by June 30, 1925.[4] This was of sufficient size to enable Rogers Caldwell to use the bank somewhat to the advantage of his company. Data are not available as to the volume of bonds sold to the bank by Caldwell and Company but it was probably considerable, nor as to the total volume of loans obtained by the company from the bank; but loans payable to the bank as of certain balance-sheet dates amounted to $37,600 on December 31, 1918, $164,000 on December 31, 1921, $242,000 on December 31, 1922, and $250,000 on December 31, 1923.[5] In no instances do these amounts exceed the legal maximum for national bank loans to one party but they do indicate a growing volume of loans made by the bank to Caldwell and Company. Further, the company's investment in the stock of this bank yielded relatively large dividends which were appropriated by Rogers Caldwell himself, until this practice was noted by auditors in 1927. To straighten up the accounts a dividend equal to the income from the Fourth and First National Bank stock was declared by the directors of Caldwell and Company and, since all of this dividend went to Rogers Caldwell, his account with the company so far as the appropriated dividends on the Fourth and First National stock were concerned was paid.[6] Finally Caldwell and Company was benefited by the rise in the market price of its Fourth and First National stock from $225 a share in 1920 to $321 in 1925.[7]

Meanwhile the bank was enjoying a period of marked expansion. There was a severe shrinkage of total assets in 1921 from $38,000,000 to $22,000,000, due primarily to the sale at a good profit of Liberty bonds which the bank had bought with borrowed funds. Deposits, however, dropped less than $2,000,000, from $13,200,000 to $11,400,000. After 1921 there was a constant growth in the size of the bank and by 1925 deposits had increased to nearly $22,000,000. Capital stock was increased from

[3] Statistics relating to Fourth and First National Bank are from *Reports of the Comptroller of the Currency*, unless otherwise cited.

[4] "Audit Report of Caldwell and Company," as of dates given.

[5] *Ibid.*

[6] "Caldwell Minute Book," Meeting of the Board of Directors, June 30, 1927.

[7] *Poor's Railroad and Bank Section*, 1926.

$1,100,000 when the bank was established in 1912 to $1,250,000 in 1922, to $1,400,000 in 1924, and to $1,500,000 in 1925.

Accompanied by this growth in deposits was a growth in the bank's physical plant. It erected an elaborate banking house on the corner of Fourth and Union streets in the heart of Nashville's financial district, directly across the street from Caldwell and Company's office in the Harry Nichol Building. The bank also established a number of branch offices throughout the city and in addition established the Fourth and First Bank and Trust Company. This was a bank chartered by the state of Tennessee, all the stock of which was owned by Fourth and First National Bank. The state bank had deposits of approximately $6,000,000 and capital of $250,000.

This expansion program placed the Fourth and First National Bank among the leaders in the banking circles of Nashville, a position shared with the American National Bank which had engaged in a similar expansion program and had deposits approximately equal to those of Fourth and First National. It also had an affiliated trust institution, the American Trust Company, with deposits of $4,400,000 and capital of $500,000. An intense rivalry existed between the Fourth and First National and the American National for supremacy among Nashville banks.

The Fourth and First National Bank was the first institution affiliated with Caldwell and Company and, while the investment house did not own a majority of the stock of the bank and did not dominate its policies, the two institutions were closely related and shared alike in changing fortunes.[8]

COTTON STATES LIFE INSURANCE COMPANY

The Cotton States Life Insurance Company of Memphis, Tennessee, was organized in 1913 and licensed to operate in Tennessee, Mississippi, and Arkansas.[9] In 1922 its capital stock amounted to $128,375, admitted assets to less than $600,000, and insurance in force to slightly more than $8,000,000. A very large percentage of the company's business was weekly payment industrial insurance. It also offered special policies for Negroes with whom a substantial part of its business was done.

Caldwell and Company acquired, in 1923, 45,750 shares of the capital stock of Cotton States Life, out of a total of 60,000, for $645,379.[10] The Caldwell purchase was followed by a complete revamping of the insurance company. Its home office was moved from Memphis to Nash-

[8] See Chapters VIII and XVI, *infra*.

[9] Information concerning Cotton States Life Insurance Company has been obtained from *Unique Manual Digest of American Life Companies,* unless otherwise cited.

[10] "Audit Report of Caldwell and Company," February 28, 1925.

ville and the company was placed in charge of Charles M. McCabe and Hillsman Taylor, two men associated with Caldwell and Company. Insurance in force, which had dropped to $6,000,000 in 1923, jumped $14,000,000 to a total of $20,000,000 in 1924, with a further increase to $23,000,000 in 1925. The increase was almost entirely in industrial insurance. Admitted assets increased to $947,000 in 1924 and to $1,116,000 in 1925, represented first by an increase in cash and later by an increase in bonds. Few companies that came under the control of Caldwell and Company were ever able to maintain a very large percentage of their assets in cash, unless it was deposited in the Bank of Tennessee.

The bonds owned by the company had never amounted to as much as $75,000, most of its assets being in mortgage loans. In 1924 bonds amounted to only $8,140 but by 1925 had increased to $358,140. The $350,000 increase in bonds was represented by only four issues of bonds which, no doubt, Caldwell and Company had sold Cotton States Life since the issues were from municipalities whose bonds Caldwell and Company had bought.[11] The concentration of such a large part of the company's funds in the bonds of only four municipalities violated a basic principle of investment, diversification of risks.

In 1925 the insurance company had cash of $240,257, of which $231,159 was on deposit with the Bank of Tennessee.[12] In addition the insurance company had loaned Caldwell and Company $40,000 in 1924, which was to be secured by $50,000 of bonds pledged with a trustee. The "Audit Report of Caldwell and Company," as of February 28, 1925, called attention to the fact that the securities were not pledged, the loan being "unsecured at that time, apparently without the knowledge of the payee." Such operations convincingly indicate that to Caldwell and Company the ownership of the insurance company meant the right to subordinate its interests to the needs of the investment house, with little regard for the insurance company.

NORTH AMERICAN NATIONAL LIFE INSURANCE COMPANY

The purchase of the Cotton States Life Insurance Company was followed in the latter part of 1925 by the purchase of the North American National Life Insurance Company of Omaha, Nebraska.[13] This company had been established in 1922 as the result of a reorganization of the North American Life Insurance Company. At the time of reorganization the company had capital stock of $100,000 represented by 100,000 shares

---

[11] *Report of the Commissioner of Insurance and Banking,* State of Tennessee, 1925, p. 33.
[12] *Ibid.*
[13] Information concerning North American National Life Insurance Company has been obtained from *Unique Manual Digest of American Life Companies,* unless otherwise cited.

of $1.00 par value, $13,000,000 of insurance in force, and admitted assets of $1,768,000. By 1925 insurance in force had increased to over $20,000,000 and admitted assets to $2,140,000.

The purchase of 99,662 shares of the common stock of the company for $508,384 in 1925 gave Caldwell and Company complete control and practically complete ownership of the company.[14] The executive offices of the company were moved to Nashville and McCabe and Taylor were placed in charge of this company also. Though the officers interlocked, there was no official merger with the Cotton States Life but the effect was practically the same. The policies of management, too, were the same. This is indicated by the fact that while the purchase of control of the company was made late in 1925, by June 30, 1926, the North American National Life had $183,000 on deposit with the Bank of Tennessee.[15]

[14] "Audit Report of Caldwell and Company," June 30, 1926.
[15] *Ibid.* See also Chapter VII, *infra.*

CHAPTER V

INTERNAL DEVELOPMENT: 1918-1925

ALTHOUGH the operations of Caldwell and Company in the municipal and real estate mortgage bond fields after 1925 have already been treated, it is desirable at this point to consider the developments within the company between 1918 and 1925. In spite of the purchase of control of two small insurance companies and of stock of the Fourth and First National Bank, through 1925 Caldwell and Company's activities were primarily in the municipal and real estate mortgage bond fields. The following year, 1926, denotes somewhat of a break in the company's development. This is seen, first, in the establishment of a corporation department which first carried on substantial operations in 1926, but even more clearly is it seen in the purchase of the control of the Missouri State Life Insurance Company in the same year. These events marked the beginning of a development which resulted in Caldwell and Company's bringing under its control numerous industrial companies, several large insurance companies and banks, an investment trust, and important newspapers, as well as establishing itself as a power in Tennessee politics. Hence the period through 1925 can well be regarded as that during which Caldwell and Company emerged as a leading Southern bond house and the period from 1926 through 1929 as that during which the company's operations were of such a nature as to make it an outstanding factor in the whole financial structure of the South.

The financial growth of the company can be traced satisfactorily only by bringing in some figures from the reports of the audits which were made of the company from time to time.[1] The figures that are given refer both to Caldwell and Company and the Bank of Tennessee. This procedure is followed because of the nature of the relations between the bank and its parent concern. Assets were frequently sold from one to the other and the two corporations were for most practical purposes the same and were regarded as such by executives and employees. About the only practical difference that existed was that the Bank of Tennessee was examined by the Tennessee Department of Banking and Caldwell and

---

[1] Financial data concerning Caldwell and Company have been obtained from audit reports of the company, unless otherwise cited. Summarized balance sheets and earnings of Caldwell and Company from 1918 to 1930 are given in Appendices C and D.

Company was not. Thus, of course, the two companies kept separate sets of accounts.

Changes in total assets indicate satisfactorily the rate of growth of Caldwell and Company. On December 31, 1918, after approximately fourteen months of operation, total assets amounted to $2,138,000. Two years later they had increased to $7,973,200 and approximately $1,000,000 a year were added the next two years. On December 31, 1923, total assets amounted to $11,649,400 and on June 30, 1925, to $17,700,000. Thus in six and one-half years, from December 31, 1918, to June 30, 1925, total assets exhibited the spectacular growth from $2,138,000 to $17,700,000.

Of the individual asset items, securities owned represented the bulk of total assets at all balance-sheet dates and changes in total assets and in securities were very closely related. Cash always constituted a relatively small proportion of total assets, varying between 1 and 5.5 per cent of the total. Only in 1923 did cash equal 10 per cent of total deposit liabilities. Among the receivables held by the company, which grew from $359,000 in 1918 to $2,195,000 in 1925, should be mentioned the account of Rogers Caldwell which increased from $120,000 to $181,000 during the two periods. Finally it should be noted that the company's holdings of real estate increased with the erection of the Harry Nichol Building and the acquisition of a relatively large amount of residential and farm property on the Franklin Pike, south of Nashville.

The funds for financing this increase of assets came from three sources: net worth, loans from banks and other institutions, and deposits. Net worth grew from $128,581 in 1918 to $1,282,590 in 1925. Eliminating the capital stock of $100,000 which during this period was represented solely by a charge to Rogers Caldwell's account, and considering only surplus, the increase was from $28,581 to $1,182,590. In 1918 surplus represented 1.4 per cent of the total funds in the business, and in 1925, 6.7 per cent, showing a substantial ploughing back of earnings when the growth of assets is taken into consideration.

Though these earnings aided the company in its expansion program, outside sources were relied on primarily and, of these outside sources, deposits, obtained through the purchase of bonds under depository agreements and through directing the funds of controlled companies into the Bank of Tennessee, were of chief importance. At no time prior to June 30, 1925, were deposits as little as 50 per cent of total assets and on June 30, 1925, amounted to 70.5 per cent.

There were two chief categories of payables: loans from banks and advances from the company's New York broker, Kidder-Peabody and Company. With regard to loans from banks, the company's first audit report, in 1918, shows loans only from banks in the two cities where it had offices, Nashville and St. Louis. By 1921, however, the company was borrowing from New York banks and in the next few years began to acquire funds from an ever increasing number of banks located not only in all parts of the South but in the East as well.

The funds obtained by the company from Kidder-Peabody arose at first from the fact that the New York house handled Caldwell and Company's stock exchange business, a type of business in which it was active for a few years subsequent to the purchase of Goulding Marr and Brother. This firm had had an active stock exchange business and Caldwell and Company continued to offer this service, although the volume of this business soon dwindled to small proportions. At first, though, Caldwell and Company carried a good many stocks on margin for its customers, which stocks were in turn carried for Caldwell by Kidder-Peabody. Later the New York firm began to take up Caldwell's participations in various syndicates and carry them until Caldwell could market the securities.[2] The relations with this house gave Caldwell and Company a strong connection in the East and enabled it to finance more easily its participations in the syndicates it was invited to join.

Caldwell and Company's total current liabilities during this period were at all times roughly equal to total current assets. For industrial concerns such a relationship would indicate an extremely poor financial condition. However, it is normal for bond houses to borrow heavily and as long as borrowed funds are invested in liquid assets no trouble should arise. On the whole, Caldwell and Company had built up a net worth as large or larger than its non-liquid assets and was investing borrowed funds primarily in liquid assets.

The expediency of Caldwell and Company's expansion policy must be appraised in the light of earnings, just as the expansion policy of any company must be judged on such a basis. Combined net earnings of Caldwell and Company and the Bank of Tennessee varied appreciably from year to year. In the first full year of operations, 1918, earnings amounted to $38,265 and the following year to $48,496. The depression in the early twenties cut earnings to $11,498 in 1920 and to $12,906 in 1921. During the remainder of the period down to June 30, 1925, earnings were much higher, amounting to $233,302 in 1922, $127,705 in 1923, $257,583 in 1924, and for the six-month period, January 1 to June 30, 1925, to $464,095. The large increase indicated for this last period was due

[2] "Report of the Special Commissioner upon the Intervening Petition of Devonstreet and Company for the claim of Kidder-Peabody and Company in the case Dean *v*. Caldwell." Cited hereafter as "Petition of Devonstreet and Company."

in part to the fact that certain accumulated profits on sales of securities were closed into the surplus account during the six-month period, although a part had been earned during 1924.

A comparison of earnings and surplus[3] indicates on the whole an extremely high rate of return. In 1918 earnings were 133.9 per cent of surplus, due to the very small surplus that had been previously accumulated. In 1920 the rate was 14.5 per cent and in 1921, 13 per cent, while in 1922 it jumped to 70 per cent. The following year, 1923, the rate declined to 27.7 per cent, but for the first six months of 1925 it was back to 39.2 per cent, indicating an annual rate for that year of almost 80 per cent. In short, Caldwell and Company had an excellent earnings record from 1918 through June 30, 1925, the period under consideration at present. When it is remembered that the company began operations with no capital of its own and in slightly less than eight years accumulated a surplus of $1,182,590 from earnings, the financial success of the company appears in its true light and the feasibility of its expansion program cannot be seriously questioned.

There were evidences of growth other than those shown through changes in the financial size of the company. Perhaps most obvious was the change of location of the business in Nashville. The rapid growth of the volume of its business and of its personnel made the offices obtained from Goulding Marr and Brother entirely inadequate, hence the occasion for the erection of the Harry Nichol Building at the corner of Union Street and Fourth Avenue—400 Union Street—into which Caldwell and Company moved on Thanksgiving Day, 1923. Not having expanded sufficiently to need all eight floors of the new building, the banking house at first occupied only the first floor, mezzanine, and basement. Later, however, as the company expanded still further it occupied the entire building with the exception of the seventh floor which was leased to its legal counsel.[4] The new offices were elaborately and luxuriously furnished, the lamps on the desks costing seventy-five dollars each.[5] Particularly well was Mr. Caldwell provided for, his first floor office being a richly furnished suite very suitable for this rapidly rising young Southern financier, and later his eighth floor office was even more elaborate and no doubt more difficult of access.

Another evidence of the company's growth was the establishment of branch offices in many of the larger cities of the country, these springing up at the rate of about one every six months. By the end of 1925 there

---

[3] Surplus rather than net worth is used because capital stock had not been paid in.
[4] "Caldwell Bill of Exceptions," v, 16.
[5] Statement to the writer by V. H. Kennedy.

were fourteen of these offices. They were located in Chattanooga, Knox-ville, Memphis, Birmingham, New Orleans, Greensboro, Louisville, St. Petersburg, St. Louis, Chicago, Detroit, Cincinnati, New York, and Los Angeles.[6] The following year the New York office became a separate corporation, Rogers Caldwell and Company, Incorporated, all the stock of which was owned by the Nashville company. While these offices were instrumental in developing the business of the company, none of them, at any time, handled as large a volume of business as did the Nashville office.

Some attempts were made to keep the efficiency of the internal organ-ization of the company increasing as rapidly as its physical and financial size, though internal efficiency continually, and to the company's decided detriment, lagged behind. One such attempt, however, was the division of the business into functional departments, the four principal ones being the buying department, the sales department, the local securities depart-ment, and the accounting department. Rogers Caldwell, as president, was directly in charge of and responsible for the company's operations but a large part of his time was spent in making outside contacts which necessitated the placing of subordinates at the head of each department. His two executive vice presidents, E. J. Heitzeberg and J. D. Carter, the latter having been advanced from bookkeeper to vice president between 1918 and 1921, were in charge of purchases and sales respectively. Heitze-berg was aided in the municipal field primarily by H. C. Alexander who, as the former's time became completely taken up in the purchase of cor-poration issues, became head of the municipal buying department. Frank D. Marr headed the local securities department, having charge of sales of securities of local corporations as well as of sales to local buyers, both individual and institutional.[7]

The accounting department was by far the weakest spot in the busi-ness. For many years there was no semblance of organization in this department and no logical system of accounts. The affairs of the depart-ment were handled in a very haphazard manner, each employee making whatever entries he thought should be made and the department more or less running itself. The first audit of the company's records was made by Grannis-Blair Audit Company of Nashville, covering operations to December 31, 1918. Another audit was not made by outside auditors until three years later when Homer K. Jones and Company of Memphis audited the records as of December 31, 1921. Ernst and Ernst were called in for audits as of December 31, 1922, and 1923, but the next one was

[6] "Audit Report of Caldwell and Company," February 28, 1925.
[7] "Caldwell Bill of Exceptions," IV, 87-89.

not until February 28, 1925. In 1925 the fiscal year was changed to end on June 30 and another audit was made as of June 30, 1925, after which time audits were made regularly every year by an outside firm of accountants. Not only were audits of Caldwell and Company at first made irregularly but the accounting department made no trial balances. Haphazard internal accounting was thus accompanied by infrequent external audits, neither policy being sound, especially for a rapidly growing concern.

The audit reports submitted by Ernst and Ernst in 1925 called the attention of the officers of the company to the condition of its accounting department in no uncertain terms. The report of February 28, 1925, said in part:

Apparently no effort had been made to correctly keep the Notes Receivable record of the Company as many items were not entered therein. . . . During our examination and verification of the Accounts Receivable balance we noted a large number of incorrect charges and credits, several transactions had not been entered and the aggregate of the detailed accounts had not been in balance with the controlling account for a number of months. The record of collateral pledged on customers' margin accounts was found to be incomplete and inaccurate. . . . No complete record was maintained either at the Nashville office or the branch offices showing the securities for which the company was accountable or the location of the securities. . . . It is essential that the actual securities be balanced against the records at least monthly, however, no attempt has been made by your employees to do this in the past.

We noticed instances of bonds having been received and used without being paid for or entered on the Company's records, and securities deposited with customers to guarantee delivery of other securities purchased, but no entry recorded therefor, and your attention is directed to the importance of immediately recording any securities received or delivered by the company.

The report as of June 30, 1925, was in practically the same tenor.

Our examination of accounts receivable disclosed numerous errors which we have corrected. A number of trades, purchases and sales were not entered on the Company's records although the securities had been received or delivered. This condition is unnecessary and can easily be corrected by due diligence on the part of the employee handling such transactions. . . . We found a very large number of errors in postings to the security ledger sheets—par values of purchases were entered in the sales column and vice versa; incorrect amounts were entered in the par value or share column; transactions were frequently posted to the wrong account, etc.

We noted some improvement in your accounting procedure, especially in regard to the securities, however, the bookkeeping has been unsatisfactory due in part to the incorrect data on entries received by the bookkeepers and to the fact that they are inexperienced, particularly in your business.

We have placed the records in excellent condition as of June 30, 1925, but we don't believe they will remain so unless greater diligence is exerted in supervising the accounting procedure. In this connection it is our opinion that it is essential that you place a competent and experienced man in charge of your accounting department in the capacity of auditor to make a continuous internal check of your records thereby eliminating the numerous errors which at present remain undetected for long periods.

The laxness with which the accounting department was run meant not only that the officers did not know the results of the company's operations but that a bad impression was given customers, who would come into the office to get or pay for securities and have to wait quite a long time because of delays in the accounting department. Sometimes bills would be wrong and occasionally customers sent in checks to cover mistakes in their bills. The company did not know how many mistakes it was making which the customers did not notice and correct.[8]

The situation became so bad that steps had to be taken to improve matters. In 1925 Caldwell asked Carter to take over the general supervision of the accounting department and attempt to bring some order out of the chaos that existed. Carter brought in Timothy Graham Donovan, who had formerly been in the accounting department of Western Union, to help straighten out the department. After several months' work correcting entries and installing a workable system of accounts, in September, 1925, the accounting department made its first trial balance. Thus a beginning was made toward materially improving the conditions in this department and later the records were placed in excellent condition, an accomplishment which resulted in Donovan's being made secretary of the company and placed in direct charge of the accounting department in 1926, under the general supervision of Carter.

Not only was there deplorable laxness in the accounting department but certain other internal policies of the business were questionable. Although the firm was a corporation, directors' or stockholders' meetings were never actually held, minutes of fictitious meetings simply being drawn up when necessary. While it is true that Rogers Caldwell owned all the stock of the company and could therefore dictate policies, nevertheless a more careful administration of the business might have resulted from regular directors' meetings.

Another practice which hindered the smooth operation of the business and showed a complete disregard for internal efficiency was the way the correspondence files of the company were handled. The auditors in 1925 reported considerable difficulty in "locating various letters in the cor-

---

[8] *Ibid.*, p. 85.

respondence files due to the practice of removing correspondence from the files of one month and refiling same in with letters of a later month."[9] In addition to this the officers and employees made a practice of keeping correspondence files in their desk drawers rather than returning them to the company files.[10] Desk drawers can furnish a hiding place for a large volume of correspondence.

The chief explanation of this lax internal organization can be found in the fact that there was no one with sufficient authority to devote his time to supervising completely the internal operations of the business. Caldwell spent too much of his time making outside contacts to do this, while Heitzeberg was concerned only with buying. It fell to Carter, more than to anyone else, to direct internal operations. This, together with sales, was a little more than he could effectively manage. The size of the company was obviously outgrowing the capacity of its three executive officers to manage efficiently.

Despite deplorable internal conditions, during the period from 1917 to 1925 Caldwell and Company was apparently successful in its operations. If reliance can be placed in the accounts, it was marketing a large volume of securities at high profits and the business had been brought into a position of leadership among Southern investment bankers. The House of Caldwell and its slogan, "We Bank on the South," had, by 1925, become widely known to most purchasers of Southern securities.

[9] "Audit Report of Caldwell and Company," February 28, 1925.
[10] Statement to the writer by V. H. Kennedy.

Chapter VI

EXPANSION INTO INDUSTRIAL FINANCING

CALDWELL and Company's expansion into the industrial securities field came at a time when the investing public was seemingly willing to put larger and larger proportions of its funds into securities of this type while, at the same time, the rapid industrialization of the South was needing ever increasing quantities of funds that could be had through the sale of such securities. The company was thus taking advantage of very favorable conditions when it added this line. Its first experience with new industrial securities was in participations in selling syndicates. As it developed its selling organization and became better known in Eastern financial circles, the company was given these participations by a number of leading houses. While this was a profitable type of operation, it did not have the same potentialities as actually originating and underwriting new securities. A $600,000 issue of 7 per cent bonds for the Harlan-Wallins Coal Corporation of Pineville, Kentucky, in 1924 was the first of Caldwell and Company's own industrial issues, but it was not until 1926 when it established a corporation department to finance industrial enterprises that its operations in this field became of substantial importance. In that year four new issues were offered to the public by the company, and during the three following years it continued to carry on a considerable volume of business of this type.

During the four years, 1926-1929, it originated and underwrote bond and note issues of twenty-four companies, the total amount of which was $25,826,000. It participated in the underwriting syndicates of a number of issues, probably the most important of which was a $13,000,000 issue of 6 per cent bonds of the Pennsylvania-Dixie Cement Company, which resulted in a profit of $547,000 to Caldwell and Company in one year.[1] Furthermore, the company financed at least eight companies having only stocks outstanding. Some of these were securities of Southern companies. The rest were to finance expansion into the South. They represented a wide variety of industries, of which the most important groups were textile and clothing mills, mines and other heavy industries, and distribution and service industries.

[1] "Audit Report of Caldwell and Company," June 30, 1927.

With regard to the companies financed solely by Caldwell and Company, certain features are characteristic of their capital structures. In the first place most of the companies had at least three types of securities outstanding: either debenture or mortgage bonds, preferred stock, and no par common stock. Some of the companies had two types of bonds or two grades of preferred stocks as well as common stock. Usually, however, the capital structure consisted, in the first place, of an issue of bonds equal roughly to one half the value at which the fixed assets of the company were carried. Since most of the company's financing was done during a time when the art of writing up the value of assets was at its height, there is no reason to doubt that the assets of many of the companies were carried at excessive values. Support for this view is found in the relatively large number of issues that arose to finance mergers and to reorganize old companies profitably operating. But considering book values alone, the bonds were usually well backed. They carried high coupon rates, with all issues having rates of either 6.5 or 7 per cent, except two 6 per cent short-term note issues.[2]

In practically all capital structures there was an issue of preferred stock. The relation between the size of the preferred issues and the bonds outstanding varied, but they were usually about equal, the two together amounting roughly to the book value of the fixed assets. Most of the preferred issues were cumulative with dividend rates of $7.00 a share or higher. Finally, there was an issue of no par common stock which, in some cases, represented working capital, but in the great majority of cases little but water, for large blocks normally went to Caldwell and Company as a bonus for financing the various enterprises.[3]

The current financial position of some of the firms was apparently quite satisfactory; on the other hand, there were some that were constantly pressed for funds. Included in this latter class were the Fair Stores Company, Harlan-Wallins Coal Corporation, and the Apex Oil Company. The current positions of some of the companies were weakened to an appreciable extent by Caldwell and Company's policy of virtually compelling them to keep a large part of their unused cash on deposit with the Bank of Tennessee. Probably the outstanding example of a company whose financial position was seriously impaired when its control passed to Caldwell and Company was Cooper, Wells and Company, the entire capital stock of which was bought by Caldwell and Company in July, 1929, for $1,800,000. At the time the purchase was made Cooper, Wells had cash on hand amounting to $800,000. A cash dividend of $700,000 was declared immediately after the company passed into Cald-

---

[2] A complete list of industrial bonds originated and underwritten by Caldwell and Company is given in Appendix E.   [3] See *infra*, this chapter.

well's hands, this amount being used to make the first payment on the purchase.[4] Earnings of the companies varied; at least five of them failing to earn bond interest the first year of operation.

In some of the enterprises it financed, Caldwell and Company took very little active part in management, allowing these companies to pursue their own policies, and satisfying itself by holding a seat on the board of directors to foster, if possible, its own interests. Important among such companies were Saratoga Victory Mills, Tennessee Products Corporation, Layne and Bowler, and Wertham, Morgan, Hamilton Bag Company.

On the other hand, there were many companies over which Caldwell and Company exercised rather close control, either through domination of the boards of directors or through the selection of the active managers. Control of these companies arose by Caldwell and Company's either receiving as a bonus a majority of the common stock or buying a controlling interest and installing management of its choice before the stocks were offered to the public. In at least five companies, Kentucky Rock Asphalt Company, Harlan-Wallins Coal Corporation, Atlanta Laundries, Spur Distributing Company, and Southern Department Stores, Caldwell and Company's control was increased by the use of voting trust agreements. In the Kentucky Rock Asphalt agreement the three voting trustees were the three executive officers of Caldwell and Company, while in the other agreements only one trustee was an officer of the banking house.

A list of the industrial companies that can be considered as controlled by Caldwell and Company is given in the following table, along with the percentage of the common stock owned by Caldwell and Company and the total assets of the companies, both as of approximately December 31, 1929. Some of these companies merit individual treatment.

INDUSTRIAL COMPANIES CONTROLLED BY CALDWELL AND COMPANY

Company and Type of Industry	Percentage of Common Stock Owned by C. & Co.	Total Assets 1929
Textile Mills and Clothing Manufacturers		
Alligator Company—Approximately 40%		$ 1,031,000
Alabama Mills Company—Over 50%		8,065,000
Cadet Hosiery, Inc.—Approximately 33%		2,500,000
Mark Henderson Company—Over 60%		94,500
Oak Manufacturing Company—Approximately 50%		931,000
Cooper, Wells and Company—All		2,237,000
Frank Silk Mills—Approximately 50%		500,000 (est.)
Rock Hill Printing & Finishing Co.—Approximately 25%		2,132,000
Total		$17,490,500

[4] Memorandum prepared for the Receivers of Caldwell and Company. Not dated.

Heavy Industries
 Cumberland Portland Cement Co.—Approximately 33%.$ 1,940,000
 Harlan-Wallins Coal Corp.—Over 33%............... 2,150,000
 Kentucky Rock Asphalt Co.—Over 50%.............. 6,257,000
  Total...$10,347,000
Distribution and Service Companies
 Apex Oil Company—Approximately 45%.............$ 1,799,000
 Atlanta Laundries, Inc.—Approximately 25%.......... 4,055,000
 Cloverland Dairy Products Corp.—Approximately 50%.. 1,835,000
 Fair Stores Company—Approximately 33%............ 1,779,000
 Southern Department Stores, Inc.—All............... 3,115,000
 Spur Distributing Co.—Approximately 33%............ 345,000
  Total...$12,928,000
Nashville Enterprises
 Nashville Baseball Association—90%.................$ 250,000
 Nashville Suburban Development Co.—All............ 57,000
  Total.....................................$ 307,000
  Grand Total...............................$41,072,500

Sources: "Audit Report of Caldwell and Company"; memoranda covering the
various companies prepared by officers of Caldwell and Company for the
Receivers; and John Moody, *Manual of Investments, Industrial Securities*,
cited hereafter as *Moody's Industrials*.

ALLIGATOR COMPANY

The Alligator Company was organized in 1926 to take over the assets
of the Alligator Clothing Company of St. Louis, makers of the well-
known brand of "Alligator" raincoats. The predecessor company was
in bankruptcy and Caldwell and Company agreed to finance the new one.
A loan to the company of $250,000 was made in 1926, which was imme-
diately sold to the Missouri State Life Insurance Company. This loan
was funded in 1928 with an issue of $250,000 ten-year, 7 per cent deben-
tures, which Caldwell and Company offered at 102½. For its services,
Caldwell and Company received 7,750 shares, or 51.66 per cent, of the
common stock of the company. A stock dividend of 200 per cent was
declared in March, 1929, after which Caldwell and Company offered the
stock it held to the public, selling 15,181 shares at an average price of
$29.50 a share, which netted the investment house a profit of $449,089.[5]

ALABAMA MILLS COMPANY

The Alabama Mills Company was incorporated in 1927 to construct
ten cotton mills in various towns in northern Alabama. The $3,000,000

[5] Data obtained from *Moody's Industrials*, 1930; "Audit Report of Caldwell and Company"; and statements to the writer by T. G. Donovan.

of first sinking fund 6.5 per cent fifteen-year bonds were offered at 99 by Caldwell and Company in May, 1928. The preferred stock was subscribed largely by a few individuals interested in the formation of the company and the Alabama Power Company. Of the 180,000 shares of common stock, approximately 95,000 shares went to Caldwell and Company as a bonus, relatively little of which was ever sold. The company was not financially successful, failing to earn interest on its bonds in 1928, or in subsequent years. Caldwell and Company was forced to come to its rescue with advances of $150,00 in 1929 and $175,000 in 1930.[6] Obviously the project was very unsound financially and the company became a very weak affiliate for its banker.

FRANK SILK MILLS, INCORPORATED

The Frank Silk Mills, Incorporated, was organized in 1928 to operate a plant at Murfreesboro, Tennessee, making several types of staple silk fabrics. The $250,000 issue of 7 per cent, ten-year, first mortgage bonds were bought by Caldwell and Company at 90, in August, 1928, and offered to the public at around 100. Each bond bore a detachable warrant entitling the holder of each $1,000 of bonds to purchase twenty shares of class "A" common stock at prices ranging from $10 to $20 a share, depending upon the date of purchase.[7] This company was prominent among the weak enterprises financed by Caldwell and Company. By the early part of 1930, with all bonds still outstanding, the plant was abandoned and efforts to locate any officers of the company failed. The insurance company notified Caldwell and Company of the cancellation of the fire insurance because the power had been shut off and the sprinkler system would not work. The property which had been valued at $405,000 was placed in the hands of a receiver and sold, the machinery and equipment bringing $2,500 and the land and building approximately $40,000.[8]

KENTUCKY ROCK ASPHALT COMPANY

The Kentucky Rock Asphalt Company was incorporated in Delaware in 1926 to acquire the property of the Kentucky Rock Asphalt Company of Kentucky, which was engaged in the quarrying, crushing, and marketing of bitulithic rock asphalt under the trade name of "Kyrock." The company had extensive properties and mineral rights in and around Edmonson County in south central Kentucky. The former company had

[6] *Ibid.* Also, Memorandum concerning company prepared for Receivers of Caldwell and Company. Not dated.

[7] "Report of Receivers of Caldwell and Company," Part I, p. 167.

[8] Statement of Cecil Sims, Nashville attorney, before the Special Master, appointed in the case *Dean* v. *Caldwell*, with reference to the claim of the Receiver of the Holston-Union National Bank; filed September 16, 1932.

outstanding $52,300 of first mortgage bonds, $30,000 par value of preferred, and $1,304,600 par value of common stock. Caldwell and Company proposed to the common stockholders to pay them par for their stock and give them in addition one share of preferred in the new company for each share of common in the old. The proposal was accepted and the new company took over the assets of the old. A first mortgage was placed on the property and $1,500,000 of 6.5 per cent bonds were issued, the proceeds of which were used to pay for the common stock and retire the bonds and preferred stock of the old company. To the purchaser of each $1,000 bond a detachable stock warrant was given which entitled the holder to buy twenty-five shares of common stock at $15 a share at any time prior to June 1, 1936. The new company also issued 13,046 shares of preferred which were given to the old common stock holders.[9]

The 105,000 shares of common stock of the new company were bought by Caldwell and Company for ten cents a share and it was from the sale of this stock that the investment house expected its principal return from the transaction. The company's operations proved to be profitable, bond interest being earned 5.31 times in 1928, 5.69 in 1929, and 6.25 in 1930. Preferred dividends were regularly met and an initial dividend of twenty-five cents a share was paid on the new common stock on January 3, 1928. This amount was paid quarterly until April 1, 1929, when the rate was increased to forty cents and a 5 per cent stock dividend was declared.[10]

The company's earnings and dividend policy, coupled with an aggressive stock-selling campaign, enabled Caldwell and Company to profit handsomely from this promotion. After distributing stock to the participants in the syndicate formed to underwrite the bonds and selling some 3,800 shares to the public, on June 30, 1927, the investment house had on hand 73,292 shares, the market value of which was estimated to be $806,212, or $11 a share. During the next year, 1927-1928, the company sold 11,660 shares for $57,206, or at an average price of $4.90 per share. In the following fiscal year, 1928-1929, Caldwell and Company sold 42,567 shares of Kentucky Rock Asphalt at a profit of $1,567,049, or at an average profit per share of $36.80. The remaining 20,500 shares held by the company were carried at a book value of $1,644 and estimated to have a market value of $694,855.[11] Thus, in two years Caldwell and Company made a gross profit on this stock of $1,624,255, which was equal to more than 25 per cent of the total assets of the asphalt company. The frequently cited

---

[9] *Plan of Reorganization of Kentucky Rock Asphalt Company,* filed in District Court of the United States for the Western District of Kentucky, June 29, 1935.

[10] *Moody's Industrials,* 1931, p. 726.

[11] "Audit Report of Caldwell and Company" for years mentioned.

underwriting profit of $62,500,000 on the promotion of United States Steel Corporation amounted to less than 5 per cent of its original capitalization of $1,400,000,000.

One other advantage gained by Caldwell and Company from its purchase of the old Kentucky Rock Asphalt Company came from the issuance at the time of the reorganization of $200,000 of 6 per cent five-year notes, due June 1, 1931. These notes were purchased by Caldwell and Company for a $200,000 unsecured deposit in the Bank of Tennessee. The notes were never offered to the public but, on the other hand, none of the $200,000 on deposit with the Bank of Tennessee was ever withdrawn.[12] The transaction, in effect, gave Caldwell and Company $200,000 additional collateral which it used to pledge on loans.

APEX OIL COMPANY

Apex Oil Company operated a chain of filling stations in Nashville and neighboring Tennessee communities. Its capitalization consisted of $300,000 of ten-year, 6.5 per cent debenture bonds, 4,050 shares of $7.00 cumulative preferred, and 116,834 shares of common stock, approximately 53,000 shares of which went to Caldwell and Company as a bonus. The value of the assets of the company were written up unjustifiably, the item, controlled business, being carried at $810,000.[13] Since the company had to rely frequently on Caldwell and Company to obtain funds to meet pay rolls and was unable to meet its preferred dividends after 1929, it of course is obvious that its controlled business was not worth the amount given in the balance sheet. Although the company paid its bond interest, this is one of the numerous cases where Caldwell and Company loaded a speculative enterprise with a fixed charge security.

FAIR STORES COMPANY

Fair Stores Company, with its home office in Little Rock, Arkansas, operated a chain of eighty-four retail merchandise stores in Arkansas, Mississippi, and Louisiana. In February, 1929, Caldwell and Company bought half the common stock of the company, 25,000 shares, for $450,000, or $18 a share, and offered it to the public at $25 a share. The somewhat profitable operations of the company in the first ten months of 1929, together with the condition of the security market, enabled Caldwell and Company to sell approximately 15,000 shares of the stock. In the last

[12] *Ibid.* For the later history of the company see Chapter xx, *infra.* The most interesting part of the company's relations with Caldwell and Company arose through the latter's interest in Tennessee politics. See Chapter xi, *infra.*

[13] Memorandum in files of Receivers of Caldwell and Company, by E. J. Heitzeberg, January 2, 1931.

two months of 1929, sales of the stores fell off badly and continued to do so all during the next year. This fact, combined with poor management, forced the company into bankruptcy in December, 1930. The assets of the company were such that the creditors received about ten cents on the dollar, and the stockholders, consequently, nothing.[14] Thus Fair Stores Company makes a strong bid for being the weakest of all the enterprises financed by Caldwell and Company.

SOUTHERN DEPARTMENT STORES, INCORPORATED

Southern Department Stores, Incorporated, was chartered in August, 1928, and its organization was completed late in 1929. It was a holding and management company which brought several large department stores into one chain. The stores included were H. E. Bacon Company, Evansville, Indiana; the Drennen Company, Birmingham, Alabama; Lebeck Brothers, Nashville, Tennessee; John C. Lewis Company, Incorporated, and Herman Straus and Sons Company, both of Louisville, Kentucky. A subsidiary of Southern Department Stores was the Southern Realty and Investment Company which owned the property occupied by Straus in Louisville. Steps toward forming the company were taken as early as 1927 when Caldwell and Company bought 1,500 shares, or 50 per cent, of the stock of Lebeck Brothers for $157,400. In 1928 Caldwell and Company acquired half the common stock of the Drennen Company, while control of the other stores was purchased in 1929 with funds advanced by the banking house.

The securities offered to the public in January, 1930, consisted of $1,000,000 three-year, 6 per cent notes at 98; 14,000 shares of callable preferred, with a par value of $25 and a dividend rate of 7 per cent; 21,800 shares of no par cumulative preferred with annual dividend rate of $1.50; and 100,000 shares of no par common stock. Since the securities were offered after the stock market crash, none of them sold very rapidly, with none of the common stock moving.

The stores making up the chain had sales in 1927 and 1928 of about $4,600,000 and in 1929 of about $4,000,000 while net profit during the three years averaged around $175,000. Earnings of this amount were approximately three times as great as fixed charges of $60,000 and gave a substantial margin over fixed and contingent charges of $127,200. In spite of its good earnings for these three years, business fell off in 1930, and in the fall of that year Southern Department Stores defaulted the interest payments on its note and passed preferred dividends, and a re-

[14] "Report of Receivers of Caldwell and Company," Part I, p. 382; Memorandum in files of Receivers of Caldwell and Company. Not dated.

organization followed. This was the last industrial enterprise financed by Caldwell and Company.[15]

Nashville Suburban Development Company

The two Nashville enterprises show more clearly than anything else the diversity of the investments made by Caldwell and Company. In 1929 Caldwell and Company financed the construction of an eight-inch water main from the city limits of Nashville four and one-half miles out the Franklin Pike. Located on this pike were the homes of many rich Nashville people, including James E. Caldwell, and practically all the officers of Caldwell and Company, as well as large tracts of land owned by the Bank of Tennessee. The water main, of course, enhanced the value of all the property. Its construction cost approximately $57,000, $30,000 of which was recovered by the sale of taps to the residents along the route of the main, leaving a net cost to Caldwell and Company of $27,000. A corporation, the Nashville Suburban Development Company, was created to operate and own the main and was capitalized at $60,000, represented by 600 shares of common stock, with par value of $100. A share of stock was sold to every one who connected with the main to cover the costs of construction. While Caldwell and Company's investment would no doubt have been profitable to it in the long run in enhancing the value of the Bank of Tennessee's real estate, it produced no immediate returns whatever.[16]

Nashville Baseball Association

Caldwell and Company was indeed getting very far away from the municipal bond business when it bought control of the Nashville Baseball Association, a member of the Southern Association. Control was obtained when Caldwell and Company purchased, in 1926 and 1929, 629 out of a total of 700 shares of stock in the association for $195,400, at an average price per share of $310. A new grandstand was built in 1927 at a cost of $75,000, which Caldwell and Company obtained by selling bonds to the Missouri State Life Insurance Company.

The club showed a profit in 1926 of $16,800 and in 1927 of $38,000. A new manager was brought in after that who, thinking that Rogers Caldwell as a millionaire sportsman would meet all deficits, spent large sums trying to build up the team. The result was an operating loss in

[15] Memorandum prepared for the Receivers of Caldwell and Company by E. J. Heitzeberg, not dated; "Report of Receivers of Caldwell and Company," Part 1, p. 483; "Audit Report of Caldwell and Company"; and *Moody's Industrials,* 1933, p. 2161. See Chapter xx, *infra,* for an account of the reorganization of this company.

[16] Memorandum prepared for the Receivers of Caldwell and Company by L. B. Stevens, December 16, 1930.

1928 of over $10,000 and in 1929 of almost $18,000, as well as loans from the Fourth and First National Bank of $70,750, and advances on open account by Caldwell and Company of $49,000.[17] In brief, the free passes that were the only return to Caldwell and Company from its investment in the baseball world were indeed costly.

SUMMARY

These summary sketches of the more important industrial companies controlled by Caldwell and Company show the wide variety of the investments it made, the great differences in the financial conditions of the companies, and the differences in the profitableness of the companies to the underwriter.

Advantages were obtained by Caldwell and Company from the financing of industrial companies, both those considered as controlled and those not in that category, from three sources. The first was the spread between the purchase price and the offering price on the industrial bonds sold by the company. Normally, Caldwell and Company paid around 90 for the bonds and offered them at par, making a ten-point margin. Against this has to be offset the fact that there were always relatively large amounts of these bonds in the company's inventory, most of which could usually be hypothecated on loans or deposits. A second advantage was the deposits the industrial companies kept with the Bank of Tennessee, which amounted to $1,100,000 on June 30, 1929. Offset against this amount was the sum of $182,000 advanced to industrial companies at that date, leaving a net amount of funds furnished to Caldwell and Company by its controlled industrial companies of over $900,000.[18]

The final and most important source of profit to the company from its industrial financing came from bonus stocks. The profits arising from this source in some individual cases have already been noted. Bonus stocks were received by the company as soon as it began financing industrial companies, but profits on the sale of these stocks did not become appreciable until the fiscal year ending June 30, 1927. At the beginning of that fiscal year, Caldwell and Company had on hand 59,415 shares of bonus stocks, the chief items of which were 30,170 shares of Houston Gulf Gas and 9,000 shares of Tennessee Products. During that year 142,248 shares were received, consisting principally of Kentucky Rock Asphalt, Pennsylvania-Dixie Cement, Alligator Company, and Rio Grande

---

[17] Letters to Receivers of Caldwell and Company from R. L. Voss, December 16, 1930; "Report of Receivers of Caldwell and Company," Part I, p. 476.

[18] "Audit Report of Caldwell and Company," June 30, 1929. Not included are deposits from the company's controlled newspapers; see Chapter x, *infra.*

Valley Gas. Some 33,465 shares were sold at a gross profit of $462,600 and 46,874 shares distributed to various parties as bonuses, leaving on hand at the end of the year 120,889 shares with an estimated total market value of $1,545,800.[19]

During the next fiscal year, 1927-1928, 271,984 shares of bonus stocks were received by Caldwell and Company, the principal items being Alabama Mills, Atlanta Laundries, Cloverland Dairy Products, Inland Gas, National Cotton Seed Products, and Oak Manufacturing Company. Approximately 47,000 shares, consisting primarily of Kentucky Rock Asphalt, National Cotton Seed Products, and Pennsylvania-Dixie Cement, were sold at a total gross profit of $291,174. Also there were 77,537 shares in all distributed to members of syndicates participating in the under-writing of the various securities from which the bonus stocks arose, leaving on hand on June 30, 1928, 268,242 shares with an estimated market value of $2,334,452.[20]

During the following fiscal year, 1928-1929, the company received 246,688 shares of bonus stocks, composed primarily of 10,000 shares of Alligator Company, 52,120 shares of Apex Oil, 72,000 shares of Aviation Corporation, 11,900 shares of Cumberland Portland Cement, 14,500 shares of Frank Silk Mills, 25,000 shares of Memphis Natural Gas, and 10,000 shares of Saratoga Victory Mills. There were 42,000 shares distributed to syndicate participants without profit to Caldwell and Company. Yet there were sold 81,040 shares which yielded the company a gross profit of $2,238,000. Of this amount, $1,567,000 came from the sale of 42,567 shares of Kentucky Rock Asphalt, $449,000 from the sale of 15,181 shares of Alligator Company, and $119,000 from the sale of 10,000 shares of Memphis Natural Gas common stock. After these changes in the bonus stock account during the year, there were on hand on June 30, 1929, 391,000 shares of various common stocks, the market value of which was estimated to be $1,838,000.[21] Thus, in three fiscal years Caldwell and Company made a total gross profit from the sale of bonus stocks of $2,991,774 which was sufficient to make this easily one of the greatest sources of profit to the banking house, if not the greatest, and to make industrial financing one of the most important phases of the business.

A final point that should be mentioned concerning the industrial financing carried on by Caldwell and Company is that it placed the company in a strategic position with regard to several strong industrial companies in the South and gave it control over industrial assets of more than $40,000,000. It thus became an industrial capitalist whose influence in Southern industry was very powerful.

[19] "Audit Report of Caldwell and Company," June 30, 1927.
[20] Ibid., June 30, 1928.   [21] Ibid., June 30, 1929.

CHAPTER VII

GROWTH OF INVESTMENTS IN INSURANCE
COMPANIES

THE COMPARATIVELY small investments that Caldwell and Company made
to obtain control of the Cotton States and North American National
Life Insurance companies were forerunners of investments in the insurance field that were the most important of any that the company made.
One very important company, the Missouri State Life Insurance Company, was soon brought under Caldwell control, as were several smaller
and less important companies. The operations of these companies and
their history under Caldwell control are discussed in this chapter.

MISSOURI STATE LIFE INSURANCE COMPANY

The Missouri State Life Insurance Company of St. Louis was established in 1892 as an assessment association and reorganized in 1902 as a
legal reserve company with capital stock of $100,000. The company en-
joyed a period of rapid growth and by 1925 had insurance in force of
$587,587,000, admitted assets of $61,890,000, and capital stock of $2,000,000.[1]
Its operations were profitable, dividends of $1 per share of $10 par being
paid each year from 1920 through 1922 and $1.20 per share thereafter
through 1925. Its stock sold for from $40 to $55 a share.[2]

In the latter part of 1925 Rogers Caldwell approached M. E. Singleton,
president of the company, with a proposition to buy the controlling interest in the company from him and other stockholders. An agreement
was reached on January 2, 1926, providing for the purchase by Rogers
Caldwell of 86,000 shares of stock from Singleton and members of his
family for $100 a share and up to 64,540 shares from other stockholders
at $75 a share. Supplemental agreements the following month reduced
the purchase price approximately $5 per share.

The purchase of all the stock covered in the contract would have
given Caldwell 150,540 shares out of a total of 200,000 outstanding.
Slightly less than this number was purchased, a total of 148,158 shares
being obtained by Caldwell on February 28, 1926, under the terms of the

---

[1] Alfred M. Best, *Life Insurance Reports*, pp. 518-20. Cited hereafter as *Best's Reports*.
[2] John Moody, *Manual of Investments, Banks and Finance*, 1930, p. 2510. Cited hereafter as *Moody's Banks*.

contracts.[3] The total amount due the selling stockholders was $12,462,000.[4] Thus stock with a book value of approximately $25 a share and a former market value of $55 was bought for approximately $85, which was seventy times the dividend payment. Obviously Caldwell and Company was seeking the same advantages that accrue to investment bankers from the control of insurance companies as were enjoyed twenty years before when Charles Evans Hughes investigated for the state of New York the motives behind offers as great as $7,000,000 for 502 shares of stock of the Equitable Life Assurance Society, the annual dividend on which was limited to $3,514.[5]

The contract for the purchase of control of Missouri State Life was entered into personally by Rogers Caldwell, but was sold by him to the Insurance Securities Corporation, formed expressly for the purpose of buying it. This company was incorporated under the laws of Delaware on January 5, 1927, with an authorized capital stock of 2,250 shares with no par value. Its three stockholders, each owning 750 shares, were: first, Caldwell and Company; second, the Fourth and First National Company, the security affiliate of the Fourth and First National Bank; and, finally, the American National Company, the security affiliate of the American National Bank.[6] Each of the stockholders paid approximately $750,000 into the corporation. The holding company's investment in Missouri State Life stock was increased in April, 1927, when stockholders were given the right to subscribe to one share of stock in the insurance company at $10 a share for every two shares previously held. The amount going to the Insurance Securities Corporation was 73,300 shares, calling for an additional outlay of $733,000 and bringing its total investment to $13,425,000. The original contributions of the stockholders amounting to $2,250,000 had been applied to the purchase price of the stock. The balance which was to have been paid in annual installments was settled in a lump sum when Insurance Securities Corporation borrowed from New York banks $11,250,000 on its one-year, 5 per cent notes, dated February 1, 1927, and secured by the company's entire holdings of Missouri State stock.[7]

The effects of Caldwell control of Missouri State Life became significant in the early part of 1927. At that time M. E. Singleton was replaced as president by Hillsman Taylor, who had been president of

[3] "Audit Report of Caldwell and Company," June 30, 1926.

[4] "Audit Report of Insurance Securities Corporation," June 30, 1928.

[5] See Report of Legislative Committee of State of New York appointed in 1905 to investigate the affairs of insurance companies.

[6] "Audit Report of Insurance Securities Corporation," June 30, 1926.

[7] Ibid.

Cotton States Life Insurance Company, and James E. Caldwell was made chairman of the board of directors. Rogers Caldwell and Paul M. Davis, the latter representing the American National Company, were also elected to the board. Further, Caldwell and Company's expansion fever was soon contracted by its new company. In 1928 the Missouri State Life reinsured the business of the International Life Insurance Company of St. Louis, whose capital and surplus were exhausted and reserves impaired to the extent of $1,500,000 through the manipulation of the company's assets by its president, Roy C. Toombs. This company had insurance in force of $309,116,000, its assets were of a somewhat questionable nature, and Missouri State Life was not in a condition to assume the liabilities involved in the reinsurance but, in order to keep the company in Missouri and to make it appear that the Missouri State Life was growing rapidly, the step was taken.[8]

This transaction was followed in 1929 by Missouri State's purchase of the control of the Southwestern Life Insurance Company of Dallas, Texas. This was considered one of the strongest companies of the Southwest, having admitted assets of $33,154,000, and insurance in force of $271,669,000. Its capital of $2,000,000 was represented by 20,000 shares of $100 par value.[9] On July 19, 1929, the board of directors of Missouri State Life approved a contract under which the company agreed to purchase 10,500 shares of the capital stock of Southwestern Life, at a price of $700 per share, which was approximately three and a half times its book value of $205, or a total price of $7,350,000. The first block of 1,500 shares was delivered to the Missouri State Life for $1,059,000 in cash, while the balance was to be delivered at the rate of 2,250 shares annually for four years.[10]

The growth of the Missouri State Life Insurance Company can be seen in the increase of its admitted assets from $61,900,000 in 1925 to $143,000,000 in 1929 and the increase in insurance in force from $587,000,000 to $1,233,000,000 during the same period.[11] Of its assets, the volume of bonds held grew more rapidly than any other item, increasing from 1 per cent of total assets in 1925, or $1,085,000, to 25 per cent in 1929, or $36,364,000. Missouri State Life purchased around $12,000,000 of bonds in 1927, a large part coming from Caldwell and Company and the Fourth and First National Company. During 1928 and 1929, the company bought $23,370,500 of bonds, $17,478,000 coming from the same two houses. In

[8] "Missouri State Life Insurance Company," in *Best's Insurance News (Life Edition)*, xxxiv (October 2, 1933), 318 ff.   [9] *Best's Reports*, 1930, p. 1114.
[10] Report of Examination of Missouri State Life Insurance Company, as of December 31, 1929, *Best's Insurance News (Life Edition)*, xxxi (October 1, 1930), 306 ff. Cited hereafter as *Mo. State Report of 1929.*   [11] *Best's Reports*, 1930, p. 701.

1929 alone, these two Caldwell-controlled firms sold Missouri State Life $5,309,000 of bonds on which a profit of $55,000 was realized.[12]

A second important advantage gained by Caldwell and Company from the purchase of control of Missouri State Life was the funds it obtained from the deposits and loans of the insurance company. On June 30, 1926, less than six months after Caldwell and Company obtained control, the insurance company had a deposit with its new owner of $40,000 and had loaned the investment house $1,190,000. The amount of loans a year later was $1,592,000 while on June 30, 1928, Missouri State's unsecured deposit account with Caldwell and Company amounted to $235,000 and on June 30, 1929, to $503,000.[13]

The large purchase of bonds from Caldwell and Company and the advances to this house by Missouri State Life resulted in a special examination of the insurance company early in 1928 by the insurance departments of Illinois, Kentucky, Missouri, and Tennessee. Concerning the purchase of bonds by the Missouri State Life, the report of this examination stated that "from the best information at hand, it appears that the company [Missouri State Life] has paid somewhat higher prices for some bonds than quoted elsewhere. If the company persists in purchasing bonds from interested parties, it should realize that careful inspection of such purchase prices will follow and if the purchase price continues to be high, publicity of such fact will be detrimental to the company."[14]

The report also criticized the large loans to Caldwell and Company and the excessive cash balances of Missouri State Life, a large part of which were kept in Caldwell banks. These criticized practices continued to such an extent that the company was subjected to a second special examination by the insurance departments of several states in 1930. While the report of this examination did not criticize the relations of Missouri State and Caldwell and Company quite as severely as the former report, it pointed out that large quantities of bonds were still being sold to Missouri State Life by the Nashville house at prices, some of which were above and some below market. Commenting on these sales, it said that the examiners considered "the purchase of securities from investment firms which directly or indirectly control the stock of a life insurance company a practice in which the resulting transactions are as likely to be colored by the financial interests of the banking firms as that of the insurance company itself."[14a] This was, indeed, a mild statement on the

---

[12] *Mo. State Report of 1929.*

[13] "Audit Report of Caldwell and Company," as of dates mentioned.

[14] *Best's Insurance News (Life Edition),* xxix (December 1, 1928), 445 ff.

[14a] *Ibid.,* xxxi (October 1, 1930), 306 ff.

nature of the sale of bonds to Missouri State Life by Caldwell and Company.

Further advantages arising from the control of Missouri State Life were the dividends on the stock and stock subscription rights, which came to Caldwell and Company indirectly through Insurance Securities Corporation. The cash dividend per share amounted to $1.20 annually, while in addition to the stock subscription rights of April, 1927, were those granted in December, 1928, giving the privilege of purchasing at $20 one new share for every three shares already held. Insurance Securities Corporation received the bulk of the dividend payments and of the new stock purchase rights. This company, by June 30, 1927, had paid off $1,415,250 of its $11,250,000 of notes, leaving $9,834,750 due. The funds for paying off these notes had been raised from the sale of stock of Missouri State Life to the three stockholders of Insurance Securities Corporation, who, in turn, had sold it to the public. Less than six months after its incorporation, by June 30, 1927, the corporation had sold 23,400 shares of Missouri State stock at a profit of $468,912, and had received dividends of $43,980 on its holdings.[15]

The American National Company, which owned one third of the stock of Insurance Securities Corporation, withdrew in the latter part of 1927, placing the company completely under the control of Caldwell interests. Insurance Securities bought its stock held by the American National Company for approximately $1,800,000 and retired it, the necessary funds being raised by marketing a part of the Missouri State Life stock. Thus, the American National Company, after deducting its original contribution of $750,000 to the capital of Insurance Securities Corporation, made a profit of over $1,000,000 when it withdrew from the company.[16]

Reflecting gradual public distribution of Missouri State Life stock, Insurance Securities Corporation, on June 30, 1928, held 100,000 shares, or one third the total capital stock, which was carried on its books at $6,163,000, or $61.63 a share, and estimated to have a market value of $93 a share. In addition the holding company had cash of $779,000 and other assets sufficient to bring the total to $7,079,000. Its notes payable as of this same date had been reduced to $5,000,000. From its incorporation to this time, the company had made a profit on the sale of Missouri State Life stock of $1,490,000, and had received dividends and interest of $323,000, or a total income of $1,813,000, while expenses of $675,000, largely

[15] "Audit Report of Caldwell and Company," June 30, 1927.
[16] "Audit Report of Insurance Securities Corporation," June 30, 1928.

taxes and interest, left a net profit of $1,032,000. The following fiscal year, ending June 30, 1929, added $1,159,000 to the company's net profit and by December 31, 1929, the purchase money notes of the company had been reduced to $3,000,000 and cash balances amounted to $1,467,000, a large part of which was on deposit with Caldwell and Company.[17] Thus in less than three years Insurance Securities Corporation had retired $8,250,000 of notes, accumulated sufficient cash to pay off half the remaining $3,000,000, and still held sufficient Missouri State Life stock to allow the Caldwell interests to dominate that company.

This was done, in brief, by the granting of rights to the stockholders to purchase stock at prices decidedly below market, a proportionate part of the shares being bought by the dominant stockholder, Insurance Securities Corporation, which company in turn sold these new shares and a part of its original holdings to Caldwell and Company and the Fourth and First National Company at prices decidedly above cost. These latter companies distributed the stock of Missouri State Life to the public in relatively small blocks, thus enabling Insurance Securities Corporation to continue to control the insurance company even though it held less than 50 per cent of the outstanding stock.

In spite of the sale by Insurance Securities Corporation of its Missouri State stock to Caldwell and Company and Fourth and First National Company above cost, the price charged these companies was always below market, thus enabling them to make a profit on the sale of the stock to the public. Caldwell and Company's profit obtained in this way netted $187,618 in the three years, 1927-1929.[18]

The investment of $750,000 which Caldwell and Company made in the stock of Insurance Securities Corporation had by the end of 1929 proved to be of tremendous advantage, due to the sale of a large volume of securities to the insurance company, profits from the sale of Missouri State Life stock, and deposits of Insurance Securities Corporation and Missouri State Life with Caldwell and Company which together were providing the company with $1,973,000 on June 30, 1929.[19] Finally, the investment gave the bond house direct or indirect control of assets totaling $176,416,000, Missouri State Life having assets of $143,262,000, and Southwestern Life, assets of $33,154,000. To be charged against these advantages were the $3,000,000 of notes still outstanding at the close of 1929 which alone was not a particularly great debt but which when taken with other debts was an important amount.

[17] *Ibid.*, as of dates mentioned.
[18] "Audit Report of Caldwell and Company," June 30, 1929.
[19] *Ibid.*

Inter-Southern Life Insurance Company

A short time after the control of the Missouri State Life Insurance Company was purchased, Caldwell and Company began negotiations for the purchase of Inter-Southern Life Insurance Company of Louisville, Kentucky, which had been organized in 1915 by a Louisville attorney, James R. Duffin, who became the company's president. Certain charges questioning Duffin's honesty were brought against him in the latter part of 1924 which, although disproved, resulted in a great deal of unfavorable publicity for his company. The company was also having trouble with the Kentucky Insurance Department over the valuation of certain of the company's assets.[20] The result of these various difficulties was to place the company in an unsatisfactory light with the financial and business interests of Louisville.

While the company was thus in a doubtful condition, early in 1926 Caldwell and Company offered to buy its control from Duffin and other Louisville interests. The Caldwell offer was to buy approximately half of the $750,000 capital stock of Inter-Southern, represented by a like number of shares with par value of $1, at $1.25 per share, and to pay an additional $300,000 into Inter-Southern's surplus, thereby strengthening the company. The offer was accepted and by June 30, 1926, Caldwell and Company owned 356,954 shares of Inter-Southern stock which had cost, including expenses, a total of $760,000.[21] Caldwell and Company had expected to sell the controlling interest in the company to the Missouri State Life Company and it was with this in view that the purchase was made, but the Insurance Commissioner of Missouri objected and control of Inter-Southern remained with Caldwell and Company.[22]

Caldwell and Company attempted to improve and expand the business immediately. Duffin was replaced as president by Carey G. Arnett, who had been superintendent of agents with Missouri State Life. The territory in which the company was licensed to do business was increased from ten states in 1925 to twenty-four by 1929. Insurance in force, which had amounted to $106,584,000 at the end of 1926, increased to $122,823,000 during 1927, and stood at $158,460,000 at the end of 1929.[23] A part of this growth came from the reinsurance of the business of both the Cotton States and North American National Life Insurance companies which Caldwell and Company instigated and carried through early in 1928.[24]

[20] *Best's Reports*, 1926, pp. 386-87.
[21] "Audit Report of Caldwell and Company," June 30, 1926.
[22] "Caldwell Bill of Exceptions," v, 44.
[23] *Best's Reports*, 1930, p. 491.   [24] See Chapter IV, *supra*.

The admitted assets of Inter-Southern reflected the growth of the business, increasing from $12,803,000 in 1925 to $20,204,000 at the end of 1929. The asset item showing the largest percentage growth was stocks and bonds which increased from 4 per cent of total assets, or $472,750, in 1925, to 25 per cent, or $5,248,000, at the end of 1929. A conservative estimate of the amount of securities sold this company by Caldwell and Company, based upon the security holdings of Inter-Southern, is $2,120,000, an amount not approaching the volume sold to Missouri State Life. Nor were there any dividends paid to Caldwell and Company on its Inter-Southern stock. By June 30, 1928, however, Caldwell and Company was receiving benefits from its investment in the form of Inter-Southern deposits kept with it, which amounted at that time to $222,855, and a year later to $207,000.[25]

The principal advantage arising from the purchase of Inter-Southern, however, was the profits Caldwell and Company made from trading in the shares of the company. The expanding size of the insurance company led to an increase in its capital stock to $1,250,000 in 1928. Using the company's growth as a basis, Caldwell and Company promoted the sale of Inter-Southern stock and obtained a profit of $444,000 in the two years, 1928-29. At the same time the investment house held more than half the stock of Inter-Southern, and hence retained its control.[26] The control of the company added assets of $20,204,000 to the insurance interests of Caldwell and Company.

The Inter-Southern Life Insurance Company itself was materially strengthened from the time it passed into Caldwell control until the end of 1929. Its assets had increased markedly and were much better diversified, and it was gradually living down the reputation it had acquired under Duffin. On the other hand the more conservative financial interests saw danger in the alliance of the company with an investment banker whose issues were becoming more and more speculative.[27]

SOUTHERN SURETY COMPANY

Rogers Caldwell's entrance into the investment banking business was preceded by several years' experience writing surety bonds, hence it was rather to be expected that one of the companies coming under his control should be a surety company. This company was the Southern Surety

[25] "Audit Report of Caldwell and Company," as of dates mentioned.

[26] *Ibid.*

[27] An indication of the improved condition of Inter-Southern Life Insurance Company is seen in the improved rating given the company by Alfred M. Best Company in 1929 as compared with 1928, the year the ratings were first given. In the earlier year, the rating was "C," or good; in the later, "B," or very good.

Company of Des Moines, Iowa, which wrote all types of casualty insurance.

Caldwell and Company's first contact with this enterprise was in 1926 when it purchased, together with W. S. Aagaard and Company of Chicago, 2,700 shares of a new stock offering of the company at $200 a share, which in turn were offered to the public by the bankers at $235 a share. The money raised by the sale of this stock met only temporarily the increasing needs for funds on the part of the surety company, and at the close of 1927 Caldwell and Company entered into an agreement with Kidder-Peabody and Company to underwrite a thorough reorganization of it.[28]

This reorganization was completed in June, 1928, when a new company, the Southern Surety Company of New York, was set up with its home office in St. Louis. The company had a capital of $2,500,000, represented by 250,000 shares with a par value of $10, and assets of $11,698,000. The stockholders of the old company were given six $10 par value shares in the new company for each old $100 par value share, an exchange which required 90,000 shares of the new stock. A part of the remaining stock was offered to stockholders of Missouri State Life at $35 a share.[29] The old management of the company was removed and Norman P. Moray, who had formerly been with the Hartford Accident and Indemnity Company, was made president, and as such began an ambitious expansion program.[30] Caldwell and Company was in a position to send a considerable volume of business to the company in the form of surety bonds written to cover both municipal and private construction projects financed by issues it purchased. The result was that in 1929 the net insurance premiums written by the company increased to $12,113,000, as compared with $8,832,000 in 1926.[31]

A part of Moray's expansion program was the establishment in April, 1929, of the Southern Fire Insurance Company, with a home office in New York City. This company's capital stock of $1,000,000, represented by 100,000 shares of par value $10, was offered to the holders of Southern Surety stock in April, 1929, at $33 a share on the basis of two shares of the fire insurance company for five shares of the surety company. By the end of 1929 this company had insurance in force of $30,858,000 and admitted assets of $3,022,000.[32]

Moray conducted the business along the lines he had been accustomed to in the Hartford Company, a much larger and stronger one. He was

---

[28] Memorandum in files of Receivers of Caldwell and Company compiled by J. D. Carter, December 22, 1930. Cited hereafter as "Memo., Southern Surety."

[29] *Moody's Banks,* 1930, p. 1933.   [30] "Memo., Southern Surety."

[31] *Moody's Banks,* 1930, p. 1933.   [32] *Ibid.,* p. 2468.

also, no doubt, influenced by the thought that his bankers would be able to furnish him with additional capital whenever needed. The company's large underwritings necessitated the constant transfer of surplus to unearned premium reserve and in the latter part of 1929 it was imperative that additional capital stock be sold at a price above par, thereby increasing the surplus and obviating the necessity of transferring sums from the capital stock account into the unearned premium reserve. At this time, therefore, Caldwell and Company and Kidder-Peabody underwrote an offering of 25,000 shares of the stock to the stockholders on the basis of one share of the new stock for every five of the old at a price of $25. This offering occurred late in 1929 and was not successful, hence the bankers had to carry the greater part of it.[33] In order to do this Kidder-Peabody borrowed the necessary funds from the Chase National Bank, and at the end of 1929 Caldwell and Company owed the New York house $1,115,000 as a result of their various undertakings in Southern Surety stock.[34]

The Southern Surety venture, however, was not without its advantages to Caldwell and Company. The bond house no doubt sold its affiliate at least $2,000,000 of bonds, and in addition made a profit from the earlier sales of Southern Surety stock, which amounted to $168,500 for Caldwell and Company's fiscal year ending June 30, 1929, while in the same year a profit of $79,000 was made on the sale of Southern Fire Insurance Company stock.[35] Caldwell and Company's relationship with Southern Surety Company and Southern Fire Insurance Company was close enough to include the assets of these companies in the total controlled by the banking house. At the end of 1929 Southern Surety had assets of $14,500,000 and Southern Fire, $3,022,000, making a total of $17,522,000.

Associated Life Companies

Caldwell and Company's first insurance holding company, Insurance Securities Corporation, was followed by a second, though of an entirely different type, Associated Life Companies, Incorporated. This company was chartered in Delaware on July 5, 1929, and authorized to issue 1,000,000 shares of no par common stock. It was organized by Caldwell and Company and Carey G. Arnett, president of Inter-Southern Life, who was made president of the new company. Its creation was formally announced on July 8, 1929, as a $20,000,000 holding company established to acquire controlling interests in some of the leading life insurance companies of the South.[36]

[33] "Memo., Southern Surety."   [34] "Petition of Devonstreet and Company."
[35] "Audit Report of Caldwell and Company," June 30, 1929.
[36] From copy of press release of July 8, 1929.

The plans for the company were indeed auspicious. It was to be financed by the sale of its 1,000,000 shares of stock at around $20 a share. On the day of its incorporation it contracted to purchase control of the Southeastern Life Insurance Company of Greenville, South Carolina, and control of Inter-Southern was to pass to it as soon as sufficient funds could be raised to buy Caldwell and Company's interest. This exchange would leave control of Inter-Southern with Caldwell and Company while at the same time relieving the banking house of its rather large non-income producing investment in Inter-Southern. The purchase of other companies for Associated Life Companies was planned and it can probably be justifiably assumed that it was planned to sell the control of Missouri State Life to the holding company at some later date.

The Southeastern Life Insurance Company was a profitable company with a good reputation in the Southeast, the region to which its operations were limited. At the end of 1928, six months before Associated Life Companies purchased its control, its admitted assets amounted to $3,652,000, insurance in force to $40,124,000, and capital stock of $200,000 represented by 2,000 shares of $100 par.[37] Associated Life Companies agreed to purchase the entire 2,000 shares of the capital stock of Southeastern Life from its president, C. O. Milford, and other stockholders for $1,150,000, of which $850,000 was to be paid in cash and $300,000 in the stock of Associated Life Companies at $22 a share. Thus Associated Life Companies agreed to pay $425 in cash and $150 in its stock for each share of Southeastern stock which had a book value of only $175. It was expected that the cash would be raised by the sale of Associated Life stock to the public but, until this could be done, Caldwell and Company loaned the holding company 120,172 shares of Inter-Southern stock with which it borrowed $225,000, while Inter-Southern advanced $383,000. These funds were used to pay $600,000 of the cash payment for the Southeastern stock and the payment of 13,636 shares of Associated Life Companies stock was made, leaving a balance due the old Southeastern stockholders of $250,000 which was secured by 1,300 shares of Southeastern stock. The other 700 shares of Southeastern stock were delivered to Associated Life Companies which pledged them to Inter-Southern to secure the advance of $383,000 it had made.[38]

The outcome of these transactions was that the controlling block of Southeastern stock was pledged with the old stockholders pending payment of $250,000; Inter-Southern held 700 shares of Southeastern Life

[37] Best's Reports, 1930, pp. 1087, 1090.
[38] Memorandum in the files of Receivers of Caldwell and Company by T. W. Goodloe. Not dated. Cited hereafter as "Memo., Asso. Life Cos."

which had cost it $383,000; and Caldwell and Company had turned over 120,172 shares of good collateral to the holding company for which it held nothing in exchange. Obviously the banking house had come out at the little end.

The second company purchased by Associated Life Companies was the Shenandoah Life Insurance Company of Roanoke, Virginia. This company, which had been formed in 1916, was a very strong and rapidly growing institution, its admitted assets having increased from $1,128,000 in 1920 to $5,437,000 in 1929, while insurance in force for the same years amounted to $12,112,000 and $86,205,000, respectively. The stockholders since 1921 had received dividends of between 5 and 9 per cent.[39] Robert H. Angell, president, and other large stockholders of Shenandoah Life, on October 19, 1929, agreed to sell 20,000 shares or 40 per cent of the outstanding capital stock of the company for $1,040,000, payable in two equal installments on October 19, 1929, and January 2, 1930.[40] The purchase price of $52 a share was more than two and a half times its book value of $20 a share and decidedly above its market value of $37. The control of insurance companies appears to have been very dear to Caldwell and Company. Associated Life Companies had sold no stock, had no funds, and hence had to borrow to meet the payments on the purchase contract. The source of funds for this transaction was Lehman Brothers, this house advancing $520,000 on October 19, 1929, and the same amount on January 2, 1930, when the other half fell due. The 20,000 shares of Shenandoah Life were pledged as collateral for the loan and in addition half of the loan was guaranteed by Caldwell and Company.[41]

The acquisition of Shenandoah Life was announced just prior to the crash of the New York stock market in October, 1929. Had this latter event not occurred, the stock of the Associated Life Companies would, no doubt, have been offered for sale to the public by Caldwell and Company in a very short time. But the crash came too soon; the stock was not offered to the public and, instead of Caldwell and Company's being relieved of its investment in Inter-Southern, it was burdened with other obligations it was in no position to carry. If Caldwell and Company had evaluated these transactions at the end of 1929, it would have had to mark its proposed Associated Life Companies an almost complete failure. It had not had control long enough to sell either the Southeastern or Shenandoah companies any securities nor did either keep deposits with the Bank of Tennessee. Finally, the dividends paid on their stock were not sufficient to pay interest on the loans necessary to carry the invest-

[39] *Best's Reports*, 1930, pp. 1080, 1084.   [40] "Memo., Asso. Life Cos."

[41] Copy of letter from Rogers Caldwell to Lehman Brothers, January 25, 1930.

ments in their stock. The only advantage, if such it was, to Caldwell and Company was that control was secured over additional assets of insurance companies totaling $9,415,000 and hence enhanced somewhat its prestige in the insurance world.

The Arkansas Venture

The remaining group of insurance companies that came under the control of Caldwell and Company were the Home Life, Home Fire, and Home Accident Insurance companies of Little Rock, Arkansas, which had been organized and were operated by A. B. Banks and his two principal associates, Vann M. Howell and J. J. Harrison. The Home Life Insurance Company at the close of 1928 had admitted assets of $3,817,000 and insurance in force of $43,063,000. The accident company during the same year wrote business the net premiums from which amounted to $2,569,000 and had assets of $2,770,000; while the fire company had assets of $2,726,000 and insurance in force of $208,409,000. The assets of all the companies were heavily loaded with bank stocks, the life company holding $763,000 of assets of this type, the fire company $1,381,000, and the accident company $730,000.[42] The fire and accident companies owned also rather large holdings of common stocks of lumber companies.

The banks, the stock of which was owned by the Home Companies, constituted what was known as the A. B. Banks chain, which included some fifty-five banks located throughout Arkansas. The American Southern Trust Company and the Exchange National Bank, both of Little Rock, were the largest, their combined resources amounting to $26,886,000, while the total resources of the banks in the chain outside Little Rock approximated $25,000,000. The soundness of Banks' insurance and banking firms was questioned by the more conservative bankers and business men of Little Rock. It was felt that country bank stocks, to say nothing of stocks of small lumber companies, were not a proper investment for insurance firms. Outside of Little Rock the people of Arkansas seemed to have more confidence in the companies, judging from the amount of business done over the state.

Caldwell and Company became interested in the purchase of the Home Life Company for Associated Life Companies early in 1929.[43] The transaction as worked out called for the purchase of an interest in all three insurance companies, and on March 7, 1929, Caldwell and Company agreed to pay Banks, Howell, and Harrison $3,780,000 for a 60 per cent stock

[42] Data on Home Life from *Best's Reports*, 1930, pp. 490, 494; data on other two companies from *Moody's Banks*, 1930, p. 2131.
[43] "Report on Examination of Home Life Insurance Company," June 30, 1929.

interest in each of the three companies.[44] Of the total purchase price, $750,000 was to be paid in cash in three equal installments on March 7, 1929, September 7, 1929, and March 7, 1930. The remaining $3,030,000 was to be paid Banks and his associates with assets taken out of the three companies by Caldwell and Company. In place of these assets taken out, Caldwell and Company was to turn over to the three companies securities or cash of the same total amount, these substituted securities to be approved by the Arkansas Insurance Department. The $3,030,000 was to be paid in three annual installments of $1,010,000 beginning May 1, 1930, the deferred payments being secured by the stock of the three companies. Caldwell and Company made its first payment of $250,000 in cash on the date of the contract, March 7, 1929, and the second payment of a like amount on September 7, 1929. These funds were raised by selling temporarily to Insurance Securities Corporation that part of the stock of the Home Companies released when the payments were made.[45]

An additional feature of the transaction was the working out of a plan for a merger of the American Southern Trust Company and the Exchange National Bank. This merger was deemed desirable, for in this way certain doubtful assets could be removed from each bank and a new, strengthened bank would result. The merger was completed and a new bank, the American Exchange Trust Company, was set up, with capital of $1,000,000, and assets of $20,408,000. The new capital was raised by sale of stock to the old stockholders of the American Southern Trust Company, with Banks and Caldwell and Company buying the stock not thus sold.

Had the contract for the purchase of the Home Companies been completed,[46] these companies would have been materially strengthened. The stock of most of the banks and lumber companies as well as other less desirable holdings were to be removed and replaced with sounder assets, thus resulting in a much more acceptable portfolio for the insurance companies. From the standpoint of Caldwell and Company, however, the project had no such marked advantages and by the beginning of 1930 was proving costly indeed. The Associated Life Companies was in no position to take over the contracts for the purchase of the Home Companies, and Caldwell and Company itself was becoming pressed for funds, so Insurance Securities Corporation had to be called into the breach. Further, in the merger of the banks, Caldwell and Company had lost an investment of $75,000 in the stock of the Exchange National Bank which it had purchased in January, 1929, and had, in addition, put $25,000

[44] From copies of original and subsequent contracts entered into between Caldwell and Company and Banks and associates for the purchase of the Home Companies.

[45] Balance Sheet of Insurance Securities Corporation, December 31, 1929.

[46] See Chapter XIV, *infra*.

into the stock of the new bank.[47] On the other hand, the banking house gained control of insurance assets of $9,373,000, of one bank with assets of $20,408,000, and, until their stocks could be taken out of the Home Companies, of a chain of banks with assets of approximately $25,000,000.

SUMMARY

Caldwell and Company's investments in, and advances to, its insurance companies amounted to $2,831,000 on June 30, 1926. During the three following years, this investment showed a marked growth, standing at $3,300,000 in 1927, $4,062,000 in 1928, and $8,350,000 in 1929. Partially offsetting these investments were deposits which the companies kept with Caldwell and Company amounting in the four years mentioned, respectively, to $1,791,000, $2,853,000, $858,000, and $2,180,000.[48]

Although bought at high prices, the control of its insurance companies obtained for Caldwell and Company some tangible advantages in the form of sale of securities to the companies, profit on the sale of stock of the companies, unsecured deposits of the companies' funds, and use of its holdings of stock of the companies to secure claims. In addition there were those intangible advantages of prestige in the financial world that naturally came to the company because of the approximately $233,000,000 of insurance company assets that it controlled. This amount was made up as follows:

Company	Total Admitted Assets as of December 31, 1929
Missouri State Life	$143,262,000
Southwestern Life	33,154,000
Inter-Southern Life	20,204,000
Southern Surety	14,500,000
Southern Fire	3,022,000
Southeastern Life	3,978,000
Shenandoah Life	5,437,000
Home Companies	9,373,000
Total	$232,930,000

The control of these companies placed Caldwell and Company in a position of leadership in the insurance business of the South. At the same time, to gain the control of these companies, Caldwell and Company had assumed a large volume of obligations which at the close of 1929 amounted to $3,000,000 for Missouri State, $3,780,000 for the Home

[47] "Report of Receivers of Caldwell and Company," Part I, pp. 365, 381.
[48] "Audit Report of Caldwell and Company," as of dates mentioned.

Companies, $1,040,000 for Shenandoah Life, $850,000 for Southeastern Life, and a debt to Kidder-Peabody of $1,115,000 for its interest in Southern Surety, or a total of $9,785,000. The ability to meet these obligations depended upon the marketing of the stock of the companies or of Associated Life Companies, which was in turn contingent upon the conditions of the securities markets. The crash in the fall of 1929 meant that Caldwell and Company was to be hard put to meet obligations which it so readily assumed during the few years previous with apparently no question being raised in the organization as to the potentialities for catastrophe from such a program if the bull market should collapse.

Chapter VIII

GROWTH OF INVESTMENTS IN BANKS

The widening scope of Caldwell and Company's influence in the insurance field was paralleled by a similar penetration into banking. With the exception of the banks acquired in Arkansas in connection with the purchase of the Home Insurance Companies,[1] all the banks that the company controlled were in Tennessee. There were banks in other states, however, with which the company became closely allied through minority stock ownership and other connections.

The Fourth and First National Bank

The Fourth and First National Bank, under the guidance of James E. Caldwell as president, continued to expand during the late twenties at an even more rapid pace than in the earlier part of that decade. Deposits increased from $20,420,000 in 1926 to $40,661,000 in 1929, while total assets increased from $29,166,000 to $53,940,000 during the same period.[2] A considerable part of this growth came through mergers. In 1927 the Nashville Trust Company took over the business of the Fourth and First Bank and Trust Company, the state bank owned by the Fourth and First National Bank, this latter bank, in turn, obtaining ownership of the entire capital stock of the Nashville Trust Company and trusteeing it for the benefit of its own stockholders. The same year the Fourth and First National absorbed the Central National Bank of Nashville.

Another division of the Fourth and First group in Nashville was the Fourth and First National Company, its security affiliate, which carried on transactions which national banking laws would not have countenanced for the bank, such as the purchase with Caldwell and Company of the control of the Missouri State Life Insurance Company. The $100,000 capital stock of the company was all owned by the Nashville Trust Company, and its president was Meredith Caldwell, a younger brother of Rogers Caldwell. The Fourth and First National Company was later characterized as a mere bookkeeping and juggling department used by the Fourth and First National Bank, the Nashville Trust Company, and Caldwell and Company for their "sinister and unlawful trans-

---

[1] See Chapter vii, *supra.*
[2] Statistics from *Moody's Banks,* 1927, p. 2018; 1930, p. 1160.

actions among themselves and with outsiders who did not know the real state of affairs."[3] Outside Nashville were eight relatively small banks controlled by Fourth and First National. These various institutions brought the total assets of the Fourth and First National group to approximately $100,000,000.

This group of banks was seemingly operating smoothly when on June 20, 1929, James E. Caldwell announced to the stockholders of the Fourth and First National that the board of directors had voted to effect a closer consolidation of the Nashville units. Under the proposed plan all of these units were to be joined into one institution to be designated as the Fourth and First Bank and Trust Company, operating under the amended state charter of the Nashville Trust Company. The new institution was to have capital of $4,000,000, surplus of a like amount, and undivided profits of $2,000,000.[4] The reason for the denationalization of the Fourth and First Bank, as announced to the public, was simply that it was in line with the trend throughout the country for banks to surrender their national charters, certain large banks being cited as examples. In considering the real reason for this step, the most apparent one would be that the bank could be more easily operated according to Mr. Caldwell's policies if it were examined by the Tennessee Banking Department than by the national bank examiners, and Mr. Caldwell was choosing less strict supervision rather than sounder banking, a choice allowed bankers under the dual banking system that has contributed much to the low banking standards of this country. The bank was becoming more and more closely related to Caldwell and Company through loans to the latter, through joint ventures such as the purchase of control of Missouri State Life, and through the purchase of securities. Its assets arising from its connections with the investment house might well have been questioned by the national bank examiners.

The real motives behind the actions of James E. Caldwell are even more clouded in view of the fact that the plan for the denationalization of the bank was abandoned and on January 17, 1930, the directors of the Fourth and First National Bank and the Nashville Trust Company unanimously voted to establish another institution, Fourth and First Banks, Incorporated, as a holding company for the stock of Fourth and First National Bank, this latter institution retaining ownership of the Nashville Trust Company. This holding company was actually incor-

[3] *Original Bill of Knox County, Knox County v. Fourth and First National Bank, et al.,* No. 44871 in Part II of Chancery Court of Davidson County, Tennessee, p. 68. Cited hereafter as *Original Bill of Knox County.*

[4] Photostatic copy of Minutes of Regular Annual Meeting of Board of Directors of Fourth and First National Bank and Nashville Trust Company, January 17, 1930.

porated in February, 1930, and the stockholders of the bank were requested to exchange each share of Fourth and First National Bank stock
for one and one-third shares of Fourth and First Banks, Incorporated.
Practically all of the stock of Fourth and First National, except directors'
qualifying shares, was thus exchanged. This exchange took approximately $3,500,000 of the holding company's capital of $4,000,000, or
175,000 out of 200,000 shares of par value $20, leaving $500,000 of capital
stock to be used at the discretion of the board of directors.[5]

The reason for the changed plan was never publicly announced. The
establishment of the holding company removed personal double liability
on the ownership of the national bank stock but, since a state-chartered
bank could have been held by the holding company as well as a nationally
chartered one, this does not explain the abandonment of the plan to
denationalize the Fourth and First. A possible explanation is that the
Federal Reserve Bank of Atlanta would not accept it as a state member
bank as long as it was in such a condition and, on the other hand, would
not let it withdraw from the system until it cleared up its indebtedness
of $2,600,000 at the Federal Reserve Bank. Fourth and First Banks, In-
corporated, raising its funds by the sale of some of its stock to the public
at high prices, would have been in a position to buy some of the more
doubtful assets of the Fourth and First National Bank and thus put it in
a position to clear itself of control of the Federal Reserve Bank and the
national bank examiners. But this is speculation.[6]

The several announcements concerning impending changes in the
structure of the Fourth and First group were accompanied by stock-selling
campaigns, and since Caldwell and Company was active in marketing
the bank stock it profited from these campaigns. When the proposed
denationalization of the bank was announced, Rogers Caldwell, for his
company, made an agreement with Meredith Caldwell, for Fourth and
First National Company, to sell stock of the Fourth and First National
Bank at a commission of five dollars a share. Only Frank D. Marr, head
of Caldwell and Company's local securities department which handled
this stock, was informed of the agreement. Caldwell and Company sold
a large amount of the stock and, as the sales came in, the accounting
department, not having been informed of the agreement with Fourth
and First National Company—an example of the at times incomprehensible way Rogers Caldwell managed his business—determined the
company's profit at the difference between the cost of the stock already

[5] *Ibid.*

[6] The basis for this view is the fact that this was exactly what was happening to National
Bank of Kentucky at approximately the same time. See Chapter xiii, *infra.*

held by Caldwell and Company and the selling price. The profit thus computed amounted to $2,001,000, yet, when sales had to be covered and delivery made, Caldwell and Company found itself liable for short sales amounting to $1,400,000 which had to be met by purchases made from Fourth and First National Company at market less the five-dollar commission, reducing the company's profit to approximately $600,000.[7]

The stock-peddling efforts in connection with the establishment of Fourth and First Banks, Incorporated, were also beneficial to Caldwell and Company. The 25,000 shares of the holding company which were not exchanged for Fourth and First National Bank stock were sold for $131.17 a share to the Fourth and First National Company, which in turn formed a syndicate with Caldwell and Company to sell the stock to the public for $135 a share. Caldwell and Company made a substantial volume of sales but, instead of remitting the proceeds to Fourth and First National Company, used them as needed in its own business. By March 1, 1930, Caldwell and Company had appropriated approximately $414,000 in this manner, for which Fourth and First National Company took the investment house's demand note. The outcome was simply a loan to Caldwell and Company of $414,000 raised originally for Fourth and First Banks, Incorporated.[8]

During all of this time Caldwell and Company was relying on the Fourth and First National Bank for funds, as it had done since its inception. The amount of loans to Caldwell and Company from the bank increased rapidly from 1926 to 1929, varying at balance sheet dates between $700,000 and $1,681,000.[9] The amount directly and indirectly borrowed by Caldwell and Company as of balance sheet dates during this period was always in excess of the limit of loans by national banks to one party. The law was evaded, however, by having the Bank of Tennessee borrow funds in its name, as well as by having the Nashville Trust Company advance some of the funds, instead of having all loans made directly by the Fourth and First National Bank to Caldwell and Company.

A further relationship between Caldwell and Company and the Fourth and First National Bank was that the latter's trust department served in the capacity as trustee on many of Caldwell and Company's trust agreements covering deposits of funds and in connection with the issuance of mortgage bonds. The trust agreements covering deposits for which the bank acted as trustee were always formally in order but the bank has

---

[7] "Audit Report of Caldwell and Company," June 30, 1928, June 30, 1929; also statements to the writer by T. G. Donovan. [8] *Original Bill of Knox County,* p. 80.

[9] "Audit Report of Caldwell and Company," 1926 to 1929.

been accused of subordinating the interests of the depositors to those of Caldwell and Company.[10]

In practically every respect Caldwell and Company's relations with the Fourth and First National Bank were advantageous. This is seen clearly in the profit made on the sale of the bank's stock and the funds advanced by the bank and can at least be inferred from the relations with the trust department and the sale of bonds to the bank. Thus, while Caldwell and Company did not at any time have complete control of the bank, it was successful on the whole in using it to a considerable extent for its own financial requirements.[11]

THE HOLSTON-UNION NATIONAL BANK

The second bank in which Caldwell and Company bought a large block of stock was the Holston National Bank of Knoxville, Tennessee. This bank dated its origin from February 1, 1891, when it was chartered by the state as the Holston Bank and Trust Company. A few months later, in October, 1891, it was taken into the national banking system as the Holston National Bank. Approximately ten years after its establishment Joseph P. Gaut was made president and it was under his guidance that the bank developed.

In the latter part of 1926 the Holston National Bank absorbed the Third National Bank of Knoxville which was in financial difficulties because of irregularities in the conduct of certain officials. The cashier of the Third National, J. Basil Ramsey, was not involved in these difficulties and was taken into the Holston National as a vice president.[12] At about the same time, the Holston Trust Company was established as a wholly owned affiliate of the bank, conducting a fiduciary and bond business. By the end of 1926 the Holston Bank had total assets of $9,292,000 and deposits of $5,970,000, while the trust company had assets of around $500,000.[13]

The purchase of stock of the Holston National Bank by Caldwell and Company is significant because it was the first of a series of important joint ventures of Rogers Caldwell and Colonel Luke Lea, a prominent Tennessee publisher, politician, and business man.[14] These two men, previous to this transaction, had been jointly interested in real estate deals in and around Nashville but, when early in 1927 they went to Knox-

---

[10] *Original Bill of Knox County.* Similar charges were made in the case *Gibson County v. Fourth and First National Bank,* 96 Southwestern (2d), 184 (1936).

[11] See also Chapter xiv, *infra.*

[12] From evidence taken in the case *United States v. J. Basil Ramsey,* No. 11672, United States District Court for the Eastern District of Tennessee. Cited hereafter as "Ramsey Evidence."

[13] *Moody's Banks,* 1928, p. 605.   [14] See Chapters x and xi, *infra.*

ville and offered to buy 2,000 shares or one third of the bank's total capital stock at $225 a share, they were taking steps that led to several other even more important undertakings and resulted in tying the names of Luke Lea and Rogers Caldwell almost inseparably together, although Luke Lea neither then nor later owned any stock of, or held any position in, Caldwell and Company. However, the relations of these two men continued until the collapse of the investment house.

A few days after Lea and Caldwell had made their offer, President Gaut informed his larger stockholders and advised them to sell a part of their holdings because they could get a good price and later would be able to buy other stock in the open market at a lower price and at the same time the bank would be securing two men in a position to give it a considerable amount of business. To set an example for the others, Gaut sold 400 of his 420 shares, while the remainder of the 2,000 shares was soon offered to Caldwell and Lea.[15]

The 2,000 shares of stock cost $450,000, but 500 shares were immediately sold for $112,000, at a loss of $1 a share. The remaining $338,000 was borrowed by Caldwell and Lea from New York banks on notes endorsed by Caldwell and Company and secured by the Holston Bank stock. When the notes fell due, they were paid by Caldwell and Company, the investment house taking over its half of the stock, while Colonel Lea pledged his half on notes payable to Caldwell and Company, but permitted it to be used as the company saw fit.[16] The effect was that Caldwell and Company was financing the purchase of the control of the bank for itself and Colonel Lea, with the latter doing little more than giving his notes payable, the bulk of which was never paid, for his part of the transaction, yet at the same time gaining an important position in the control of the bank.

The results of the transference of the block of stock to Lea and Caldwell were soon felt. At the meeting of the directors in 1928, Gaut resigned, and J. Basil Ramsey, with the support of Lea and Caldwell, was elected president. Shortly thereafter Ramsey effected a merger between his bank and the Union National Bank of Knoxville, the name of the merged institution becoming the Holston-Union National Bank. Through this merger the bank, together with its controlled trust company, became the largest in the city. Ramsey proved to be an ideal bank president from the standpoint of Lea because after taking this office he directed its policies to benefit Lea as much as possible. In carrying on

---

[15] "Ramsey Evidence."

[16] Answer of Receivers of Caldwell and Company to the Petition of Colonel Luke Lea in the case *Dean* v. *Caldwell.*

his transactions with the bank, Lea made use of a number of corporations he had chartered in connection with his Nashville real estate operations, among which were the Belle Meade Land Company, Central Properties, Incorporated, and United Property Company. All of these owned property which Mrs. Lea had inherited from her father, Percy Warner, and together had issued mortgage bonds amounting to $1,350,000, for which there was little or no market but which Colonel Lea could hypothecate at friendly banks. The bonds were to be retired as the property was sold. Another corporation of Lea's was the National Investment Trust, a sort of personal holding company, with a capital of $10,000 and with Ramsey as president but with Luke Lea as boss. Lea apparently used this corporation to protect himself against personal liability in carrying on some of his activities. Ramsey permitted his bank to make large loans to the various companies, one of the more questionable items being a loan of $125,000 to the National Investment Trust, an amount over twelve times the capital of the borrowing corporation. In addition to loans, Ramsey allowed Lea to make "kiting" transactions through the bank, holding his drafts as cash items for months at a time.[17]

The relations between Lea and the Holston-Union are clearly portrayed in the following excerpt from a letter written in November, 1928, by President Ramsey to Luke Lea: ". . . in my efforts to co-operate with you, I have done a number of things, which, if my Board of Directors and the National Bank Examiners knew, it would be just cause for the Bank Examiner to call my Board together and demand my resignation."[18]

That the situation had become worse early in 1929 is evident by the strenuous objections at that time of the national bank examiner to the accommodations given Lea at the bank. Ramsey was warned that his practices with Lea could not continue without the bank examiner's taking steps to remove him from the presidency. The examiner called for a showdown in May, 1929, when he requested that either the Lea notes be cleared up or a meeting of the directors called to see what could be done. Ramsey notified Lea that he was being put on the spot and Lea immediately paid $435,000 of the obligations of himself and his companies. This served both to pacify the examiner and to make Ramsey even more confident of Lea's financial condition. Very shortly thereafter Lea was again borrowing heavily at the bank, either personally or through his various companies, which resulted in renewed warnings to Ramsey, both on the part of the examiner and the Comptroller of the Currency himself. In reply to these admonitions, Ramsey expressed his great obligations to Colonel Lea who had brought much profitable business to the

[17] "Ramsey Evidence."　　　　　　　[18] Ibid.

bank, and consequently Ramsey continued to shape the lending policies of the Holston-Union National Bank according to Lea's desires.[19]

Caldwell and Company's advantages obtained from the bank, while not insignificant, were hardly as great as those obtained by Lea, and the bank was generally regarded by Caldwell and Company as the Colonel's baby. However, Caldwell and Company earned a profit of around $125 a share on a part of its Holston-Union stock sold to the Inter-Southern and to its controlled investment trust, Shares-in-the-South, Incorporated,[20] thus enabling the company to retain the same amount of control over the bank while shifting the burden of the investment to other companies. Also, Caldwell and Company looked to the bank for a considerable volume of funds. Thus, on June 30, 1928, Holston-Union had an unsecured deposit with the Bank of Tennessee amounting to $500,000, but this had been reduced to $100,000 a year later,[21] possibly on the advice of the national bank examiner. There is no evidence of advances on notes until the latter part of 1929 when the Holston-Union loaned Caldwell and Company $100,000 and the Bank of Tennessee the same amount, at the same time, however, withdrawing its deposit from the latter institution. In December, 1929, Holston-Union bought $250,000 of bonds from Caldwell and Company under a repurchase agreement. The bonds were all speculative industrial issues, the market for which was very uncertain, yet Holston-Union was willing to subordinate the interests of itself and its depositors to the extent of buying the entire lot of bonds at par, thereby benefiting one of its important stockholders. At the close of 1929, through repurchase agreements and loans to Caldwell and Company and to the Bank of Tennessee, the Knoxville bank was advancing $450,000, or more than twice the amount of loans a bank with the capital and surplus of the Holston-Union could advance to one party under the Federal banking code.

From the standpoint of Colonel Lea and Caldwell and Company, the purchase of the control of the Holston-Union was indeed justifiable. From the standpoint of the bank, it was a most unfortunate event, for the lowered banking standards that followed the passage of the control of the bank into the hands of the two Nashville men placed it in a precarious condition.

THE MEMPHIS BANKS

The extension of Caldwell and Company's banking interests into Memphis, Tennessee, placed it in a strategic position with regard to the banking systems in three of the four largest cities of the state, thus en-

---

[19] *Ibid.* [20] See Chapter IX, *infra.*
[21] "Audit Report of Caldwell and Company," as of dates mentioned.

abling it to become by far the strongest influence in Tennessee banking. Caldwell and Company entered Memphis banking in May, 1928, when Rogers Caldwell for his company, Luke Lea for himself, and Edward Potter, Jr., for the Commerce-Union Company, the security affiliate of the Commerce-Union Bank of Nashville, purchased 751 shares, or 51 per cent, of the capital stock of the Manhattan Savings Bank and Trust Company, from the heirs of I. Samelson, thus gaining control of the bank. The group paid $400 a share, or a total of $300,400, for the stock, borrowing the funds from the National Park Bank of New York.[22] The Manhattan Bank was considered the strongest small bank in the city. It had had a long and profitable existence and its stock was regarded as a desirable investment. At the close of 1928 it had deposits of $8,613,000 and assets of $9,866,000.[23]

Not content with the control of a small bank in the city, the group sought a larger one. Late in 1928 the Union and Planters Bank and Trust Company, one of the three largest banks of the city, suffered a run. Its immediate liquidity was not threatened and it came through the one-day run unharmed. But basically the bank was in a rather unsound condition because of its large volume of slow and doubtful assets and a thorough reorganization was desirable. Knowing that this condition existed, the men who had bought control of the Manhattan together with two Memphis bankers, Frank Hayden, who was already connected with the bank, and William White, executive vice president of the Manhattan, offered to reorganize the Union and Planters with a view toward improving its condition. The offer was accepted and shortly after the undertaking was begun, James E. Caldwell, through the Fourth and First National Company, was asked to join the group, which he did. To carry out the transaction, Rogers Caldwell, James E. Caldwell, Luke Lea, and Edward Potter, Jr., of Nashville, and William White and Frank Hayden of Memphis established the Bank Securities Corporation on February 25, 1929, with capital stock of $12,000, represented by 120 shares of par value $100, 20 shares of which went to each of the six in the group.

The reorganization plan of the Union and Planters called for increasing the capital of the bank from $2,500,000 to $3,500,000, the surplus from $200,000 to $3,500,000, and undivided profits from approximately $830,000 to $1,750,000, while slow and doubtful assets totaling $1,700,000 were to be removed and replaced by cash. The Manhattan Bank was to become an affiliated institution of the Union and Planters with all of the Manhattan stock trusteed for the stockholders of the larger banks. The cap-

[22] Letter from Edward Potter, Jr., to E. A. Goodloe, February 9, 1929.
[23] Moody's Banks, 1929, p. 625.

ital of the Manhattan was to be increased from $150,000 to $700,000, surplus to $700,000, and undivided profits to $1,050,000.[24] Finally, the new bank was to apply for a Federal charter and, until this was granted, it was to operate as the Union Planters Bank and Trust Company, thus dropping the first "and" from its former title.

Under the reorganization plan approximately $5,220,000 was needed to increase the net worth items of the Union and Planters Bank, $1,450,000 for the same purpose in the Manhattan Bank, and $1,700,000 to replace the assets to be removed from the Union and Planters, thus making a total cash requirement of approximately $8,370,000 which the reorganization group expected to raise by the sale of Union Planters stock. The par value of the stock in the new bank was set at $10, in place of the old par of $100, and the stockholders of Union and Planters Bank were given the option of selling their old stock at $250 a share or exchanging it for new stock. There were 115,000 out of a total of 350,000 shares of stock of the new bank thus offered, while the stockholders of the Manhattan were given the privilege of exchanging their stock for 14,000 shares of the new bank. In all, 129,000 shares of the new Union Planters Bank were offered in exchange for the shares of the old Union and Planters Bank and the Manhattan Bank.

The old stockholders expressed their approval of the plan by taking almost all the stock offered them, thus requiring a negligible cash payment to them. Of the remaining 221,000 shares, Bank Securities Corporation was to hold 75,000 as its permanent investment while 146,000 shares were offered to the public at $63 a share early in 1929 by Caldwell and Company, Fourth and First National Company, and Commerce-Union Company in Nashville, and by Union and Planters Company and Manhattan Securities Company in Memphis. The sale of all of this stock would have raised $9,198,000, which would have been sufficient to carry through reorganization, and to give to the promoting group a cash profit of over $800,000 and the $1,700,000 of slow assets to be removed from the bank, at the same time allowing the group to retain enough stock to control the bank.

The Union and Planters stock was not absorbed in the market as readily as anticipated, some 109,000 shares having been sold by February 28, 1929, the date set for the reorganization, rather than the 146,000 expected. This was learned only after the Nashville group, headed by James E. Caldwell and Luke Lea, had reached Memphis to conclude the deal, and the necessity of obtaining $700,000 was pressing. This obstacle was overcome by the Bank of Tennessee's advancing the needed amount,

[24] Letter from Hirsch Morris, president of the Manhattan Savings Bank and Trust Company, to the stockholders of the bank, January 4, 1929.

this action being taken by T. G. Donovan, who came to supervise the details of the transaction. The actual transfer of funds to the credit of the Union Planters Bank was made by Donovan's giving the bank duplicate deposit slips on the Bank of Tennessee, Fourth and First National Bank, and Commerce-Union Bank. Had the representatives of the old bank asked that checks be given rather than deposit slips, as they could and probably should have done, the whole deal might have fallen through for Donovan had no power to sign checks for the various banks and the Bank of Tennessee was in no position to honor the checks that would have been drawn on it without first borrowing from other sources. But no questions were asked and the deal was completed.[25]

The new Union Planters Bank and Trust Company was a materially improved institution after its reorganization. The paying in of cash to increase its net worth and to replace its $1,700,000 of doubtful assets had placed it in a very sound condition. Frank Hayden, a leading Memphis banker who had taken part in the reorganization, was made president while William White remained as executive vice president of the Manhattan Savings Bank, the wholly owned affiliate of the Union Planters Bank. At the close of 1929 Union Planters had total assets of $38,537,000 while the Manhattan had assets of $10,830,000,[26] the two combined constituting by far the largest banking group in the city.

As soon as the new bank was organized Caldwell and Company began seeking funds from it. In fact, on the way back to Nashville, after buying the bank, Donovan persuaded Luke Lea that the Bank of Tennessee should be rewarded for its services by a deposit from Union Planters of $500,000, which amount was immediately transferred by wire. By June 30, 1929, this deposit had been reduced to $238,000 but the Manhattan Bank had on deposit at that time with the Bank of Tennessee $605,000, making a total unsecured deposit of $843,000. At the same date Caldwell and Company had sold $616,000 of notes and bonds under a repurchase agreement to the Union Planters and $259,000 to the Manhattan, or a total of $875,000 to the two banks. Further, the Union Planters Bank had loaned Caldwell and Company $720,000 of Memphis, Tennessee, Revenue Anticipation Notes which Caldwell and Company used to secure several of its deposit accounts. Thus, in all, the two Memphis banks were advancing Caldwell and Company the astoundingly large sum of $2,438,000 as of June 30, 1929, four months after the reorganization had been completed.[27]

[25] The method of paying for the bank was related to the writer by T. G. Donovan.
[26] *Moody's Banks,* 1930, pp. 1160, 1161.
[27] "Audit Report of Caldwell and Company," June 30, 1929.

Certain of the Memphis directors of the bank soon became concerned lest the new owners after placing it on a sound basis would proceed virtually to wreck it. Their opportunity to protect the bank came when it secured a national charter on July 9, 1929, and became the Union Planters National Bank and Trust Company. These directors insisted that the Comptroller of the Currency exercise his power to protect the bank, which led to the agreement contained in the following letter:[28]

MEMPHIS, TENNESSEE
April 9, 1929

COMPTROLLER OF THE CURRENCY
WASHINGTON, D. C.

DEAR SIR:

In a meeting held in Memphis, Tennessee, with your examiners, Wm. R. Young and John S. Wood, the matter of the application of the Union Planters Bank and Trust Company to convert into a national bank was discussed at length and in detail. The five undersigned, Rogers Caldwell, Luke Lea, Edward Potter, Jr., Frank Hayden and William White, are members of a group that underwrote the reorganization of the Union Planters Bank and Trust Company.

After a full discussion of the matter, the undersigned expressed the opinion that in view of their large stock interest in the Union Planters Bank and Trust Company it would be to the interest of the bank that they would not jointly, nor severally, nor individually, nor any of their corporations, firms, enterprises or underwritings either directly or indirectly, by accommodation loans or otherwise use any of the funds of the proposed Union Planters National Bank and Trust Company or the Manhattan Savings Bank and Trust Company; and it is further provided and agreed that if on the date of the conversion of the Union Planters Bank and Trust Company into a national bank the said Rogers Caldwell, Luke Lea, Edward Potter, Jr., Frank Hayden, or William White, or either of them, jointly or severally, individually, or through any of their corporations, firms, enterprises or underwritings, directly or indirectly owe the Union Planters Bank and Trust Company or the Manhattan Savings Bank and Trust Company, or both, that all of the said indebtedness will be paid within six months from the date said Union Planters Bank and Trust Company converts into a national bank.

This agreement on the part of the undersigned is to remain in full force and effect until modified or abrogated by the Comptroller of the Currency.

Respectfully,

ROGERS CALDWELL
LUKE LEA
EDWARD POTTER, JR.
FRANK HAYDEN
WILLIAM WHITE

[28] From a copy of the original in the files of the Receivers of Caldwell and Company.

Thus, the Union Planters National Bank and Trust Company was rendered of little use to Caldwell and Company as a source of funds and the investment house was faced with the necessity of repaying the advances the bank had already made.

Moreover, the transaction necessitated the raising of large amounts of cash to carry the investment in the stock of Union Planters National Bank. Bank Securities Corporation, after the promotion had been completed, owned 131,396 shares of Union Planters stock which it carried at its cost of $2,342,000, including payment of $50,000 to L. K. Saulsbury of Memphis, who had acted as agent for the group. The remainder of its assets were primarily the $1,700,000 of slow and doubtful assets taken from the Union Planters Bank.[29] To liquidate these assets, a subsidiary, the West Tennessee Company, was organized, its entire stock being owned by Bank Securities Corporation, and some progress was made toward realizing on this property. The funds obtained from this source were used to replenish the reserves for accrued interest and taxes of the two banks which had been added to surplus when the reorganization took place and also to buy out the interests of Hayden and White in the undertaking. Hayden was let out as president of the bank in October, 1929, and his stock in Bank Securities Corporation was bought from him by the holding company and retired. White then became president, but in July, 1930, he was removed, his stock of Bank Securities Corporation bought and retired, and an outsider, E. P. Peacock of Clarksdale, Mississippi, was selected to head the bank.

At the close of 1929 Bank Securities Corporation owed a total of $4,288,000, which was secured by its stock in Union Planters National Bank. Its holding of this stock had increased as a result of efforts to peg the price which could be financed only by additional borrowings. Of its total debts $2,045,000 was owed to Caldwell and Company and the Bank of Tennessee, which meant that Caldwell and Company had had to borrow from some other sources to provide these sums. Bank Securities borrowed the remaining funds from other Nashville banks as well as from New York banks. Thus, by the end of 1929 the promotion had become exceedingly burdensome to Caldwell and Company. It was having to borrow large sums in an effort to maintain a market for Union Planters stock, and other banks which would lend money directly to Caldwell and Company were advancing funds to Bank Securities Corporation, thus reducing the amount of funds Caldwell and Company could expect to borrow from them, while at the same time it was precluded from borrowing from the Memphis banks by the agreement with

[29] Balance Sheet of Bank Securities Corporation, March 31, 1929.

the Comptroller of the Currency. There was in all about $4,500,000 locked up in the stock of Union Planters National Bank that might otherwise have been available to Caldwell and Company. As the financial condition of the investment house became steadily weaker, the need for these funds was felt very strongly. Thus in many respects the Union Planters transaction can be regarded as an important factor in the downfall of Caldwell and Company.

OTHER BANKING INTERESTS

While the banks already discussed in this chapter, together with those acquired in the purchase of the Home Insurance Companies, were the only ones to come under the actual control of Caldwell and Company, the company bought considerable stock interests in the Commercial National Bank and Trust Company of New York and the Canal Bank and Trust Company of New Orleans. Also, through its relations with Luke Lea, Caldwell and Company became aligned with the Liberty Bank and Trust Company of Nashville and the Central Bank and Trust Company of Asheville, North Carolina, but the investment house did not own stock in either of these banks. The Liberty Bank was a small state bank organized in 1925 and dominated by Luke Lea and its president, R. E. Donnell. Lea used this bank in the same way he did the Holston-Union National in Knoxville. His cold checks would be held as cash items and later paid by checks which were "kites" on other banks. It was later estimated that the volume of transactions handled in this manner for Lea approximated $10,000,000.[30]

The Central Bank and Trust Company of Asheville deserves a more detailed account. This was the largest bank in western North Carolina, having deposits of around $15,000,000. It had loaded itself very heavily with real estate loans at the time of the Asheville real estate boom and, with constantly dropping realty values in that section, its financial condition became increasingly desperate. Connected with the bank as a securities affiliate was the Central Securities Company, which had taken over a large part of the property on which the bank had foreclosed and issued mortgage bonds secured by this property. In this way the bank hoped to shift the carrying of the real estate to the investing public, but, in general, it was unsuccessful. The bank was able to continue operations largely because the city of Asheville and Buncombe County kept rather large deposits with it. In spite of these deposits, the officers of the insti-

[30] *Interim Report of the Special Legislative Committee,* appointed by the 67th General Assembly of Tennessee, January, 1931. Report dated March 16, 1931. Reprinted in *House Journal of 67th General Assembly of State of Tennessee,* 1931. Cited hereafter as *Interim Report.*

tution realized that if they were to keep operating they must secure help from some quarter.[31]

Wallace B. Davis and J. Charles Bradford, president and cashier respectively of the Asheville bank, thought they had found the needed source of help when, early in 1930, with their bank in an insolvent condition, they made a contact with Luke Lea, who had the reputation of being both a big banker and a very rich man. Lea thought that through this contact he was going to be able to expand his sphere of influence in the banking world in an important way into North Carolina and Kentucky. With this in mind Lea worked out a plan to save the Central Bank as well as to increase his power.

The details of Lea's plan have never been completely disclosed for the organization was never perfected. It involved, however, the establishment of a holding company with an original capital of $7,500,000 which would own the controlling interest in the Central Bank. Lea at least hoped to bring the Wachovia Bank and Trust Company into the picture for the plan contemplated "the guarantee by the controlling shareholders of Wachovia Bank and Trust Company of the assets transferred into the merged bank."[32] There is no evidence to the effect that the Wachovia even casually considered Lea's overture. From the data available it can be inferred that the new institution was to be called the Union Trust Company, for in May, 1930, the Central Bank loaned $200,000 to such an institution with which Luke Lea was connected. It can be further inferred that this money was used to buy the controlling interest of the First City Bank and Trust Company of Hopkinsville, Kentucky, for it was about this time that the control of this bank passed to Lea and Davis. Later, in October, 1930, Luke Lea, Jr., was writing Davis that

our Kentucky representative, Mr. E. W. Bryan, Vice-President of the First City Bank and Trust Company at Hopkinsville, was here today for our weekly conference, and we have discussed with him some parleys he has recently had with the First National Bank, of Greenville, Kentucky, also the Farmers State Bank at Greenville, and some at Central City, Kentucky.[33]

Continuing, Lea said:

I am sending herein copy of the last printed statement of the First National Bank of Greenville, showing resources of $2,139,401.46, bonds and securities $958,000.00, also Central City statements.

[31] All information concerning Lea's relations with the Central Bank and Trust Company is from the *Record* in the case *State* v. *Wallace B. Davis, Luke Lea, and Luke Lea, Jr.*, No. 585, in the Supreme Court of North Carolina, 1931, unless otherwise noted. Cited hereafter as *Lea Record*.

[32] Letter from Luke Lea to Wallace B. Davis, May 5, 1930.—*Lea Record*, p. 636.

[33] October 8, 1930.—*Lea Record*, pp. 694, 695.

This is one of the strongest and most successful banks in Central Kentucky, and the controlling spirit, Mr. Reynolds, wishes to retire from active participation in the bank as he is now a wealthy man, and wishes to take things a little easier. He also owns control in the other bank at Greenville, which shows resources of approximately $500,000.00. Also he controls the Citizens Union at Central City, resources $487,000.00, and being in the same county as Greenville.

I believe we could pay a 300 per cent cash dividend at Greenville and could buy control of the bank with an investment of $60,000, and with nearly $1,000,000.00 in bonds on hand we could sell a good part of them and substitute our issues instead.

This letter probably more than any other one written document illustrates the methods used by the Leas in their banking deals. No comment need be made as to the basic honesty of such transactions. Suffice it to say that these Kentucky banks were not brought under the control of Lea and Davis because their little empire along with the larger one of Caldwell and Company began toppling before any action could be taken. Lea and his corporations borrowed heavily from the Central Bank, usually on notes secured by bonds of Lea's real estate companies, with total borrowings between May and November, 1930, the dates between which Lea was carrying on transactions with the bank, amounting to $825,150. Toward the end of this period, Lea made desperate though futile efforts to raise funds for the bank—a story to be told later.[34]

SUMMARY

Caldwell and Company had from its very beginning been interested in banks. Indeed, its first investment of a permanent nature was in the stock of a bank, the Fourth and First National. By the end of 1929 it had built up the largest chain of banks then in the South with assets of over $213,000,000.[35] These banks, together with their assets as of December 31, 1929, are listed in the following table:

THE CALDWELL CHAIN OF BANKS, DECEMBER 31, 1929

BANKS	ASSETS
Fourth and First Group (Nashville)	
Fourth and First National Bank	$41,078,000
Nashville Trust Company	12,863,000
Trust Departments	39,863,000
Country Banks (estimated)	7,000,000
Total	$100,804,000

[34] See Chapter xiv, *infra*.

[35] The Bankers Trust Company, which failed in 1926, had controlled more individual banks, having 120 in Georgia and 60 in Florida. See Gaines T. Cartinhour, *Branch, Group and Chain Banking*, pp. 85-87; also pp. 66-69.

Holston-Union Group (Knoxville)

Holston-Union National Bank	$16,535,000	
Holston Trust Company	1,155,000	
Total		$ 17,690,000

Union Planters Group (Memphis)

Union Planters National Bank	$ 38,537,000	
Manhattan Savings Bank	10,830,000	
Total		$ 49,367,000

Home Insurance Companies' Banks (Arkansas)

American Exchange Trust Company	$20,408,000	
Country Banks (estimated)	25,000,000	
Total		$ 45,408,000
Grand Total		$213,269,000

Development of this chain of banks yielded returns to Caldwell and Company in the form of loans, unsecured deposits, outlet for securities, dividends received on stocks, and profits from sale of stocks. Yet on the whole its banking chain was not a successful venture. It had had to raise large sums of money for the reorganization of the Union Planters National Bank in Memphis and the American Exchange Trust Company in Little Rock, money which Caldwell and Company could have used to a much better advantage in strengthening its own financial condition. Also, the domination of the Holston-Union National Bank by Luke Lea had created a very unhealthy condition in that bank, which, because of the increasing number of joint ventures of Rogers Caldwell and Luke Lea, did not enhance the reputation of Caldwell and Company. From the standpoint of the banks and their depositors, the domination of Lea and Caldwell meant tying up their fortunes with two reckless financiers, a condition certainly not to be desired by a sound bank.

Chapter IX

THE ORGANIZATION OF A SOUTHERN INVESTMENT TRUST

AN IMPORTANT development of the bull market of the twenties was the creation of investment trusts by investment banking houses, one important purpose being to unload the bankers' unmarketable securities on the trust and then sell the securities of the trust to the public. Through such activities the bankers were creating what they hoped would be a perpetual buyer for their securities. The question as to whether it was ethical for the buyer and seller to be controlled by the same party does not seem to have been given a great deal of consideration, judging from the number of investment houses that established their own investment trusts. Among these houses were Dillon Read and their United States and Foreign Securities Company and their United States and International Securities Corporation, Lehman Brothers with their Lehman Corporation, Goldman Sachs with their Goldman Sachs Trading Corporation, to say nothing of Kidder-Peabody's Kidder Participations, Incorporated, Numbers 1, 2, and 3.[1]

Not to be outdone by the larger and older investment houses, Caldwell and Company in 1928 established its investment trust. Having done so much to popularize the securities of the South, and having progressed so rapidly under its slogan, "We Bank on the South," it christened its new venture "Shares-in-the-South, Incorporated." The trust was chartered under the laws of Delaware on August 9, 1928, as a general management trust and authorized to issue 250,000 shares of no par common stock. It was completely dominated by Caldwell and Company with Rogers Caldwell serving as president for $5,000 a year, J. D. Carter and E. J. Heitzeberg holding offices as vice presidents, and all other officers and directors selected from the Caldwell personnel. The only thing about the company that was non-Caldwellian was that the securities bought had to be kept with the trust department of the National Park Bank of New York.

At the start only 50,000 of the authorized 250,000 shares of stock were issued. This stock was offered to the public by Caldwell and Company

[1] See John T. Flynn, *Investment Trusts Gone Wrong*, particularly Chapters IV to VII.

as fiscal agent for the investment trust at a price of $40 a share, with some 37,000 shares being taken at this price. The employees of Caldwell and Company were offered the stock at $33 a share under a partial payment plan, with Caldwell and Company agreeing to repurchase it on demand. Under considerable pressure the employees responded and purchased 8,000 shares. In all, approximately 45,000 shares were sold to over 900 stockholders in twenty-seven states,[2] leaving Caldwell and Company with 5,000 shares.

The future of the trust was painted in brilliant colors by T. W. Goodloe, secretary of Shares-in-the-South and a minor executive of Caldwell and Company, in an address before the sales convention of Caldwell and Company in Louisville, Kentucky, on December 10, 1928, while the original sales campaign was being carried on. Goodloe pointed out that the sale of 50,000 shares would net the trust $2,000,000. *If* Shares-in-the-South issued $5,000,000 of 6 per cent preferred stock and $5,000,000 of 5 per cent debenture bonds, making a total capital of $12,000,000, and *if* the company earned 10 per cent on its invested capital, which he considered a conservative estimate based on the past performance of leading investment trusts, total earnings would be $1,200,000. After deducting bond interest of $250,000 and dividends on preferred stock of $300,000, $650,000 would be available for the common stock, or 32.5 per cent on the original offering price of $40 a share. Now, with the stock earning $13 a share, and since, it was contended, there was no good reason why it should not sell at twelve times earnings, the price of the stock in the near future should amount to $156 a share. The future of Shares-in-the-South was limited only by the industrial and agricultural growth of the South and it was not at all impossible that it might grow to be a corporation with more than $50,000,000 of invested capital, said Goodloe, speaking for Caldwell and Company. The reader should keep in mind that the late twenties was a period of rather remarkable optimism with respect to all things financial.

This glowing future, needless to say, was not realized. The company at the start did have its $2,000,000 which Caldwell and Company paid it for its capital stock, the payment being made with securities which Caldwell and Company had on hand and which Shares-in-the-South held until funds could be raised from the sale of stock to the public. On November 30, 1928, a month after the shares had been offered for sale, Shares-in-the-South had securities of $1,722,000, cash of $302,000, and total assets of $2,047,000. It had bills payable of $50,000 and net worth of

[2] Letter to Stockholders of Shares-in-the-South, Inc., February 11, 1929.

$1,997,000. It had lost $3,500, or seven cents a share, and its stock had a book value based on market value of its securities of $42.50 a share.[3]

A few months later, however, Shares-in-the-South reported to its stockholders a much better picture. The company's first report for the fiscal year ending January 31, 1929, showed earnings of $24,300, or twenty-one cents a share, after deducting current expenses of $11,000 and $10,000 of the total organization expense, a large part of which went, no doubt, to Caldwell and Company. In addition, the company reported a net unrealized enhancement in the market value of its securities of $117,000, which, added to earnings, equalled a per annum return of approximately 22 per cent. The operations to that date had been so successful that the stockholders were notified that the board of directors had authorized the sale of an additional 50,000 shares of the company's stock with the provision that 25,000 of the new shares were to be offered to the old stockholders at $42.50 a share, with the balance to be sold by Caldwell and Company, for the trust, "through channels which will interest new shareholders in the stock of the company, thereby broadening the market on the outstanding stock, which will tend to make it still easier for the company to increase its capital from time to time as it expects to do."[4] The stockholders were thus denied their usual right of subscribing to all the new stock of a corporation in proportion to the amount already held.

When this offer was first made, the stock was selling at $45 a share. In spite of the spread of only $2.50 between the market price and subscription price, the old stockholders bought 17,103 of the 25,000 new shares offered. On March 6, 1929, the directors authorized the sale of the remaining 32,897 shares by Caldwell and Company at not less than an average price of $49 a share, the approximate market price at the time; but of these shares, only 35 were sold, bringing the total number outstanding to 67,138.[5]

The faith of the stockholders in the company seems to have been little justified, for by July 31, 1929, after nine months of operation, the trust showed profits of only $1.27 a share and its earnings were at a rate of 4.1 per cent per annum rather than the anticipated 10 per cent.[6] At that time the company held $2,376,446 of securities, of which 11.3 per cent were bonds, 9.1 per cent preferred stock, and 79.6 per cent common stock. The bulk of the bonds and preferred stocks were industrial issues sold the

[3] Balance Sheet of Shares-in-the-South, Inc., November 30, 1928.
[4] Annual Report to Stockholders of Shares-in-the-South, Inc., February 5, 1929.
[5] From memoranda in files of Receivers of Caldwell and Company.
[6] Report on Shares-in-the-South, Inc., July 31, 1929, by the assistant secretary, Lee Davis, prepared for the officers of the company.

trust by Caldwell and Company, although it did hold relatively small blocks of railroad and public utility issues which had been obtained in the open market. Of the common stocks, bank, insurance company, and industrial stocks were the most important types, with those issues handled by Caldwell and Company bulking large. In all, Caldwell and Company had sold the trust $1,583,161 of securities, or 66.6 per cent of its portfolio, at a reasonably estimated profit of $600,000, a large part of which came from industrial common stocks which Caldwell and Company had received as bonuses. It is rather evident that Caldwell and Company was using the trust as a convenient dumping ground for these securities.

The price of the stock of Shares-in-the-South reached its high of 51 in March, 1929. After this time, some six months before the stock market broke, the price drifted downward slowly. In June Caldwell and Company attempted to peg the stock at 42½, the level held until October, 1929, when, following the crash of the stock market, the pegged price was lowered to 40. In its effort to maintain the market for these shares, Caldwell and Company, between June 30 and December 31, 1929, bought 13,861 shares at an average price of 40¾, with its investment in the stock of Shares-in-the-South increasing from $544,000 to $1,108,000 between the two dates.[7] In addition, on December 31, 1929, Insurance Securities Corporation was carrying 4,780 shares of the stock at a book value of $201,000, bringing the total number of shares carried directly or indirectly by Caldwell and Company up to 31,051.

The cause of the decline in the price of the shares in this company before the stock market crash is somewhat difficult to ascertain. A logical explanation seems to lie in the fact, however, that the stock of Shares-in-the-South, more than any other security issued by Caldwell and Company, reflected the standing of Caldwell and Company itself in the estimation of the security-buying public, for the trust was more closely tied to Caldwell and Company than any of its other affiliates with securities in the hands of the public. The decline in the value of these shares even before the stock market crash indicates that the prestige of Caldwell and Company was declining somewhat. The decline after the stock market crash can, of course, be partly explained by the general collapse of security prices. But even then the continued fall in price cannot be divorced from the weakening condition of Caldwell and Company.

The stock market crash, of course, materially affected the condition of Shares-in-the-South, just as it did all investment trusts. On December

---

[7] Caldwell and Company's holdings from "Audit Report" as of dates mentioned. Price data are from reports of Shares-in-the-South, Inc., in files of Receivers of Caldwell and Company.

31, 1929, the trust showed a loss of $425,000 on the market value of its securities, over $405,000, or 95 per cent, of which was from the decline in the value of its common stocks. It had at that time cash of $434,000 and securities with a book value of $2,386,000. The time was approaching when the auditors would inspect the books of the company and prepare their annual report as of January 31, 1930. With this in mind, the report of the condition of Shares-in-the-South as of December 31, 1929, drawn up by the accounting department of Caldwell and Company, contained the following comments which throw considerable light on the basic policies of Caldwell and Company at that time:

Of the $434,014.87 shown in the balance sheet as cash in bank, $392,949.00 is in the Bank of Tennessee; $38,230.98 is in the Fourth and First National Bank; and but $2,834.89 is in the Chase National Bank. As Price, Waterhouse and Company know the close relationship existing between Shares-in-the-South and the Bank of Tennessee, we believe they will want to comment upon this in the report which they will render as of January 31, for the coming stockholders' meeting. We would like to suggest, therefore, that some of the funds on deposit with the Bank of Tennessee be transferred to the Chase National Bank of New York during the period of the audit.

We also would like to call your attention to the loss in market values. We believe that Price, Waterhouse and Company will wish to reserve for this condition and if such is done that not only the operating profit and surplus will be charged off but that a deficit of approximately $200,000 will be created. Therefore, if this situation is to be remedied it should be within the next few days so as not to be too apparent to the auditors.

Whether or not the funds were transferred before the audit was made cannot be ascertained from the Price, Waterhouse report, but no comment was made by that firm on the large deposit in the Bank of Tennessee. A few minor changes, however, were made in security holdings, which reduced the loss on total holdings by approximately $35,000. In spite of this, the net loss totaled $390,590. The auditors, however, were less exacting than had been feared. The balance sheet drawn up carried the securities at cost, the only mention of the loss being a short statement in the report that market value of all securities held at January 31, 1930, was $390,590 less than cost. After this brief statement the profit and loss account was drawn up, showing net profit for the year of $103,400, which gave the company a surplus of $155,000. No reserves of any kind were set up.[8] Such accounting procedure, though it possibly conformed to standards then current, obviously failed to portray effectively the actual situation.

[8] "Audit Report of Shares-in-the-South, Incorporated," January 31, 1930.

At the close of 1929 Shares-in-the-South had come to be no unmixed blessing for Caldwell and Company. Organized primarily because Caldwell and Company thought it could sell stock in the investment trust more easily than the securities owned by Shares-in-the-South, the trust had at first proved beneficial. The investment house sold the trust a large volume of securities at a handsome profit and also obtained relatively large cash deposits from the trust. On the other hand, its efforts to peg the market for the stock of Shares-in-the-South, which resulted in its holding 31,051 of the 67,138 shares outstanding, necessitated the raising of funds which it needed badly for other purposes. This growing investment in the stock of Shares-in-the-South was becoming one of several millstones around the corporate neck of Caldwell and Company.

Chapter X

INVESTMENTS IN NEWSPAPERS

Colonel Luke Lea, who was associated with Rogers Caldwell in two banking ventures, was, despite all of his other interests, primarily a politician, his political power resting at least partially upon his newspapers, the *Nashville Tennessean* and the *Evening Tennessean.* These two papers were published by the Tennessee Publishing Company, of which Lea had become president in 1907, and had been used by him to promote his position in Tennessee state politics.[1] He was aided in the administration of these papers by his son, Luke Lea, Jr., who was business manager of the publishing company.

Lea shared the newspaper field in Nashville with one strong competitor, the *Nashville Banner,* which was edited and published by one of Lea's bitterest political enemies, E. B. Stahlman. They clashed on every major issue in Tennessee and Nashville politics. That they both usually supported the Democratic nominee for president was perhaps due to the fact that no Republican daily could thrive in Nashville. It was generally conceded that the *Tennessean* dominated the morning newspaper field but Lea had made small inroads into the *Banner's* control of the evening field.

Caldwell and Company had no financial interest whatever in the Tennessee Publishing Company at any time, it remaining solely a Luke Lea enterprise. However, when Luke Lea desired to expand his newspaper business outside Nashville and build up a powerful group of papers, he turned to Rogers Caldwell for financial aid and these two men purchased two large newspapers in the state, the Memphis *Commercial Appeal* and the *Knoxville Journal,* and attempted to purchase a large paper outside of the state, the *Atlanta Constitution.*

The Memphis Commercial Appeal and Southern Publishers, Incorporated

The *Commercial Appeal,* published by the Commercial Publishing Company of Memphis, Tennessee, was one of the oldest and strongest newspapers in the state. Its predecessor, the *Commercial,* had been established in 1839, and the *Commercial Appeal* arose out of the consolidation

---

[1] See Chapter xi, *infra.*

of this and two other Memphis papers in 1894. Edited for many years by C. P. J. Mooney, it had grown in influence and circulation until it had become one of the leading papers of the South. Its hold on the morning newspaper field in Memphis was unchallenged. In 1923 the publishing company established the *Evening Appeal,* which shared the evening field in Memphis with a Scripps-Howard paper, the *Press-Scimitar.* The *Evening Appeal* never approached the high level of its older kinsman and was, from the start, a money-losing proposition.

The death of Mr. Mooney in 1926 and the failure to secure an editor that could approach his ability resulted in a slow but perceptible weakening of the *Commercial.* The stockholders of the Commercial Publishing Company, some twenty prominent residents of Memphis, realized that if their investment was to be protected and the paper was to continue to hold its former position a strong editor must be obtained or the paper sold to other interests. The latter way out was chosen when Rogers Caldwell and Luke Lea in the early part of 1927 offered to purchase the *Commercial Appeal* and *Evening Appeal.*

The offer of Caldwell and Lea was to pay $3,600,000 to the stockholders for all of the assets of the publishing company except the building. A new company, Memphis Commercial Appeal, Incorporated, was to be created to take over the assets of the old company and carry on the publication of the papers. Its capital structure was to consist of $2,500,000 of 6.5 per cent debenture bonds, 20,000 shares of 7 per cent $100 par value preferred stock, and 150,000 shares of common stock with no par value.[2] The reorganization was completed by the latter part of April, 1927, when the complete ownership of Memphis Commercial Appeal, Incorporated, passed to Luke Lea and Rogers Caldwell.

In the meantime, Lea and Caldwell had formed Southern Publishers, Incorporated, to hold the stock of the new company. This holding company was incorporated on April 22, 1927, under the laws of Delaware, as usual, and was authorized to issue 1,000 shares of common stock with no par value. Luke Lea and Caldwell and Company each bought half of this stock at $1 a share and Lea was elected president of the holding company at the fantastic salary of $50,000 per annum.[3]

The funds necessary to pay for the *Commercial Appeal* amounted to some $3,260,000, not including $340,000 of cash on hand that was used.

[2] *Moody's Industrials,* 1929, p. 2492.

[3] "Audit Report of Southern Publishers, Incorporated," covering the period April 1, 1927, to February 23, 1931, made in connection with the receivership of Southern Publishers, Inc., arising from the case *Nashville Trust Company, et al.* v. *Southern Publishers, Inc., et al.,* No. 42737, in Part II of Chancery Court, Davidson County, Tennessee (1931). Cited hereafter as "Audit of Southern Publishers."

The purchase money was raised by two bond issues. One was the $2,500,000 of debentures of Memphis Commercial Appeal, Incorporated, which Caldwell and Company and Halsey, Stuart and Company of Chicago underwrote at 90, thus netting the issuer $2,250,000 and the underwriters a profit of $250,000, since the bonds were easily sold at par. The second bond issue was $1,500,000 of 6 per cent collateral trust debentures of Southern Publishers, Incorporated, dated May, 1927, $1,000,000 of which matured on May 1, 1932, and $500,000 a year later. These bonds were secured by the entire preferred and common stock issues of Memphis Commercial Appeal, Incorporated. This collateral was placed in trust with the Nashville Trust Company, and the entire issue of bonds sold to the Minnesota and Ontario Paper Company, which sold newsprint to the *Commercial Appeal* and to Lea's *Tennessean*.[4] As this company was in turn controlled by the Minnesota and Ontario Power Company, the newspapers through the sale of these bonds became financially tied up with power interests.

The sale of both issues yielded a total of $3,750,000, which was almost $500,000 more than needed to complete the purchase. The cash balance was not turned over to the publishing company but, instead, Lea and Caldwell interests retained the cash and paid the publishing company in bonds of Lea's real estate companies and Caldwell issues. Lea was made president of Memphis Commercial Appeal, Incorporated, and publisher of the paper and although he retained his office in Nashville and was not particularly active in the management of the company, except in dictating its policies on political matters, he was paid a salary of $24,000 a year, in addition to the $50,000 he received as president of Southern Publishers.

Financially, the operations of Memphis Commercial Appeal, Incorporated, were successful. Total profits from operations during the period from March 31, 1927, to June 30, 1930, amounted to $995,000, or average annual profits after interest of approximately $306,000.[5] These earnings were more than sufficient to pay the dividend on the company's preferred stock, amounting to $140,000 annually, which in turn would have allowed Southern Publishers to pay the $90,000 annual interest on its collateral trust bonds. But no dividends were paid on the preferred stock and Southern Publishers was forced to borrow to meet every interest payment. All of these funds came from Caldwell and Company or the Bank of Tennessee, these two houses, on May 1, 1929, holding $270,000 of the notes of Southern Publishers covering its bond interest payments for a period of three years.[6]

[4] Minutes of the stockholders' meeting of Southern Publishers, Incorporated, May 10, 1927.—"Minute Book of Southern Publishers, Incorporated."
[5] "Audit of Southern Publishers."   [6] *Ibid.*

In return for advancing these funds, Memphis Commercial Appeal maintained an unsecured deposit in the Bank of Tennessee which was always greater than the amount of funds advanced to Southern Publishers for the *Commercial Appeal* transaction. On June 30, 1929, this deposit amounted to $866,000.[7] At that time, in addition to the $270,000 loaned to Southern Publishers, Caldwell and Company had advanced Memphis Commercial Appeal $340,850 with which it purchased a like amount of securities from Luke Lea.[8] Thus, in the *Commercial Appeal* deal alone, Caldwell and Company was advancing $630,850 while obtaining a deposit of $866,000, netting $233,150 in cash to the investment house, which was a real advantage to Caldwell and Company arising from the transaction.

From the standpoint of Memphis Commercial Appeal, Incorporated, its ownership by Southern Publishers was rather unfortunate. Instead of the company's using its earnings to pay dividends on its preferred stock as it normally would have done, its funds were simply being deposited with Caldwell and Company and used by Lea and Caldwell in furthering their other enterprises. Further, the publishing company was saddled with Lea's salary of $24,000, as well as an absurd and wholly unjustified management charge of Southern Publishers set at $5,000 in 1928 and raised to $10,000 the following year.[9] The paper became the spokesman of Luke Lea in Memphis and West Tennessee and he naturally used it to attempt to expand his influence in state politics. In spite of its circulation increasing from 100,000 in 1926 to 113,000 in 1929, the paper did not retain the same prestige it had enjoyed under the Mooney editorship.

THE ATLANTA CONSTITUTION

In 1927, about the same time that Luke Lea and Rogers Caldwell were closing the *Commercial Appeal* deal, they began negotiations for the purchase of another large Southern newspaper, the *Atlanta Constitution,* edited and published by Clark Howell, and the leading morning newspaper of that Georgia city. Negotiations, carried on between Lea and Caldwell and the Howell family which owned 3,025 shares of the total 5,000 shares of the Constitution Publishing Company, were based upon balance sheets and income accounts of the publishing company furnished by the Howells. The latest available balance sheet was as of March 31, 1927, and the latest income account was for the first three months of 1927. The latter indicated earnings for this three-month period of $107,028, or slightly more than $21 a share, earnings which were obtained before setting up a reserve for unfulfilled prepaid subscriptions. The omission

---

[7] "Audit Report of Caldwell and Company," June 30, 1929.
[8] "Audit of Southern Publishers."   [9] *Ibid.*

of this reserve account was mentioned to the Howells, but they claimed that such a reserve was unnecessary because these subscriptions increased the good will of the paper and hence the value of advertising space. Lea and Caldwell made no particular issue of this point and the sales contracts were made.[10]

The contracts, drawn up by Luke Lea and entered into by him and Caldwell and the Howells, stated that the assets of the Constitution Publishing Company, exclusive of good will, amounted to $1,028,624, and that liabilities, exclusive of common stock and surplus, amounted to $845,172. For the payment of $10, Lea and Caldwell obtained an option on the 3,025 shares owned by the Howells at a price of $1,050,000. Notice of the desire to exercise the option had to be given on or before July 1, 1927, and when the option was exercised 3 per cent of the purchase price, or $31,500, had to be deposited with the Citizens' and Southern National Bank at Atlanta. If notice of the desire to exercise the option was given, Price, Waterhouse, and Company was to make an audit of the Constitution Publishing Company to be completed not later than August 1, 1927. If the transaction was then to be carried out, the buyers were to pay an additional $100,000 on the purchase price of the paper. Then in October of the same year the balance was to be paid and the Citizens' and Southern National Bank, as escrow agent, was to turn over the stock to Lea and Caldwell. If the audit made by Price, Waterhouse showed earnings for the first three months of 1927 to be lower than $20 a share, the buyers were to have the option of either being released from the transaction or of buying the stock at a price to be determined in relation to the company's earnings, as ascertained by the auditors. The price so determined was to be the percentage of the original purchase price of $1,050,000 that the earnings per share were of $20.[11]

The notice of the desire to exercise the option was made immediately after the contract was signed, the $31,500 earnest money was deposited, and Price, Waterhouse made the audit of the company, which was completed by July 1, 1927, when the additional $100,000 payment was made. The audit, with two major exceptions, indicated a substantially similar financial condition to that shown by the reports submitted by the Howells to Lea and Caldwell. One difference was that the value of the assets of the paper was placed at an amount $268,200 greater than that submitted by the Howells. The second startling discrepancy was that, according to the auditor's statement, the Constitution Publishing Company earned, dur-

[10] *Lea, et al.* v. *Citizens' and Southern National Bank, et al.,* 27 F (2d) 385 (1928).

[11] From original contract for the purchase of the stock of the Constitution Publishing Company, dated May 27, 1927.

ing the first three months of 1927, $5,529.14, or $1.01 a share, instead of $107,028, or $21 a share, as represented by the Howells. The difference arose because Price, Waterhouse set up a reserve of approximately $100,000 for unfulfilled prepaid subscriptions.[12]

On October 15, 1927, the date set for the completion of the deal, Caldwell and Lea offered the Citizens' and Southern National Bank $54,350 of their deposit of $131,500, which, under the contract, would be the purchase price if earnings were $1.01 a share, and requested that the 3,025 shares deposited by the Howells be turned over to them. When the bank refused to release the stock, Lea and Caldwell entered suit in the United States District Court at Atlanta against the Citizens' and Southern National Bank and the Howells to enforce the delivery of the stock, claiming that Price, Waterhouse, and Company was authorized by the contract to set up the unfulfilled prepaid subscription reserve. The Howells contended that under the contract the auditors had no right to set up any additional reserve accounts, but only to verify the representations made by them to Caldwell and Lea, and to ascertain the profit in the way in which it had always been computed by the Constitution Publishing Company.

The suit as applied to the Citizens' and Southern National Bank was dismissed by Judge Sibley of the District Court but the Howells were required to answer the bill. A decision was rendered in July, 1928, setting aside the contract and holding in favor of the Howells. The concluding paragraph of the decision is significant:

The results that actually flow from the construction claimed by Lea and Caldwell, all of which could have been easily foreseen, emphasize its unreasonableness. On the basis of the facts represented by the Howells, Lea and Caldwell were willing to pay $1,050,000 for the stock and did put in the bank $131,500 thereof. The audit finds the facts were all basically true except that the physical property was worth much more than was claimed, but on a debatable interpretation of the status of the paid subscriptions, whose existence was really the greatest element of value in the paper, that the price should be reduced by $1,000,000. When it is remembered that these very subscriptions were to be, in the main, fulfilled at little additional cost before the property was to be delivered, the result is little short of shocking.[13]

The absurdity of the position taken by Lea and Caldwell is further shown by the fact that the $54,000 offered for the paper was slightly more than twice as much as the $25,000 they had agreed to pay their representative in Atlanta, Forrest Adair, Jr., of the Citizens' and Southern National Bank, when the purchase of the Howell stock was completed.[14]

[12] *Lea, et al.* v. *Citizens' and Southern National Bank, et al.,* 27 F (2d) 385 (1928).
[13] *Ibid.*   [14] Original Contract between Lea and Caldwell and Adair.

The inconsistency of their position is shown by the fact that their own publishing company, Memphis Commercial Appeal, Incorporated, carried reserves only for accrued interest and taxes.[15] As the transaction progressed, it seems to have become little more than an effort on the part of Lea and Caldwell to buy the *Constitution* at a ridiculously low price, whatever may have been their original intention.

While the amount of the purchase price was being fought out, on May 31, 1928, Caldwell and Lea transferred the contract for the purchase of the *Atlanta Constitution* to Southern Publishers, Incorporated, for which company the transaction was being made from the start. At that time, the deal had cost approximately $180,000, made up of audit fees, legal expenses, and the $131,500 of earnest money placed in escrow. Southern Publishers raised $169,000 of the total amount by borrowing from the Bank of Tennessee, and the balance from other sources.[16] The whole transaction was finally brought to a close on October 4, 1928, when Southern Publishers received the entire amount which had been placed in escrow with the Citizens' and Southern National Bank, which amounted, with interest, to $142,000. This left Southern Publishers with a loss of $38,000 on the deal, which was finally charged off.[17] The funds recovered by Southern Publishers were used not to repay the Bank of Tennessee which had originally advanced them but to pay off its notes at the Holston-Union, leaving the Bank of Tennessee with an unsecured loan of $169,000. This $38,000 was the total direct financial loss sustained from the venture, but the nature of Judge Sibley's decision was given wide publicity, especially in Tennessee, and caused some people to question the character of the transactions that were being carried on by Lea and Caldwell.

THE KNOXVILLE JOURNAL

The *Knoxville Journal* differed from other papers purchased or attempted to be purchased by Caldwell and Lea in at least one respect; namely, that this paper was definitely Republican, carrying on its masthead "the only Republican Daily South of the Ohio River." Located in the Republican section of East Tennessee, it traced its genealogy back to the *Whig,* published before the Civil War by Parson Brownlow, who later became Tennessee's reconstruction governor.[18] In 1898 the *Journal* was consolidated with the *Tribune* and Captain William Rule, a staunch Republican, was made editor. The controlling stock of the publishing

---

[15] *Moody's Industrials,* 1928.
[16] "Audit of Southern Publishers."   [17] *Ibid.*
[18] See Ellis M. Coulter, *William G. Brownlow, Fighting Parson of the Southern Highlands.*

company, the Knoxville Journal and Tribune Company, was owned by the Sanford family, distinguished Knoxville residents.[19]   The desire of Luke Lea to control a Republican newspaper in a Republican section can be partially explained on the grounds that many Tennesseans vote Democratic in state matters and Republican in national elections.   Probably more important was the fact that Lea thought he was getting a bargain.[20] Whatever the reason, in 1927 Lea and Caldwell approached A. F. Sanford, who was president of the publishing company, with a proposition to purchase the *Knoxville Journal,* and a contract for its sale was drawn up and signed August 13, 1927.

The contract provided for the formation of a new company to be known as the Knoxville Journal Company which was to take over the plant and equipment, good will and franchises, and certain other assets of the old company, but was to have no initial cash, nor any debts except $500,000 of bonds.   The capital structure of the new company was to be made up of $500,000 of fifteen-year, 6.5 per cent debenture bonds, 5,000 shares of no par, $7 preferred stock, and 10,000 shares of no par common stock.   For organizing the new company and transferring all of its securities to Lea and Caldwell, the Sanfords were to receive $735,000.   To seal the contract the buyers placed $100,000 in escrow with the Holston Trust Company and later deposited an additional $100,000 with the same institution, funds which were advanced to the buyers by their already owned Memphis Commercial Appeal, Incorporated.

As with the other papers, the *Knoxville Journal* was bought for Southern Publishers, Incorporated, and hence when the Sanfords turned the company over to Lea and Caldwell, 5,000 shares, or half of the common stock and all of the debenture bonds of the Knoxville Journal Company, were taken by the holding company.   Memphis Commercial Appeal got 2,000 shares of common and 2,000 shares of preferred for the advances it had made on the purchase.   Southern Publishers pledged its 5,000 shares of common and its $500,000 of debentures with Caldwell and Company on a loan of $500,000, which together with the $200,000 advanced by the Memphis Publishing Company provided $700,000 of the total purchase price of $735,000.   Caldwell and Company, in turn, pledged the debentures with the Canal Bank and Trust Company of New Orleans on a loan of $400,000.   Then, on April 22, 1928, at the time Southern Publishers bought the Constitution Publishing Company contract, it also bought Commercial Appeal's holdings of Knoxville Journal stock at

[19] Testimony of A. F. Sanford, in "Ramsey Evidence."

[20] Such a statement was made by Lea to J. B. Ramsey, president of the Holston-Union National Bank.—"Ramsey Evidence."

$200,000 plus interest, with Caldwell and Company advancing this sum to Southern Publishers to pay Memphis Commercial Appeal.[21] The net result of these various transactions was that Southern Publishers held $500,000 of bonds, 7,000 shares of common and 2,000 shares of the preferred stock of Knoxville Journal Company, all of which was hypothecated, and that Caldwell and Company had advanced $300,000 and the Canal Bank and Trust Company $400,000 of the funds with which to buy the paper.

The remainder of the purchase price and the funds necessary to furnish some working capital for the company were raised by the sale of 1,125 shares of common and 1,013 shares of preferred stock of the publishing company to other parties Lea was able to interest. The Lea controlled Holston Trust Company was directed to purchase $25,000 of the stock. Also certain advertisers in both of Knoxville's leading papers were offered a proposition whereby, if they would subscribe to Journal stock and give all their advertising to the *Journal,* half of the money paid for advertising would be credited on the purchase of the stock, and thus their advertising would soon pay for their investment.[22] By such means the necessary $35,000 for the remainder of the purchase price and approximately $150,000 of working capital were raised.

The operations of Knoxville Journal Company under Lea-Caldwell control were not financially successful. Although at first it earned bond interest, net profit before payment of preferred dividends amounted to only $335 for the fiscal year ending March 31, 1929.[23] Preferred dividends, hence, could not be met in that or in the following year and the only income to Southern Publishers from the paper was the interest it received on its journal company bonds. No management fees were charged this paper; but Luke Lea received a salary of $12,000 a year for his services as president of the Knoxville Journal Company and publisher of the *Knoxville Journal,* a capacity in which he was no more active than in the same position he held with the *Commercial Appeal.*

The Holston-Union National Bank was relied upon to provide some working capital for the Knoxville Journal Company. At almost every time that interest was due on the company's debentures, the Holston-Union was called upon for another loan. These loans were, however, usually reduced before the following interest date, and were not excessively large, the total amount outstanding reaching $77,500 toward the end of 1930.[24] But many of the loans were made without any security to a company whose earnings hardly justified such accommodations.

[21] "Audit of Southern Publishers." [22] "Ramsey Evidence."
[23] Audit Report of Knoxville Journal Company, as of March 31, 1929, in "Ramsey Evidence." [24] "Ramsey Evidence."

From the standpoint of Caldwell and Company, the purchase of the *Knoxville Journal* was a definite loss. The bulk of the funds for this purchase was raised by the investment house. A portion of such funds was obtained by pledging the debentures of Knoxville Journal Company to the Canal Bank, but in addition Caldwell and Company had $300,000 tied up in the deal. Moreover, Caldwell and Company was responsible for the repayment of the $400,000 advanced by the Canal Bank for it was advanced on a Caldwell note. The only offsetting item was an unsecured deposit of the Knoxville Journal Company in the Bank of Tennessee of approximately $100,000, which the Caldwell organization could use practically as it desired.[25] The result was that Caldwell interests advanced a net amount of $200,000 of the purchase price of the paper and borrowed an additional $400,000 for this purpose, which reduced by that amount the funds that Caldwell and Company could secure from the Canal Bank for other purposes.

From the standpoint of the *Journal,* the passage of its control to Lea and Caldwell meant great changes in policy. In the contract for the purchase of the *Journal,* it was agreed that an independent paper would be published. It is almost inconceivable that a staunch Democrat like Colonel Lea would allow a paper which he controlled to continue to give hearty support to the Republican party, no matter what its background had been. Captain William Rule, who had long given guidance and support to the Republicans of the section, "was relegated to a half-column stature, and what he wrote had to be signed and credited to him personally. The *Journal's* editorial department was immediately devoted to discussions of academic questions and the old-time rock ribbed and undeviating Republican organ was laid away in moth balls."[26] Captain Rule died on July 26, 1928, and thus his influence on the editorial policy of the paper ceased altogether. The effect of this is clearly seen in the contest for the Democratic nomination for governor in the summer of 1928 when the *Journal* advised all Republicans to vote in the Democratic primary for Colonel Lea's candidate.[27]

SUMMARY

Caldwell and Company's excursion into the newspaper field, from a financial standpoint, had not proved successful by the end of 1929. The failure of Memphis Commercial Appeal, Incorporated, to pay dividends on its preferred stock held by Southern Publishers, although earned,

---

[25] "Audit Report of Caldwell and Company," June 30, 1929.
[26] *Chattanooga Daily Times,* July 7, 1928. [27] See Chapter XI, *infra.*

necessitated advances by Caldwell and Company to meet the interest on Southern Publishers' collateral trust bonds at every interest date. The Knoxville Journal Company paid interest on its debentures regularly to Southern Publishers but this was not sufficient even to pay the interest on the loans made to buy the paper, much less to reduce these loans, while the journal company was not in a position to pay dividends on its preferred stock. Hence, the only source of revenue to Southern Publishers, other than the amounts received as management fees from Memphis Commercial Appeal, was the interest on the Knoxville Journal Company debentures. These funds were quite insufficient for the needs of the holding company so Caldwell and Company was called on to advance the necessary working capital. The only advantages accruing to Caldwell and Company from these transactions was the profit on the sale of the Memphis Commercial Appeal debentures and the unsecured deposits the two publishing companies kept with it. These deposits, however, were never as large as the total amounts advanced by Caldwell and Company to Southern Publishers, the excess of advances over deposits being $147,358 in 1927, $660,191 in 1928, and $431,381 in 1929.[28] From a political standpoint, the control of these papers helped to initiate Caldwell and Company, and particularly Rogers Caldwell, into Tennessee state politics to such an extent that the political machine controlled by Luke Lea came to be considered as the Lea-Caldwell machine.[29]

For Luke Lea the purchase of the two papers and the formation of Southern Publishers had both financial and political advantages. His total annual salaries from the holding company and the two publishing companies, amounting to $86,000, were the first and quite substantial financial advantage. The sale of the practically worthless bonds of his property companies to Memphis Commercial Appeal was a second. The control of the editorial policies of these two newspapers, together with his *Tennessean,* gave Lea a position in the press of the State that could by no means be approached by his political foes. The domination of these papers by Lea meant that the readers of the *Commercial Appeal* and the *Knoxville Journal* had issues presented to them in the way that Lea saw fit, the papers becoming his mouthpiece instead of the strong, public-spirited institutions they had been under the leadership of their former editors, Mooney and Rule.

In summing up the whole series of transactions, it can be said that Caldwell and Company was financing deals which yielded Luke Lea huge salaries and increased political power and placed the company in an

[28] "Audit Report of Caldwell and Company." The amounts given are as of June 30, in each of the years.   [29] See Chapter XI, *infra.*

undesirable position. Over a period of years, the investments in the two papers might have become extremely profitable from a financial standpoint alone, but Caldwell and Company was beginning to be faced with problems that could be met only with present funds and not with future profits.

POLITICAL AFFILIATIONS

THERE WERE three forces which made it difficult for Caldwell and Company, had it desired to do so, to keep itself free from politics. These were, first, the relations of the company with states and municipalities growing out of the purchase of their bonds; second, the control of Kentucky Rock Asphalt Company which was trying to sell its product, Kyrock, to the various civil units carrying on extensive road building programs during the period; and finally, and more important, the business and personal relations between Rogers Caldwell and Luke Lea which, of necessity, developed into political affiliations. With these forces operating there is little wonder that the company became extensively involved in politics.

A brief picture of the Tennessee political layout is necessary to understand the forays into politics made by Caldwell and Company. Tennessee is geographically divided into three parts. East Tennessee is predominantly Republican in its politics. This is particularly true of the northern counties of this section clustering around Knoxville and Johnson City. As one goes further south in the State toward Chattanooga, the hold of the Republicans becomes gradually less, but their strength is still sufficient to necessitate some unity on the part of the Democrats, and the existence of powerful conflicting machines within the party is not usual. While Caldwell and Company was just as much an issue in East Tennessee as in other parts of the state, it was primarily in the machines of Middle and West Tennessee that the company found its way into politics.

In both of these sections of the State, the Democrats have such a hold that there is room for the various factions within the party to be fighting constantly among themselves and still usually give enough votes to the party nominees for state and national offices to overcome the Republican advantages in East Tennessee. The foremost of these conflicts comes between the machines whose activities are centered primarily in Memphis in West Tennessee, and Nashville in Middle Tennessee.

There were two powerful machines in Nashville during the time of Caldwell and Company's activities in politics, one of which was controlled by Luke Lea, a native of Nashville and a protégé of the great Tennessee politician, editor, and statesman, Edward Ward Carmack. Lea made his entrance into Tennessee state politics just before the murder of Carmack in 1908, and attempted to build his political power upon the following of his late leader. Using his *Tennessean,* which had been Carmack's paper, to further his political interests and possessing a very winning personality and convincing manner, Lea built up a powerful political organization, not only in Nashville but in much of Middle Tennessee, which elected him to the United States Senate in 1911. Defeated for re-election in 1916 by K. D. McKellar, Lea in 1917, shortly after the United States entered the World War, organized the 114th Field Artillery, became its lieutenant colonel and, just before his regiment sailed for France, became its colonel. He served ably and well during the war and after the Armistice, before leaving for America, led a small unsuccessful expedition into Holland to kidnap the Kaiser as a present for President Wilson when he arrived in Paris for the Peace Conference.[1] This escapade naturally gained for Lea a great deal of publicity and also a threatened court-martial, the latter, according to Colonel Lea, due to the influence of his political enemy and newspaper competitor in Nashville, E. B. Stahlman, the editor of the *Banner.*

After the war Lea returned to Nashville and resumed again the active editorship of the *Tennessean* and the development of his political power, not with the objective of obtaining offices for himself but primarily to control the selection of those who would fill state offices. In addition to his newspaper and political interests, he expanded into banking and real estate, primarily with Rogers Caldwell, but in some cases with other parties. The extent of his influence in the banking field is indicated by his election as a director of the Federal Reserve Bank of Atlanta.

The Lea political opposition in Nashville was centered in the machine headed by Hilary E. Howse who, during his life, served very frequently as mayor of Nashville; E. B. Stahlman, the editor of the *Nashville Banner;* and K. T. McConnico, a prominent Nashville attorney. This group and Lea were in eternal conflict, the editorial columns of both the *Tennessean* and *Banner* being used to carry on this struggle at all times, and particularly during the contests for Democratic nominations for public offices.

The dominant political figure in Memphis was (and is) Edward H. Crump who had come there as a young, red-haired boy from northern Mississippi.[2] His first business was the E. H. Crump Buggy and Harness Company, but as the demand for these products decreased he turned partly

---

[1] See T. H. Alexander, "They Tried to Kidnap the Kaiser," in *Saturday Evening Post,* ccx (October 23, 1937), 5 ff.

[2] See James Street, "Mista Crump Keeps Rollin' Along," in *Colliers,* ci (April 9, 1938), 16.

to real estate, insurance, and investment banking, but primarily to politics. His political influence at first was limited to the city of Memphis, where he became a member of its Board of Public Works in 1905, its fire and police commissioner in 1907, and by 1915 had been elected its mayor three times. His last term as mayor was marred by ouster proceedings for corrupt administration. This move, supported by an audit of the affairs of the city by Haskins and Sells,[3] was becoming successful when in 1915 Mr. Crump suddenly resigned. By no means politically impotent, the next year he was elected as county trustee of Shelby County, an office he continued to hold until 1924, when he voluntarily stepped down and put one of his machine men in his place. During the time of his county trusteeship he established the most powerful county and city machine in the state, and one of the most powerful in the South. Hated and feared by politicians outside of his own county, his influence in state politics was limited for many years to his power to throw the vote of Shelby County to his favorite candidate for state offices, a power, however, which was by no means negligible, for the vote of his county was by far the largest of any in Tennessee.

The Crump opposition which had led the ouster proceedings in 1915 had become definitely weaker by 1920 when Crump's chief opponent in Memphis became Clarence Saunders of Piggly-Wiggly fame. Saunders' political power rested upon his personal fortunes, the first of which he made from Piggly-Wiggly stores and lost when he tried to buck Wall Street in the early twenties by getting a corner on Piggly-Wiggly stock, only to see the rules of the New York Stock Exchange suspended in order to allow the "bears" to cover their short sales. His second fortune was made from the rapid promotion of "Clarence Saunders, Sole-Owner-of-my-Name, Stores" during the middle and late twenties. His challenge to the hegemony of the Crump organization in Shelby County usually came in connection with contests for the Democratic nomination for governor.

A reference to the governor's election in 1918 will introduce all the characters that later played a rôle in the political drama of Caldwell and Company. In that year A. H. Roberts, with the support of the Howse-Stahlman-McConnico machine in Nashville and Crump in Memphis, received the Democratic nomination over Austin Peay, who had Luke Lea's support, and was elected governor. In 1920 Roberts was renominated over his opponent, Crabtree, but, in the general election in November, was defeated by the Republican, Alfred Taylor, who had taken part in Tennessee's political "War of Roses" against his brother, Bob Taylor, many years before. Roberts' defeat was partly due to the Harding

[3] See Chapter XVII, *infra*.

landslide, partly to his support of the nineteenth amendment, and partly to Luke Lea's opposition. The vigor of Lea's opposition and the nature of his tactics are seen in his charges in the *Tennessean* that Roberts had had illicit relations with his secretary, had insulted "reputable women of highest character," and was a "habitué of disreputable houses."[4] The result was naturally bitter personal animosity between the two men.

The Democratic nomination in 1922 went to Austin Peay. Peay had the support of Luke Lea in Nashville and of Clarence Saunders in Memphis and had won the nomination by a small majority over former Governor Benton McMillan, who had been supported by the other Memphis and Nashville machines. Governor Taylor was the Republican nominee again and, although he had the support of the Crump and Howse machines who called themselves "Taylor Democrats," Peay was elected by a 40,000 majority and Luke Lea had again placed his candidate in the governor's chair.[5]

Peay had little opposition in 1924 and was easily renominated and re-elected on his record as governor. In 1926, however, when he ran for a third term he was opposed by Hill McAllister, who made the chief issues of the election the tobacco tax imposed under Peay and the fact that Peay was running for a third term. In Peay's efforts for the third nomination he retained the support of Lea, but Saunders allied himself with Crump to oppose the Governor, stating that his changed position was due solely to the fact that Peay was running for a third term. The nomination went to Peay by the small majority of 8,000, and in the election in November he was re-elected governor for a third term.

Austin Peay is recognized generally as one of the outstanding governors of Tennessee since the Civil War. Throughout his administration he was backed by Lea and was very friendly toward him but in no sense of the word was he dominated by Lea. Peay's greatest contributions were his tax reforms, the reorganization of the State's governmental machinery in the Reorganization Act of 1923, and the extension of the road system. In this last program Peay had insisted upon a pay-as-you-go policy financed by a gasoline tax and bridge tolls. There was a great deal of agitation in 1924 for a $75,000,000 bond issue for roads but, being opposed to this, Peay in 1925 compromised with the adherents of the issue by supporting the policy of selling short-term notes to supplement highway revenues. In that year the legislature authorized the State Funding Board to issue $5,000,000 of these notes with their maturity limited to five years to be

[4] August 3, 1920.
[5] T. H. Alexander, "Austin Peay: A Brief Biography," in *Austin Peay . . . A Collection of State Papers and Public Addresses*, p. xxiii.

retired from current highway revenues, while two years later the legislature authorized the issuance of an additional $10,000,000 of these notes.[6]

In Peay's Reorganization Act of 1923 seven commissions were created to administer the business of the State, each headed by a commissioner who served at the pleasure of the governor, except the commissioner of education, who had a definite term of office. Among these commissions was that of highway and public works, which, after 1925, was headed by C. Neil Bass, who was developing a very good state highway system. In September, 1927, after Caldwell and Lea had entered into several large deals together, Lea approached Bass with the suggestion that he specify without competition the use of Kyrock, the product of the Caldwell affiliated Kentucky Rock Asphalt Company, in the building of certain roads. Bass was not in sympathy with such a proposition, however, and refused.[7]

A month after this incident, on October 2, 1927, Governor Peay died very suddenly. Under the succession laws of Tennessee, the speaker of the senate becomes governor in case of a vacancy. This official at that time was Henry H. Horton, a staunch supporter of Peay but unknown politically outside his district, east of Nashville. There is a story to the effect that Austin Peay would not consent to the election of Horton to the speakership before obtaining from him a promise that, if the office of governor became vacant, he would resign his position as speaker, thus giving up his right to become governor. Whether or not this was the case, Horton did not resign but was sworn in as governor in the presence of a few leading citizens, including Rogers Caldwell and Luke Lea. It was afterwards claimed that he raised his hand toward heaven but placed his eyes upon Lea and Caldwell.[8]

The effect of the change in governors was soon felt, at least by some. Pressure was now brought upon Bass to use the Highway Department for political ends. In a talk with Bass's father-in-law, who was an old friend, Horton suggested that he convey to Bass the idea that he was not using the Highway Department to the best political interests of the Governor and that his policies be directed more toward that end. In January, 1928, Bass was approached by Herbert Carr, the Nashville representative of Kentucky Rock Asphalt Company, who informed him that his company expected Kyrock to be specified without competition for a

[6] *Tennessee Taxation and Public Finance*, Report of the State Tax Committee, November 29, 1930, pp. 26, 27.

[7] *Second Report of the Special Legislative Committee*, appointed by the 67th General Assembly of Tennessee, January, 1931. Report dated May 25, 1931. Reprinted in *House Journal of 67th General Assembly of State of Tennessee*, 1931, p. 660. Cited hereafter as *Second Report*.   [8] *Nashville Banner*, December 31, 1930.

Federal aid road in West Tennessee. One of the employees of the department became so indignant that he ordered Carr out of the office. A few
days later Governor Horton called in Bass and suggested that it would
make for smoother operation of his department if another man were
appointed commissioner and Bass were to give his time completely to
its engineering duties. Such an arrangement was not agreeable to Bass
and on February 13, 1928, Horton asked for and received his resignation.[9]

Horton appointed Colonel Harry S. Berry, a lifelong friend of Luke
Lea, to fill Bass's place. Before he was given the appointment Lea told
Berry that Horton's chances for obtaining the nomination in August were
negligible unless the Highway Department could be operated in sympathy
with him and it was with this in mind that Berry took the job. Thereafter, Kyrock was specified for a number of roads, assuring a good market
for a Caldwell product.[10]

ELECTION OF 1928

Between Peay's last nomination in 1926 and the race for the Democratic nomination for governor in 1928, Rogers Caldwell and Luke Lea
had together bought a large interest in the Holston-Union National Bank,
had secured control of the *Commercial Appeal* and *Knoxville Journal,*
and were negotiating for the control of the *Atlanta Constitution.* These
transactions had been given wide publicity in the press of Tennessee and
the names of Luke Lea and Rogers Caldwell became closely connected
in the minds of a large majority of people. The fact that one was primarily a politician and the other an investment banker was not popularly
recognized, and Rogers Caldwell came to be regarded along with Lea
as a politician. The gubernatorial campaign of 1928 did more than anything else to foster this opinion.

There were three candidates for governor in 1928. One of them,
Lewis Pope, was making his first bid for the office and attracted little
support. Horton was up for re-election early in the spring and Hill
McAllister, who had given Peay such a close race two years before, threw
his hat in the ring shortly thereafter. In Nashville, Horton had the
support of Luke Lea and his *Tennessean* while the *Banner* and the
Howse-Stahlman-McConnico group were equally as strong for McAllister, partly at least because he was opposed by Luke Lea. Saunders
again changed sides and, although his political power was very definitely
on the wane, came out in favor of Horton, while Crump threw his power
behind McAllister.

The leading issue of the election was soon clarified by McAllister and

[9] *Second Report,* p. 661.   [10] *Ibid.,* p. 662.

his supporters. It was that Horton was backed by Lea and Caldwell and that for the good of the State a candidate with such support, and hence under such control, should not be nominated. Collateral issues arising from this were the use of Kyrock in the construction of the roads of the State, the firing of Neil Bass, and the effort of Caldwell and Company to get the State to assume the debts of drainage districts and thus raise the market value of numerous Caldwell and Company assets.[11] Lea's paper, the *Tennessean,* tried to shift the issue to the power question, charging that the *Banner* was under the control of power interests. The public did not respond to this issue and it was a dangerous one for Lea to raise in view of the fact that his purchase of the *Commercial Appeal* had been financed partially by power interests.

The Lea-Caldwell support of Horton was agitated more in Nashville than anywhere else, with the *Banner* being unrelenting in its assaults upon Horton, Lea, and Caldwell. In a series of cartoons in this paper Caldwell was referred to as "Kid Kyrock" and always pictured with the money bags, Lea became Musso-LEA-ni, and the Governor was usually mired up in Kyrock. The assumed correspondence between Luke Lea, "Governor-in-Fact," and Henry Horton, "Governor-in-Name," was carried daily by the *Banner.* Assuring the public of Horton's defeat in the primary on August 4, the *Banner* on July 30 pictured Lea and Caldwell on the deserted ship "Horton," aflame on a sea of Kyrock, and rimed:

> The Kid stood on the burning deck
> Whence all but Luke had fled.
> Alas, 'tis the flame first lit by Bass,
> Each to the other said.

Lea, in harmony with his rôle as the would-be kidnapper of the Kaiser, fought back with the accusation that Stahlman, the editor of the *Banner,* was not an American citizen, a charge the latter denied. Through his *Knoxville Journal,* Lea advised Republicans to vote in the Democratic primary and based his position on his claim that the *Banner* and the two Scripps-Howard papers in the State were all three Republican and yet were involving themselves in a Democratic primary.

To further discredit Horton and his supporters, McAllister claimed that Caldwell had offered him his support if he would back a bill providing for state assumption of drainage district bonds. Caldwell was brought into the campaign to such an extent that one of the leading ministers of Nashville, Dr. James I. Vance, issued a public statement saying that Rogers Caldwell "is a citizen of highest standing in personal

---

[11] See Chapter II, *supra.*

character, business integrity and service to the public." A group of young businessmen in a much more exaggerated statement claimed that "Rogers Caldwell is the Moses that will lead us out of that bondage and make possible for us a new freedom such as the old South has struggled for since the days of the Confederacy."[12] Finally Caldwell himself issued a public statement saying,

> It is neither pleasant nor proper for a private citizen to be made an issue and to be used as a target for abuse and misrepresentation. But that is what the opposition to Governor Horton has done. The opposition to Governor Horton first sought my support, and is now bitter and hostile because this support was refused. It has been unfair enough to condemn me for supporting Governor Horton exactly as it begged me to support its candidate. Therefore, it has made this statement necessary.[13]

To all of which the *Banner* replied that Rogers Caldwell was not acting as a private citizen when he was trying to get the bonds of drainage districts assumed by the State and trying to get Kyrock specified for Tennessee roads without competition.

In West Tennessee a more or less private fight was taking place between Crump and Saunders. It reached its peak when the Crump organization arranged a big McAllister rally in Covington, the county seat of the adjoining county, thinking it better for McAllister not to speak in Memphis. A holiday was declared for all employees of Memphis and of Shelby County, who turned out en masse for the event. During the address of McAllister, an airplane flew over and dropped on the meeting handbills with the words "Horton is the man," a touch added to the political rally by Saunders. The following Sunday, Saunders had a full-page advertisement in most of the leading newspapers of the State carrying a story entitled, "Mr. Ed Crump Gets Mad—and the Buzz of a little Airplane Did It." It said in part: "Mr. Crump in utter disregard of the Public's business, issued orders for these men to quit their jobs—leave the business of the taxpayers of Shelby County and strut their stuff like martial peacocks forty miles to Covington so Mr. Hill McAllister might before such a worshipful audience pay tribute to the uncrowned red-headed king of Shelby County."[14] Crump immediately answered, claiming that Saunders could not even vote and dragged out once again the fraud and embezzlement charges that were brought against Saunders when he lost control of Piggly-Wiggly.

As the time for the August primary approached, the chances for Horton's nomination appeared less and less favorable and a slush fund of

---

[12] *Nashville Tennessean*, July 18, 1928.
[13] *Ibid.*, July 23, 1928.   [14] *Ibid.*, July 22, 1928.

tremendous size was needed if McAllister were to be defeated. Just how much was raised or how much all the Caldwell-Lea enterprises contributed it is impossible to say. But there is little doubt that a considerable amount was raised. Three cement companies contributed $65,000,[15] two of which, Cumberland Portland Cement Company and Pennsylvania-Dixie, had been financed by Caldwell and Company. Caldwell and Company advanced $27,500 on notes signed by Horton Headquarters and G. H. Keaton, Horton's campaign manager,[16] which, however, were later sold to Southern Publishers, thus transferring the burden of the contribution to that organization.[17] When the likely contributions of the Lea-Caldwell newspapers, Kentucky Rock Asphalt Company, Caldwell and Company itself, and other Lea-Caldwell enterprises that were probably called upon are added, the total funds from the Lea-Caldwell domain were no doubt quite large.

The fact that these interests were allied on the side of Horton had its effect and the nomination went to the Governor. It was one of the closest primaries in Tennessee history. Horton received 95,278 votes, McAllister, 90,014, and Pope, 23,985. McAllister immediately claimed that if Pope had withdrawn from the race Horton would have been easily defeated. McAllister carried Davidson County, the home county of Lea and Caldwell, receiving 11,388 votes to Horton's 4,455, and the Crump organization in Shelby County delivered 23,939 votes to McAllister to the 3,649 for Horton.[18] In the November general election, Horton was easily re-elected in spite of the State's swinging to Hoover in the national arena. Thus the pre-eminence of Lea in Tennessee politics for another two years was assured as well as the fact that the interests of Caldwell and Company would be well served.

HORTON'S POLICIES

Shortly after Horton's re-election differences between the Governor and his new Highway Commissioner, Harry S. Berry, arose. This was not so much over the use of Kyrock, because Berry had proved himself quite willing to co-operate in that respect, but involved the location of certain roads which Horton in his campaign for the nomination had promised to construct. One of these roads was to go through property owned by Luke Lea, thus enhancing its value. Another proposed road was in the western part of the State which had been promised in exchange for the support of a local politician. It was with regard to this road that the final break between Berry and the Governor came. Horton

[15] Testimony of Harry S. Berry before Tennessee Investigating Committee, 1931.
[16] "Audit Report of Caldwell and Company," June 30, 1928.
[17] "Audit of Southern Publishers."   [18] *Nashville Tennessean*, August 5, 1928.

informed Berry that under the Reorganization Act the governor could locate all roads and bridges and that this particular road had to be built where he had promised it even if he had to build it with his own hands. Berry then realized that his services were no longer desired and shortly thereafter he was discharged. Expressed in his own words, he was "crucified in a 'road-for-votes' trade by disciples of the cross and double-cross."[19]   On leaving office Berry said Colonel Lea was the sole owner of the state government of Tennessee and he attributed his discharge primarily to the growing breach between himself and the Colonel.

Another example of the extent to which Lea dominated Horton's policies was the selection of a superintendent of banks. Under the incomprehensible Tennessee law, the State Bankers' Association recommends five men for this position and the governor makes his choice from this group. The new superintendent appointed was D. D. Robertson, a minor official of the Lea-Caldwell controlled Manhattan Savings Bank of Memphis. William White, executive vice president of this bank, asked Robertson if he would like to have the place and a few days later Lea called Robertson to Nashville and took him to see Horton. Robertson had never met the Governor before but in a few minutes Horton assured him that he would be appointed. It was charged later that Robertson informed Lea when banks in which he was interested were going to be examined so that Lea could warn them in advance.[20]

Meanwhile, the regular session of the General Assembly of 1929 had met and provided for the issuance by the State Funding Board of $28,796,000 of bonds and notes, $25,000,000 of which were for roads and bridges. The Funding Board at that time was composed of the governor, the state treasurer, the comptroller, and the secretary of state. It had power to offer for sale all state bonds which had been authorized by the General Assembly, at times it thought appropriate and at interest rates it could obtain. After the General Assembly of 1929 there were, in addition to the bonds authorized by that assembly, bonds authorized by the legislatures of 1925 and 1927 still unissued. The Funding Board met to determine its course of action with regard to the sale of these bonds and a sharp issue arose as to whether there should be one large bond sale or several smaller ones which would provide the funds as needed for the construction projects. The Governor was decidedly in favor of the one large issue while the treasurer, John F. Nolan, favored the other course. The Secretary of State would not commit himself for a while but at the second meeting of the board he gave in to the desires of Horton on the

[19] Testimony of Harry S. Berry before Tennessee Investigating Committee, 1931.
[20] *Second Report*, p. 656.

ground that it was his administration and he did not want to block any of his policies. Accordingly, the board approved the offering for sale of $21,000,000 of bonds and notes on June 4, 1929.

There was only one bid submitted for the bonds and this was by a syndicate headed by Caldwell and Company and the American National Company of Nashville which offered to buy the entire lot at par with interest rates varying on the specific issues between 4.5 and 4.75 per cent. The bid was made with the condition that

after the various State depositories have been fully supplied with funds, first from other sources and then from the proceeds of these sales, under the provision of Chapter 54 of the Acts of 1913, the surplus proceeds shall be deposited with such good and solvent banks in the State of Tennessee and in such amounts as we [Caldwell and Company and American National Company] may designate, such banks to pay three per cent interest on the average daily balances, such interest to be payable semi-annually, as required by law, guaranteeing the safety and security of the several deposits and their prompt forthcoming when demanded, the said deposits to be withdrawn from said banks proportionately and only as funds are needed to pay for Highway and Bridge Projects contemplated in the issuance of said securities.[21]

The bid was accepted under the conditions stated and the syndicate in turn sold the bonds to a New York syndicate headed by Lehman Brothers. As a matter of fact the bonds were signed in New York by the proper state officials and delivered directly to Lehman Brothers. The commissions from the sale of the bonds totaled $169,894, of which Caldwell and Company received only $7,417.[22]

The real gain to Caldwell and Company from the issue was the deposits of the State that were placed in the Bank of Tennessee. The Act of 1913, mentioned in the bid for the bonds, provided for the deposit of state funds in banks pledging approved surety bonds of twice the size of the deposit with the amount of the deposit in any one bank not exceeding one fourth of its paid-up capital stock.[23] The State Treasurer requested an opinion from the State Attorney General as to whether he could, under the law, abide by the condition set out in the bid for the bonds. In his opinion the Attorney General said that the Funding Board had no power to bind the Treasurer to deposit the funds from the sale of the bonds in accordance with the conditions of the bid, but that the buyers would have to rely upon the good faith of the Treasurer to obtain these funds and that he could not allow them to remain with the pur-

[21] Copy of letter from Caldwell and Company and American National Company to the Treasurer of the State of Tennessee, June 4, 1929.

[22] Testimony of T. G. Donovan before Tennessee Investigating Committee, 1931.

[23] *Public Acts of Tennessee*, 1913, Chapter 54.

chasers any longer than his judgment and sense of fairness dictated. It
was clear that the amount of funds arising from the bond sale would be
larger than could be accommodated by the regular state depositories,
hence the Attorney General recommended that after all state depositories
had received their part of the funds, then any surplus funds, and only
such surplus, could be deposited according to the judgment of the Treasurer. The Treasurer was reminded that the depositories were to make
bonds with sureties satisfactory to him and it was stressed that sound
judgment would suggest for such suretyship some well-known and qualified surety company, "the continued solvency of persons being more
difficult for you to be kept informed about, and there being surety companies of well known and established responsibility in the State, unless
you should conceive that the State's interest can as well be protected by
individual bonds if by that method a better rate of interest may be
secured."[24]

Despite this opinion the deposit of funds was made according to the
conditions of the bid and on June 30, 1929, the Bank of Tennessee had
$2,269,000 of state funds, all of which, except $200,000 of special funds
secured by collateral, were secured only by the personal surety bonds
signed by the officers of Caldwell and Company.[25] There was one bond
for $3,000,000 signed by Rogers Caldwell and all the vice presidents of
the firm, namely, Carter, Heitzeberg, Alexander, and Marr, and four
other bonds totaling $3,500,000, each of which was signed by Rogers Cald-
well and at least three of the vice presidents.[26]

THE SPECIAL SESSION OF THE GENERAL ASSEMBLY IN 1929 AND THE SECOND BOND ISSUE

In his efforts to be of further assistance to Caldwell and Company
Governor Horton called a special session of the Tennessee General Assembly for December 2, 1929, to consider certain measures he thought
were necessary. Among these were four that were of considerable importance to Caldwell and Company. Two authorized the sale of $15,000,000
of bonds.[27] These were in addition to those bonds already authorized by
previous general assemblies but still unissued by the Funding Board.

The third act of importance to Caldwell and Company increased the

[24] "On Duty of Treasurer as to Proceeds from Sale of Notes and Bonds by State Funding Board," June 4, 1929, in *Opinions of Attorney General L. D. Smith*, 1926-1930, pp.
137-42.
[25] "Audit Report of Caldwell and Company," June 30, 1929.
[26] Testimony of Assistant State Attorney General Nat Tipton, before Tennessee Investigating Committee, 1931.
[27] *Public Acts of the Extraordinary Session of the General Assembly of Tennessee*, 1931,
Chapters 4 and 14.

membership of the State Funding Board from four to five by adding the commissioner of taxation and finance.[28]   At that time this office was held by Charles M. McCabe, who had been president of the Caldwell controlled Cotton States and North American National Life Insurance companies until they had been reinsured by Inter-Southern Life.   McCabe had been appointed to his state office shortly after Horton became governor.   The Peay appointee to this office, Frank H. Hall, had offended Lea in July, 1927, by issuing a distress warrant to collect delinquent taxes due by Lea's Tennessee Publishing Company.   Horton, after becoming governor, attempted unsuccessfully to get Hall to have a talk of reconciliation with Lea.   When Horton persisted in the idea that this be done, Hall resigned,[29] and the more acceptable McCabe was given the position.   Placing McCabe on the Funding Board packed it in favor of Caldwell and Company's interests.   The sale of the $21,000,000 issue in June had almost been held up because of the opposition of Treasurer Nolan and it was not desirable from the standpoint of Caldwell and Company that such happen again.   The final act of the special session that should be mentioned gave the Funding Board power to choose, within certain limits, depositories for bridge and highway funds.   Under the new law, after the approval of a project and the estimated cost of it had been determined, the Funding Board was to notify the Treasurer of this fact and direct him to place these funds in a state depository chosen by the Funding Board located in the county in which the project was situated.   If there was no depository in that county, the Funding Board could designate any other depository it desired.   This meant that the Funding Board could direct deposits into the Bank of Tennessee or any other Lea-Caldwell bank at any time that it had approved a project in a county having no state depository.

While the General Assembly was still in session, the Funding Board began considering the sale of additional bonds.   Under the guidance of Lea and Caldwell, the Board decided to issue $31,050,000 of bonds for sale on January 9, 1930, and this offer was accordingly advertised.   When the board met on that date, it had two bids.   One was from Lehman Brothers offering to buy $29,050,000 of the bonds at par with interest averaging 4.80 and no strings attached.[30]   The other bid was from a

[28] *Ibid.*, Chapter 9.

[29] *Articles of Impeachment Against Henry H. Horton, Governor of Tennessee,* presented to the House of Representatives of the General Assembly of 1931, Article I, Section a.   Reprinted in *House Journal of General Assembly,* 1931, p. 896.   Cited hereafter as *Horton Articles of Impeachment.*

[30] Testimony of John F. Nolan, state treasurer, before Tennessee Investigating Committee, 1931.

syndicate headed by Caldwell and Company and the American National Company offering to buy the same $29,050,000 of bonds at par with average interest rates of 4.676, with the usual Caldwell strings attached; namely, that the funds be deposited by the Funding Board in banks designated by the buyers in compliance with "Chapter 33 of the Public Acts, Extra Session of 1929" which had just been passed.[31] As might well be expected, the Caldwell bid, strings and all, was accepted.

The same procedure in the delivery of the issue was carried out as was employed with the $21,000,000 issue in June. The bonds were printed and sent to New York where the officials of the State went to sign them and delivered them not to Caldwell and Company's syndicate but to Lehman Brothers' syndicate which, purportedly, had offered the only original competitive bid. It is not difficult, in the light of these events, to believe that the two bidders for the issue had made an agreement to the effect that the Lehman bid would be at a higher interest rate than the Caldwell bid and that Lehman Brothers would buy the bonds as soon as they were sold to the Caldwell syndicate.

Before the funds from the sale of the bonds were received, the Treasurer asked the Attorney General to interpret the new law regarding deposits of state funds. In this opinion it was pointed out that the law merely gave the Funding Board power to designate depositories of highway and bridge funds and that the banks so designated must furnish security as required by the older law covering all deposits of state funds. It was further said that the law indicated that the Funding Board should make reasonable regulations uniform throughout the State and divide the funds among those banks qualifying as depositories for highway funds on the basis of capital and surplus.[32] Again, however, when the funds came into the state treasury they were apportioned out among the banks according to the instructions from the Caldwell syndicate and not on the basis of the capital and surplus of the respective banks. As at first apportioned, the Bank of Tennessee's share was $2,000,000, while the other Lea-Caldwell banks got deposits as follows: Fourth and First National, $5,000,000; Union Planters National, $2,000,000; Manhattan Savings Bank, $1,000,000; the Holston-Union National, $2,000,000; and the Liberty Bank, which had had no part whatever in the syndicate but which got a deposit through Colonel Lea's influence, $150,000.[33]

[31] Letter to Funding Board from Rogers Caldwell, for Caldwell and Company, and Paul M. Davis, for the American National Company, January 9, 1930.

[32] "On State Depositories for Highway Funds Required by Highway Department in Road Building," January 31, 1930, in *Opinions of Attorney General L. D. Smith*, 1926-1930, pp. 158, 159.

[33] Testimony of John F. Nolan before Tennessee Investigating Committee, 1931.

The Effect of Its Political Operations on Caldwell
and Company

That there were some very great advantages obtained by Caldwell and Company because of its political operations cannot be denied. One advantage was the business it was in a position to throw to its affiliated Kentucky Rock Asphalt Company, business which no doubt increased the profits of this company and made it easier for Caldwell and Company to make its huge profit of $1,625,000 from the sale of the stock of this company.[34] Similarly, Caldwell and Company was in a position to throw some business to the cement companies it financed, Cumberland Portland Cement and Pennsylvania-Dixie.

But by far the greatest advantage that Caldwell and Company obtained from its political connections was the state deposits in the Bank of Tennessee. The fact that these deposits were secured only by personal surety bonds of the officers of the company made them of even greater benefit, for they were, in effect, unsecured advances to the company by the State at 3 per cent interest. The Bank of Tennessee was first designated as a state depository in 1927, and the deposits of the State in that bank on June 30, 1927, amounted to only $40,000, and a year later to only $50,000. At the close of the following fiscal year, June 30, 1929, shortly after the sale of the $21,000,000 of bonds, the State's balance with the Bank of Tennessee had jumped to $2,269,000.[35] The amount of cash credited to the State's account monthly from August, 1929, through October, 1930, is as follows:[36]

MONTH	AMOUNT	MONTH	AMOUNT
August, 1929	$ 359,000	March, 1930	$ 71,900
September	586,400	April	653,900
October	324,700	May	1,068,900
November	345,500	June	576,500
December	170,600	July	784,500
January, 1930	2,003,100	August	284,300
February	382,800	September	576,800
		October	149,700
Total			$8,338,600

In addition to these sums, $406,000 was credited to the account in November, 1929, from the proceeds of a small bond issue bought by Caldwell and Company, and a total of $107,100 in interest was also credited to the account during this period. On November 6, 1930, when the Bank of

---

[34] See Chapter VI, *supra.*

[35] "Audit Report of Caldwell and Company," as of dates mentioned.

[36] These data were obtained from a confidential, though reliable, source.

Tennessee was closed, the State had a deposit balance of $3,418,400. Until March 30, 1930, the Bank of Tennessee carried the State's funds as demand deposits against which reserves of 10 per cent were legally required. By that date, cash had become so scarce with the bank and Caldwell and Company that the deposits were transferred to time deposits against which a legal reserve of only 3 per cent was needed, though the deposit was, needless to say, just as active as ever.

An additional consideration was given the needs of Caldwell and Company by the State Funding Board when, on August 14, 1930, it passed a resolution calling for the deposit of $245,000 of bridge funds in the Bank of Tennessee because there was no bank in the county where the bridge was being constructed large enough under the law to receive the deposit. In passing the resolution the Funding Board "unanimously designated the Bank of Tennessee as a depository to disburse bridge funds." This resolution was interpreted by the State Treasurer to mean that all bridge funds should go to the Bank of Tennessee and such was done. In this way the bank received funds that would be withdrawn more slowly because of the usually rather long period used in the construction of bridges.[37]

The funds which the Bank of Tennessee obtained from the State without having to give collateral enabled it, as well as Caldwell and Company, to continue operations at least four or five months longer than they otherwise could have done. Even though this was the case, the costs at which these funds were acquired were extremely high. Few companies and certainly no investment house, no matter what its previous reputation had been, could have had its owner and chief executive dragged into a mud-slinging political campaign as Rogers Caldwell was in the Tennessee gubernatorial race of 1928 without a severe loss of prestige. The charges of political pillage that were hurled against Caldwell naturally reflected upon his company. He was definitely linked in the minds of many people with Luke Lea and a large part of the people of the State probably thought Lea held a high position in Caldwell and Company and owned a large interest in the business. Lea's foes, and his tactics had gained for him many unremitting ones, became foes of Rogers Caldwell and Caldwell and Company, a condition which was certainly detrimental to the company's efforts to sell its securities, especially in its own state. Many who desired Lea's political downfall would not have regretted the downfall of Caldwell and Company because of the financial assistance this company was giving Lea in expanding his influence through his newspapers and banks and felt that if the power of Lea were to be

[37] *Second Report*, p. 653.

diminished, the support of his financial backer must be cut off. They saw such a step necessary if Tennessee were to be rescued from the abysmal depths of corruption in public office and the subordination of its financial affairs in the interests of Lea and Caldwell. It was generally accepted that Henry Horton, while basically honest, was not able to see where his policy of following Lea and Caldwell would lead and that with such a weak governor the danger that the State's finances would be unwisely, if not dishonestly, managed was imminent. In short, the political operations of Caldwell and Company had resulted in the feeling on the part of many Tennesseans, partisan though many of them were, that the State could be saved only through reducing the financial power of Caldwell and Company.[38]

[38] These conclusions are based upon the general tenor of the opposition press, upon conversations with various former officials of Caldwell and Company who were trying to sell its securities, and upon the fact that while the company's sales increased 36 per cent from June 30, 1927, to June 30, 1928, they increased less than 10 per cent from June 30, 1928, to June 30, 1929, which covered one of the most active periods in the history of security trading in this country.

Chapter XII

CALDWELL AND COMPANY AT THE END OF 1929

In an interview in 1927, when asked the question, "And you have made this tremendous success in ten years?" Rogers Caldwell is reported to have answered: "Success? Who knows whether he has made a success at all until he comes to die?"[1] If Rogers Caldwell had doubts in 1927 that his achievements would be permanent, he had, by 1929, sufficient cause for grave concern as to the continued existence of his financial empire. That there were numerous evidences of success in the development of Caldwell and Company down to the end of 1929 cannot be denied. These achievements were reflected in the aid given by Caldwell and Company to the development of the South and in the progress of the company itself.

During the entire life of Caldwell and Company the South was experiencing a marked economic development, which was financed partly by outside capital and partly by capital accumulating within the region. Caldwell and Company aided in attracting outside capital by the sale of Southern securities in other parts of the country and by borrowing from banks outside of the South. A conservative estimate of the volume of funds attracted through the first channel, based upon sales of branch offices in other regions in years for which data are available, is $120,000,000. This amount does not include issues such as those of the state of Tennessee in 1929 and 1930 for which Caldwell and Company was merely an intermediary between the issuing government and Eastern financial houses. It is impossible to estimate the volume of funds brought into the South by Caldwell and Company through its borrowing from Eastern banks, but the total was doubtless substantial. While these funds were in the nature of temporary advances rather than permanent investments, they helped supply a part of the working capital for the South's industrial development.

Caldwell and Company also aided in Southern development by acting as the necessary intermediary between the small saver within the South and the public and private organizations needing funds. It tapped these sources of capital by issuing types and denominations of securities that would appeal to all investors. The company's sales force and its network

[1] Alexander, "A Rich Man's Son Earns His Own Success," in *The New South*, I, 23.

of branch offices, which at the close of 1929 numbered around twenty-five, were designed to secure a considerable portion of the savings of the region.

The funds placed in investment channels through Caldwell and Company were used in the construction of a wide variety of permanent capital goods, both public and private, the nature of which has already been pointed out. Suffice it to say that many public and private improvements in the South would never have been undertaken unless Caldwell and Company or some other Southern investment banker had been willing to underwrite the securities necessary to finance the projects. Particularly is this true for most private industries and smaller municipalities in whose securities Eastern underwriters were then generally uninterested.

From the standpoint of Caldwell and Company itself there were unmistakable evidences of success. In only twelve years it had grown from an insignificant municipal bond house in Nashville to the dominant investment banker of the South. Its total assets had increased from $2,138,000 in 1918 to $17,700,000 in 1925 and to $38,075,000 by the close of 1929. Similarly, its annual sales had jumped from less than $10,000,000 in 1918 to $74,000,000 in the fiscal year ending June 30, 1929, and earnings from $38,265 to $1,907,522 between these two dates. It had pushed itself through strategic investments into the insurance, banking, industrial, and newspaper fields until it had become an important factor in each of these lines of Southern business. The total assets of the companies controlled by Caldwell and Company at the close of 1929 amounted to slightly less than $500,000,000, distributed as follows:

Insurance Companies	$232,930,000
Banks	213,269,000
Industrial Companies	41,072,500
Newspapers	6,966,000
Investment Trust	2,924,000
Total	$497,161,500

When assets of $20,000,000 of Caldwell and Company and the Bank of Tennessee, other than their investments in these controlled companies, are added, total assets controlled by Caldwell and Company pass the half-billion-dollar level. The organization had become a large holding company, controlling other holding and operating companies affiliated with it, thereby permitting the practice of all the abuses that can accompany the extensive use of holding companies. These intercorporate relations are depicted in the accompanying chart. To put tersely the achievements of Caldwell and Company it can be said that it had so

THE CORPORATE AFFILIATIONS OF CALDWELL AND COMPANY

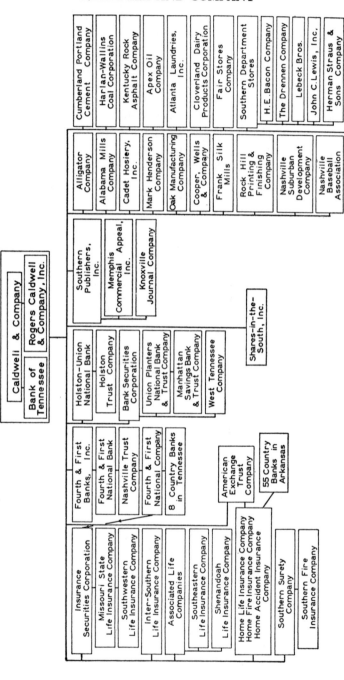

SOURCE—Compiled by author.

increased in size and built up such prestige in financial circles that it was referred to as the "Morgan of the South."[2]

This same expansion, however, that had placed Caldwell and Company at the top among Southern investment bankers carried with it the cause of the company's ultimate destruction for it was accomplished at a time when practically all securities were selling at extremely inflated prices and Caldwell and Company necessarily had had to agree to pay these prices in the building of its domain. In so doing it had loaded itself with obligations that were to become progressively more difficult to meet. This was true primarily because Caldwell and Company was expanding in the main on borrowed funds and relying only to a small extent on reinvested earnings and permanent capital. Reinvested earnings and capital stock, for which Rogers Caldwell finally paid in 1927 when it was called to his attention by the auditors of the company that he had never done so, amounted to 10.1 per cent of total assets on June 30, 1926, but, by the end of 1929, to only 4.7 per cent. Since total assets had increased from $17,700,000 to $38,000,000 between these two dates, ever increasing quantities of funds had to be obtained from outside sources. These funds from outside sources were primarily loans from banks and deposits, with the latter always the more important. Deposits of municipal funds secured through the purchase of municipal bonds under depository agreements constituted at all times from 1926 to 1929 the most important single source of capital. Deposits from controlled companies, however, increased absolutely and relatively throughout the period, jumping from 10 per cent of total assets in 1926 to 20 per cent in 1929. Bank loans varied between 20 and 30 per cent of total assets.[3] This reliance by Caldwell and Company on deposits of municipalities and controlled companies constituted from a social standpoint the most undesirable condition in the whole organization. It resulted in making the financial condition of the controlled companies, municipal depositors, thousands of individual depositors in Caldwell banks, holders of policies of Caldwell insurance companies, holders of securities of Caldwell industrial companies, as well as the interests of countless taxpayers unjustifiably dependent upon the precarious financial condition of Caldwell and Company.

This pernicious effect would not have existed to the extent that it did if the funds obtained from outside sources had been invested in liquid assets. But accompanying Caldwell and Company's expansion was the

[2] Testimony taken in the case *Laurent* v. *Akers, et al.,* No. 206688, Jefferson County (Kentucky) Circuit Court, Chancery Branch. Cited hereafter as *Laurent Evidence.*

[3] "Audit Report of Caldwell and Company," for years mentioned.

relative and absolute growth of the nonliquid assets held by the company. These assets may be divided into three categories, the first of which was composed of slow-moving securities. On June 30, 1929, the company had $922,000 of securities which had been on hand from six months to a year and $2,240,000 which it had held for over a year. Together they amounted to approximately 20 per cent of the company's inventory at that time, other than its investments in affiliated companies.[4] The second category of nonliquid assets consisted of the investments of a permanent nature that the investment house had made in its affiliated companies. While many of these investments were of a type that might prove profitable in the long run, most of them were not readily marketable for the obvious reason that controlling interests in large insurance companies, banks, and industrial enterprises cannot usually be sold upon short notice without a loss. Assets of this type, on June 30, 1929, were over $14,000,000, or 40 per cent of the total assets of the company.

The third group of nonliquid assets, while not so large as the second group, were much more tightly frozen than any of the others. Exclusive of the home office building of the company which was financed by long-time bonds, the principal items in this group were past-due bonds and coupons; overdue and, in many cases, because of the company's lax collection policies, uncollectible notes and accounts; and real estate not used in operations. Defaulted bonds and coupons increased from a par value of $270,500 in 1926 to $978,000 in 1928 and to $1,164,000 in 1929; but liberal write-offs after 1928 reduced the book value of these securities to $215,045 at the end of 1929. Part of the overdue notes and accounts were those of individuals not directly in the employ of Caldwell and Company but closely connected with it. Outstanding items of this class in 1929 were Luke Lea's debts of $150,000; those of Hillsman Taylor, president of Missouri State Life, amounting to $130,000; and $110,000 owed by Meredith Caldwell, Rogers Caldwell's brother and president of Fourth and First National Company. An equally important part of frozen receivables were debts of the officers of the company. On June 30, 1929, Rogers Caldwell owed $380,000; E. J. Heitzeberg, $93,000; and J. D. Carter, $70,000. Heitzeberg's and Carter's indebtedness arose from securities they had bought on credit from the company and from loans made to them to purchase rather expensive homes. Rogers Caldwell's debt was due largely to the fact that he was drawing more from the business for his personal expenses than he was receiving in dividends and salaries.[5]

[4] *Ibid.*, June 30, 1929. See Appendix C for balance sheets.

[5] Rogers Caldwell's salary as president of Caldwell and Company, Bank of Tennessee, and Rogers Caldwell and Company, Incorporated, increased from $54,000 in the fiscal year

Part of these funds was used to finance Brentwood Stables, his private venture in horse racing.

Rogers Caldwell, too, built a home, but he financed his somewhat differently than the company's two vice presidents had financed theirs. The Bank of Tennessee had acquired a substantial amount of residential and farm property on the Franklin Pike south of Nashville, one 216-acre block of which adjoined the property of James E. Caldwell. In 1927 Rogers Caldwell decided to build a home commensurate with his financial standing and chose a beautiful location, supposedly on the block of land owned by the bank. The building, known as Brentwood House and modeled after the "Hermitage," the home of Caldwell's reputed ideal, Andrew Jackson, was begun in 1927 and completed in 1928. The house cost approximately $350,000 and the lands around it, not the actual site, cost $80,000. The funds to meet these costs were provided by the Bank of Tennessee which carried the property as an asset valued at $430,000 and paid taxes on it. Rogers Caldwell's account with the bank was charged $5,000 annually as the rent on the place, or slightly more than 1 per cent of the cost. Brentwood House, however, was not erected on land belonging to the bank but just across the line on land belonging to James E. Caldwell. This fact was not made known to other officers and employees of the bank, all of whom thought the bank had a clear title to the property, an idea which was impressed successfully on the state bank examiners. If this asset had been taken off the books of the bank, as it should have been, on December 31, 1929, the Bank of Tennessee, instead of having a surplus of $316,000 would have had a deficit of $114,000. The method of financing Brentwood House and the advances to Brentwood Stables constitute probably the outstanding instances in which Rogers Caldwell used his business resources to finance purely private projects, regardless of the ultimate effect upon the business. It can with certainty be stated that the company was not abiding by one of its original bylaws; namely, that no officer or employee should be retained whose expenditures exceeded his known income.[6]

At the close of 1929, of Caldwell and Company's total assets, approximately $19,500,000, or 55 per cent, were definitely of a nonliquid character, a condition which was all the more serious in view of the fact that

---

ending June 30, 1927, to $90,000 during the next two fiscal years. In addition he received $5,000 as president of Shares-in-the-South. Cash dividends paid by Caldwell and Company to Rogers Caldwell as sole stockholder amounted to slightly more than $300,000 between June 30, 1926, and June 30, 1929. Carter and Heitzeberg, as executive vice presidents, received $31,500 in the fiscal year, 1928-1929.—*Ibid.*

[6] See Chapter I, *supra*.

outside sources were providing around 90 per cent of the company's total funds.

In addition to these frozen, or at best nonliquid, assets some of the company's funds were siphoned off through useless expenditures. Included among these was a part of the additional sums spent equipping the Harry Nichol Building, including an infrequently used kitchen and dining room, as Caldwell and Company expanded up to the point that it used practically all of the building. Further, the maintenance of a Fifth Avenue apartment in New York for the convenience of the company's officers and their families, an addition made late in 1928, cost approximately $4,000 a month. Perhaps outstanding among such expenses, though, were the losses Caldwell and Company sustained in the stock market. In 1927 Rogers Caldwell evidently decided the New York stock market was ready to start downward and began selling short such outstanding performers as American Can, American Telephone, Coca-Cola, General Electric, General Motors, New York Central, Southern Pacific, U. S. Steel, and U. S. Rubber, the blue chips of the bull market.[7] Losses resulting from these transactions amounted to $197,000 in 1927, $184,000 in 1928, and $304,000 in 1929, or a total of $685,000.[8] The short account was closed in June, 1929, and, sad to relate, was not reopened. By these operations the company sustained losses which amounted to 21 per cent of its net worth as of June 30, 1929.

That Caldwell and Company was becoming financially imperiled was made evident in many ways other than through the growing volume of frozen assets and the increasing reliance upon outside sources of funds. The deficiency in the Bank of Tennessee's legal cash reserve strongly suggests such a condition. These deficiencies on June 30, 1927, 1928, and 1929, respectively, amounted to $163,000, $135,000, and $182,000.[9] The auditors of the company in their report of June 30, 1929 "strongly urged that a consistent effort be made to strengthen the company's cash position." The impaired cash reserve reflected a generally unsatisfactory condition in the Bank of Tennessee, which has been characterized as a "dummy" corporation, as Rogers Caldwell's vest-pocket bank, and by other deprecatory phrases, and which was conducted almost solely to aid Caldwell and Company in whatever manner possible. The bank always had large payables since it was used by its parent organization, Caldwell and Company, to borrow funds from those banks where the parent, in its own

[7] "Caldwell Minute Book," Meeting of the Board of Directors, June 30, 1927, and June 30, 1928.

[8] "Audit Report of Caldwell and Company," as of dates mentioned.

[9] Ibid.

name, had already borrowed up to the legal limit. The funds thus obtained were then made available to Caldwell and Company by the bank's purchasing securities from it. All such purchases of securities, after June 30, 1927, were covered by a general repurchase agreement which the bank and Caldwell and Company entered into on that date. In this contract it was agreed:

1. That from time to time, Caldwell and Company will sell and the Bank of Tennessee will purchase from Caldwell and Company bonds and other securities at such prices as may be agreed upon, said prices to be indicated by entries on the books of the Bank of Tennessee, and, thereafter, upon demand of the Bank of Tennessee, Caldwell and Company will repurchase, and the Bank of Tennessee will sell back to Caldwell and Company, said bonds and securities at their respective purchase prices plus accrued interest on the bonds.

2. That, unless otherwise indicated by contract in writing as to any specific security or securities, this general contract and agreement shall apply to all purchases of bonds and securities by the Bank of Tennessee from Caldwell and Company.[10]

Since Caldwell and Company completely controlled the bank, no repurchase demands would be made except those agreeable to Caldwell and Company. Under this agreement the bank purchased from Caldwell and Company $86,353,000 of securities and sold back $82,659,000, amounts indicating the extent to which the companies were trading with each other.

This agreement, it should be noted, arose out of an examination of the bank by the Tennessee Banking Department in 1927. Finding the bank in poor condition and knowing its close relationship with Caldwell and Company, the Superintendent of Banks insisted that such an agreement be drawn up, thereby attempting to protect the depositors in an institution he was examining by tying its solvency to Caldwell and Company which he did not examine and about whose financial stability he knew little. The efficacy of such a policy was indeed questionable and reflects the inadequacy of the recommendation.

A further evidence of the shaky financial condition of the company can be seen in the violated trusts for which both Caldwell and Company and the Bank of Tennessee acted as trustees. Violations of trusts resulted from the company's lack of sufficient collateral of the type called for to be hypothecated on trust agreements. Securities were substituted which were not eligible under the terms of the agreements and no notices were given to the depositors of such substitutions. This practice is well sum-

[10] "Caldwell Minute Book."

marized in the following excerpt from a memorandum from E. A. Goodloe, cashier of the Bank of Tennessee, to Carter and Heitzeberg:

We have not been notifying municipal authorities in cases where I feel
certain they would question the collateral. Just at present we would [sic]
better let well enough alone. When authorities write for lists (which is sel-
dom) I send them a list which I feel certain will be approved. The list is,
however, supported by actual temporary physical substitution of the collateral
listed; thus I do not legally misrepresent the situation in my letters. I am
satisfying all concerned in this respect and just as soon as conditions change,
I will take steps to keep up collateral exactly in line with trust agreements.[11]

The continued presence of violated trust agreements meant that there
was criminal negligence on the part of some individual or group of
individuals.

The source of a substantial part of Caldwell and Company's funds,
namely, the deposits of the state of Tennessee in the Bank of Tennessee,
necessarily resulted in an unsound situation. During the latter part of
1929 and even to a greater degree in 1930, the company relied considerably upon these deposits for cash. The withdrawal of these funds would
have been disastrous, yet they would unquestionably have been withdrawn
if an unfriendly administration were elected. Thus the company's liquidity was dependent to a great extent upon the results of the biennial
gubernatorial races in Tennessee which in turn were dependent upon the
changing alignments of political machines, only one of which Caldwell
and Company could rely upon for aid.

Also, there were decidedly unsatisfactory conditions in Caldwell and
Company at the close of 1929 which were not primarily financial in character but which resulted from the failure of the executives of the company to exercise proper and sufficient management over the internal
operations of the business. There were no clearly defined lines of responsibility and authority fixed and recognized by the company's head. Rather,
Rogers Caldwell conducted his business largely as the exigencies of the
situation demanded, a policy which resulted in clashes between himself
and other officials, particularly Carter, and in detriment to the company's
best interests.[12]

Caldwell allowed his company to be carried along with the general
trend in investment banking toward the wholesale and disastrous relax-
ation of standards of safety and the underwriting of securities of the most
speculative nature.[13] This trend, so far as Caldwell and Company is

[11] December 19, 1929.
[12] Letter from J. DeWitt Carter to Rogers Caldwell, May 20, 1930. See Chapter xv,
infra.   [13] See Graham and Dodd, op. cit., p. 9.

concerned, can be seen in its expansion from underwriting municipal bonds exclusively to real estate and industrial bonds, and toward the end of the twenties the selling of common stocks as its dominant field of operation. The company lacked safeguarding traditions and standards acquired through many years of service. It was an essentially young bond house which through rapid growth had gained for itself a substantial clientele. The policies and administration of the company were entirely in the hands of young men, none of whom had been seasoned in the investment banking business by long years of experience covering all kinds of business weather. Rather, they had obtained practically all their experience in investment banking with this one house during the extremely fair weather of the twenties when securities were not usually critically evaluated by either the issuing house or the investing public, and hence they did not have the maturity which would have equipped them to guide the house more ably through whatever difficulties might arise.

The existing weaknesses in the company had been brought to a head by the stock market crash in the latter part of 1929. At that time it had made several large investments in insurance companies, the success of which depended upon the marketing of the stock of its new insurance holding company, Associated Life Companies. Substantial holdings of the stock of certain banks were becoming burdensome. Its efforts to peg the price of Shares-in-the-South after the stock market break were even more difficult than they had been in the summer of 1929. Finally, the company had several issues of industrial bonds, including $1,000,000 of Cadet Hosiery and $1,100,000 of Rock Hill Printing and Finishing Company, which had never been offered to the public, as well as large blocks of other bonds and bonus stocks of various corporations which could be sold only under the market conditions that had existed in the earlier part of 1929. From the standpoint of Caldwell and Company, the stock market crash came at the most inopportune time possible, for it found the company with a greater volume of commitments than at any other time in its history and obviated all chances of its meeting these commitments in the manner planned.

Thus at the close of 1929 numerous defects existed which placed Caldwell and Company in a woefully vulnerable position. With an extremely weak cash position, it could withstand only a small net reduction of its demand liabilities. Even a slight run would bring disaster. The securities markets were such that the company could expect little relief through the sale of its inventory, a sales campaign in October, 1929, having shown the futility of this. If the company was to be saved, extreme measures had to be taken immediately.

CHAPTER XIII

THE MERGER WITH BANCOKENTUCKY COMPANY

Rogers Caldwell in the latter part of 1929 and early in 1930 recognized the tottering condition of his company and was prepared to take drastic and far-reaching steps in his efforts to prevent its impending collapse. His major effort to strengthen his institution began in the early part of 1930, when, on January 29, he wrote the following letter[1] to James B. Brown, president of BancoKentucky Company, a holding company controlling the National Bank of Kentucky of Louisville:

My dear Mr. Brown:

I have been wondering lately whether it would be feasible to consider a consolidation between the BancoKentucky Corporation and the banks in which we are interested. If I could discuss the matter with you I have a suggestion to make which, in my opinion, might be very helpful to the market situation on BancoKentucky stock. As you know, the banks in which we are interested already have deposits of above $150,000,000 and I believe that a combination of our interests would make one of the most formidable situations in the country.

I am leaving tonight for St. Louis to attend the annual meeting of the Missouri State Life Insurance Company and if you think this suggestion is worthy of our getting together you might wire me there, care of the Missouri State Life Company and I could come back by way of Louisville.

With assurance of my regard and looking forward to discussing this matter with you, I remain

Very truly yours,

Rogers Caldwell

Mr. Brown's reply was evidently favorable, for during the greater part of the next four months negotiations were carried on between Caldwell and Brown which resulted in the merger of BancoKentucky Company and Caldwell and Company.

The National Bank of Kentucky and BancoKentucky Company

The National Bank of Kentucky traced its origin back to an act of the Kentucky legislature in February, 1834, which established the Bank of Kentucky in Louisville, a part of the stock of which was bought by

[1] Exhibit to testimony taken in *Laurent Evidence*. Joseph S. Laurent was appointed receiver of BancoKentucky Company and, as such, sued the directors of the company to recover losses suffered by the company due to their negligence. See Chapter xix, *infra*.

the State. In 1872 the State sold most of its bank stock and in 1900 the Bank of Kentucky applied for and received a national bank charter and became the National Bank of Kentucky. The bank increased in size and influence under its national charter and in February, 1919, after merging with the National Bank of Commerce and the American-Southern National Bank, both of Louisville, had total resources of $52,568,000 and deposits of $43,988,000. Its directors formally congratulated themselves, as noted in the minutes of their meeting, that their bank was the largest south of the Ohio River.[2]

The directors might well have congratulated themselves upon the success of their bank. By that time it had enjoyed a continual existence of eighty-five years. It had weathered all financial storms, state and national, including those incident to the Civil War and reconstruction. It had attracted depositors from the small towns and rural areas of Kentucky as well as great numbers from Louisville, and held the reserves of many of the banks in the smaller towns throughout the State. Further, it was a very important depository of the state of Kentucky. It had acquired a reputation for unswerving conservatism, unshaken stability, and unquestioned safety, which had been earned through its long and honorable record, and its achievements merited the confidence of several thousand customers.

The merger of the National Bank of Kentucky with the other two national banks in 1919 brought into the bank an individual, James B. Brown, whose policies proved to be inconsistent with those to which the bank had previously adhered. Brown, who had been president of the National Bank of Commerce of Louisville and had quite a reputation as a financier, was made president of the consolidated bank. He had been appointed by President Wilson to the War Finance Corporation and held directorships in the Louisville and Nashville Railroad Company, the Standard Oil Company of Kentucky, the Southern Bell Telephone and Telegraph Company, the Louisville Gas and Electric Company, the Kentucky Jockey Club, and later the American Turf Association.[3] He acquired control of the *Herald-Post,* a daily paper in Louisville, which, although operated at a loss, enhanced Brown's political power and placed him in a position to obtain many political favors. In addition to

---

[2] These and other facts in the following paragraphs concerning the National Bank of Kentucky, unless otherwise cited, are from the Original Bill of Paul C. Keyes, receiver of the National Bank of Kentucky, in the case *Keyes* v. *Akers, et al.,* No. 649, in equity, in the United States District Court for the Western District of Kentucky at Louisville. Keyes was relieved by Anderson and the case became *Anderson* v. *Akers, et al.* Cited hereafter as *Original Bill of Keyes.* See Chapter xix, *infra.*

[3] *Laurent Evidence.*

these activities, he carried on extensive security speculation through a Louisville brokerage firm, Wakefield and Company, which was little more than Brown's private agency. Many of Brown's activities, especially those connected with the *Herald-Post,* the Turf Association, and Wakefield and Company, called for large sums of money, and Brown, in turn, called on the National Bank of Kentucky to help foot the bill.

Brown's effect on the policies of the National Bank of Kentucky had become apparent by 1923. In 1921 he had been made chairman of its board of directors while continuing to hold his position as president, thus becoming the dominant figure in the bank's affairs, dictating its policies on every matter and ruling it with an iron hand. In January, 1923, his salary, which had been $13,500 when he first came with the bank and had later been increased to $25,000, was raised to $50,000. His entrenched position is shown by the fact that the next highest paid official received $12,000 a year. After his election to the chairmanship of the board, Brown became less and less regular in his attendance at directors' meetings and indulged to a much greater extent his personal inclinations and idiosyncrasies with respect to his presence at or absence from the bank during business hours; yet through his dominance over the other officers his control of the funds of the bank increased.[4] Finally, it became Brown's custom to devote his nights to the affairs of the bank, using a desk at one of the branches. There he held such conferences as he permitted with the other officers. Charles F. Jones, cashier and later vice president of the bank, was the main connecting link between Brown and his institution, and, through Jones, Brown communicated his desires and instructions to the other officers.[5]

The affairs of the bank took a definite turn for the worse in 1925. An examination by the national bank examiner in April of that year disclosed losses of $109,000, which were written off, and slow and doubtful assets of $1,860,000 and $244,000, respectively. Despite this write-off, the examination in November, 1925, by the chief national bank examiner for the eighth Federal Reserve District, John S. Wood, found its affairs in a decidedly more unsatisfactory condition. Losses of $334,000 had to be charged off at that time and thirteen other specific criticisms were directed against the management. At every examination from that time on losses of considerable size were charged off, slow and doubtful assets were criticized, and the dominance of the bank by Brown and his utter disregard for the law and the regulations of the Comptroller's office were stressed.[6]

[4] *Original Bill of Keyes.*

[5] *Plaintiff's Brief on Law,* in the case *Anderson* v. *Akers, et al.,* p. 308.

[6] J. W. Pole (Comptroller of Currency of the United States), "National Bank of Kentucky, Louisville, Kentucky: Brief of Reports of Examinations and Actions Taken by the

In spite of and perhaps because of its unsatisfactory loan policies, the National Bank of Kentucky during the middle and late twenties was making substantial gains in business. Total assets, which had amounted to $38,720,000 in September, 1921, reached $55,362,000 by the close of 1926. In 1927 the affiliation of the bank with the Louisville Trust Company, which had total assets of $8,465,000 and deposits of $5,794,000, was announced. Under this arrangement, the shares of both institutions were deposited with six trustees and exchanged for Trustees' Participation Certificates. By the end of 1929 the combined assets of these two institutions amounted to $75,000,000 and deposits to $48,900,000.[7]

Meanwhile, the criticisms directed against the bank's management by the Comptroller continued and finally became so severe that the directors of the bank began considering its denationalization and the carrying on of the operations of the bank under the state charter of the Louisville Trust Company. During 1929 the directors decided definitely to do this, informed the Comptroller of the proposed step, and took measures to be admitted to the Federal Reserve System as a state member bank. The Federal Reserve Bank of St. Louis advised the board that it could not be thus admitted, though as a national bank it already possessed membership, unless it eliminated from its assets certain loans aggregating $4,023,000, while on the other hand it could not withdraw from the system until it had repaid rediscounts of approximately $8,000,000 at the Federal Reserve Bank.[8] The National Bank of Kentucky was in no position to meet either of these requirements so the plan of running away from its difficulties through denationalization was postponed until some measures could be taken that would enable it to meet the requirements of the Federal Reserve Bank.

It was thought that these requirements could be met if some other institution could be formed which would take the doubtful assets out of the bank and replace them with cash. Such a step was agreed upon and the institution created for this purpose was the BancoKentucky Company. There was also the additional advantage that such an institution could unify the management and control of enough banks in the Ohio Valley to make it the most powerful financial organization and its president, James B. Brown, the most powerful banker in a large region.

With these ends in view, BancoKentucky Company obtained a Delaware charter in July, 1929, which authorized a capital stock of $20,000,000,

Office of the Comptroller of the Currency," in *Hearings on the Operations of the National and Federal Reserve Banking Systems*, Part v, pp. 631-35, Seventy-first Congress, Third Session. Cited hereafter as *Comptroller's Report on National Bank of Kentucky*.

[7] *Moody's Banks*, 1930, pp. 1133, 1134.   [8] *Original Bill of Keyes*.

represented by 2,000,000 shares of $10 par value, and which gave the corporation the almost unlimited powers granted in the usual Delaware charter. Brown was, of course, elected president of the company and its directorate was composed of the members of the National Bank of Kentucky and Louisville Trust Company boards. The holders of Trustees' Participation Certificates of the two banks were offered two shares of BancoKentucky stock for each certificate held and were given the option of subscribing to as many additional shares at $25 a share as they desired, which was no special consideration, for the shares were offered to the public at that price. The whole plan was conditioned upon the acquiring by Banco of a majority of the certificates. With the certificates then selling at $45, the exchange of one certificate for two shares of Banco would net the holder a paper profit of $5. In addition to this present monetary consideration, the certificate holders were strongly advised to exchange their certificates for the Banco stock on the ground that the new institution would expand the facilities of the banks and make the operations of the entire group much more profitable. The holders of 540,384 certificates out of a total of 570,550 succumbed to the plea of the directors and exchanged their holdings for 1,080,768 shares of the Banco stock. At a price of $25 a share, the control of National Bank of Kentucky and Louisville Trust Company thust cost Banco $27,019,200 in stock.[9]

After making this exchange Banco had more than 900,000 authorized shares of stock which it desired to sell for cash or exchange for other assets. The officers of the company were requested to solicit subscriptions at $25 a share, and, in addition, a contract was entered into by Banco with Blythe and Company, H. M. Byllesby and Company, and Wakefield and Company to market the stock. The shares were listed on the Chicago Stock Exchange and these brokers agreed to handle market operations to create a demand for the stock and effect its wide distribution to the public. Banco was to offer 100,000 shares for market trading purposes and to keep the balance as unissued stock. The brokers were given the option of purchasing up to 250,000 shares of the stock by June 1, 1930, at a price of $26 to February 1, 1930, and $26.50 thereafter.[10] Between September 25 and November 7, 1929, Banco sold for cash 394,786 shares of stock, receiving $9,869,650.[11]

The purchase of these shares was financed largely by the National Bank of Kentucky and the Louisville Trust Company. Hundreds of persons who subscribed to Banco stock applied for loans at the banks and were accommodated up to $25 a share. By December 31, 1929, the

[9] Original Bill of Laurent in the case *Laurent* v. *Akers, et al.* Cited hereafter as *Original Bill of Laurent.*

[10] *Laurent Evidence.*   [11] *Original Bill of Laurent.*

National Bank of Kentucky had loaned $5,853,000 secured in whole or in part by 225,000 shares of Banco, a policy which necessitated a $5,800,000 increase in payables. The Louisville Trust Company, on the same date, had loaned $2,700,000 secured wholly or partly by 100,000 shares. Together, the two institutions had loaned approximately $8,500,000 of the $9,869,650 received by Banco from the sale of its stock. This practice continued in 1930. In September of that year the bank had loans of $6,136,000 secured wholly or partly with 230,000 shares while the trust company had $3,376,000 of such loans secured by 91,000 shares. These loans, which were made largely without reference to the financial standing of the borrower, were secured by 321,000 shares, or 80 per cent of the entire amount of the stock sold to the public for cash. It is interesting to note that the bank made loans equal to its entire net worth on notes largely secured by an amount of Banco stock which represented only 1.98 per cent of the net worth of the bank and .797 per cent of the net worth of the trust company.[12]

Shortly after the acquisition of the control of the National Bank of Kentucky and Louisville Trust Company, BancoKentucky Company began buying other banks and brought eight more under its control. These banks had total assets of $56,244,000 and were purchased for an expenditure of $6,561,555 in cash and $5,067,850 in stock, or a total of $11,629,405. They are listed in the accompanying table together with the purchase

SMALLER BANKS ACQUIRED BY BANCOKENTUCKY COMPANY. 1929-30

Bank and Location	Date of Acquisition	Assets	Net Worth	Percentage of Stock Bought	Cost in Stock	Cost in Cash	Total Cost
		(In thousands)					
Cincinnati, Ohio							
Brighton Bank........	Sept. 27, 1929	$15,500	$ 939	89	$ 786,475	$3,323,410	$ 4,109,885
Pearl Market Bank...	Sept. 27, 1929	13,400	1,883	80	1,373,400	2,200,400	3,573,800
Covington, Kentucky							
Central Savings Bank.	Nov. 22, 1929	2,640	248	91	....	329,372	329,372
Peoples-Liberty Bank .	Jan. 10, 1930	9,040	1,022	32	....	491,136	491,136
Louisville, Kentucky							
Security Bank........	Mar. 27, 1930	2,800	682	90	732,350	217,200	949,550
Ashland, Kentucky							
Ashland National Bank..............	Mar. 27, 1930	6,800	1,109	89	1,423,000	37	1,423,037
Paducah, Kentucky							
First National Bank...	Mar. 7, 1930	4,234	390	92	623,250	....	623,250
Mechanics Trust and Savings Bank......	Sept. 19, 1930	1,830	158	58	129,375	....	129,375
Totals.........	....	$56,244	$ 6,431	....	$5,067,850	$6,561,555	$11,629,405

SOURCE—Compiled from *Original Bill of Laurent; Moody's Banks, 1930;* and *Report of State Banking Commissioner of Kentucky.*

[12] *Original Bill of Keyes.*

price of each. In all, BancoKentucky obtained control of ten banks with assets of approximately $136,300,000 and net worths at the time of purchase of $15,926,000 for $6,561,555 in cash and $32,087,000 in stock. The control of all of these banks was acquired at prices higher than earning power or net worth warranted, the purchases being negotiated by Brown whose chief consideration seems to have been to bring a large number of banks under the control of BancoKentucky, and hence of himself, regardless of cost.

In addition to the banks, Banco acquired an astoundingly large note of $2,000,000 of Wakefield and Company, endorsed by Brown, dated November 13, 1929, and due May 13, 1930. The note, which was made by Brown to take up some loans in certain Chicago banks secured by obligations of the American Turf Association, was supposedly secured by 40,000 shares of stock of Standard Oil Company of Kentucky and 60,000 shares of Banco. Actually it had the 60,000 shares of Banco but only 22,500 shares of Standard Oil. Brown reported to his board that Banco had made a broker's loan of $2,000,000 and, when asked what the collateral was, replied Standard Oil of Kentucky stock. No director knew until the following October that there were only 22,500 shares of Standard Oil securing the note, which fact shows a complaisant, if not a negligent, directorate.[13]

BancoKentucky Company's statement just prior to the Caldwell deal showed total assets of $40,351,000 against which the only claims were taxes of $6,000, giving a net worth of $40,345,000. The inflated condition of this statement is shown by the fact that the total net worth of all the banks it controlled amounted to less than $16,000,000 and it did not own all the stock of any of these banks. It had outstanding 1,610,267 of its 5,000,000 authorized shares of stock, its authorized capital having been increased from $20,000,000 to $50,000,000 on January 14, 1930.[14]

Meanwhile, the public was not absorbing the stock of Banco according to the plans worked out by Brown, and the brokers who had agreed to create a market for it were having little success. After the stock had been listed on the Chicago Stock Exchange in October, 1929, its price went as high as 34½, reaching that price on October 15 and 16; but by the end of the month it was down to 22½. By December it had reached a low of 18½.[15] This break in the price of its stock materially hindered the ultimate aim of BancoKentucky to raise cash with which to buy certain doubtful assets from the National Bank of Kentucky.

[13] *Laurent Evidence.*

[14] *Minute Book and Organization Records of BancoKentucky Company,* copy in *Laurent Evidence.* [15] *Laurent Evidence.*

Further, the National Bank of Kentucky was still having its difficulties with the Comptroller and the national bank examiners. The second examination of the bank in 1929 had been delayed because of the repeated promises of the officers that the bank was going to surrender its national charter, but when it became apparent that this was not being done, in December, 1929, the bank was again examined. At this time slow assets of $5,000,000 and doubtful paper of $725,000 were criticized and losses of $386,000 were written off. The examiners reported that Brown continued to dominate the bank and criticized particularly loans to directors, officers, and employees, and to corporations in which directors were interested. The Comptroller notified the directors of the condition of the bank and asked that immediate steps be taken to remedy the situation. At the examination in April, 1930, losses of $139,000 were written off and the examiner obtained a promise from the directors to write off additional assets amounting to $128,000 on or before June 16, 1930, and $976,000 by September 1. The large volume of loans secured by Banco stock was the subject of particular criticism in the report of this examination.[16]

Such was the background and present condition of the institution Rogers Caldwell approached when he saw his own company nearing financial ruin. It seems as if it were a case of one drowning man calling to another for aid.

The Terms of the Merger

Negotiations for the merger of Caldwell and Company and Banco-Kentucky Company were carried on almost solely by Rogers Caldwell and James B. Brown, the latter relying somewhat on the aid of Charles F. Jones, who was then vice president of the bank, but Caldwell playing his rôle practically alone until the deal was made.[17] Caldwell at no time during the negotiations presented a balance sheet of his company to Brown but simply told him of the conditions of his company and its affiliates. He justified this policy on the ground that if Brown saw a statement of Caldwell and Company and then the deal did not materialize the standing of his company might be jeopardized. In relating to Brown the condition of his firm, Caldwell did not point out that of the company's liabilities several million dollars were deposits subject to withdrawal on demand. He did reveal, however, that among Caldwell and Company's assets were his home and his debts which were carried at more than $900,000. Brown insisted that these debts be paid and that

---

[16] *Comptroller's Report on National Bank of Kentucky.*
[17] Material in this and the following paragraphs concerning the negotiations for and terms of the merger is from *Laurent Evidence,* unless otherwise cited.

Brentwood House be removed from the assets of the business, which Caldwell agreed to do. Caldwell further indicated to Brown that his company would need some financial assistance from the National Bank of Kentucky, to which Brown agreed. In fact, on April 14, before the contract had been drawn up, National Bank of Kentucky advanced Caldwell and Company $500,000 secured by stock of Inter-Southern Life.

Brown reported to the directors of BancoKentucky from time to time on the progress being made in the transaction, and on April 15, 1930, the board unanimously authorized Brown to draw up a contract for the purchase of a half interest in Caldwell and Company. During the next month Brown and Caldwell higgled back and forth, Brown doing a certain amount of insisting that he be shown a statement of Caldwell and Company. Caldwell consistently refused to do so. At the meeting of Banco's directors on May 26, Brown reported that he was not quite satisfied with the contract that Caldwell had drawn up nor had he yet satisfied himself as to the value of Caldwell and Company's assets. Three days later, however, on May 29, Brown's doubts seem to have dissolved for he brought to his board a very favorable report upon the proposed merger. He reported that Rogers Caldwell had stated that his company had assets in the neighborhood of $20,000,000 and owed $11,000,000, making a net worth of approximately $9,000,000. An appraisal of the assets of the company might indicate a net worth as large as $11,000,000. He expressed the view that if Caldwell and Company had no net worth whatsoever he would be willing to pay $5,000,000 in cash for half interest in the business, for its sales force and branch offices would aid in marketing Banco stock, thus providing cash for the company through the sale of its stock, and because its affiliates would keep large deposits with National Bank of Kentucky. Missouri State Life Insurance Company alone had an income averaging $5,000,000 a month, a large part of which, Brown was sure, would be deposited in the Kentucky bank. Another point in favor of the merger was that Caldwell and Company's earnings in the past three years had amounted to $2,300,000, one half of which would permit the payment of a substantial dividend on Banco shares. As a result of these various advantages, Brown stated that he believed the connection with Caldwell and Company would enhance the market price of Banco stock five or six dollars a share. His arguments convinced the directors that the merger was desirable and they authorized him to carry out the transaction without seeing a statement of Caldwell and Company, only one director opposing the step.

On the night of May 29, the same date the directors authorized Brown to proceed with the deal, a merger contract was signed at Brown's residence by Rogers Caldwell for Caldwell and Company and by James B. Brown for BancoKentucky Company. Under this contract Caldwell and Company agreed to increase its capital stock from 10,000 to 20,000 shares and to exchange the 10,000 new shares for 900,000 shares of Banco stock. Of these 900,000 shares, 100,000 were to be given to the National Bank of Kentucky for the $2,700,000 of obligations of the Kentucky Wagon Company and National Motor Company, assets of the bank which had been severely and repeatedly criticized by the bank examiners. Caldwell and Company was then to reorganize or liquidate these companies and to pay to BancoKentucky any funds thus obtained. Another 200,000 shares of the Banco stock were to be placed in escrow with the Louisville Trust Company pending valuation of Caldwell and Company's assets. As to the financial conditions of the two companies, Banco-Kentucky Company listed the banks which it controlled and the amounts of stock of each owned, and stated that on May 1 it had no liabilities, cash of $1,298,000, and "good and collectible notes" of not less than $2,000,000. Caldwell and Company merely claimed that on the date of the contract its assets were of "such fair aggregate value" that after deducting all liabilities it had a net worth of $9,000,000.

BancoKentucky was given a year in which to "satisfy itself" as to the value of Caldwell and Company's assets, with Brown and Caldwell to set the values on the assets, provision being made to select an arbitrator in case of disagreement. If by such valuation it was found that Caldwell and Company did not have a net worth of $9,000,000, it was to pay Banco $2.22 for each $1 of shortage, the amount to be paid either in cash or in Banco stock at $25 a share. If, on the other hand, Caldwell and Company had a net worth of more than $10,000,000, Banco was to pay $1 in Banco stock for each $1 of excess.

In the less significant clauses of the contract, Banco agreed not to sell its Caldwell and Company stock without having offered it to Rogers Caldwell, and the latter not to sell his half interest in Caldwell and Company without first offering it to BancoKentucky Company. Each company agreed not to dispose of any material portion of its assets, pending consummation of the transaction, without consent of the other and Caldwell and Company was to retain a substantial investment in the insurance field while Banco was to maintain a working agreement between the security departments of its banks and Caldwell and Company in the distribution and underwriting of securities.[18]

[18] This has been summarized from the merger contract and supplemental agreements between BancoKentucky Company and Caldwell and Company, copy of which is in *Laurent Evidence*. The complete contract is found in Appendix G. While the contract is dated May 28, it was actually signed on May 29.—*Ibid.*

The merger of the two companies was formally announced in the press and was hailed by some as the financial accomplishment of the age. Brown's *Herald-Post* of June 2, 1930, characterized it as the creation of

by far the largest and most important financial structure ever built in the Middle Western or Southern States and one that will undoubtedly stand out in the future as one of America's greatest financial institutions.

The importance of the association of the BancoKentucky Company and Caldwell and Company to this section cannot be over estimated. It brings to the Middle West, the Eastern Central and the Southern States capital that will be sufficient to meet every requirement of business, industry and development in this entire section of the country and will be a great stabilizing factor in the financial structure of all this territory.[19]

Among the more conservative elements of Louisville, however, the merger was regarded at least with suspicion. It was made by two men, both of whom were presidents of institutions then in dire distress, both of whom were regarded by the informed as speculatively if not dishonestly inclined, and neither of whom had acted in good faith in the merger of the companies. Brown had represented the value of his banks at the inflated prices which he had paid for them and doubtless never indicated in any way to Caldwell that the National Bank of Kentucky was having difficulties with the Comptroller of the Currency; while Caldwell represented his company's net worth at $9,000,000, when the highest net worth its books had ever shown, that of June 30, 1929, was only $3,255,000.

As has already been indicated, the advantages that BancoKentucky Company expected to obtain from the deal were: (1) the creation of a market for its stock by Caldwell and Company's sales force which would enable it to raise cash in order to improve the condition of the National Bank of Kentucky, (2) the removal from the bank of the Kentucky Wagon Company and National Motor Company obligations which had been the subject of much criticism, (3) the obtaining of deposits from many of the companies controlled by Caldwell and Company, and (4) the funds that would be received from Caldwell and Company in the form of dividends. The last expectation did not materialize at all and the amount of funds obtained from the controlled companies was extremely disappointing, Caldwell and Company itself wanting and getting the bulk of such deposits. The assets of the wagon and motor companies were removed after the merger but the national bank examiners criticized the Banco stock which took its place in the bank's portfolio. And finally, Caldwell and Company was unable to create a market for Banco stock

[19] Exhibit in *ibid.*

and could not even assist BancoKentucky in its efforts to peg its stock at 23, an effort which resulted in Banco's buying 106,000 shares of its own stock between March and July, 1930, and necessitated the borrowing of $1,000,000 from the Chemical Bank and Trust Company. The pegging operations had to be abandoned, however, and the price of the stock fell to 16 in August and 11¾ in October.[20] In short, BancoKentucky obtained practically none of the ends it sought from the deal.

The advantages that Caldwell and Company hoped to obtain from the transaction were the financial support of the National Bank of Kentucky and the use of Banco shares as collateral on its obligations; or better, the cash sale of these shares, the latter proving impossible, however, in view of the market for Banco stock. The stock was, though, used extensively as collateral and the National Bank of Kentucky advanced $2,400,000 to its Nashville affiliate.[21] Caldwell and Company was thus the decided winner in the merger and Rogers Caldwell must be credited with carrying through a shrewd bargain.

Steps Taken by Caldwell and Company to Meet the Terms of the Contract

There remains to be considered the action taken by Caldwell and Company to meet three provisions in the merger contract; namely, (1) the removal of the personal indebtedness of Rogers Caldwell from the company, (2) the attainment of a net worth of $9,000,000, and (3) the increase of the company's capital stock to $2,000,000. All three are closely related as they directly involve the net worth of the company.

The personal indebtedness of Rogers Caldwell and Brentwood House were eliminated by a highly suggestive method from the assets of the company. It will be recalled that Brentwood House was carried as an asset of the Bank of Tennessee. Caldwell and Company obtained this by selling securities to the Bank of Tennessee in an amount equal to that at which the house was carried, namely, $430,000. To remove this from the assets of Caldwell and Company, the house was sold to Rogers Caldwell and charged to his account, increasing his total indebtedness to his company to $925,772.[22] A dividend of $1,200,000 was then declared as of May 1, 1930, payable to Rogers Caldwell as sole owner of the stock of the company on that date and credited to his account. This wiped out his indebtedness and left an amount due him sufficient to meet the federal income tax that would be payable the following March on an income of that size. This transaction obviously reduced the net worth of Caldwell and Company by the amount of the dividend.

[20] *Ibid.*   [21] See Chapter xiv, *infra.*
[22] Working papers of Caldwell and Company, May 30, 1930.

Prior to the declaration of this dividend, on April 30, 1930, instead of the books of the company showing a net worth of $9,000,000, the surplus and capital stock accounts had been completely wiped out and a net deficit of $255,730 existed. On May 31, after paying the dividend, the company's statement showed a net worth of $2,567,300, exclusive of the $20,000,000 added by the acquisition of the 800,000 shares of Banco. This amount was obtained by the following changes:[23]

Changes increasing book net worth:
Transference of reserves for contingencies and sustained security
   losses to surplus...$1,950,000
Write up of stocks in controlled companies.................... 2,263,896
Write up of other stocks......................................   630,791
      Total...$4,844,687
Changes decreasing book net worth:
Dividend to Rogers Caldwell...............................$1,200,000
Reduction of inventory to market...........................   544,001
Write off of worthless securities and May operating losses.........   268,656
      Total...$2,012,657
Excess of changes increasing net worth over changes decreasing net
   worth $2,832,030
Less deficit as of April 30................................   255,730
    Net worth as of May 31 before other write-ups and addition of
     Banco stock...$2,576,300

The controlled companies whose stocks were written up and the amounts of the increases were Cloverland Dairy Products, common, $207,482; Insurance Securities Corporation, $1,756,414; and Kentucky Rock Asphalt, common, $300,000. Other stocks written up were Commercial National Bank of New York, $175,200; Cumberland Portland Cement, preferred, $75,591; and Rock Hill Printing and Finishing, common, $380,000.[24] With the write-up of these six stocks and the transference of reserves to surplus, the book net worth of Caldwell and Company was increased enough to pay a dividend of $1,200,000 and still have a balance of $2,567,300 in place of a deficit of $255,700. This, however, was but the beginning of the upward revaluation of securities held by the company as the net worth was still $6,500,000 short of that specified in the contract.

This additional amount was obtained by swapping securities at increasing prices back and forth between Caldwell and Company and the Bank of Tennessee, thus getting the securities on the books of Caldwell and

[23] Compiled from *ibid*.
[24] "Audit Report of Caldwell and Company," June 30, 1930.

Company at a much higher figure than that at which they had been previously carried. This process was carried on until an increment of $6,907,479 had been added to the book value of the securities held by Caldwell and Company, after the initial write-up of the six stocks listed above. The bulk of this additional increment, or $6,162,190, came from increasing the carrying prices of stocks of affiliated companies from $8,109,305 to $14,271,495. Among these stocks, the values of which were thus written up, were 80,051 shares of Alabama Mills, common, from $8,837 to $80,051; 21,620 shares of Atlanta Laundries, common, from $2 to $216,200; 5,000 shares of the Bank of Tennessee from $843,728 to $2,807,280; 1,328,108 shares of Inter-Southern Life from $4,764,463 to $6,640,541; 47,292 shares of Southern Department Stores, common, from $1 to $472,950; and 500 shares of Southern Publishers from $719 to $750,000.[25]

The 800,000 shares of BancoKentucky Company were entered on the books of Caldwell and Company at $20,000,000 as an investment in controlled and affiliated companies. Of this amount, $19,000,000 was credited to surplus and $1,000,000 to the capital stock account, thus raising capital stock to $2,000,000. The additional $1,000,000 of capital stock was authorized by an amendment to the charter of Caldwell and Company, and 10,000 shares with a par value of $100 each were issued to BancoKentucky Company.

After placing the Banco stock on its books and after completing the write-up of the value of its securities, Caldwell and Company's balance sheet showed a net worth of $29,483,797.[26] The company had therefore obtained a book net worth of more than the $9,000,000 specified in the contract, not including the $20,000,000 obtained from the receipt of the Banco stock.

The question of the actual value of the securities of the company and hence of its real net worth remains unsettled. It is impossible to say just what the values of Caldwell and Company's holdings on May 28, 1930, were. Developments since that date, of course, would lead unmistakably to the conclusion that they did not have sufficient value to give the company a net worth of $9,000,000. However, the contract was not drawn on the basis of future values and most all securities fell in price after that date; but not as much, fortunately, as the securities in Caldwell and Company's inventory. The contract between Caldwell and Company and Banco-Kentucky Company used as a basis for evaluating the former's assets the term "fair value," which can have as many interpretations as interpreters. If market value were intended, the statement of Caldwell

[25] *Ibid.*, May 31, 1930.   [26] *Ibid.*

and Company after the increased valuations were given effect showed an extremely inflated condition because few of the stocks could then have been sold for sums approaching their rewritten prices. On the other hand, many of these securities did have market values in excess of the amount at which they were carried prior to any increased valuation. This was particularly true of one or two issues of bonus stocks which were carried at the low value of one dollar for the entire block.

It has been contended in litigation that has arisen since the failure of Caldwell and Company[27] that the company at the time of the Banco deal was insolvent, having quick liabilities of over $38,000,000 and total assets of approximately $37,000,000, these figures being based upon an audit made of Caldwell and Company as of May 28, 1930, by Price, Waterhouse, and Company in 1931.[28] If the assets were given a "fair value" in this audit, Caldwell and Company was insolvent when the merger was made. Even though the valuation of assets in this audit may have been low, a logical conclusion seems to be that Caldwell and Company did not have a net worth approaching $9,000,000 and that Rogers Caldwell obtained an interest in BancoKentucky Company by grossly, though perhaps unintentionally, misrepresenting the true condition of his firm to James B. Brown.

[27] See Chapter XIX, *infra.*

[28] The audit referred to was made for Joseph S. Laurent, receiver of BancoKentucky Company, for the case *Laurent* v. *Akers, et al.,* cited above. The audit was not, however, filed in court, the case being settled outside of court through a compromise. A trip to Louisville by the writer in an attempt to inspect the report of the audit was futile. It was learned from the attorneys for the receiver of BancoKentucky that the audit was made under very strict rules covering its use. The amounts given above were not, therefore, taken directly from the audit but from an amended petition of Laurent filed after the audit was made, the amounts used in this petition being based presumably on the audit. Price, Waterhouse, and Company obtained values for the various assets with the aid of certain former officers of the company, particularly Carter. Just how these values were reached and what was the difference in the methods of valuation at the time of the audit and the time of the merger, it is impossible to say.

CHAPTER XIV

THE SCRAMBLE FOR CASH

CALDWELL AND COMPANY had obtained some advantages from its merger with BancoKentucky Company but these did not strengthen the organization sufficiently and Rogers Caldwell was faced all through 1930 with the necessity of staving off increasing insolvency. The critical financial condition of the company can be traced directly to its lack of permanent capital which had resulted in its expansion being financed primarily with funds from outside sources, a considerable part of such funds being payable upon demand. Of its total liabilities on December 31, 1929, of $36,290,400, demand deposits accounted for $10,394,400, demand loans for $6,631,000, and demand liabilities on repurchase agreements for $2,503,300, making total demand liabilities of $19,528,700, a call for the payment of which the creditors of the company could issue at any time.[1] With stocks of controlled companies and industrial stocks and bonds accounting for more than $19,000,000 of its $22,607,000 inventory on this same date, and with market conditions for these securities such that they could be sold only at terrific losses, if at all, the probability of Caldwell and Company's raising funds to meet any appreciable part of its demand liabilities through the sale of inventory vanished.

The crucial situation is seen even more clearly when demand liabilities are compared with cash and unpledged, readily marketable securities—United States government bonds, certificates of deposits, and municipal bonds. On December 31, 1929, cash amounted to $1,194,200 while securities of the type mentioned amounted to $781,300, or a total of only $1,975,500 which could be immediately applied to meet calls for payment of its $19,528,700 of demand liabilities. The situation six months later, on June 30, 1930, was even more hopeless. At that date demand liabilities had increased to $21,881,800 while cash and unpledged, readily marketable securities had fallen to $834,500, giving the company a liquid reserve of less than 4 per cent of its demand liabilities.[2] That even a

[1] Balance Sheet of Caldwell and Company, December 31, 1929. For representative balance sheets during the year 1930, see Appendix C.

[2] Balance Sheets of Caldwell and Company as of dates mentioned; and Schedule of Total and Unpledged Securities held by Caldwell and Company by months, June, 1929, to September, 1930.

small net withdrawal of funds from the company would be fatal is evident.

Caldwell and Company was faced with this crisis at a time when the forces that ultimately resulted in the complete breakdown of the banking system and in the banking holiday of 1933 were beginning to make themselves felt in a decidedly upward movement of bank failures. This naturally contributed to the investment house's difficulties. It is during times when the banking system is being subjected to unusual pressure from its depositors for funds and with institutions similar to Caldwell and Company that the serious danger of combining investment and commercial banking is seen most clearly. Certainly the securities in Caldwell and Company's inventory were not of a type in which a commercial banker could with safety invest the funds of his depositors; but with Caldwell and Company, as with many other institutions carrying on both types of banking, demand deposits were invested in such securities, seemingly with little regard for the safety of the depositors' funds, and with sometimes tragic losses to the depositors when the market for the securities all but disappeared. Unquestionably such a result followed from the uses to which Caldwell and Company put the funds it received through its commercial banking operations and the practices of the company in this respect provide a rather striking argument for the necessity of the banker-opposed legislation of 1933 which attempted to separate commercial and investment banking.[3]

That its large volume of demand liabilities and small volume of unpledged liquid assets were giving rise to grave concern on the part of some of the officers of the company is seen in the following memorandum from Eddie Goodloe, cashier of the Bank of Tennessee, to the three chief executives of the company, setting forth very clearly the problems that faced the banking house at this time.

With approximately $14,000,000 of deposits in Caldwell and Company and the Bank of Tennessee we should have at least one per cent daily withdrawals. This obviously amounts to $140,000 per day.

Shipments are not averaging $40,000 per day. This differential of $100,000 per day must be met in one of two ways, namely by securing additional cash deposits or through loans.

It has been practically impossible to borrow from the money centers on anything other than municipal bonds of larger cities and municipalities. With our very limited supply of such collateral we have been extremely pushed to satisfy the wishes of such banks as Chase National, Chemical Bank and Trust Company, Equitable Trust Company, and others. With such large loans

[3] See U. S. Congressional Hearings on Banking Act of 1933.

with these banks it is impossible to pledge solely municipal bonds of any type, much less of larger cities and counties.

We are in some instances permitted to use on the above loans a few selected stocks at an attractive margin including Missouri State Life, Union Planters National Bank and Fourth and First Stocks. We have pledged in each case as much of such stocks as the bankers will take.

The main point I wish to stress in this memorandum, however, is the matter of bank balances. In spite of the fact that we are pledging high grade collateral on wide margins our correspondents without exception expect and are demanding that we keep a twenty per cent supporting balance against our borrowings. This has been impossible, our bank balances being ridiculously small in comparison with our borrowings.

Our inability to keep these balances up is forcing us into an unfavorable light in the eyes of our bankers. My greatest concern is that due to our inability to keep balances considered satisfactory to our correspondent they may either call our demand loans or refuse our time loans.

The lack of cash funds at the present cannot be laid to the fact that we utilized too great an amount of the $2,000,000 State money to pay off loans rather than use same to increase cash balances. We have reborrowed practically all sums paid off with this deposit.[4]

With the company thus pushed for cash it was impossible to correct the long-standing problem of violated trusts. The practices responsible for the condition of the trusts had begun years before and had been given official sanction by the executive officers inasmuch as they knew of the condition and in many cases had initiated the procedure leading to the violations. The violations were doubtless considered of a temporary or emergency nature but when some progress was made in improving the situation another deal would be concluded under circumstances requiring irregular action and resulting in the same old condition. The practice of the Bank of Tennessee's acting as trustee for deposits with Caldwell and Company and vice versa had been engaged in so long and trusts arising under this procedure violated so regularly that these deposits were regarded practically as free.[5]

This condition was called to the attention of the executives of the company by auditors and minor officials so frequently that some steps had to be taken to try to remedy the situation. It was decided that Goodloe, as cashier of the Bank of Tennessee, should make reports to the three executives on the state of the trusts and to facilitate these reports a classification of trust violations was worked out: the "A" trusts were flagrantly violated; the "B" trusts, seriously violated; and the "C" trusts, less seri-

[4] Memorandum to Messrs. Caldwell, Carter, and Heitzeberg, February 6, 1930.
[5] *Ibid.*, March 18, 1930.

ously. On June 30, 1930, the report on the state of the trusts showed a total of fifty-two trusts, twenty-seven of which were violated in no respect. Of the remaining twenty-five, five were of the "A" type, seven of the "B," and thirteen of the "C."[6] Some progress had been made in improving conditions when the report of September 16 was made, at which time there were five trusts of the "A" variety covering deposits of $1,457,-000; six of the "B" type covering deposits of $522,600, and four "C" trusts covering deposits of $525,000, or a total of $2,504,600.[7] Some of the larger trust violations of the "A" and "B" type were corrected through the use of surety bonds; hence somewhat improved conditions existed on October 23 when $1,696,400 of deposits were not properly secured, divided as follows: five "A" trusts, $732,000; five "B" trusts, $325,400; and five "C" trusts, $639,000.[8]

When the company failed, less than a month later, one of the trusts in the "A" category on October 23, namely, that covering a deposit of the state of Arkansas for $150,000, had been paid out; another, covering a loan from the Charlottesville (Virginia) National Bank was secured with Cadet Hosiery bonds instead of state of Tennessee bonds, while two trusts in the "B" group had been secured with surety bonds. There were in all about twelve trust violations at the time of the failure of the company.[9] Thus a condition, which had been repeatedly called to the attention of the executives of the company ever since the audit report of 1926, was allowed to continue during times when it could have been corrected, until the evil became unmanageable. The policy that was adhered to with respect to the trusts constituted legal, moral, and financial malpractice and portrays the responsible officers of the company in a very bad light.

Accumulating weaknesses in Caldwell and Company meant necessarily that the Bank of Tennessee was becoming endangered. The precarious condition of this latter institution was discovered by the Tennessee bank examiners late in September, 1930. On September 24, prior to the examination, Luke Lea called Caldwell and Company and, on learning that Rogers Caldwell was out of town, told Carter that the bank would be examined the following day.[10] Lea's information had come, no doubt, from the superintendent of banks, D. D. Robertson, who owed his appointment largely to Colonel Lea. The bank was in no condition for a favorable examination, its cash reserve being below the legal mini-

---

[6] Report on Condition of Trusts, June 30, 1930, exhibit to *Original Bill of Knox County.*
[7] *Ibid.,* September 16, 1930.   [8] *Ibid.,* October 23, 1930.
[9] Memorandum concerning the condition of Caldwell and Company's trusts, prepared by Eddie Goodloe after the failure of the company.
[10] *Second Report,* p. 656.

mum to a greater extent than usual. To obviate this, the bank discounted its note with Caldwell and Company for $500,000, giving it additional reserves on deposit of that amount, which was sufficient to improve its condition as shown on its books. On September 25 the examiners descended, as Lea had said, and found the bank in spite of its faked increase in reserves in the throes of insolvency, a condition Robertson reported to the officers of Caldwell and Company. The latter were of course eager to keep the bank open and readily agreed to Robertson's requirement that Caldwell and Company turn over to the Bank of Tennessee approximately $3,840,000 of securities to cover the depreciation in the value of its assets.[11] The securities Caldwell and Company delivered to the bank, while not of the gilt-edged variety—few of Caldwell and Company's securities at this time fell into this somewhat ephemeral category—were, however, of sufficient value to improve materially the condition of the bank.

Nothing was said to Robertson about the subsequent substitution of securities turned over to the bank but Caldwell and Company had developed this art to such a high degree that the securities had hardly been pledged before substitutions began to take place, and a month later the character of the entire list was changed. Some securities were pledged with the bank which had formerly been written off as valueless and others which had defaulted interest and principal payments were pledged at par plus accrued defaulted interest. Perhaps the most absurd substitution was the handing over to the bank of 1,600 shares of its own stock and the entire capital stock of Southern Banks, Incorporated.[12] These substitutions were in no way hindered by the Tennessee Banking Department, which, having satisfied itself as to the bank's stability by the original transaction, made no further examination. Perhaps Colonel Lea's influence was being used.

These extremely alarming conditions accumulated in spite of many unusual maneuvers made by Rogers Caldwell to bring cash into his company and to shift the burden of many of the investment house's commitments to its affiliates, both of which in general were accomplished only by impairing the financial status of the affiliates.

Aid Obtained from Insurance Companies

Rogers Caldwell's outstanding accomplishments in the shifting of burdensome commitments were in the insurance field. As has been pointed

[11] Statement of D. D. Robertson, appended to Financial Statements of Bank of Tennessee, November 6, 1930.

[12] List of securities pledged with the Bank of Tennessee and substitutions were given in exhibits filed in the case *Nashville Trust Company, et al.* v. *Southern Publishers, Inc., et al.* Concerning Southern Banks, Incorporated, see this chapter, *infra.*

out, at the close of 1929 the company owed approximately $9,000,000 on contracts to purchase controlling interests in insurance companies. The collapse of the stock market had prevented the transference of the burden to the investing public as planned and Caldwell and Company was faced with the problem of attempting to retain control of its insurance interests and yet, at the same time, shift the financial load to some other institution.

The company chosen to assume this burden was the Inter-Southern Life Insurance Company, the only one of the controlled insurance companies for which Caldwell and Company had completed payment. Early in 1930 Caldwell told Carey G. Arnett, president of Inter-Southern, that he planned for Inter-Southern to take over the control of Missouri State Life and the other Caldwell insurance companies. Arnett was quite agreeable and, when his directors met on April 9, an increase in the capital stock from $1,250,000 to $3,500,000, represented by shares of $1 par, was authorized to enable the Inter-Southern to acquire an interest in the Missouri State, Southeastern, Shenandoah, and Home Insurance companies, for the controlling interest of each of which Caldwell and Company still owed considerable amounts.

The Home Fire, Home Life, and Home Accident companies of Arkansas were the first to pass into the control of Inter-Southern.[13] Caldwell and Company, the year before, had agreed to pay $3,780,000 for 60 per cent of the stock of each of these companies. After adding interest to May 1, 1930, and expenses incurred in making the purchase, the total price amounted to $3,893,585. Caldwell and Company had paid $750,000 on the contract plus the expenses, leaving $3,030,000 due to A. B. Banks and his associates. A payment of $1,010,000 was due on May 1 which Caldwell and Company was in no position to meet. Seven days before the payment became due, Inter-Southern bought the contract for the purchase of the Home Companies for an amount equal to the original purchase price plus interest and expenses, namely $3,893,585.

Of this amount, $2,020,000 due in 1932 and 1933 was paid with 538,666.67 shares of Inter-Southern stock at $3.75 a share, which were issued to Caldwell and Company and substituted for the stock of the Home Companies in escrow in the American Exchange Trust Company of Little Rock, the Home Companies stock being delivered to Inter-Southern. The remainder of the purchase price was delivered to Caldwell and Company in cash and securities, $1,010,000 of the latter being paid to the Home Companies, and a similar amount of the Home Companies' holdings being

---

[13] All facts concerning the purchase of the Home Companies by Inter-Southern are from petitions in the case *Dean* v. *Caldwell*.

turned over to Banks in accordance with the terms of the contract. The Home Companies thus received securities that had formerly been in the portfolio of Inter-Southern in place of the stocks of lumber companies and smaller banks controlled by Banks through his insurance companies, an exchange which materially strengthened the Arkansas companies.

The next company to pass into the control of Inter-Southern was the Missouri State Life, and with it the control of Southwestern Life. This transfer was brought about to allow Insurance Securities Corporation to meet the payment due on $3,000,000 of notes. The transaction agreed upon on May 21 provided for the purchase by Inter-Southern of 116,000 shares of Missouri State Life stock, 87,000 shares of which were owned by Insurance Securities Corporation, 20,245 by Caldwell and Company, 2,000 by Shares-in-the-South, and the balance by Fourth and First National Company.[14] Inter-Southern agreed to buy the stock, which had a book value of $18.11, for $88 a share, paying $43 a share in cash or acceptable securities and $45 a share in Inter-Southern stock valued at $4.00 a share, bringing the total purchase price for the controlling interest of Missouri State Life to $4,988,000 in cash and securities and 1,305,000 shares of Inter-Southern.

The securities, which were delivered to the Nashville Trust Company for the account of the sellers, were covered by a repurchase agreement under which Inter-Southern agreed to repurchase upon demand all or any of the securities with all funds it had or could make available for investment purposes. The repurchase would naturally be a long process and the sellers of Missouri State Life desired to obtain cash immediately. This end was gained by having Missouri State Life agree to buy $3,997,764 of the securities, obtaining at the same time Inter-Southern's repurchase agreement. The effect of this was to place Missouri State Life in the position of financing at least temporarily Inter-Southern's purchase of its control. Of the approximately $4,000,000 of mortgages and bonds Missouri State Life agreed to purchase, it had actually purchased and paid cash[15] for $1,635,847 of mortgages and $417,630 of bonds, or a total of $2,053,477 when the Missouri Insurance Commissioner ordered it to stop purchasing the securities and to demand repurchase by Inter-Southern and the Nashville Trust Company of those already obtained. Such demand was made but no securities were repurchased.[16]

[14] All facts concerning the purchase of Missouri State Life by Inter-Southern are from petitions in the case *Dean* v. *Caldwell*, unless otherwise cited.

[15] Missouri State Life had obtained $1,550,000 of the cash from the sale of United States Treasury Certificates.

[16] "Report on Missouri State Life Insurance Company," in *Best's Insurance News (Life Edition)*, xxxiv (October 2, 1933), 404.

These transactions produced enough funds together with those already on hand for Insurance Securities Corporation to retire its $3,000,-000 of notes. After doing this, on May 31, 1930, this company had cash of $1,106,000; 900,000 shares of Inter-Southern carried at $3,600,000, or $4.00 a share; and other stocks and bonds amounting to $1,440,000, making total assets of $6,146,000. Its only liabilities were accrued interest and taxes amounting to $113,522, giving it a net worth of well over $6,000,-000.[17] The company was liquidated during the summer and early fall, its Inter-Southern stock divided between its two owners, Caldwell and Company and Fourth and First National Company, the funds on deposit with these companies turned over to them, and Caldwell and Company took its choice of the stocks and bonds.[18] Thus was ended probably the most profitable single venture made by Caldwell and Company during its entire life. The control of Missouri State Life had furnished it with a needed source of funds and an outlet for a large volume of securities, and its operations in the stock of this company had yielded a substantial profit. Insurance Securities Corporation, half interest in which had cost Caldwell and Company $750,000, paid the bond house a liquidating dividend in stocks, bonds, and cash of over $3,000,000. And yet Caldwell and Company obtained this last-mentioned advantage without giving up control of Missouri State Life since it completely controlled the new owner, Inter-Southern Life Insurance Company.

On October 9 Inter-Southern agreed to buy two other companies controlled by Caldwell and Company, namely, the Shenandoah Life and Southeastern Life. Inter-Southern agreed to pay $850,000 for 74 per cent of the capital stock of Southeastern, a part of which was already pledged to it by Associated Life Companies on a loan of $383,000; and $1,040,000 for a 40 per cent interest in the Shenandoah, plus any expenses that had been incurred in the purchase of these companies by Associated Life Companies the previous year. One half of the purchase price was to be paid in Inter-Southern stock at $3.75 a share and the balance in cash.[19] But this agreement was drawn up too late to be carried out before the collapse of Caldwell and Company.

The effect of selling the various insurance companies to Inter-Southern was literally to loot the portfolio of the latter company. In its purchase of the controlling interest in Missouri State Life and the Home Companies, securities and cash amounting to $6,845,100 were taken out

---

[17] Balance Sheet of Insurance Securities Corporation, May 31, 1930.
[18] Memoranda in files of Receivers of Caldwell and Company.
[19] Best's Reports, 1929 and 1930.

and replaced by the stocks of these companies. The change in the nature of the company's assets resulting from these transactions is seen in the decrease of its bonds from 21 to 1 per cent of total assets, of its mortgage loans from 21 to 8 per cent, and the increase of stocks from 6 to 47 per cent.[20] The decline in the price of Missouri State stock from the $88 a share Inter-Southern paid for it to $26 a share on November 1 necessarily meant heavy losses for the Louisville company. Inter-Southern, consequently, was left ill prepared to cope with the problems that faced insurance companies in general, and Caldwell companies in particular, in the next few years.

It is interesting to note that Inter-Southern, which had first been purchased by Caldwell and Company for Missouri State Life but could not be turned over to it because of the objections of the Missouri Commissioner of Insurance, through the series of transactions just described, became, in effect, a holding company for the other Caldwell insurance companies, controlling even Missouri State Life. Further, through these transactions, Inter-Southern relieved Caldwell and Company of commitments it could not directly meet.

An effort was made by Caldwell and Company to sell its interest in Southern Surety Company and thereby release $1,125,000 invested in the stock of this company. Kidder-Peabody and Company had an investment of the same size and both bond houses were eager to sell. Kidder-Peabody, in March, 1930, negotiated an agreement whereby the Home Insurance Companies of New York[21] would pay $3,414,000 for the control of Southern Surety and its subsidiary, Southern Fire Insurance Company. A formal contract, however, was not drawn up and repeated efforts on the part of Caldwell and Company failed to bring about the consummation of the sale and the release of its urgently needed funds.[22]

Not only did Caldwell and Company seek relief with its various attempts to shift its investments in insurance companies but also looked to these companies to furnish it funds through deposits in the Bank of Tennessee. Inter-Southern, because it had to use its funds to carry out the purchases of the various Caldwell insurance holdings, reduced its deposit in the Bank of Tennessee from $490,000 on June 30, 1930, to $200,000 when the bank closed, while Southern Surety Company had a deposit balance of $124,000 at this latter date.[23] Missouri State Life's deposit was by far the largest of any of the companies, varying between

[20] *Ibid.*
[21] Not to be confused with the Home Companies of Arkansas.
[22] "Memo., Southern Surety."
[23] Balance Sheet of Bank of Tennessee, November 6, 1930.

$800,000 and $1,000,000 during 1930 and standing at $873,000 when the Bank of Tennessee failed.[24]

USE OF BANKING INTERESTS TO OBTAIN CASH

Caldwell and Company attempted to shift to the public its investment in Union Planters National Bank of Memphis as one means of alleviating its financial condition. Bank Securities Corporation, which owned the controlling interest in the Memphis bank, owed Caldwell and Company $1,895,000 during the first few months of 1930, a debt which could be paid if a portion of the Union Planters stock it held could be marketed. But the demand for this stock, in 1930, was very weak and there was little possibility of selling enough to pay Caldwell and Company. The market for the stock of Fourth and First Banks, Incorporated, was somewhat more active and it was arranged for this company to acquire Bank Securities' holdings of Union Planters stock at the rate of 1 share of Fourth and First Banks for 2.84 shares of Union Planters and, on the basis of the placing of the control of both Union Planters National Bank and Fourth and First National Bank with Fourth and First Banks, Incorporated, to attempt to sell to the public substantial blocks of the stock of the latter company. To carry out the transaction, Fourth and First Banks increased its capital from 200,000 shares of $20 par to 300,000,[25] and advertised widely that the acquisition of 176,000 shares of Union Planters stock gave it control of banks with total resources of $150,000,000. As a matter of fact, Fourth and First Banks actually acquired only 126,000 shares of Union Planters stock but the public was not advised of this discrepancy.

Bank Securities Corporation received approximately 45,000 shares of Fourth and First Banks stock of which it was able to market less than 6,000 shares, leaving it with 39,429 shares carried at $3,479,700. In addition it owned 19,662 shares of Union Planters stock carried at $645,800, giving the securities corporation an investment of $4,125,500 in the two stocks, all of which was pledged on its loans which totaled $3,906,000.[26] Although Bank Securities Corporation was not able to reduce materially its indebtedness through the exchange of its Union Planters stock for Fourth and First Banks stock, in the shift that was made it did reduce its indebtedness to Caldwell and Company from $1,895,000 to $450,600 as well as its indebtedness to other Nashville banks by shifting a larger part of its loans to Eastern banks when it received the Fourth

---

[24] *Ibid.*, and confidential source.

[25] Letter to Stockholders of Fourth and First Banks, Incorporated, from James E. Caldwell, president, April 15, 1930.

[26] Balance Sheet of Bank Securities Corporation, December 31, 1930.

and First Banks stock which could be pledged with these banks more readily than the Union Planters stock.[27] Thus Caldwell and Company obtained $1,445,000 in cash from the transaction.

It was not, however, through shifting its investments in banks that Caldwell and Company attempted to raise cash, but primarily through borrowing from its affiliated banks. Of these, the ones most extensively exploited were the National Bank of Kentucky and the Fourth and First National Bank.

LOANS FROM THE NATIONAL BANK OF KENTUCKY

During the negotiations for the merger with BancoKentucky and Caldwell and Company, Rogers Caldwell had intimated to Brown that his company would need financial assistance from the National Bank of Kentucky. The bank at that time held a note signed by Caldwell, Carter, and Heitzeberg for $265,000 which had been made when Caldwell and Company helped finance a reorganization of the Murray Rubber Company at the insistence of the National Bank of Kentucky, the note amounting to the par value of the bonds of the rubber company which Caldwell and Company had not been able to sell to the public and being secured by these bonds. Since the note was signed by the officers rather than in the name of Caldwell and Company, it was not considered by the bank as affecting the amount of loans it could legally make to Caldwell and Company. The capital and surplus of the bank at that time was $6,000,000; hence, under the national banking code, the limit of loans to one party was $600,000.

The first loan to Caldwell and Company came on April 14, when negotiations for the merger had progressed far enough to indicate its final accomplishment. This loan was for $500,000 and was secured by 200,000 shares of Inter-Southern stock, at a collateral value of $2.50 a share, which was under the market price, the stock on that day being quoted at a bid price of $3.50.[28]

The next aid came in connection with a $500,000 participation of Caldwell and Company in a $6,000,000 issue of Louisville Street Railway bonds. A call was made on Caldwell and Company for $321,000 on July 7 and $33,000 on July 18. Since it was in no condition to meet these calls, the National Bank of Kentucky paid the amounts, taking the bonds just as if they were an investment. Caldwell and Company drew out these bonds as they were sold, eventually selling all except $143,000

[27] Ibid.

[28] Material Pertaining to Caldwell and Company Loss, in the case Anderson v. Akers, et al., p. 58.

and making a profit on the transaction of approximately $28,000.[29] Since the funds thus advanced were regarded as an investment in bonds, the amount the bank could legally advance to Caldwell and Company was not affected.

The next loan by the National Bank of Kentucky to the Caldwell organization was on July 29. This was for $400,000 and was secured by the following collateral:

5,000	Shares-in-the-South @ 30	$150,000
2,500	Kentucky Rock Asphalt @ 12	30,000
1,000	Union Planters Bank @ 32	32,000
1,100	Fourth and First Banks, Inc., @ 120	132,000
$150,000	Southern Department Store Notes	142,000
$100,000	Municipal Bonds @ par	100,000
	Total	$586,000

Regarding this loan, Carter wrote Charles F. Jones, of the National Bank of Kentucky, "As explained to you we might make this loan with other of your banks than the National Bank of Kentucky, or we might arrange it in the name of the Bank of Tennessee if this would be more convenient to you."[30] Apparently the latter alternative was chosen, for the loan was made in the name of the Bank of Tennessee.

This loan was followed by one for $500,000 on August 21, obtained in the name of Associated Life Companies. Caldwell and Company loaned the insurance holding company a varied list of securities which were used as collateral at the bank. This loan was made in the form of two certificates of deposit for $250,000 each, issued under the condition that they would not be presented for payment except to cancel or reduce the loan. These certificates were turned over to Caldwell and Company by Associated Life Companies in place of the securities it had borrowed, and Caldwell and Company, in turn, sold them to Missouri State Life Insurance Company.[31] The effect of this transaction was to take $500,000 away from Missouri State Life in exchange for certificates of deposit issued with specific limitations as to their payment. This loan increased the amount which the National Bank of Kentucky had advanced, directly and indirectly, to Caldwell and Company, to $1,400,000, exclusive of the funds advanced to carry the Louisville Street Railway and Murray Rubber Company bonds.

About the time of this loan, Rogers Caldwell furnished James B. Brown, president of the National Bank of Kentucky and BancoKentucky

[29] *Report of Special Master*, in the case *Anderson v. Akers, et al.*, p. 200.
[30] Letter of July 22, 1930, exhibit in *Laurent Evidence*.
[31] *Laurent Evidence*.

Company, with a statement of Caldwell and Company's financial condition, the first Brown had seen. Nothing had been done up to this time concerning the valuation of Caldwell and Company's assets called for under the merger contract. The statement revealed to Brown the desperate financial straits of his associated company; it also revealed to him that he had been nothing short of a sucker. He saw for the first time that Caldwell and Company had large deposit liabilities payable on demand and that the sudden withdrawal of any large percentage of these would result in its collapse. Thus, he was confronted with the alternative of letting Caldwell and Company shift for itself, leading no doubt to its failure and the probable loss by the National Bank of Kentucky of the sums already advanced as well as to other damaging effects on his institutions, or of giving the company further financial assistance in an effort to save it. To discuss this problem with Rogers Caldwell, a conference was arranged between the two men for Sunday, August 24, at Bowling Green, Kentucky, a point about half way between Nashville and Louisville. C. F. Jones accompanied Brown to the meeting and Carter accompanied Caldwell. Brown reported his shock on seeing the statements which had been furnished him, pointing out that they did not at all reflect the condition Caldwell had represented to him; but he did agree to have the National Bank of Kentucky advance additional funds to Caldwell and Company if it would place 400,000 additional shares of Banco stock in escrow with the Louisville Trust Company, pending valuation of its assets, thus bringing the total shares in escrow to 600,000 of the 800,000 received by Caldwell and Company in the merger. Caldwell regarded Brown's demands as unfair and contended that the National Bank of Kentucky should advance an additional $1,000,000 on secured notes to Caldwell and Company without additional Banco stock being pledged. Carter insisted that the company would need between $6,000,000 and $7,000,000 if it was to be saved and advised Brown and Caldwell to call in outside men big enough to be of real assistance. Neither Brown nor Caldwell thought this suggestion worthy of being followed, both preferring to work out their own salvation. But no agreement could be reached as to just what steps should be taken.[32]

About ten days later, however, with Caldwell and Company daily being pressed harder for funds, Rogers Caldwell agreed to deposit an additional 200,000 shares of BancoKentucky stock with the Louisville Trust Company provided Brown would have the National Bank of

---

[32] *Material Pertaining to Caldwell and Company Loss,* in the case *Anderson* v. *Akers, et al.,* pp. 60-69.

Kentucky lend an additional $1,000,000. Brown consented to do this if the funds would be taken out only as absolutely needed, and on September 4 the 200,000 shares of Banco were sent to Louisville.[33] Of this $1,000,000 which was to be advanced, $400,000 was loaned on September 9. Brown had agreed to increase the collateral value of Inter-Southern from $2.50 to $3.00 a share, in spite of its decline in price to $2.00 a share, thus giving Caldwell and Company a margin of $100,000 on its April 14 loan of $500,000, secured by 200,000 shares of Inter-Southern. The Bank of Tennessee at this time obtained $200,000 on 67,000 shares of Inter-Southern; and the Associated Life Companies exchanged the collateral on its $500,000 loan for 200,000 of Inter-Southern and obtained an additional advance of $100,000. These increased sums brought the loans to Caldwell and Company, the Bank of Tennessee, and Associated Life Companies to $600,000 each.

By the first of October, Caldwell and Company was back again at the door of the bank asking for help and again the bank was willing but legally could make no more loans to the Caldwell corporations already borrowing. But this proved to be no hindrance because Caldwell and Company had prepared itself for just such an emergency. On September 2 Southern Banks, Incorporated, had obtained a Tennessee charter. The company issued 2,000 shares of stock with no par value, all of which were sold to Caldwell and Company for $50,000, an amount Caldwell and Company borrowed from the Bank of Tennessee and which was left on deposit with this bank by Southern Banks. Southern Banks then purchased from Caldwell and Company 265 shares of Holston-Union National Bank stock for $82,972.80, of which $49,000 was paid with its deposit in the Bank of Tennessee and the balance covered by a demand note payable to Caldwell and Company and secured by the entire amount of Holston-Union stock which Southern Banks had purchased. This stock, incidentally, was used by Caldwell and Company as collateral on one of its own obligations. The only actual cash that had passed in the establishment of Southern Banks was $33 for organization expenses.[34] Southern Banks may well be considered the outstanding dummy corporation created by Caldwell and Company.

Caldwell and Company loaned this newly created affiliate 100,000 shares of Inter-Southern and the affiliate, in turn, on October 6 pledged these shares as collateral for a loan of $300,000 from the National Bank

[33] Letters from J. D. Carter to Louisville Trust Company, September 4, 1930, and from Rogers Caldwell to James B. Brown, September 8, 1930, exhibits in *Laurent Evidence.*
[34] Balance Sheet of Southern Banks, Inc., October 31, 1930.

of Kentucky, turning over the money thus obtained to Caldwell and Company. Two weeks later, on October 20, the process was repeated, bringing the total loans to Southern Banks to $600,000. The two days these loans were made the bid prices for Inter-Southern stock were $1.75 and $1.50.[35]

The National Bank of Kentucky in making these loans was engaging in unsound banking of the rankest sort. It made loans of $2,400,000 to Caldwell and Company and subsidiaries, with all funds going directly to the parent corporation, thus violating the spirit if not the letter of the national banking act restricting the size of loans to one party to 10 per cent of a bank's capital and surplus; the evasion being carried out by using subsidiary corporations, one of which was formed solely to borrow funds from the National Bank of Kentucky. In addition, $2,000,000 of these loans were secured only by Inter-Southern stock which was accepted as collateral at $3.00 a share when its market price had fallen as low as $1.50.

Meanwhile the long-standing issues between the National Bank of Kentucky and the Comptroller of the Currency were becoming sharper and sharper. On September 12 the Comptroller's office was notified by the chief examiner of the eighth Federal Reserve District that the National Bank of Kentucky had substituted Banco stock for the obligations of the Kentucky Wagon Company and National Motor Company and also that it was lending large sums to Caldwell and Company. The Comptroller thought these developments warranted an immediate examination which was begun on September 17 and lasted until October 24. At this time, losses aggregating $1,356,000 were written off and slow and doubtful assets amounting to $4,542,000 and $686,000 respectively were criticized.[36] The examiner found that, in addition to taking the obligations of Kentucky Wagon Company and National Motor Company from the bank in exchange for the 100,000 shares of Banco stock as provided for in the Caldwell deal, losses of $242,500 sustained by the bank on the sale of Van Camp Packing Company stock had been offset by an arbitrary appreciation of the shares of BancoKentucky. The examiner held two meetings with the directors of the bank, pointed out to them the desperate condition of the bank, insisted that no additional loans be granted Caldwell and Company or its controlled enterprises, and ordered that the loss on the Van Camp stock be returned to the bond account and charged to profit and loss for, he said, ". . . action

[35] *Material Pertaining to Caldwell and Company Loss*, in the case *Anderson* v. *Akers, et al.*, p. 58.
[36] *Comptroller's Report on National Bank of Kentucky.*

of the officers in capitalizing this loss . . . was entirely irregular if not in fact a violation of law." To improve the condition of the bank the examiner insisted that BancoKentucky buy approximately $1,000,000 of the bank's doubtful assets. This move was opposed by the directors but they compromised on the transference of $600,000 of these assets, the purchase being financed by Banco's borrowing $600,000 from the Chemical Bank and Trust Company on the 22,500 shares of Standard Oil of Kentucky which were pledged on Brown's $2,000,000 note and the stock of several of its smaller controlled banks. The examiner also succeeded in getting appointed an executive committee to control the affairs of the bank, but Brown was one of the five members of this committee.[37]

In defiance of the warning of the examiner, the second loan to Southern Banks of $300,000 was made just before the examination was completed. This was done solely by Brown and entirely without the approval of the executive committee or board of directors. When the examiner discovered this he brought it to the directors' attention and forced them to adopt a resolution specifying that no additional credit would be granted Caldwell and Company interests and ordering the bank to demand payment of at least a part of the loans already made. However, they did not comply with this latter order.[38]

About the time the examination of the bank was completed, but with the warnings of the examiner still fresh in the minds of the officers and directors, Caldwell and Company made a request for an additional $500,000, the loan to be made in the name of Memphis Commercial Appeal, Incorporated. Brown had evidently approved the loan, for on October 22 a draft was drawn by Memphis Commercial Appeal through Fourth and First National Bank for $500,000 with its note and collateral attached. The collateral consisted of $200,000 of Alabama Mills bonds, $200,000 of Cadet Hosiery bonds, and $100,000 of Frank Silk Mills bonds. On October 23 Caldwell and Company wrote the bank about the collateral, which indicated clearly that the loan was for Caldwell and Company. The warnings of the examiner evidently prevented Brown from handling this loan without bringing it before his directors. In so doing he pointed out the importance of continued support to Caldwell and Company. But the board refused the loan on the advice of one of its members. Caldwell and Brown did not, however, give up hope and, at the request of Brown, a financial statement of Memphis Commercial Appeal was sent to him. A representative of Caldwell and Company

[37] *Laurent Evidence.*
[38] *Comptroller's Report on National Bank of Kentucky,* and *Laurent Evidence.*

also went to Louisville to see what could be done. But the jig was about up then and on October 29 Caldwell and Company wired National Bank of Kentucky to return the note and collateral.[39]

LOANS FROM FOURTH AND FIRST NATIONAL BANK

The assistance given Caldwell and Company during its entire life by the Fourth and First National Bank was continued and enlarged during 1930. Although the conditions surrounding the loans made by this bank are not as definite as is the case with those made by the National Bank of Kentucky, the support of the Nashville bank was as important as that given by the Louisville bank. In fact, on one occasion Brown used as an argument for a loan to Caldwell and Company the statement that the Fourth and First National Bank had agreed to continue to support Caldwell and Company if the National Bank of Kentucky would do likewise.

Fourth and First National Bank aided Caldwell and Company by lending it and the Bank of Tennessee funds and by buying bonds from it, both outright and under repurchase agreements. The latter type of advance enabled the bank to evade the law limiting size of loans. This was also evaded by making some loans in the name of the Bank of Tennessee and by having some of the advances made by the Fourth and First National Company and the Nashville Trust Company. At the time of the failure of Caldwell and Company, the Fourth and First National group was advancing directly and indirectly at least $2,202,000 to the investment house.[40] These advances were secured largely by the general run of corporate stocks and bonds originated by Caldwell and Company, the market for which had virtually disappeared. Fourth and First National, no doubt, recognized that it was so closely tied with Caldwell and Company that it could not stand the shock that would most certainly be incident to the collapse of Caldwell and Company. Self-interest, therefore, necessitated the granting of maximum aid to the investment house.

AID OBTAINED FROM THE CENTRAL BANK AND TRUST COMPANY OF ASHEVILLE

The Central Bank and Trust Company of Asheville, North Carolina, connected with Caldwell and Company largely through Colonel Lea,

[39] *Material Pertaining to Caldwell and Company Loss,* and *Report of Special Master,* in the case *Anderson* v. *Akers, et al.,* pp. 96, 222, respectively.

[40] Compiled from "Report of Receivers of Caldwell and Company," Part I, pp. 588-94, 625, and Balance Sheet of Bank of Tennessee, November 6, 1930.

came to its assistance in a transaction which was neither a loan nor a repurchase agreement in the usual sense of the term and, while the amount involved was not particularly large, the nature of the transaction is of sufficient interest to warrant an account of it.

The various efforts Colonel Lea had made during the summer of 1930 to reorganize this bank on a sounder basis had all failed and in October, 1930, while the bank was literally fighting to keep open, Lea attempted to supply it with funds on a day-to-day basis. During this month the bank issued cashier's checks and drafts totaling some $781,000, which were turned over to him. Most of these checks were delivered personally to Lea in Nashville by employees of the Central Bank and Trust Company. Frequently the only records of the checks would be a debit ticket in the issuing teller's cage which would be carried as a cash item for as long as a week, while sometimes they would be charged directly to Colonel Lea's account, thus causing it to be overdrawn for large amounts. Lea would deposit the cashier's checks with other banks with which he had accounts and transfer the proceeds of the deposit by wire to the Central Bank. In this way the Central Bank got the proceeds as soon as the cashier's checks were deposited, while the banks in which they were deposited would present them for collection through the regular channels which would take from three to five days, thus giving the Central Bank the use of the funds from the time that the wire transfer came in until the checks were presented for payment.[41] Although it would seem that Colonel Lea was getting control of the funds of the Central Bank without any security, the checks were all used by him in the manner described and in no case for his own personal benefit.

Similarly, Lea tried to sell the certificates of deposit of the Central Bank, a total of $780,000 of these certificates being handled by him.[42] He negotiated for the sale of some of them to the Liberty Bank and Trust Company, the Nashville bank he completely controlled; some of them he could not sell; but $600,000 of them were issued in connection with a transaction between Caldwell and Company and the Central Bank and Trust Company.

An agreement was entered into between these two institutions for Central Bank to issue $300,000 of certificates of deposit payable to the Bank of Tennessee in exchange for the following bonds which were to be delivered to the Fourth and First National Bank as trustee:[43]

[41] *Lea Record, passim.*
[42] *Ibid.*, p. 75.   [43] *Ibid.*, p. 740.

$75,000 Southern Department Stores @ 95......$ 71,250
 75,000 Rock Hill Printing and Finishing @ 95.. 71,250
 40,000 Oak Manufacturing Company @ 96.75.... 38,750
 50,000 Cadet Hosiery Company @ 95.......... 47,500
 75,000 Alabama Mills @ 95.................. 71,250
     Total.......................$300,000

The bonds were to be covered by a repurchase agreement in which Caldwell and Company was to agree to buy back upon demand at the sale price any or all bonds. The certificates were to yield 4 per cent interest while the Central Bank was to get 6 per cent on the bonds, thus gaining net interest of 2 per cent. The fact that the bonds were to be delivered to the Fourth and First National Bank instead of to the Asheville bank indicates the temporary nature of the transaction. As a matter of fact the transaction seems to have been simply an accommodation by Central Bank, giving Caldwell and Company certificates of deposit it could pledge on trusts which specified such collateral. It was entered into, no doubt, because of the close connections of Colonel Lea with both institutions. The bank was assured by Caldwell and Company that the certificates would never be used in such a manner as to come into the possession of some third party which would present them for payment and that Caldwell and Company itself would not so present them.[44]

After the agreement had been made, on October 8 Central Bank issued $300,000 of certificates of deposit payable to the Bank of Tennessee and delivered them to that institution. Instead of using these certificates, Bank of Tennessee "inadvertently"[45] returned them to Central Bank and Trust Company and they were cancelled. When the mistake was discovered on October 23, certificates of the same amount were issued and sent to the Bank of Tennessee, the bonds were turned over to the Fourth and First National Bank as trustee, and Caldwell and Company pledged the certificates on trusts.[46]

Another transaction in October, 1930, between Caldwell and Company and the Central Bank involved the purchase by the former of $300,000 of 4.5 per cent Revenue Anticipation Notes of Asheville, dated October 25, 1930, and due April 15, 1931, from Central Bank. Caldwell and Company agreed to buy these notes on October 25, subject to legal opinion of New York attorneys, and directed Central Bank to send one $5,000 note to New York and the balance to Nashville. This was done and Cald-

[44] Petition of the Commissioner of Banks of North Carolina in the case *Dean* v. *Caldwell*, filed June 30, 1931.
[45] This was the term used by Rogers Caldwell in an affidavit filed in *State of North Carolina* v. *Luke Lea, et al.*, 203 North Carolina (1932). Cited hereafter as *State* v. *Lea*.
[46] *Lea Record, passim.*

well and Company advanced the bank $250,000 before receiving the legal opinion, thus leaving Caldwell and Company with $45,000 of the notes for which it had paid nothing. The entire $295,000 of notes, however, were used by Caldwell and Company on its obligations.[47]

It should perhaps be stressed that both of these transactions aided Caldwell and Company. It gained net securities of $45,000 in the bond transaction which it could use as collateral; and, in the transaction involving the certificates of deposits, it obtained cover for trusts and with it was able to correct some violations, at least technically.

Aid from Other Banks

Caldwell and Company was unable to call on all of its affiliated banks for aid. The Union Planters National Bank and Manhattan Savings Bank of Memphis were fortunately protected by the agreement with the Comptroller prohibiting loans to Caldwell and Company or any of its interests. The Holston-Union National Bank, although under the supervision of the same Federal officer, had no such protection and, while it was in no condition to increase its loans to Caldwell and Company, the $450,000 which it had advanced through loans and repurchase agreements during 1929 was not reduced. The Caldwell controlled American Exchange Trust Company of Little Rock loaned Caldwell and Company $100,000 of additional funds during the summer of 1930, bringing its total advances to the investment house to $340,000.[48]

There were banks not affiliated with Caldwell and Company which came to its aid during the last few months of its operations. In Nashville the American National Bank, the strongest competitor of the Fourth and First National, loaned Caldwell and Company $350,000 as late as October 23, 1930, on a note secured by BancoKentucky stock and Harlan-Wallins Coal Corporation bonds; while the Tennessee-Hermitage National Bank, a much smaller institution, loaned $50,000 on September 15, secured by BancoKentucky stock and miscellaneous corporation bonds. In the East the Chase National Bank advanced $740,000 to Caldwell and Company and the Bank of Tennessee, at least $50,000 of which was loaned as late as November 1, 1930. It is interesting to note, however, that this later loan was secured by municipal bonds while one of the earlier loans for $325,000 made on April 14, 1930, was collateraled by common stocks. Chemical Bank and Trust Company loaned Cald-

[47] Petition of the Commissioner of Banks of North Carolina.
[48] "Report of Receivers of Caldwell and Company," Part I, p. 579, and Balance Sheet of Bank of Tennessee, November 6, 1930.

well and Company and the Bank of Tennessee each $100,000, the loan
to the former having been made on October 22. From the Middle West
funds were obtained from the First National Bank in St. Louis, which
advanced a total of $660,000, at least $465,000 of which came between
September 16 and October 9. Further south, the First National Bank
of Dallas had loaned a total of $450,000, $300,000 of which was advanced
on August 5 and the balance on October 6.[49] While there were numerous
other banks with Caldwell and Company and Bank of Tennessee notes
at the time of their failures, the above list is significant in that it shows
banks scattered over a wide section of the country advancing funds at
a time when both of these institutions were in a hopelessly insolvent
condition. Some of the loans were secured by sound collateral, others by
stocks and bonds of very doubtful value. It is impossible to say whether
the loans were made by the banks, knowing that Caldwell and Company was in desperate financial straits and trying to help save it and
thus prevent a crisis in the South which might imperil their own stability, or whether they were made simply because the banks believed the
collateral behind the loans was good, regardless of the condition of Caldwell and Company. The advances of the Nashville banks were, no doubt,
made with the former consideration in view because much of the collateral accepted was of little value. Loans of the other banks were probably made partly because of the one consideration and partly because of
the other. It might be said that the action of the banks places Caldwell and Company in a very favorable light inasmuch as it was in a
position to ask for and receive the assistance of many widely scattered
banks when its difficulties became serious; but in reality the bank loans
serve more to discredit the lending institutions than to stamp the seal
of approval on Caldwell and Company. Indeed, the banks had furnished
a substantial part of the funds which had enabled Caldwell and Company to extend its influence into many financial and industrial institutions which were so closely interwoven with each other and with Caldwell and Company that when the investment house became endangered
so many other institutions were involved that a serious financial crisis
was threatened. Thus, the banks were presented with the alternative of
continuing to advance funds or of being endangered themselves by the
crisis that was sure to follow the collapse of the Nashville house. If some
of these same banks had been more careful in supplying funds to Caldwell and Company when it was rapidly expanding its scope of influence,
they would not have been faced with this problem.

[49] *Ibid.*, pp. 579-613, and Balance Sheet of the Bank of Tennessee, November 6, 1930.

Funds from the State of Tennessee

The inflow of funds from the treasury of the state of Tennessee into the Bank of Tennessee and hence into Caldwell and Company during 1930 has already been noted. It bears repeating at this time, however, that during 1930 the State deposited a total of $6,552,400 in the bank and had a balance of $3,418,400 when the bank failed, and that these funds enabled the institution to continue to operate at least several months longer than it could have done otherwise.

The Bank of Tennessee was not the only Caldwell bank to be benefited by state funds. From July 1 to November 1 state funds totaling $3,262,500 were deposited with the Holston-Union National Bank,[50] the State having $2,630,000 in its account there when the bank closed in November. In addition, the Holston Trust Company, which was not authorized to accept deposits, received a $250,000 state deposit on June 30, 1930, at the request of Luke Lea. Lea was also looking after his Liberty Bank in Nashville, the bank having a state deposit of $354,000, or three times its capital, when it failed.[51] The state deposits in these institutions were made during a time when they were all becoming progressively weaker and unquestionably aided in temporarily relieving them from considerable pressure.

The danger of these funds being removed from the Lea-Caldwell banks was obviated by the renomination and re-election of Henry H. Horton as governor in 1930. In the Democratic primary Horton not only had the support of Lea and Caldwell but had built enough roads in the vicinity of Memphis to gain Ed Crump's support. His opponent in the primary, L. E. Guinn, secured the support of Stahlman and his *Banner,* which enabled him to carry Nashville. The support of Horton by both Lea and Crump was too much for Guinn to overcome, however, and Horton received the nomination on August 8 by a majority of 40,000.[52] The primary campaign was not nearly as bitter as it had been in 1928 nor were Caldwell and Company and its affiliated Kentucky Rock Asphalt Company brought into the campaign as much. It was known by all, however, that Horton still had the support of both Lea and Caldwell, a fact which was used against him by his opponent wherever possible. In the general election in November Horton easily defeated C. Arthur Bruce, the Republican nominee, who tried unsuccessfully to make an issue out of the large amount of state funds in Lea-Caldwell banks.[53]

[50] Testimony of Nat Tipton, assistant attorney general of the state of Tennessee before Legislative Investigating Committee, 1931.   [51] *Interim Report*, pp. 471-73.
[52] *Nashville Tennessean*, August 9, 1930.   [53] *Second Report*, pp. 674-76.

AID FROM MEMPHIS COMMERCIAL APPEAL, INCORPORATED

During the summer and early fall of 1930 the account of Memphis Commercial Appeal, Incorporated, in the Bank of Tennessee was allowed to accumulate until it reached $1,128,786 on September 30, 1930.[54] On this same date Southern Publishers, Incorporated, the holding company owning all of the stock of Memphis Commercial Appeal, owed Caldwell and Company and the Bank of Tennessee $1,311,000, a debt which could not be paid because Commercial Appeal had paid no dividends on either its preferred or common stock. To enable Southern Publishers to pay these notes, a series of transactions took place in October which actually but legally robbed Memphis Commercial Appeal of its funds.

On October 23 dividend on the 20,000 shares of the $7.00 preferred stock of Memphis Commercial Appeal from July 1, 1927, to July 1, 1930, amounting to $420,000, was declared and paid to Southern Publishers. Six days later, on October 29, the directors of the paper, in a special meeting in Nashville, declared the quarterly dividend on the preferred stock for the period July 1 to October 1, 1930, amounting to $35,000, and a dividend of $2.25 a share on the 150,000 shares of common stock which amounted to $337,500. Thus a total of $792,500 of dividends was declared and paid to Southern Publishers in less than a week. With these and other funds the holding company paid $811,000 of notes owed to Caldwell and the Bank of Tennessee. Moreover, Caldwell and Company obtained $335,500 by selling Commercial Appeal securities of that amount. Thus, in all, the investment house received $1,128,000 from Memphis Commercial Appeal and Southern Publishers in one week in October. After these various transactions, Southern Publishers still owed Caldwell and Company $500,000 borrowed when the Knoxville Journal Company was purchased.

In addition to meeting these obligations due Caldwell and Company, Southern Publishers also paid its president, Luke Lea, his salary of $50,000 a year which had not been paid since May 15, 1927, and amounted to a total of $175,000. This sum was paid primarily with securities Lea had previously sold Southern Publishers.

The dividend payments all but financially wrecked the Memphis publishing company. On September 30, 1930, the company had cash of $1,307,892 and total current assets of $1,747,847 while total current liabilities amounted to $544,373. On October 31, after these transactions, the company had cash of only $76,296 and current assets, including the

---

[54] Facts concerning the transactions that took place between Memphis Commercial Appeal, Inc., Southern Publishers, Inc., and Caldwell and Company during October, 1930, are from "Audit Report of Southern Publishers."

$335,500 of practically worthless securities, of $629,389. The effect of the dividend payments was partly hidden on the company's balance sheet by writing up intangible assets from $4,000,000 to $4,575,000. Even with this increase, which was based upon the doubtful ground that the money-losing *Evening Appeal* had circulation and good will worth the additional $575,000, the net worth of the company was reduced in the space of one month by $240,000.

Aid from Shares-in-the-South, Incorporated

Although not involving as large sums as the deals with Memphis Commercial Appeal, the manipulations in 1930 of the assets of Shares-in-the-South were of a nature to command brief notice. Caldwell and Company's efforts to peg the price of the stock of the investment trust proved ineffective in 1930 even though its holdings of this stock increased from 31,057 shares on December 31, 1929, to 63,535 shares in November, 1930.[55] Included in this latter amount were all the shares of the investment trust which had been sold to the employees of Caldwell and Company under repurchase agreements and which Caldwell and Company, certainly to its credit, had bought back upon demand.

During the summer of 1930 the portfolio of Shares-in-the-South included an even larger percentage of securities originated by Caldwell and Company since many of the marketable securities of the trust were sold and the funds deposited in the Bank of Tennessee. Under the by-laws of the trust these funds had to be secured and Caldwell and Company hypothecated any type of asset it had available, pledging with the trust some of its very slow and doubtful notes. Through this process of selling out its portfolio, Shares-in-the-South deposited $765,000 in the Bank of Tennessee during the four-month period, July-October, 1930.[56] While it withdrew a part of these funds, the major portion was used by Caldwell and Company, Shares-in-the-South having a deposit balance of $616,418 in the Bank of Tennessee on November 6, 1930.[57] Further, the stock of the trust which Caldwell and Company bought and which was of little value because of the nature of the assets behind it was practically all pledged to unsuspecting depositors.

Other Suggested and Attempted Methods of Saving the Company

While most of the steps discussed above which were taken in an effort to save Caldwell and Company were of a rather unusual nature, all during this time the company was still relying on one of its usual and accus-

---

[55] "Report of Receivers of Caldwell and Company," Part 1, p. 480.
[56] Confidential source.
[57] Balance Sheet of Bank of Tennessee, November 6, 1930.

tomed sources of funds, namely, deposits obtained by the purchase of bonds under depository agreements. The amount of funds thus obtained totaled more than $11,000,000 on September 30, or approximately one third of the company's total current liabilities. During 1930 the need for funds became so great that very frequently issues would be purchased under depository agreements and sold the following day at a price below that paid for the bonds. In this way the company could quickly obtain funds which would be withdrawn only as needed to pay for construction projects. They were costly funds but the fact that the company was willing to do this indicates perhaps as clearly as any other one thing its desperate financial condition.

In addition to the various measures taken to obtain cash, other suggestions were made by officials of the firm as to how it could be saved. Carter insisted that some outside party be called in who had sufficient financial backing to restore the company's solvency, a step Rogers Caldwell consistently opposed and refused to take. Donovan thought a less drastic measure would bring material aid; he suggested that Caldwell and Company issue collateral trust bonds with its unpledged notes and securities as collateral and exchange these bonds for the better grade securities owned by some of the Caldwell controlled insurance companies.[58] Just why this proposal was not carried out cannot be definitely said, for it was certainly in line with the general policy of Caldwell and Company at this time; but it may be presumed that after the Inter-Southern Life Insurance Company had exchanged a large part of its securities for the stocks of the other insurance companies it had no very great amount of salable securities available to be exchanged for such bonds, and it is most likely that the Missouri Commissioner of Insurance would have prevented Missouri State Life from engaging in such an activity. In none of the other insurance companies had Caldwell and Company established dominance sufficient to enable it to effect the proposed exchange.

When no permanent relief was afforded the company by any of the transactions carried out or proposed, Rogers Caldwell agreed that the only remaining step that could save his company was the sale of its controlling stock of Inter-Southern Life Insurance Company. Although practically all of Caldwell and Company's holdings of this stock was pledged, it was pledged to affiliated institutions which would accept other collateral and hence it was thought that its sale would furnish enough free funds to enable Caldwell and Company to continue operations. Several possible buyers were considered. Fourth and First Banks, Incorporated, was

[58] Confidential Report to J. D. Carter from T. G. Donovan, August 1, 1930.

prominently mentioned as a buyer within the Caldwell organization but it was in no condition to undertake such a large transaction. J. B. Brown was approached about the matter and he agreed to attempt to form a syndicate of banks with National Bank of Kentucky as a prominent member to finance the purchase of Inter-Southern by Associated Life Companies which would still leave control of Inter-Southern in the hands of Caldwell and Company. These efforts, though, bore no fruit and, as their failure became apparent, Caldwell and Company's early demise became increasingly evident.

RESULTS OF ATTEMPTS TO RAISE CASH FOR THE COMPANY

The large inflow of funds into the sinking Caldwell organization during 1930 proved no more than a temporary stimulant but the condition was too grave for a temporary stimulant to do any good. The reason for this can be found in two immediate conditions: first, the losses from operations sustained by Caldwell and Company; second, the heavy withdrawals of funds from the company. In the fiscal year ending June 30, 1930, Caldwell and Company operated at a loss of $2,511,000 before providing for all losses in value of inventory and excluding the arbitrary write-up of security values in connection with the BancoKentucky merger. During the remainder of 1930 the company continued to operate at a loss, which, during the three months, July, August, and September, amounted to $550,000, without taking into account depreciation in value of inventory.[59]

Much more important as a cause of the company's increasing distress was the steadily accumulating net withdrawals of funds. From July 1, 1929, until the failure of Caldwell and Company and the Bank of Tennessee, $15,851,000 more was withdrawn from than was advanced to them. Certain liability accounts showed increases during the period, which indicated a greater inflow than outflow of funds from these sources. Notes payable to banks, obligations to repurchase securities on demand, and funds held in trust subject to withdrawal increased $5,231,000. On the other hand, net decreases in demand deposits of $11,570,000 and of time deposits of $440,000, payments to Kidder-Peabody of $4,706,000 more than received, a decrease in notes payable other than to banks of $1,411,000, a net withdrawal of $567,000 by controlled companies, and important decreases in several other liability items brought the total of these decreases to $21,082,000 and the net decrease to $15,851,000.[60] It was in this huge withdrawal of funds that the basic factors bringing about the downfall of Caldwell and Company made themselves felt.

[59] Income Accounts of Caldwell and Company for the months mentioned.
[60] From confidential source.

The general financial condition of the company during this period is very adequately summarized in a report of Donovan to Carter which said in part:

On June 30 [1930], we had free and unpledged securities in the box amounting to $6,000,000, notes amounting to $4,500,000, or a total, excluding BancoKentucky stock, of $5,000,000, of $10,500,000. This represents notes and securities unacceptable to banks and others as collateral on loans, trusts, etc. Our assets are $36,000,000 made up of cash in banks, notes receivable, and inventory, against liabilities of $34,000,000. The cash in banks represents about 3 per cent of our total liabilities and during the month of June the deposit withdrawals exceeded the deposit income by about $1,000,000, which in a large measure accounts for the present money situation; as well as the present class of our inventory preventing to a large degree our arranging loans to meet our demands without strains.

Our operating expenses and other losses for the past year average $194,000 per month which makes it necessary for us to earn $2,400,000 annually before making a profit. Decided cuts have been made during the past month which will materially affect this situation; but others seem quite necessary.

It seems that the present state of our inventory cannot be definitely placed upon any responsible party, but this situation should be remedied in the future by placing definite responsibility for the purchase of all securities. As a suggestion, we recommend that no issue be purchased in excess of $50,000 without the approval of the president and now operating executive committee. We further recommend that the Committee follow up more closely than before the movement of sales from inventory.

To meet withdrawals at present, we must get additional deposits or make new loans on the released collateral in case of secured deposit withdrawals. The source of additional deposits seems uncertain. I do not believe that during the next five years [he was indeed an optimist] we shall receive a great deal of deposit money from Tennessee issues, but there remains a large amount of road construction work in the States of Alabama, Kentucky, Mississippi, and Arkansas, which may produce funds available for deposits but it seems doubtful if we can obtain a sufficient amount to replace a very large part of the money now on deposit with us and which may be withdrawn.

Our greatest concern at present is, therefore, how steady will be the withdrawals of funds now held as deposits. Our notes payable are well secured and it is not thought that many of the larger notes will be called for payment nor will we be entirely unsuccessful in getting present notes renewed.

Our greatest danger is in the small reserve of cash or liquid or available assets we hold to meet the demands made on us through clearings and largely without much notice.[61]

[61] From Confidential Report, August 1, 1930.

Chapter XV

INTERNAL CONFLICT

During this period when Caldwell and Company was having such great trouble in meeting its cash requirements, it was confronted with another difficulty, which, while of a less serious nature, impaired the company's morale at a time it could ill afford it. This was a conflict between Rogers Caldwell and DeWitt Carter which involved differences of opinion both as to how the business should be run and how the spoils should be divided.

During the more prosperous years of Caldwell and Company's operations, Carter became dissatisfied with his position with the company. Beginning as a bookkeeper at $175 a month, he had been steadily advanced until he became executive vice president at an annual salary of $35,000. Though a responsible officer, he owned no stock in the company and shared in no dividends. The ownership by Rogers Caldwell of all the stock of Caldwell and Company prior to the BancoKentucky merger and half of it after the merger placed him in a position to dictate completely even to the highest officials of his firm, one of whom was Carter. Carter resented this situation and felt that since he and E. J. Heitzeberg had had such important rôles in the development of Caldwell and Company they should be given a chance to acquire a substantial part of its stock. Heitzeberg may have taken the same attitude but he was not aggressive in the matter. Carter, however, was, and several years prior to 1930 had approached Caldwell on the issue, claiming that since he had shared in the responsibilities of the company he should be given some means of participating in its earnings and of protecting himself against dismissal at any time Caldwell might order. Caldwell refused to give in to Carter's desires, and while Carter remained with the firm, retaining hopes that some day he would convince Caldwell of the justness of his views, he felt that he had been greatly wronged and naturally a coolness developed between the two men.

There seems to have been no sharp clash between Carter and Caldwell until the early part of 1930. This arose in connection with the sale of the controlling interest of Missouri State Life Insurance Company to Inter-Southern. A meeting to discuss this proposed sale was held at the home of Rogers Caldwell, with Carter, Rogers Caldwell, James E. Caldwell,

Meredith Caldwell, and Carey G. Arnett, president of Inter-Southern, present. The matter was discussed at great length and Carter expressed his emphatic disapproval of the transaction on the ground that it was not fair to Inter-Southern or its policyholders to exchange stock of Missouri State Life for its diversified investments. Finally, Meredith Caldwell said, "Rogers, as long as you and father and I are in favor of this thing why discuss it any longer?" With that Carter asked that he be excused, and left seriously aggrieved.[1]

A few days later, on March 17, 1930, Carter sent Caldwell a letter of resignation stating that developments of the past few weeks, such as the incident with regard to the sale of Missouri State Life to Inter-Southern, had served to clarify his mind and hasten the decision which he had made. He said in part, "On the one hand I have been confronted with the desire to be loyal to you and the employees of Caldwell and Company and the people with whom it is doing business and to help fight the burdens that exist. On the other hand my conscience constantly dictates that I should not continue to make myself a party to principles and actions that are unsound and unfair, and which so affect my spirit and loyalty that my effectiveness is seriously impaired."

Rogers Caldwell was in the midst of trying to swing the Banco-Kentucky merger and several of the other deals that were made about that time and he recognized that if his executive vice president resigned while these transactions were in progress their consummation might not be effected. Therefore he asked Carter to withdraw his resignation, at least tentatively. Carter was willing to do this on the basis that he be given an interest in the business. Caldwell then suggested that it might be best to accept the resignation sometime after the Banco deal was completed and let Carter take charge of the securities affiliate of the Union Planters National Bank in Memphis, but when Carter declined to do this the matter was dropped for the time and Carter continued in his old capacity.[2]

About two months later, on May 20, just before the BancoKentucky merger was completed, Carter handed Caldwell two letters and asked that they be carefully read. Since they were rather long and since the Banco deal was then consuming all of his time, Rogers Caldwell laid them aside, thinking probably that he would read them soon; but as a matter of fact, according to Caldwell himself, he neglected them entirely and they were filed away unread.[3] One of the letters was addressed "Dear Rogers" and the other "Dear Mr. Caldwell." In the for-

---

[1] "Caldwell Bill of Exceptions," IV, 247-49.
[2] Ibid., V, 73-76.   [3] Ibid., pp. 90-92.

mer, which was much briefer and in a way explained the contents of the other much longer one, Carter assured Caldwell that he had the best interests of the business at heart. In this letter Carter mentioned three items that he objected to particularly. These were: first, the statement by Caldwell that he felt Caldwell and Company was justified in using the assets of Inter-Southern Life to its own advantage rather than to the utmost advantage of Inter-Southern's policyholders; second, the instructions that men in the employ of Caldwell and Company sign a false receipt for bonds in connection with the $250,000 loan made to Caldwell and Company by the National Bank and Trust Company of Charlottesville, Virginia; and third, the use of $1,000,000 of East Jefferson Parish, Louisiana, bonds as collateral before Caldwell and Company had paid for them. Carter said further: "Possibly if the financial affairs of Caldwell and Company were in splendid condition these matters would not have disturbed me so greatly, because I might have felt that no real risk existed for these innocent parties in their dealings with us, but when we get so calloused as to do things of this sort in the face of our present position and the consequent great risk involved for innocent parties who deal with us, I cannot help but feel that the very foundations on which a business of this sort must rest are being shaken."

In the longer letter to Caldwell, Carter went at great length into what he considered the principal weaknesses of the business, giving on the whole a very splendid analysis of the situation.[4] He pointed out that the problems which faced the company had their origin many years before and could not be laid entirely to the break in the stock market. The unsatisfactory condition of the business was largely due, he stated, to the failure to manage the company properly and to the lack of sufficient permanent working capital. A solution could be worked out by a recognition on the part of Caldwell that a proper organization was necessary. In achieving this, some individual should be selected and given the proper authority to organize the business "so that its affairs can be handled in an efficient, economical, and concerted way." Then Carter went into some detail as to how the man should be selected, the attributes he should have, and the nature of the task he would have to perform.

With regard to the lack of capital, Carter suggested that there were assets totaling $4,000,000 on March 31 which could be turned into cash if the company would adopt a firm attitude with regard to the collection of certain notes and accounts receivable and would push certain stocks and bonds which were in Caldwell and Company's inventory but which had been originated by other houses. He raised a doubt as to whether

[4] See Appendix H.

the company was in a position to seek outside capital at this time but strongly advised that this be done as soon as it put "its house in order."

The last matter discussed in the letter concerned Carter's long-standing grievance, namely, that he owned none of the stock of Caldwell and Company. He pointed out why the "older associates" in the business should be enabled to acquire an interest in it and stated that he knew there were two principal executives who had expected for six or seven years that such would be done. He also said that he was sure some satisfactory plan could be easily worked out if Caldwell wanted to do so.

Though Caldwell presumably did not read Carter's letters, he did take one step in line with Carter's ideas when an executive committee was created. This committee was set up on July 12 under an agreement between Rogers Caldwell, DeWitt Carter, and E. J. Heitzeberg, who composed the committee's personnel, covering "plans for future conduct, management, and control of the business and policies and operations of Caldwell and Company." The policy outlined in the first two sections of the agreement is informative. It was agreed:

1. That the operations of the company in the future should be guided by the combined efforts and judgments of the heads of the organization acting as an executive committee, rather than through individual action as has been largely the case in the past.

2. That sounder and more thorough methods of organizing the business throughout should be pursued in the future, so that the conduct and operations of the business would tend toward its functioning as the result of organized and systematic effort and control rather than as the result of individual decision, recognizing, however, that though organized effort and action is to be stressed, the qualifications and capacities of individuals will determine the character and effectiveness of the organization and hence the theory of the importance of the system and organization is not to be exaggerated to the extent that individual capabilities are to be unreasonably subordinated to some iron clad system. That efforts be made to eliminate from the business any unsound practices or policies which may have gradually developed during prosperous years, and that serious effort be made toward putting the company on the soundest basis possible, not only as to its own affairs and that of its affiliated companies, but as to the issues it has handled in the past and will handle in the future.[5]

As to the functions of the three responsible officers, Caldwell was to be occupied mainly with the maintenance of "our more important contacts," and Heitzeberg was still primarily to take care of buying issues. Carter was to continue as head of the sales department but also was charged with "seeing to it that the plans to be determined upon for

[5] From a copy of the agreement setting up this committee.

improving the organization and co-ordinating the work of individuals and departments, and the general questions of policy to be worked out from time to time, are effected and made known as necessary throughout the organization." In spite of the formal acknowledgment that the company was to be run in accordance with the general policies outlined in the agreement, there seems to have been little change in actual practices. Its immediate influence, however, was to bring about a temporary truce between Carter and Caldwell, but it left unsolved the issue of participation by Carter in the ownership of the business.

There was another factor which no doubt caused Carter to be temporarily better satisfied with his position in Caldwell and Company. It will be recalled that when Caldwell and Company merged with Banco-Kentucky, one of the agreements made was that the debts Rogers Caldwell owed to his company should all be paid, and that actually these debts were paid by declaring a dividend of $1,200,000. Caldwell evidently decided that some of his older employees should, along with himself, obtain some direct advantages from the merger, and while he did not give them any part of the dividend he did cancel the indebtedness to the firm of Carter, Heitzeberg, Donovan, and E. A. Goodloe, cashier of the Bank of Tennessee. Their indebtedness arose from securities they had bought on credit, and, in addition, Carter and Heitzeberg owed to the company considerable sums which they had borrowed to purchase homes. Carter's indebtedness amounted to approximately $65,000 and Heitzeberg's to approximately $90,000, while that of the other two was much less.[6] When Carter accepted this favor he wrote Caldwell another letter, on September 16, stating just why he was doing so, making it very clear that he was not satisfied. He said in part:

I expect to accept these stocks because I feel that I am entitled to them in view of my efforts in the past and present for the Company, and because of the unusual nature of some of the services I have been called on to render the Company. . . .

While the memorandum states that it is full settlement up to and including January 1, 1930, I feel certain that you did not mean for it to cover your promise to me, made a few weeks ago, in regard to an interest for me in your one half interest in Caldwell and Company, and I accept these stocks only with the distinct understanding that this promise is still in effect and is to be carried out by you at some later and convenient date and in keeping with our conversation on the subject.

It appears from this letter that Caldwell had promised Carter an interest in the business, probably in July when the executive committee

[6] Balance Sheet of Caldwell and Company and records in the case *Dean* v. *Caldwell.*

was formed. In September when Carter wrote the above letter nothing had been done about the matter. The company at that time had only two more months to operate. With such insistence by one of the high officials that he be permitted to acquire an interest in the business, it would seem that there is some evidence for the view that the officials of the company themselves really did not know that the end was so imminent.

Another month elapsed without Caldwell's doing anything about Carter's demands. By this time it must have become clearly evident that the remaining life of the company was very short and Carter did not then seem to be pushing his old claims. He did, though, break very sharply with Caldwell on the question of bringing in outside aid, a step the latter refused to consider. As a result, on October 11, Carter again handed in his resignation. The letter containing this, which seems to have been his last to Caldwell, was as follows:

MY DEAR ROGERS:

As you know, for some weeks it has been my thought that we needed some strong outsider to come in to help us out of our present situation. My reasons for feeling this way are because I have felt that a fresh viewpoint of our situation would be of great help and because there does not exist in our group any one in whom outsiders who might be of financial aid would have the utmost confidence for one reason or another. This idea has not been adopted mainly because you gentlemen who are most interested in the business do not admit to yourselves that you cannot cope with the situation or are unwilling to let some outsider see our real picture. At times when some new turn of our thoughts offered some ray of hope, I have felt maybe that this would not be necessary, because of my optimistic hopes that something would be accomplished. All such hopes, however, have been dissipated by the unnecessary delays encountered, due mainly to your failure to aggressively pursue some definite line of action without deviation. Two weeks ago, we, at what I thought was almost the last moment, hit upon the plan of selling the insurance holdings. With time the most important factor a whole week was lost in aimless discussion here at Nashville. Then about two weeks ago, you and Mr. Brown discussed a plan and were to, by the end of this week, complete the means by which the Associated Life Company would acquire our insurance holdings from us for as much as $5,000,000 in cash to us. After a week, apparently, nothing definite has been accomplished notwithstanding the extreme urgency of the situation.

Frankly speaking, Rogers, you and Mr. Brown and for that matter your father are playing with a situation that is full of dangers to many institutions and individuals without either of you applying yourselves to a straightforward and persistent effort towards a solution. You know that I do not mind fighting for a just cause or doing everything within my power in any situation possible of solution, but for me to continue my efforts under the conditions which have existed for weeks is utterly useless to you or to any one else.

It was our distinct understanding when we settled our differences the first of July that there were to be no more violations of trusts. Last week, contrary to my specific instructions, the Arkansas Trust was violated. I do not think you or any one else, no matter what the conditions are, has a right to expect me to disregard my self-respect sufficiently to sit and be deliberately a party to such as this. Furthermore, the proposed correction in view of what Colonel Lea said yesterday about the Bank at Asheville is a mere subterfuge no better than the present condition.[7]

My conclusions are: That I shall not continue another day in my present position under the present conditions. You, Mr. Brown, and your father represent the control of large resources and are charged with the proper safeguarding of large institutions which are in great danger at present because of our situation. If you gentlemen cannot arrange to take care of the situation you should call in for assistance some one, or more, able to help out in such a situation. My suggestion would be Mr. Couch, Mr. Watts, or Mr. Davis,[8] who, no doubt, would want to see a calamity averted. You will have the balance of today, all day tomorrow, and in a way, Monday (because it is a partial holiday), in which to make some definite plans which will relieve our needs and correct the Arkansas Trust. Unless you can make such plans I shall not continue my efforts any longer.

I do not take this as a means of ducking a responsibility but simply of bringing to a head an aimless and unavailing program which has lasted for weeks and which if it continues can have only one ending.

DeWitt Carter

Just what was done to retain the services of Carter, other than to get the certificates of deposit of the Central Bank and Trust Company of Asheville and pledge these on the Arkansas trust until this account was withdrawn, cannot be said, but it was about this time that National Bank of Kentucky made its second loan to Southern Banks and Brown was attempting to get the bank to furnish even more funds. Possibly Carter was persuaded to remain with Caldwell and Company by the assurance that the National Bank of Kentucky would continue to give support and possibly some assurance was given him that the insurance holdings

[7] The trust covering the deposit of the state of Arkansas funds referred to no doubt allowed as collateral the certificates of deposit of solvent banks. The certificates of deposit obtained from the Central Bank and Trust Company of Asheville were pledged first on the Arkansas trust and, after this deposit was withdrawn, on other trusts. Lea had evidently told Caldwell and Company that the Asheville bank was insolvent. See Chapter XIV, *supra*.

[8] Harvey C. Couch, chairman of the board of the Louisiana and Arkansas Railway and later a director of the Reconstruction Finance Corporation; Paul M. Davis, president of the American National Bank of Nashville; and Frank O. Watts, president of the First National Bank of St. Louis.

would actually be sold. Whatever the reason, Carter continued in his capacity as executive vice president of the company until it closed, without ever having his desire to hold a part of the stock of Caldwell fulfilled. When the company did close, it became apparent that he was deeply embittered against Rogers Caldwell, since he so willingly offered his services wherever needed in the prosecution of his former employer.[9]

[9] See Chapters XVII and XVIII, *infra*.

CHAPTER XVI

THE CRASH OF THE EMPIRE

THE EFFORTS of Rogers Caldwell to save his company through the sale of its controlling stock of Inter-Southern Life Insurance Company continued into November. The plan being primarily relied upon was the purchase of the stock by Associated Life Companies which was to be financed partially by the National Bank of Kentucky and partially by St. Louis banks.[1] This plan was rumored in financial circles, and in St. Louis was mentioned to a national bank examiner who rather casually and tactlessly, perhaps, replied that the National Bank of Kentucky was in no condition to carry through such a deal for it had been practically insolvent for about five years. The examiner's statement spread rapidly and affected Caldwell and Company as well as the National Bank of Kentucky for it was now generally known among bankers how dependent Caldwell and Company was upon the Kentucky bank for support. Thus the proposed sale of Inter-Southern was completely checked.[2]

The net withdrawal of funds from Caldwell and Company and the Bank of Tennessee that had been steadily mounting since the first of 1930 continued at an accelerated pace. During October, deposits in the Bank of Tennessee were reduced more than $2,000,000 and, in the first six days of November, approximately $650,000. Caldwell and Company had approximately $1,665,000 of deposits and other demand liabilities withdrawn during October and $1,346,000 during the first twelve days of November.[3] Rumors as to the shaky financial condition of the institution became so widespread that they could no longer be ignored.

On Wednesday, November 5, 1930, the morning papers of the State carried an article branding as false the rumors concerning the weak financial condition of Caldwell and Company. Incidentally, these same papers carried the news that Henry H. Horton the day before had been re-elected governor of Tennessee over his Republican opponent. The news about Caldwell and Company, however, reported that a meeting of the Nashville Clearing House Association had been called on the previous day to discuss the condition of the investment house and that

[1] "Caldwell Bill of Exceptions," v, 52.
[2] Statement to the writer by T. G. Donovan.
[3] Balance Sheets of Caldwell and Company and Bank of Tennessee as of dates mentioned.

Governor E. R. Black of the Atlanta Federal Reserve Bank had attended. After this meeting the Clearing House issued a public statement that, through an investigation, they had found all the loans of Caldwell and Company in the banks in Nashville well secured and in no case exceeded the limit allowed by law. However, the Clearing House, realizing the seriousness of the situation, had appointed a committee, with the consent of Caldwell and Company, to conserve and protect the interests of the company and its creditors. Named to this committee were Paul M. Davis, president of the American National Bank, Cornelius A. Craig, chairman of the board of the Third National Bank and president of the National Life and Accident Insurance Company, and T. D. Webb, vice president of the Fourth and First National Bank. In a statement issued to the public, this committee reported that

from statements made, we believe that Caldwell and Company is solvent and with co-operation its affairs will be worked out so that the interests of all will be conserved and protected. Its books show a large net worth; but on account of the very unusual financial condition of the entire country its securities are difficult to dispose of at this time at a fair price. The affairs of Caldwell and Company have been placed in our hands as a committee for the purpose of conserving and protecting the interests of that institution and all concerned and we ask and invite the co-operation of all interested and believe that, with same, none will suffer.[4]

In a separate statement Governor Black expressed his approval of the step taken and his belief in the soundness of the situation.

The bankers' committee appealed to Brown and BancoKentucky Company for assistance, asking for a loan of $6,000,000, and Brown sent W. T. Zur Schmiede, cashier of the National Bank of Kentucky, to Nashville to see what could be done, giving him a note for $6,000,000 signed by Brown as president of BancoKentucky Company with which the committee hoped they would be able to raise funds from banks outside Nashville and Louisville. This note had not been authorized by the directors of Banco, the step having been taken by Brown entirely upon his own initiative. When Zur Schmiede arrived in Nashville, the committee tried to borrow on the Banco note, but was unsuccessful and Zur Schmiede returned to Louisville, taking the note with him and leaving the committee and Caldwell and Company to work out the situation without his help.[5]

Meanwhile, the committee had called in the Tennessee superintendent of banks, D. D. Robertson, to examine the Bank of Tennessee. This examination, which was begun on November 5 and completed the fol-

---

[4] *Nashville Tennessean*, November 5, 1930.   [5] *Laurent Evidence.*

lowing afternoon, showed clearly that the only thing left to do was to close the bank; so at seven forty-five on Friday morning, November 7, Robertson filed a bill in the Chancery Court in Nashville pointing out the condition of the bank and asking that he be appointed receiver in accordance with the law of the State which then provided that the superintendent of banks be made receiver for all closed state banks, a petition which the Court granted.[6] When the bank closed it had deposits of approximately $10,000,000, roughly one third of which were those of the state of Tennessee; "due from" items amounting to $72,900; cash items of $1,000; but actual cash of only $32.55. Few, if any, of its $12,000,000 of securities were readily marketable.[7]

A report of the failure of the Bank of Tennessee was carried in the papers of the State on Saturday morning, November 8. The bankers' committee approved the step in a public statement, erroneously claiming that the Bank of Tennessee had no connection with any other banks in the State,[8] apparently not taking into consideration bankers' balances involved, nor did they mention the State's deposit of over $3,000,000. On the following day, however, it was announced that the State had deposits in the bank and Governor Horton issued a statement that he was using all of his powers to protect the State's interests.[9] One of these steps was the dispatch of H. W. Goodloe, an employee of the state treasurer's office, to Knoxville to ascertain the condition of the Holston-Union National Bank. Goodloe arrived in Knoxville on the morning of the eighth with a check for $284,000 to be used if he saw fit to withdraw that amount of the State's $2,630,000 deposit from the Holston-Union. Goodloe talked with J. B. Ramsey, president of the bank, and was convinced that the Holston-Union was sound in every respect, since it had $900,000 cash with the Federal Reserve Bank in Atlanta and $1,000,000 in Liberty Bonds with the Chase National in New York, which Ramsey said he could use if his bank suffered a run. Ramsey agreed, however, to give Goodloe additional security for the State's funds in the form of $347,000 of Caldwell and Company industrial bonds, which Goodloe accepted on the advice of State Treasurer Nolan, and returned to Nashville hoodwinked into believing the State would lose nothing in the Holston-Union.[10]

With a holiday on Sunday, the ninth, and again on Tuesday, the eleventh, for Armistice Day, the charged atmosphere in financial circles was given a chance to quiet down somewhat. But on the following day,

[6] From various petitions and decrees in the case *State of Tennessee* ex rel. *Robertson* v. *Bank of Tennessee*, No. 42644, in Part 1 of Chancery Court, Davidson County, Tennessee.

[7] Balance Sheet of the Bank of Tennessee, November 6, 1930.

[8] *Nashville Tennessean*, November 8, 1930.   [9] *Ibid.*, November 9, 1930.

[10] Testimony of H. W. Goodloe before Tennessee Investigating Committee, 1931.

Wednesday, November 12, the impending storm struck in full force, carrying in its wake almost all the banks connected with Caldwell and Company and precipitating a crisis in the Mid-South which shook its financial structure to the very foundations.

The Holston-Union National Bank and its subsidiary, the Holston Trust Company in Knoxville, failed to open their doors on the morning of the twelfth. The bank had suffered withdrawals of approximately $750,000 on Monday, the tenth, and its cash reserves were almost exhausted. This failure caused runs on all other banks in the city and several were on the point of having to suspend when a merger was carried through between the East Tennessee National Bank, the East Tennessee Savings Bank, and the City National Bank, which was announced on Thursday, November 13, at one-thirty in the afternoon.[11] This step calmed the storm so far as Knoxville was concerned but the city was left with four less banks.

In Nashville the Fourth and First National Bank had been subjected to a heavy run from the time the bankers' committee was appointed for Caldwell and Company. It had remained open on the tenth and reopened on the twelfth but its condition was becoming desperate. It had borrowed over $9,300,000 and had unsuccessfully called upon the Federal Reserve banks of New York, Chicago, and St. Louis for more funds. The American National Bank of Nashville, which had loaned $1,800,000 after the Federal Reserve banks had refused further assistance, was appealed to for additional aid and a merger between this bank and the Fourth and First National was worked out as the only means of meeting the situation.[12] A committee from each bank was appointed at noon on November 12 and at four that afternoon it was announced that details for the merger of the two institutions had been agreed upon and carried out. On Thursday morning, November 13, papers carried announcements of the merger, characterizing the new bank as an "impressive financial structure, coming not as an accident or incident, but as the proof and product of growth."[13] Incidentally the same papers in Nashville which announced the merger incongruously carried the regular advertisement of the Fourth and First National Bank and Nashville Trust Company, stating that for sixty-seven and forty-one years, respectively, these two institutions had been open every business day. That morning, however, the Fourth and First National opened as the American National Bank.

[11] Memphis *Commercial Appeal*, November 14, 1930.
[12] Letter from P. M. Davis, president of American National Bank, to stockholders of Fourth and First Banks, Inc., 1933.   [13] *Nashville Banner*.

Meanwhile, the condition of Caldwell and Company itself was becoming more and more crucial. Cash had fallen to $67,000 and unpledged, readily marketable securities amounted to certainly no more than $25,000, while at the same time the withdrawal of deposits mounted. Since it was apparent it was a question of voluntary or involuntary receivership, the company chose the former, and on November 13 had one of its bond buyers, Fred Dean, petition in the United States District Court in Nashville for the receivership of the company on the grounds that it could not raise sufficient funds to continue operations in spite of its substantial assets which, although at a fair value, probably more than enough to pay its liabilities, could not be readily sold on account of the condition of the security market. Caldwell and Company, in its answer to Dean's petition, admitted its inability to meet its debts but held that an orderly liquidation of its assets would realize enough to pay its creditors more than was owed. The only way to properly conserve its assets, the answer concluded, was through the appointment of a receiver.[14]

Judge John J. Gore of the United States District Court in Nashville, on the same day the petition was filed and answered, appointed a friendly receiver, former United States District Attorney Lee Douglas, and, as attorney for the receiver, the firm of Price, Schlater, and Price. Douglas was connected by marriage with the Caldwell family, a fact which was generally known, and his appointment as receiver was looked upon critically by many. On November 15 the state of Tennessee, because of its material interest in the affairs of Caldwell and Company, asked that a co-receiver be appointed. The court allowed this request and on November 17 appointed Major Rutledge Smith, an official of the Tennessee Central Railway, as co-receiver.[15]

The receivership of Caldwell and Company was publicly announced on Friday morning, November 14. At the same time the resignation of the bankers' committee was noted, it no longer being in a legal position to be of service. This committee had made a futile effort to do something for the company, but in fact had merely served to postpone failure long enough to enable Caldwell and Company itself to make a final effort toward solvency and, failing in this, to get itself in a condition that would be less embarrassing when receivership finally culminated.

The same morning the receivership of Caldwell and Company was announced the Liberty Bank and Trust Company of Nashville, which Luke Lea had dominated so completely, failed to open. Its president, R.

[14] From Petition of Fred Dean and Answer of Caldwell and Company in the case *Dean* v. *Caldwell*.
[15] From court records in the case *Dean* v. *Caldwell*.

E. Donnell, blamed the bank's collapse upon the "raging financial storm" in Nashville. The bank had had to suspend operations after an unsuccessful attempt to cash certificates of deposit of the Central Bank and Trust Company, which Lea had sold it. The remaining banks in Nashville were being subjected to runs that were growing more and more severe. Lines a block or more long formed around them with the banks attempting to protect their resources somewhat by allowing only one customer to come in the bank at a time to withdraw his deposit. The Tennessee-Hermitage National Bank was on the verge of collapse when the Commerce-Union Bank agreed to take it over with the co-operation and financial support of the other banks in Nashville, a merger which was announced on Saturday, November 15, at one-thirty.[16] This merger helped to settle conditions in Nashville and so far as that city was concerned the worst of the storm was over, only one more bank, a Negro institution, closing its doors after that. During the four days, November 13 through 16, however, Nashville had seen one bank close, the largest investment banking house in the South fail, its largest commercial bank saved by a merger, and another smaller bank saved in a similar manner.

The Caldwell banks in Memphis, the Union Planters National Bank and the Manhattan Savings Bank, were also subjected to some pressure but not to the same degree as those in Nashville. The officers of these banks made a public statement on November 6, the day before the Bank of Tennessee failed, saying that "neither Caldwell and Company nor Rogers Caldwell owes either the Union Planters National Bank and Trust Company or the Manhattan Savings Bank and Trust Company anything whatsoever; and they are not in any way indebted to any of the subsidiary companies of either bank."[17] On the day after the failure of Caldwell and Company, the officers of the Memphis banks announced the resignation of James E. Caldwell and Meredith Caldwell from the boards of directors, stating that the control and administration of the banks were entirely in the hands of officers and directors who were residents of Memphis.[18] The fact that Fourth and First Banks, Incorporated, of Nashville held the largest single block of Union Planters stock was discreetly, and justifiably, held from the public.

Outside the larger cities of Tennessee, many banks were subjected to a great deal of pressure for several weeks following the collapse of the Caldwell structure. Particularly was this true of the correspondent banks of the Holston-Union. From the time of the failure of the Bank of Ten-

[16] Memphis *Commercial Appeal*, November 16, 1930.
[17] Memphis *Press-Scimitar*, November 6, 1930.
[18] *Ibid.*, November 14, 1930.

nessee until the end of 1930, there were some sixteen state banks and three national banks in Tennessee that suspended operations, while several others were saved through mergers.[19]

The effect of the collapse of Caldwell and Company was by no means limited to Tennessee but rapidly spread to Arkansas, Kentucky, and North Carolina, and to a less extent into several other states.

In Arkansas A. B. Banks had taken cognizance of the situation on November 6 when he ran the following announcement in the Little Rock papers:

> Neither Rogers Caldwell nor Caldwell and Company owes anything whatever to the Home Insurance Companies or any of the banks in which I am interested. Caldwell and Company have only one loan in the American Exchange Trust Company well within the legal limit, amply secured by bonds and approved by the discount committee.
>
> In March, 1929, with certain of my associates, I entered into a contract with Caldwell and Company to sell 60 per cent of the capital stock of the Home Companies for $3,700,000. Of this amount $1,760,000 has been paid in cash and high grade securities. No payment of principal or interest under this contract has ever been defaulted. If for any reason Caldwell and Company or the Inter-Southern Life Insurance Company to which the contract has been assigned should not wish to complete it, my associates and I would be glad to negotiate for repurchase.[20]

This statement by Banks apparently did little to prevent a run on the American Exchange Trust Company and his chain of country banks. On Saturday, November 15, he made a further statement saying that the stock of the American Exchange Trust Company owned by Caldwell and Company had been acquired by Little Rock interests and that J. D. Carter had resigned from its board of directors. This step, said Banks, meant that the Caldwell interests had left the state of Arkansas, since they had disposed of their holdings of the insurance companies several months before and had never had an interest in any of his other banks.[21] This statement was made despite the fact that Caldwell and Company when it failed held 661 shares of American Exchange Trust Company stock.[22]

Heavy withdrawals from the American Exchange Trust Company continued throughout Saturday, the fifteenth, bringing withdrawals after the failure of the Bank of Tennessee up to $4,000,000, or approximately

---

[19] *Bulletins of the State Department of Banking.* These bulletins show that the total resources of state banks in Tennessee declined from $243,996,417 on May 19, 1930, to $192,144,256 on December 31, 1930.

[20] Memphis *Press-Scimitar,* November 7, 1930.

[21] Memphis *Commercial Appeal,* November 16, 1930.

[22] "Report of Receivers of Caldwell and Company," Part I, p. 365.

22 per cent of total deposits. The bank could not continue to operate under such conditions and after the close of business on Saturday the directors decided to suspend operations. The correspondent banks were all notified and on Monday, November 17, forty-three banks in Arkansas failed to open their doors.[23] The effect of this upon the other banks in the State is obvious. Practically all of them were subjected to severe runs, particularly those in Little Rock, and the following day, the eighteenth, nine additional banks closed. The Federal Reserve Bank in St. Louis sent $25,000,000 in currency to its Little Rock branch to aid in meeting the mounting demands for cash. The fact that only two banks suspended on the nineteenth was cited as evidence that things were returning to normal,[24] but by the next Monday, November 24, enough additional banks had failed to bring the total for the State up to seventy.[25]

Most of the banks that closed in Arkansas took advantage of the state law allowing them to suspend operations for five days. At the end of five days a few of them reopened but most of them, including the American Exchange Trust Company, remained closed. Only two units in the Banks' chain failed to close at all and of those that closed only one resumed payments after the five-day suspension.[26] The crash immediately affected the Home Fire and Home Accident Insurance companies. Since their chief assets were stocks in the banks that had failed, complete insolvency of these companies resulted and their licenses were revoked on November 24 and receivers appointed for them.[27]

On Monday, November 17, the same day the panic hit Arkansas, the Caldwell affiliated banks in Kentucky were closed. Brown, in an effort to forestall failure, had taken a course similar to Banks' and on November 6 announced in the newspapers of Louisville that "negotiations which have been in progress for several months between the BancoKentucky Company and Caldwell and Company have never been *consummated*. The BancoKentucky Company is therefore not connected in any way with the affairs of Caldwell and Company."[28] By using the word "consummated" Brown may have been technically truthful since the valuation of Caldwell and Company's assets had not yet been made, but his statement that the two companies were in no way connected could not possibly be twisted into even the appearance of veracity. The Louisville *Courier-Journal* of November 6 reminded its readers of the announcement of June 2 that the deal had been effected.

[23] Memphis *Commercial Appeal*, November 18, 1930.
[24] *Ibid.*, November 20, 1930.   [25] *Ibid.*, November 25, 1930.
[26] Data furnished writer by Arkansas Banking Department.
[27] *Nashville Banner*, November 24, 1930.
[28] *Courier-Journal*. Italics are the writer's.

The Inter-Southern Life Insurance Company was the first Caldwell holding in Louisville actually to be brought into the courts. A minority stockholder on November 13 asked that a receiver be appointed for the company on the ground that the sale of the Missouri State Life stock to Inter-Southern had cheated the company of $8,400,000. Arnett, president of Inter-Southern, branded the allegations as a "mass of falsehoods and deliberate misrepresentations" and said that the action was inspired by the former president of the company, James R. Duffin. Arnett must have been correct, at least in his latter charge, for, when the case was heard on November 15, Duffin appeared for the plaintiff. The case, however, was dismissed, the court holding there was no merit in the bill.[29]

The collapse of the Caldwell interests in Nashville and Knoxville, the action against Inter-Southern, and the statement of Brown, which was not accepted very readily by the public, had all served to shake even further the public's confidence in the National Bank of Kentucky. The slow withdrawal of deposits that had been taking place all summer and fall accelerated. This did not take the form of a precipitate run on the bank so much as the slow but steady withdrawal of funds by the larger corporate depositors and correspondent banks. After the merger with Caldwell and Company, the Standard Oil Company of Kentucky had withdrawn about $1,800,000 from the bank, even though the chairman of the board of the oil company was a director of the bank.[30] From November 5, the date of the announcement that the bankers' committee had taken charge of Caldwell and Company, to November 15, the Saturday after Caldwell and Company had gone into receivership on Thursday, the net deposits of the National Bank of Kentucky were reduced by $8,855,000, or approximately 25 per cent. Of this amount $1,833,000 was withdrawn on Friday, the fourteenth, and $2,565,000 on Saturday, the fifteenth.[31]

When the banking day ended on November 15, Bank of Kentucky had cash of approximately $17,000. It had rediscounted every possible asset with the Federal Reserve Bank and its only hope for further support was from other Louisville banks. It had started negotiations for assistance Friday morning, and on Saturday a meeting was called of about seventy-five people who were interested in the situation. A committee from the other banks was appointed to evaluate the assets of the National Bank of Kentucky and Louisville Trust Company with the idea of either tak-

[29] Ibid., November 14, 15, 1930.
[30] Material Pertaining to Caldwell and Company Loss, in the case Anderson v. Akers, et al.   [31] Laurent Evidence.

ing them over or making a loan. The officers of the National Bank of Kentucky thought a loan of $5,000,000 would enable it to stem the tide of withdrawals but, with its best assets pledged to the Federal Reserve Bank, it had little left with which to secure such a loan. The other banks, however, agreed to advance this amount if the directors of the National Bank of Kentucky would place in escrow with New York banks enough of their personal assets to secure the loan. The directors would not consent to this and on the night of Sunday, November 16, they passed a resolution to suspend operations of both the National Bank of Kentucky and the Louisville Trust Company.

The various correspondent banks of the National Bank of Kentucky were advised of this action and on Monday eight banks in Kentucky did not open for business, followed the next day by six additional banks. Of these fourteen, seven were in Louisville, all of which were relatively small except the National Bank of Kentucky and Louisville Trust Company. Nearly all Louisville banks were subjected to severe runs but the other larger banks were prepared for this, paying out deposits freely. Just across the river from Louisville, in New Albany, Indiana, two banks suspended payments, as well as several others in southern Illinois and northeastern Missouri.[32]

The announcement of the suspensions of the National Bank of Kentucky and Louisville Trust Company naturally resulted in runs on all of the other banks controlled by BancoKentucky Company, but all withstood the storm except the Security Bank in Louisville. They were able to do this in every case, however, only after local interests had bought Banco's holdings of the stocks of these banks and brought other local banks to their rescue. In no city would the other local banks come to the aid of these distressed banks until the "foreign" interests were bought out. To take charge of the sale of these banks, Banco appointed a special committee whose nocturnal journey on November 17 from Louisville to Cincinnati saved the two Banco units in that city and the two just across the river in Covington, Kentucky. Banco's interests in all of these banks were sold at small fractions of their original costs.[33] BancoKentucky Company itself went into receivership on November 18 when it was unable to repay its demand loans at the Chemical Bank and Trust Company in New York, secured by its holdings of the closed Security Bank.

[32] Memphis *Commercial Appeal,* November 21, 1930.

[33] An account of the activities of this committee, which indicates probably better than anything else the extreme tension of the time, is found in their report to the Board of Directors of BancoKentucky Company, dated November 19, 1930, and included in the *Organization Records and Minute Book of BancoKentucky Company* which is reprinted in *Laurent Evidence.*

Joseph S. Laurent, a Louisville attorney, was appointed receiver by the Jefferson County Circuit Court.[34]

The financial storm engulfed the Central Bank and Trust Company in Asheville, North Carolina, with which Colonel Lea had carried on numerous transactions of various types, on Thursday, November 20, one week after the closing of Caldwell and Company. This bank went down with $14,000,000 of deposits and, on the same day, seven other banks in western North Carolina either did not open or closed during banking hours. All seven banks, except one, were located in or around Asheville. In Asheville all banks were literally stormed by depositors, the American National Bank suffering the most severe run. On Friday, the twenty-first, this bank together with three others closed, and on Saturday three more, bringing total bank failures in this section in three days to fifteen.[35] Feeling ran so high that police guards were thrown around the Central Bank and Trust Company's building and the home of Wallace B. Davis, its president, as precautionary measures against possible mob violence from angry depositors.[36]

Approximately a hundred and twenty banks were closed and a number of others saved by mergers in seven states during the two weeks following the announcement that the affairs of Caldwell and Company had been taken over by the Nashville Clearing House Committee. It is a fair assumption that this latter event and the subsequent failures of the Bank of Tennessee and Caldwell and Company precipitated the financial panic that caused the collapse of most of these banks. At least the timing of these failures can be charged to the influence of Caldwell and Company. The question remains, however, as to Caldwell and Company's responsibility for the condition of these banks which made it impossible for them to stand the runs.

The difficulties of the banks controlled by Caldwell and Company in Tennessee, namely, the Holston-Union and the Fourth and First National, as well as of the Liberty Bank and Trust Company and the Tennessee-Hermitage National Bank in Nashville, can be almost directly charged against the influence of Caldwell and Company and Luke Lea. The relationships of the controlled banks with Caldwell and Company were so close and so well known that they were subjected to runs that only unreasonably liquid banks could have withstood. The Caldwell loans in these banks weakened them as did the Caldwell bonds they were holding and their collapse can be blamed almost entirely on the influence of Cald-

---

[34] *Laurent Evidence.*

[35] Raleigh *News and Observer*, November 21-24, 1930.

[36] Memphis *Press-Scimitar*, November 21, 1930.

well and Company. The same can be said for the Liberty Bank and Trust Company, but it was Lea rather than Caldwell and Company whose influence precipitated the run on this bank and whose activities had weakened it. The Tennessee-Hermitage National Bank was the victim of the same run that hit the other Nashville banks. Being smaller and weaker than the others, it had to obtain assistance in order to be saved.

The banks in Arkansas, Kentucky, and North Carolina that went under are hardly justified in laying the blame for their collapse completely upon Caldwell and Company. The main trouble with the North Carolina and Arkansas banks was too much real estate paper, urban in the former state and rural in the latter. The condition of the National Bank of Kentucky had long been serious. The loans of this bank to Caldwell and Company amounting to $2,400,000 gave it that much less money to meet its difficulties and the announcement of the merger between Caldwell and Company and the BancoKentucky Company in June, 1930, had resulted in slow withdrawals by the more conservative depositors. However, neither the Caldwell loans nor this slow withdrawal should have exerted sufficient pressure to cause the failure of a bank with resources of approximately $50,000,000. Essentially, this bank had to look to the dangerous developments within it prior to the Caldwell connection as the chief cause of its failure.

Regardless of the true causes of the failures of the banks, most of the blame was laid at the door of Caldwell and Company and naturally the investment house was roundly damned by many. It is without question true that the doom of many of the banks was hastened by the Caldwell failure, and had this not occurred when it did many of them probably could have continued operations until the establishment of the Reconstruction Finance Corporation which, no doubt, would have saved some of them. If this assumption is correct, then much of the bitterness toward Caldwell and Company for causing the panic is well founded, even though the company had nothing to do in many cases with the fundamental conditions that caused the bank failures. But the Reconstruction Finance Corporation came too late to be of service to these institutions and it is mere speculation to say what might have happened if it had been in existence in November, 1930.

There are certain self-evident conclusions that stand out from this tragic episode of bank failures. One is that the solution of the difficulties inherent in a unit banking system such as we now have can hardly be found in the organization of banking chains, such as the A. B. Banks chain in Arkansas, or in the organization of banks into groups, such as those under the control of BancoKentucky Company, and certainly not in linking a large number of banks, however loosely, with an investment banking house which will likely use the assets of the banks for its own rather than for the banks' interests. A second conclusion is that banks heavily loaded with real estate paper are ordinarily in no condition to withstand severe pressure; a third is that if banks are to keep out of difficulties they cannot be operated in the interest of officers or large stockholders, who have numerous other connections constantly requiring funds and who expect and direct the bank to meet these needs, as was the case with James B. Brown in the National Bank of Kentucky and Luke Lea in the Holston-Union National Bank and Liberty Bank and Trust Company. A final conclusion is that banks and all other commercial and financial institutions of any region are almost certain to encounter severe difficulties if a company built upon as shaky a foundation as that of Caldwell and Company expands its influence over the financial and commercial enterprises of the region to the extent that Caldwell and Company did over the South.

Chapter XVII

THE POLITICAL AFTERMATH

For the relatively short period when banks were actually closing in Nashville and in other parts of Tennessee, the press of the State, particularly in Nashville where the storm was severest, tried to instill a spirit of confidence into the people. It was realized that this was necessary to halt the trend that might lead to an even more complete breakdown of the financial organization of the section. The deposit of state funds in closed banks was generally known but the public was assured immediately that there were surety bonds covering all of these deposits and that the State would lose nothing, the latter statement being by no means true. The Chemical Bank and Trust Company of New York had come to Tennessee's financial assistance by wiring Governor Horton that it would advance $5,000,000 to tide the State over its difficulties. These developments helped to quiet momentarily the public and at least to stop runs on banks.

The financial situation soon became calm enough, however, for the smoldering political hates and jealousies to emerge into the open. The opponents of the Caldwell-Lea-Horton regime were given a wonderful opportunity to discredit completely the group in power and they were not long in taking full advantage of this opportunity. The public was repeatedly told that the State had on deposit $3,418,000 in the Bank of Tennessee, $2,630,000 in the Holston-Union National Bank, $257,000 in the Holston Trust Company, and $354,000 in the Liberty Bank and Trust Company, or a total of $6,659,000 in the closed Caldwell-Lea banks. The probable loss of a large part of these funds was excellent fuel to add to the fire of hatred that was soon sweeping the State. Lewis S. Pope, who had run a poor third in the gubernatorial race of 1928, branded the officials of the State as criminally negligent. Tom Taylor, a Republican legislator from East Tennessee, suggested that the impeachment of the Governor was in order.[1] Governor Horton quickly denied that anything had occurred to warrant any such suggestion.[2]

The *Banner*, the opposition paper in Nashville, thought the financial situation sufficiently quiet by November 20 to launch a bitter and con-

[1] Memphis *Press-Scimitar*, November 13, 1930.
[2] *Ibid.*, November 14, 1930.

tinuous attack against the Caldwell-Lea-Horton regime, demanding that those responsible for the misdeeds of the triumvirate be punished. On the same day Governor Horton issued a statement in which he insisted that a legal, thorough, fair, and impartial investigation would settle the slanderous charges that were being circulated and that he would demand such an investigation when the legislature convened. He promised that if the investigation revealed that any state officer had been guilty of illegal practices he would be promptly removed from office.[3]

The feeling against the administration and its advisers, Rogers Caldwell and Luke Lea, was canalized by the formation of a Public Emergency Committee on December 3. Among its members were Hill McAllister, twice-defeated candidate for governor; Lewis S. Pope; former Governor Albert H. Roberts, whom Luke Lea had fought so bitterly and effectively in 1920; K. T. McConnico, an important attorney in the Howse machine in Nashville; and C. Neil Bass, whom Horton had ousted as Highway Commissioner.[4] In a lengthy statement the committee demanded a sweeping investigation of the State's affairs. It said in part:

> There is a public emergency in Tennessee. Nearly 6 millions of the State's money are lost to the State at a time when they are doubly needed for public works and to relieve unemployment. These public funds and other county and city funds running into more millions of dollars have apparently been used to traffic and trade in companies and in speculative securities. . . . The responsibility for this disaster must be fixed and fixed quickly. . . . We propose . . . to lend our aid toward organizing the legislature to secure a fair and disinterested examination into the causes and agencies, near and remote, that have contributed to this crisis.[5]

The committee sponsored mass meetings of outraged and indignant citizens all over the State. The largest one was in Chattanooga where some four thousand people heard Luke Lea, Rogers Caldwell, and Henry Horton condemned as a "scheming triumvirate which had conspired to shame the fair name of the state." Another large mass meeting was held in Knoxville on December 21, and on December 30, a week before the General Assembly was to convene, a state-wide meeting was held in Nashville. In all, these meetings were conducted in at least twenty-five counties of the State.[6]

A large part of the public came to look upon Caldwell, Lea, and Horton as men who had robbed and cheated the taxpayers of Tennessee.

[3] *Second Report*, p. 644.
[4] Memphis *Commercial Appeal*, December 3, 1930.
[5] *Nashville Tennessean*, December 3, 1930.
[6] *Brief for the Plaintiff* in the case *Rogers Caldwell* v. *State of Tennessee*, Davidson Criminal Law No. 14, December Term, 1931, p. 97. Cited hereafter as *Caldwell Brief*.

This feeling was well caricatured by a sign that was placed in a service station in Knoxville and later in a window of the closed Holston-Union Bank, presumably showing how the State's five-cent gasoline tax was divided:[7]

Gas	14c
Caldwell	2c
Lea	2c
Horton	1c
Total	19c

Most people considered Horton as a misguided weakling who had permitted himself to be led too easily by the other two men into practices which had resulted in great losses to the State. Rogers Caldwell was considered as the scheming financier of the conspiracy who had laid most of the plans and had received most of the financial rewards. Luke Lea was looked upon as the middleman between Caldwell and Horton, the skillful politician who had seen that Caldwell's plans had been carried out by the Governor and who had reaped political rewards as well as financial returns. The three together constituted what came to be known as a "politico-bunko-busto-banko" coalition.[8]

The Sixty-seventh General Assembly of Tennessee was scheduled to meet January 5, 1931. For several weeks prior to that time, the various factions had been forming alignments for and against the administration to influence the election of the speakers of the Senate and the House. It was generally conceded, even by the Governor and his strongest supporters, that an investigation of some kind must be held. If the administration could dictate the organization of the Assembly and, hence, of the investigating committee, Horton could reasonably hope that he would be given a clean bill of health and his administration a good whitewashing. On the other hand, the anti-administration forces hoped to organize the Assembly and dominate the committee so that enough dirt could be gathered at least to discredit, if not to impeach, Horton.

Ed Crump kept tactfully quiet. He had supported Horton in 1930 but basically he opposed Luke Lea and was quite willing to get into the fight to oust Horton. But accustomed to victory as he was, he wanted to make sure that the chances for getting Horton out of the governor's chair were good. He had not joined the Public Emergency Committee and had not conducted any mass meetings in his own bailiwick of Memphis; but when on January 2 he came out with the statement that "there must be a sweeping investigation of state affairs, the guilt or innocence

[7] Memphis *Press-Scimitar*, December 13, 1930.
[8] *Time*, xvii (June 8, 1931), 19.

of any one should be determined by the facts,"[9] it became evident that
he was in the fight against Horton and his old political enemy, Luke
Lea.

The Assembly convened as scheduled on January 5 and the Democratic caucus of the two houses met to designate candidates for speakers.
In the House caucus Walter M. Haynes, an outspoken anti-Horton
man, was nominated speaker easily on the first ballot, his election having been conceded for several days. In the Senate caucus the nomination was not such an easy matter as the speaker of the Senate would
become governor if the foes of Horton were successful in removing
him, and there were quite a few who were willing to become governor
by that route. The administration's candidate was W. K. Abernathy
while the Public Emergency Committee's man was H. C. Anderson.
A. B. Broadbrent, a close friend of the late Governor Peay, and C. L.
Cornelius were both looked upon as independent candidates, yet both
men were committed to an investigation of the affairs of the State. Ed
Crump came to Nashville a few days before the Assembly convened
and at the first meeting of the caucus it was announced for the first time
that he was placing a candidate in the race, namely, Scott Fitzhugh of
Memphis.[10]

There were twenty-five Democratic members of the Senate and fifteen votes were necessary to nominate a candidate for the speakership.
The caucus met on January 5 and on the first ballot the administration's
candidate, Abernathy, had ten votes with the other fifteen scattered
among the other four candidates, Fitzhugh receiving only three. Several
other ballots were taken on that day with no change in the voting. On
the following day the five votes for Anderson went to Fitzhugh, bringing his total to eight. On the eleventh ballot, the first one taken in the
afternoon of the second day's voting, the administration support of Abernathy also shifted to Fitzhugh, giving him more than enough votes
to obtain the nomination, which was tantamount to election. The action
of the administration supporters seems to have been due to the fact that
they recognized they could not muster enough votes to elect their candidate and preferred a Crump-directed investigation to one directed by
any of the other candidates.[11] They realized there were many people in
Tennessee who would support them just because Crump was the leader
of the fight against them.

In accepting the speakership, Fitzhugh stated that he stood on
Crump's platform for a thorough investigation. But his election meant

[9] *Nashville Banner*, January 2, 1931.
[10] Memphis *Commercial Appeal*, January 7, 1931.   [11] *Ibid.*

that if Horton were impeached and convicted, Ed Crump would be in a position to dictate the policies of the State. There were many who did not like that prospect, even though they opposed the Horton administration. The Scripps-Howard papers, the Knoxville *News-Sentinel* and the Memphis *Press-Scimitar*, expressed this feeling as follows:

Will he [Scott Fitzhugh] govern his course with an eye to political advantage only? If so, the future holds nothing for him. For the people of Tennessee have had enough of puppets. They will see no advantage in exchanging a puppet of Lea and Caldwell for a puppet of E. H. Crump. Nor do the people of Tennessee see any good in swapping the Lea-Caldwell machine for the Crump machine. The Crump machine is the greater danger, if anything, for while Lea-Caldwell was a temporary tho destructive flash, Crump has been with us for years, denying the people of Shelby County a chance to express their will and thus corrupting the entire state election.[12]

Crump realized that too much apparent interference from him would engender enough discord to defeat his purpose, so when Fitzhugh was elected speaker he left Nashville and the Assembly to its own affairs.

Less than a week after the Assembly had convened it passed Senate Joint Resolution Number 1 providing for a thorough and complete investigation of all the departments of the State. This resolution set up a joint committee of twelve members, composed of five senators and seven representatives, to be appointed by the speakers, and empowered to investigate the activities of any and all private citizens, firms and corporations "who may have been directly or indirectly connected with transactions with the State or any of its officials." Further, it was instructed to employ auditors of a "national reputation" to make an audit of all state departments. The resolution was approved by the Governor on January 13.[13] A week later a bill outlining in somewhat more detail the duties and powers of the committee was passed. Included in this bill was a provision granting immunity from criminal prosecution to all who testified before the committee and who claimed this protection.[14] The members of the committee were appointed by the speakers the day the resolution was signed and at its first meeting it was decided to add the two speakers, Haynes and Fitzhugh, as ex-officio members. After some wrangling with the public accountants of the State over the choice of the auditors, Haskins and Sells were employed to make the audit of the administrative departments of the State.

The committee had a broad task assigned to it indeed. To examine all of the departments of the State would have been quite a task but,

[12] Memphis *Press-Scimitar*, January 9, 1931.
[13] *Public Acts of Tennessee*, 1931, Senate Joint Resolution Number 1.
[14] *Ibid.*, Chapter 3.

when it was empowered to investigate all individuals and corporations with which the State or its officials had had any dealings, its scope of action became so large as to be almost impossible of accomplishment. However, it set about its work resolutely. The first six weeks of its hearings were confined to investigating the passage of acts by the Special Session of the General Assembly of 1929 relative to the deposit of state funds and the organization of the Funding Board; the activities of this board with respect to the sale of the $21,000,000 and $29,050,000 bond issues in 1929 and 1930 and the deposit of the funds therefrom; the losses of the State in insolvent banks; and the conduct of the Governor, the Treasurer, Comptroller, Secretary of State, Superintendent of Banks, and Attorney General relative to the fiscal affairs of the State. Many high state officials were summoned during this time and put through a severe examination. The Nashville sessions lasted until March 5 when the committee went to Knoxville to investigate the State's transactions with the Holston-Union National Bank and Holston Trust Company. The Federal receiver of the bank would not permit the committee to question anyone connected with that institution so the committee devoted two days to the affairs of the trust company and went back to Nashville to draft its interim report. This had to be submitted to the Assembly on March 16, that body having adjourned temporarily on February 4.

Meanwhile, on March 3 Ed Crump had gone to Nashville and issued a statement saying that the committee had already unearthed enough evidence to convict many of the state officials. In his declaration he branded Horton "an easy prey for designing selfish interests, gougers in the taxpayers' money," and attacked Lea, Caldwell, and numerous high officials of the State. He indicated his willingness to "join the people in purging Tennessee of its derelict officials at the earliest possible date."[15] Simultaneously, Horton attacked bitterly the methods of the committee and challenged it to call other witnesses to find out the whole truth rather than merely the opposition's version of it.[16] The following day he answered Crump, saying that the Shelby County politician had come to Nashville with his usual bodyguard and issued his manifesto bearing all the earmarks of a Mexican revolutionist.[17] This sparring between Horton and Crump continued sporadically and branded the whole procedure as primarily a political fight between the administration forces and Crump.

[15] *Nashville Banner*, March 4, 1931.
[16] *Ibid*.   [17] *Ibid*., March 5, 1931.

When the legislature reassembled on March 16 the committee filed its interim report in which all fourteen members of the committee concurred. It was extremely critical of the administration, pointing out numerous examples of negligence, if not fraud, in the running of the State's affairs by the Funding Board, the Governor, and several other high officials. The committee desired to continue its investigation, most of the anti-administration men favoring this course, and, although Crump had announced that the committee had already done enough, he did not block the move for it to continue its hearings. The administration forces tried to halt its work but their opponents were too strong to allow this and on the day the Assembly reconvened it agreed to adjourn again from March 21 until May 25 when the committee was instructed to file another report.[18] It was expected that at this May session Horton would be impeached.

After filing its interim report and receiving instructions from the Assembly to continue its work, the committee resumed hearings. At this time it began calling former officials of Caldwell and Company, the first of which was J. DeWitt Carter. Carter's testimony showed clearly the break between himself and Rogers Caldwell. Testifying under the immunity granted him by the statute, Carter delved deeply into the shaky financial condition of Caldwell and Company and the Bank of Tennessee, pointing out that if the state deposits had not been received these institutions would have failed much sooner than they did. He presented all the letters he had written Rogers Caldwell as exhibits to his testimony, which painted Caldwell in the worst possible manner and himself in the best. He discussed the violations of trust agreements, insisting that he had been very active trying to clear up this abuse and that he had not received any co-operation from Caldwell or Heitzeberg. On the whole the testimony seems to have been an effort to discredit Rogers Caldwell as completely as possible and to create for himself a name of highest integrity and honesty.

Carter was followed on the stand by E. A. Goodloe, cashier of the Bank of Tennessee, and E. B. Smith, trust officer of the bank and of Caldwell and Company. These two men testified primarily concerning the trust violations and the substitution of the securities held by the Bank of Tennessee under the agreement entered into between Robertson and Caldwell and Company when the bank had been examined in September. They were in general more considerate of the good name of their former employer than Carter had been.

The final Caldwell officer called to testify was T. G. Donovan. Granted

[18] Memphis *Commercial Appeal*, March 16, 1931.

the same immunity as the others, Donovan proved to be completely loyal to Caldwell, the press characterizing him as a witness from whom it was very difficult to obtain any pertinent information. He denied that it was certain that the company was insolvent several months before it closed and that it could not have met the withdrawal of the State's funds in October. He insisted that the fact that Brentwood House was on the property of James E. Caldwell was unknown to any of the employees of the Bank of Tennessee and that they were all acting in good faith when they listed this house as an asset of the bank. He testified as to the earnings made by the participants in the syndicates handling the state bond issues in 1929 and 1930, but refused to admit that an agreement existed between Caldwell and Company and Lehman Brothers to handle these bonds. He in no way implicated Caldwell in the violation of the trust agreements; but his efforts to protect his former employer were largely in vain for Carter had already told enough to damn him in the eyes of most people and to start criminal action against him.[19] This was one of the desired results from the committee's work and no more Caldwell officials were called.

The activities of Caldwell and Company, however, were not allowed to recede completely from the picture for the committee next turned to an investigation of the State Department of Highways and Public Works. Former commissioners C. Neil Bass and Harry S. Berry, and the present commissioner, Robert H. Baker, were called in turn and each testified that Luke Lea had tried to get him to specify Kyrock without competition for many of the state roads. The committee then turned to other matters, investigating to some extent all the departments of the State. It found out what the State had been paying for nearly everything it bought: printing, automobile tires, road materials, dairy feed, highway signs, and other minor items. On the whole the testimony taken was extremely damaging to the Horton administration.

The partisan attitude that the majority of the committee took led in the early part of April to a break between its members. Five members were won over to the administration and tried to prevent the committee from completely discrediting Horton. Differences of opinion also arose over what powers were granted the committee as well as over the intolerance of some of the members of the committee and of the public press as to the rights and opinions of the minority. The minority unsuccessfully attempted both to get the committee to call certain additional witnesses and to ask questions of those witnesses who were called, both of which they hoped would change somewhat the nature of the commit-

[19] See Chapter XVIII, *infra*.

tee's findings. All of these things served to widen the breach between the majority and minority. The whole committee ceased taking evidence on May 8 and a subcommittee was appointed, composed solely of the members of the majority, to draft the committee's second report. This report was submitted to the committee as a whole on May 20, five days before the Assembly was to reconvene, and was adopted by the majority over the objections of the minority.[20] Thereupon, the minority members drafted another report.

On May 23, two days before the Assembly was to meet, Governor Horton, in an address dedicating a bridge, charged that Crump had already picked out the men who would get the jobs if and when the impeachment proceedings were successful. He pictured Crump as "a man who struts like a peacock with his cane on his arm and crows like a bantam rooster. I heard Mr. Crump is starting out tomorrow with a brass band. He has already rented one hundred rooms at a hotel. They are going to storm the legislature with the cry 'Oust Horton.' What has Crump done in Memphis that would justify turning the State over to him?"[21] The following day Crump gathered together a score of his lieutenants, but minus the brass band and without having rented quite one hundred rooms, and moved on Nashville.[22]

On May 25 the Assembly convened for the third time and both the majority and minority reports were submitted to it. The majority report criticized severely the State Funding Board, the failure of the Superintendent of Banks properly to examine the Bank of Tennessee, and the manner in which the Highway Department had been made a political tool. Thirteen sections of the report dealt with the activities of other departments of the State and certain of the higher officials. The final section, dealing with the chief executive, was a detailed account of the failure of Horton to conduct the affairs of the State on a high plane and a catalog of his supposed violations of his oath of office. Among the Governor's acts adversely enumerated were the sale of the bonds in 1929 and 1930 and the deposit of the funds resulting therefrom in the Bank of Tennessee; the calling of the legislature in 1929 to pass acts which aided Caldwell interests; the appointment of Robertson as Superintendent of Banks at the request of Luke Lea; the discharge of highway commissioners Bass and Berry because they would not conduct their department in a way satisfactory to Lea and Caldwell; the promising of roads and bridges for political purposes; and the granting of pardons to ob-

[20] *Minority Report*, pp. 722-26.
[21] Memphis *Commercial Appeal*, May 24, 1931.
[22] *Ibid.*, May 25, 1931.

tain votes. The majority stated at the end of its report that it had "endeavored honestly and fairly to find the facts."[23]

The minority report, signed by five of the fourteen members of the committee, attacked the majority report as an instrument based on the majority's own interpretation of the testimony and containing conclusions much stronger than the testimony justified. It charged that full credibility was given to the testimony of some witnesses which was largely "hearsay, suspicions, general rumors, and inferences." After relating the breach between members of the committee, the minority report summed up the evidence, giving particular attention to that which would tend to controvert the conclusions of the majority report. The minority report contained no reference to the actions of Governor Horton or any of the other officials of the State, claiming that the function of the committee was simply to present the evidence obtained and not to draw conclusions therefrom.[24]

Submitted along with the reports of the committee was the audit of the departments of the State which had been made by Haskins and Sells. The last witness that had been called by the committee was J. H. O'Connell, Haskins and Sells' representative in charge of the audit. The minority members of the committee had tried to introduce the fact that his firm had made an audit of certain departments of the city of Memphis when Crump had resigned as mayor in 1915 in the face of ouster proceedings, but the majority members strangled this attempt. The administration press was not so effectively bridled, the *Tennessean* pointing out that the report of the auditors made the same charges against the Horton administration that had been made against Crump fifteen years before. This paper related that:

Late in January, 1931, when "Boss" Crump was picking his auditors for his personally selected probe committee he called upon the same auditors who found plenty in support of his ouster in Memphis under a cloud of corruption and filth of government. Apparently the auditors referred to their files on the subject of public affairs and pulled out a form blank "No. 38" or whatever it was and started filling in the blanks with the names of state officials. And the funny thing again is that Haskins and Sells charged "Ousted Mayor" Ed Crump with the same crimes they now charge are so heinous in the state government. Reference to the audit of Haskins and Sells of June 25, 1916, reveals that by erasing the names of Ed Crump and his ward heelers from the 1916 report, the state probe committee is now getting the same report with the name of a state official inserted. The difference appears to be in the cost. Memphis got its audit of "Boss" Crump for $15,000 and "Boss" Crump hired

[23] *Second Report*, pp. 640-46.   [24] *Minority Report*, pp. 725 ff.

the same firm 16 years later for a mere $250,000. The report is the same—
the cost varies only $235,000.[25]

The report of the audit showed numerous violations of law and laxness
in the handling of the affairs of the State. Certain recommendations for
changes in the administrative setup were made which the administration charged would give Crump a chance to fill six additional fat jobs
if he could oust Horton. The auditors advised an improved budgetary
system to take care of the State's increasing expenditure of money, but
none of their proposals got further than that stage.

The members of the General Assembly were not particularly, if at
all, interested in improving the administrative organization of the State.
The various reports that had been submitted gave them a chance for a
much more exciting occupation, namely, trying to impeach the Governor. On May 25, the same day the reports were filed with the Assembly,
Republican Representative Tom Taylor, who had been one of the first
calling for the impeachment of Horton, introduced a resolution calling
for the appointment of a committee of the House to draw up articles
of impeachment against the Governor, and on the following day the resolution was adopted by a vote of 71 to 25.[26] It would seem that at least
up to this time there was a preponderance of sentiment in the House
against Horton. Speaker Haynes appointed John Tipton as chairman of
the committee, Tom Taylor as secretary, and three other representatives
who were opposed to Horton. The committee was ready with the first
article of impeachment on May 29, four days after its appointment.[27]

The first article charged that Horton, ever since the death of Governor Peay, had been a member of an unlawful conspiracy with Luke
Lea and Rogers Caldwell; that under this conspiracy acts had been committed which perverted and obstructed the administration of law; and
that the purpose of the conspiracy was the "personal advantage, ag-
grandizement and pecuniary gain" of the co-conspirators, and the enabling of Horton continuously "to remain in the office of Governor and
use the powers and influence of that office" for the advantages of himself and confederates. The article then went into a detailed account of
the connections between Caldwell and Lea, the financial condition of
their companies, the ways in which Horton could gain by securing the
support of Caldwell and Lea, and the advantages to these two from controlling the Governor. Ten specific charges were introduced as evidence
of the existence of the conspiracy, including the dismissal of three state

[25] May 18, 1931.
[26] House Journal, 1931, pp. 815, 834.
[27] Ibid., p. 871.

commissioners because Luke Lea desired it, the appointment of D. D. Robertson as Superintendent of Banks, the sale of the large bond issues in 1929 and 1930 and the deposit of the funds in Lea-Caldwell banks, the calling of the Special Session in 1929, and the specifying of Kyrock without competition for roads in the State.[28]

A few days later the committee brought in seven additional articles of impeachment. These articles primarily made separate counts of some of the charges that had been contained in the first, more general article. In addition, the Governor was charged with granting a pardon on a purely political basis and with being guilty of gross breaches of decorum in that he spent $2,850 for a piano for the governor's mansion which had been appropriated by the Assembly but which the Governor had said he would not spend, and in that he made a statement at the time of Caldwell and Company's failure to the effect that the State would lose none of its $7,000,000 in closed banks, which statement represented "either the willingness of the Governor to try to impose upon the supposed ignorance of the people of Tennessee, or amounts to a showing that his condition is such that he is not fit and capable longer to hold the office of Governor."[29] In general, all the articles of impeachment were based upon the relations of Horton with Lea and Caldwell, only two of the eight articles failing to mention the name of Rogers Caldwell and only one the name of Luke Lea.

While the articles of impeachment were being drawn up, the forces for and against Horton were making their alignments and strategic shifts. The public recognized the fight as one between Horton, Lea, and the administration on one side, and the anti-administration forces led by Crump on the other, a leadership which hurt the impeachment cause in some quarters. Rural legislators realized that the removal of Horton would place Speaker Fitzhugh in the governor's chair and make Crump dominant in Tennessee affairs. Most of these legislators hated and feared Crump and were unwilling to place him in power. Crump knew this and, in a move which showed that his chief desire was to oust Horton, he had Scott Fitzhugh resign as speaker on Friday, May 29, the day the first article of impeachment was presented to the House. This act was quite unexpected and created some confusion among administration forces as the question of a successor to Fitzhugh had to be settled before anything else could be done. A deal was made by some Democratic factions with the Republican members of the Senate to support Broadbrent, an avowed opponent of Crump, who had sought the position when Fitzhugh was elected. Thus when the Senate convened on Monday morn-

[28] *Ibid.*, pp. 884-936.　　　　[29] *Ibid.*, pp. 964-1006.

ing, Broadbrent's was the only name presented and he became Speaker. Nine Democrats, however, refused to vote for him, claiming that no Democratic caucus had been called and that the candidate had been hand-picked by a small group behind closed doors in the Andrew Jackson Hotel in Nashville.[30]

The second report of the committee drawing up the articles of impeachment containing Articles II to VIII was presented on June 2, the day following Broadbrent's election. A vote was not then taken and during the delay both sides tried to enlarge their voting strength. Rural legislators were appealed to by the anti-administrationists on the grounds that Crump had removed the appearance of personal advantage from the impeachment of Horton but some were not convinced. Meanwhile, the administration forces entered into an agreement with J. Will Taylor, an East Tennessee Republican boss, whereby the Republican members of the House would vote against impeachment in exchange for roads.[31] Finally, on Friday, June 5, the first article of impeachment was voted on in the House. Tom Taylor, a Republican who remained with the anti-administrationists, dramatically moved the vote "in the name of George Washington, of truth and honesty in government and of all the saints in history."[32] The result was 41 for impeachment and 58 against with the 13 Republican members who voted against impeachment wielding the balance of power. A motion to reject Article I passed by a vote of 52 to 47, thus removing it from further consideration.[33]

Over the following week end, the anti-Horton forces made a final effort to muster sufficient support to oust Horton on one of the other seven articles. The House met on Monday to consider private bills only but on Tuesday it voted on the remaining articles. The Horton opponents realized their fight was at an end when John Tipton moved that remaining articles be considered as one article and voted on accordingly. This was agreed and Tipton's motion to adopt these articles failed by a vote of 40 to 56. The motion to reject them passed by a vote of 53 to 45 and Horton had been saved from an impeachment trial before the State Senate.[34]

The failure of the House to pass the articles of impeachment probably can be laid largely at the feet of those trying to bring this about. Grave tactical blunders were made from the start. In the first place the election of Crump's candidate, Scott Fitzhugh, as Speaker of the Senate,

[30] *Senate Journal of the 67th General Assembly of the State of Tennessee,* 1931.
[31] Memphis *Commercial Appeal,* June 5, 1931.
[32] *Ibid.,* June 6, 1931.
[33] *House Journal,* 1931, p. 1068.
[34] *Ibid.,* p. 1099.

placed the Memphis politician in too prominent a position in the fight for the good of the cause. The major blunder, however, came in March when the Assembly reconvened to receive the interim report of the Investigating Committee. At that time there was harmony among the committee, all members having signed the report. Feeling against the administration was running high and if the articles of impeachment had been drawn up at that time they very probably would have passed the House. The desire of the anti-administration forces to complete the investigation proved to be a godsend for Horton. It gave him time to strengthen his defense, to distribute his patronage where it was most effective, and to gain support with jobs, pardons, and good roads.[35] The final blunders came when the Assembly met the last of May to receive the second report of the committee. There was still a possibility of the House's voting for impeachment if quick action were taken. Instead of this there was inexcusable and unexplicable delay. On one occasion after the articles had been presented, Speaker Haynes in a speech before the House developed quite a strong sentiment against Horton but instead of taking a vote at the end of his speech he allowed the House to adjourn over the week end when the wirepulling continued and the Horton forces were given the chance to get their men back in line.

In addition to these blunders, Horton gained because of sentimental considerations. Many of the older members of the House did not want to mar the name of the State with an impeachment proceeding, regardless of the justification. A general apathy among the citizens of Tennessee also helped. Crookedness in public office had long since lost its novelty and the seven months that had elapsed since the crash in November that led to the impeachment movement ameliorated much of the bitter feeling against the Governor.[36] It became clear to many that Horton was the mere pawn of Luke Lea and Rogers Caldwell and they thought he should not be too severely punished for his weakness.

The question remains, however, as to whether Horton should have been impeached. There can be no doubt that Henry Horton allowed himself to be led wherever Luke Lea and Rogers Caldwell desired. Further, there can be no doubt that some of his acts at the request of Lea and Caldwell were morally and ethically unjustified, if not illegal. The deposit of large amounts of state funds with the Bank of Tennessee secured by almost worthless personal surety bonds is an outstanding example. If civil units are ever to obtain good government they must take action against those officials who are derelict in the performance of their

[35] Memphis *Commercial Appeal*, June 6, 1931.
[36] *Ibid.*

duties and Governor Horton certainly was in this class. Mere weakness should be no excuse but, rather, the difficulties into which the weak are led more easily than the strong should deter the weak from aspiring to those places of leadership which only the most capable should occupy. The Memphis *Press-Scimitar* took a rather well-justified position when it said, "It is a sad commentary on the affairs of citizenship that a political outfit as dumb or as crooked as the one that has controlled the State of Tennessee can remain unconvicted by the judge and jury which is the Legislature."[37]

After the impeachment of Horton failed, Senate Joint Resolution Number 43 was passed, directing that in the "interest of economy and for the general welfare, peace, and good of the people" the investigation be stopped and that all expenses after June 9 cease except the payment for ten additional days to the chief auditor, his confidential secretary, and three assistants. When completed, the investigation had cost the State $261,000, the largest expense item of which was the $184,000 paid the auditors.[38]

The State gained little if anything from the investigation of the events that led to its loss of approximately $6,500,000 in closed banks. The recommendations of the auditors were in no case followed and the administration made no efforts, or at least failed, to improve its performance. The only constructive legislation arising from the entire debacle was a bill definitely setting forth how all state funds were to be deposited. Under this bill, banks could receive state deposits up to 25 per cent of their capital and surplus, to be covered either by personal surety bonds for twice the amount of the deposit or by collateral or a bond of a qualified surety company equal to the amount of the deposit, with the provision that no deposit of more than $200,000 could be secured by a personal surety bond. Banks desiring state deposits greater than 25 per cent of their capital and surplus could obtain them by pledging collateral or surety company bonds. Finally, the state treasurer could at his discretion deposit excess funds in New York banks.[39]

The legislature continued in session until July 2, and at times the impeachment of Horton was brought up but no further action was taken. The remainder of Horton's term, which expired in January, 1933, was rather uneventful. In the Democratic primary in 1932 the Horton-Lea-Caldwell issue was renewed to a degree. Hill McAllister, who had run for governor in 1926 and 1928, announced on a platform calling for wide-

---

[37] June 6, 1931.
[38] Miscellaneous Appropriation Bill, *Public Acts of Tennessee*, 1931, Chapter 86.
[39] *Public Acts of Tennessee*, 1931, Chapter 104.

spread reform in the management of the affairs of the State. He was opposed by Lewis S. Pope, who had the support of Luke Lea and was looked upon as the Horton candidate, and by former Governor Malcolm R. Patterson, who ran as an independent candidate. Patterson took enough votes away from Pope to allow McAllister to obtain the nomination, which was tantamount to election. McAllister's promised reforms, as is too frequently the case in similar situations, failed, on the whole, to materialize.

CHAPTER XVIII

CRIMINAL PROSECUTIONS

THE DEMAND that Governor Horton be impeached was accompanied by an even stronger demand that there be some "stripe wearing and chain clanging" on the part of the private individuals responsible for the financial calamity. This demand, so far as it arose in Nashville, reached its peak at the time the Investigating Committee was delving into the relationships of the state of Tennessee with the Bank of Tennessee and Caldwell and Company. While this committee was not a grand jury with the power to return an indictment against anyone, its hearings brought to light some of the activities of Rogers Caldwell and Luke Lea which to the average man were obviously criminal.

In Nashville the protagonists of vigorous criminal prosecutions were led by the *Banner* which devoted about as many front page editorials to demanding the indictments of Lea and Caldwell as to the removal of Horton. It repeatedly called attention to the fact that the attorney general of Davidson County, R. M. Atkinson, was neglecting his duty in not presenting evidence against Lea and Caldwell to the grand jury. Atkinson was generally known to be a Lea man, and his failure to obtain an indictment against either Lea or Caldwell was thought by many to be due to this fact.

In February, 1931, while the Investigating Committee was relatively new at its job, the *Banner* editorialized as follows:

The people of Davidson County, as well as the entire citizenship of Tennessee, are awaiting with a degree of apprehension some slight sign of action on the part of the Attorney General of Davidson County in presenting information in the present State probe to the grand jury of this county for such action as that inquisitorial body may deem to take under the circumstances. . . .

Since that time [the crash of the Bank of Tennessee] information has come to light that banks have been wrecked; State, county, and municipal treasuries have been looted of many millions; industrial corporations have been sent to the wall; individual fortunes have been ruined; there have been suicides in three states, including Tennessee, all the result of a politico-banco combination with which the Attorney General of this county has been affiliated in the past. . . .

With the possible exception of the Governor of the State, the Banner knows of no one who maintains an air of complete ignorance and innocence of the state of affairs in which Tennessee and her sister commonwealths find themselves just now as does the Attorney General. . . .[1]

INDICTMENTS

Criminal action against Lea, Caldwell, and other individuals connected with the collapse of the previous November was soon forthcoming, but the first indictments did not arise in Nashville. This honor fell to Knoxville where an indictment against J. Basil Ramsey, as president of the Holston Trust Company, was returned on March 6, shortly after the Investigating Committee had examined the affairs of that institution and recommended Ramsey's indictment for fraudulent breach of trust. These charges arose from the use Ramsey had made of $250,000 of Tennessee highway funds which had been deposited in the Holston Trust Company. The State charged that these funds were placed in trust and could not be handled as general deposits and that Ramsey had employed them as such.[2]

This action seems to have been the signal for a wave of indictments against everyone in a prominent position in all the larger banks that went under with Caldwell and Company. On March 8 the Federal grand jury, sitting at Greenville, Tennessee, returned two indictments against Lea, Caldwell, and Ramsey: one, for conspiracy to violate the national banking laws; and the other charging specifically that Ramsey had had the Holston-Union National Bank lend Lea and Caldwell $98,000 when Lea already owed the bank $120,000, the latter amount being the limit of loans to one party the bank could legally make at that time.[3]

The following day, March 9, Rogers Caldwell was indicted in Nashville by the Davidson County grand jury on six counts; namely, (1) fraudulent breach of trust, (2) accessory to fraudulent breach of trust, (3) grand larceny, (4) accessory to grand larceny, (5) receiving property feloniously obtained by fraudulent breach of trust, and (6) receiving stolen property. All of these charges grew out of the breach of a trust covering funds of Hardeman County, Tennessee, which were deposited with Caldwell and Company, the Bank of Tennessee acting as trustee.[4] This deposit, under the terms of the trust, was to be secured by municipal bonds, when, as a matter of fact, stocks and bonds of industrial corporations were pledged, including the stock of the Nashville Baseball Association. Rogers Caldwell was charged with the offenses as president of both the Bank of Tennessee and Caldwell and Company.

When this indictment was returned, Attorney General Atkinson announced that the "big case" growing out of the Nashville financial dis-

[1] February 19, 1931.
[2] *Nashville Banner*, March 6, 7, 1931.
[3] *Ibid.*, March 9, 1931.
[4] *Caldwell Brief*, pp. 1, 2.

aster was still under preparation.[5] This big case was evidently the indictment against Caldwell which was returned on March 20 charging that he, as president of the Bank of Tennessee, had received a deposit of $6,500 in this bank on October 28, 1930, when the bank was insolvent. This was the last indictment obtained by Atkinson against anyone connected with the Caldwell collapse. Since there were at least twelve violated trusts when Caldwell and Company failed and since millions had been lost through financial practices that, to say the least, were of a highly questionable character, it appears probable that Atkinson was protecting somewhat his political affiliates, when his big case involved a deposit of only $6,500.

The issues were not so lightly handled in Kentucky where Rogers Caldwell was indicted first by a State, and later by a Federal, grand jury. On April 3 the Commonwealth of Kentucky charged Caldwell with obtaining property by false statement in writing and on May 2 a substitute indictment was returned charging him with obtaining property by false statement. Both of these indictments were based upon the merger contract of Caldwell and Company and BancoKentucky Company in which Rogers Caldwell claimed Caldwell and Company had a net worth of $9,000,000 and thereby obtained 900,000 shares of Banco stock.[6] The Federal indictments in Kentucky did not come until June 22, when Rogers Caldwell, James B. Brown, president of the National Bank of Kentucky, and Charles F. Jones, cashier and later vice president of this bank, were all indicted on six counts. In five of these counts Brown and Jones were charged with misapplication of the funds of the National Bank of Kentucky, and Rogers Caldwell with aiding and abetting in this misapplication. These counts covered five loans made by the National Bank of Kentucky to Caldwell and Company and its affiliates from September 5 to October 20, 1930, which totaled $1,000,000. The sixth count charged the three men with conspiracy to misapply the funds of the bank. The overt acts of Rogers Caldwell listed in the last count were the formation of Southern Banks, Incorporated, and the writing of a letter concerning the loans covered in the first five counts.[7]

Meanwhile, indictments arising out of the November crash were being returned in other states. The collapse of the Central Bank and Trust Company of Asheville, North Carolina, gave rise to a series of indict-

[5] *Nashville Banner*, March 10, 1931.

[6] From Indictments against Rogers Caldwell in Jefferson County Court, Criminial Division, Louisville, Kentucky.

[7] From a copy of Indictments in the case *United States of America v. James B. Brown, Charles F. Jones, and Rogers Caldwell*, U. S. District Court for the Western District of Kentucky.

ments in March and April, 1931. First, in March, Wallace B. Davis, president of the bank, and J. A. Sinclair and C. N. Brown, two of its directors, were indicted on two counts, the first charging that they had made a fraudulent report of the condition of the bank to the Corporation Commission of North Carolina on October 18, 1930, and second, that they had published this report in the *Asheville Times*.[8] Then in April two indictments were returned which concerned Lea's activities in the Central Bank and were against Luke Lea, Luke Lea, Jr., Wallace B. Davis, and E. P. Charlet, an employee of Lea. These indictments charged that the four men had conspired with each other and with J. Charles Bradford, cashier of the bank who was then in a sanitarium in Pennsylvania, to misapply the funds of the bank and had actually misapplied them to the extent of over $1,000,000.[9]

In Arkansas, the state which had suffered the greatest number of bank failures in the Caldwell collapse, the courts found grounds for indictments arising out of these failures. On March 18, 1931, A. B. Banks was indicted by a Mississippi County grand jury for receiving deposits in the First State Bank of Osceola while it was insolvent.[10] Several weeks later Banks was indicted on the same charge with respect to the American Exchange Trust Company of Little Rock.[11]

This relatively large crop of indictments did not appease the *Nashville Banner* because Luke Lea had not yet been indicted for any of his operations in Nashville. Particularly was it felt that he should be indicted in connection with the failure of the Liberty Bank and Trust Company whose president, R. E. Donnell, had hanged himself on November 27. The *Banner*, through its editorials, prodded Atkinson to bring action against Lea. The Davidson County grand jury on May 1 issued a public statement that nothing involving the Liberty Bank and Trust Company had ever been presented to it[12] and the next day the *Banner* called for either the impeachment or resignation of Atkinson, to which Atkinson only insisted that there were no grounds on which he could bring an indictment. On July 9 Judge Charles Gilbert of the first division of the Davidson County Criminal Court ordered Atkinson to file a bill of indictment not later than July 14 against Luke Lea and Luke Lea, Jr., in connection with the failure of the Liberty Bank. Following an extension of the time to July 20, Atkinson, on July 18, appeared before Judge Gilbert and claimed that the Court had no right

---

[8] *State of North Carolina v. Wallace B. Davis*, 203 North Carolina 49-51 (1932). Cited hereafter as *State v. Davis*.

[9] *Lea Record*, pp. 3-10.

[11] *Ibid*., April 28, 1931.

[10] *Nashville Banner*, March 19, 1931.

[12] *Ibid*., May 1, 1931.

to issue a mandatory order for an indictment, and reiterated his position that there were no grounds on which to return an indictment. The court would not rescind its order, however, and while Atkinson was appealing to the Tennessee Supreme Court to set aside the order, Gilbert, on July 21, appointed Seth Walker, a prominent Nashville attorney, as attorney general pro tem to file an indictment against the Leas with the grand jury. A few days later the Supreme Court held that the lower court did have the right to order the attorney general to bring the indictment and Walker proceeded with his duties.[13]

Accordingly, on August 10 the Davidson County grand jury returned an indictment against Luke Lea, Luke Lea, Jr., J. B. Ramsey, W. S. Chappell, former cashier of the Liberty Bank, and R. B. Mosely and E. P. Charlet, employees of Lea, on charges of conspiracy to defraud the Liberty Bank of more than $150,000. Under Tennessee law, conspiracy is only a misdemeanor, carrying a maximum penalty of eleven months and twenty-nine days in jail or a fine of $500 or both.[14] Thus, with all the agitation that the Leas be indicted in Nashville, the base of their operations, and with the appointment of a special attorney general to obtain this indictment, the severest charge that could be made against them was a misdemeanor. Colonel Lea had evidently kept relatively close to the letter of the law if not to the spirit in his dealings with the Liberty Bank. The failure of Walker to bring an indictment for a felony against the Leas was at least a partial vindication for Atkinson.

The final indictments that can be traced directly to the crash of Caldwell and Company came out of the failure of the same institution that gave rise to the first, namely, the Holston-Union National Bank in Knoxville. These indictments involved Lea and Ramsey and were returned by the Federal grand jury in Knoxville on September 2, 1931. In a nine-count bill, listing many loans to the Knoxville Journal Company, to Luke Lea and to several of his controlled companies, Ramsey was charged with the willful misapplication of some $374,000 of the bank's funds and Lea charged with aiding and abetting Ramsey in this willful misapplication.[15] Rogers Caldwell was not named in this indictment as had been the case in the earlier ones returned by the Federal grand jury in connection with the failure of the Holston-Union National Bank.

Indicting the individuals connected with the crash of Caldwell and Company was only the first step. Some of the prosecutions made no further progress but several of them led to trials which will now be considered.

---

[13] *Ibid.*, July 9-27, 1931.
[14] *Ibid.*, August 10, 1931.
[15] *Ibid.*, September 3, 1931.

Rogers Caldwell's Trial in Nashville

The trial of Rogers Caldwell on the indictments against him involving the Hardeman County trust was set for June 1 by Judge Chester Hart of the second division of the Davidson County Criminal Court. Caldwell's efforts to obtain a continuance and change of venue on the ground that public feeling in Nashville against him was so great that a fair and impartial trial could not be had at that time were overruled by Judge Hart, who said that evidence presented in court and his own "private investigations and observations" convinced him that undue prejudice did not exist, even though Rogers Caldwell's trial was started at the height of the Horton impeachment fight.[16]

After some delay with preliminary hearings and the impaneling of the jury, the State began presenting evidence on June 10. The first witnesses were three officials of Hardeman County who testified concerning the size of the county, the purchase of the bonds by Caldwell and Company, the trust agreement entered into to cover the deposit of funds, and the loss the county had sustained because the collateral securing the deposit was not of the type called for under the trust agreement. The principal witnesses of the State, however, were three former officials of Caldwell and Company, E. B. Smith, former trust officer, E. A. Goodloe, former cashier of the Bank of Tennessee, and J. D. Carter, all of whom had been called before the Legislative Investigating Committee earlier in the year. T. G. Donovan, who had also testified before this committee, was not called as a witness, a fact which may be explained by Donovan's reticence to tell anything to the committee that would harm his former employer and also because it was established in the trial that Donovan had nothing to do with the trusts.[17] The introduction as state witnesses of these three men who had been formerly connected with Caldwell and Company added bitterness to the trial that would have probably been lacking otherwise. Smith and Goodloe could hardly be classed as effective witnesses for the State since their testimony tended to show that Rogers Caldwell was not familiar with the condition of the trusts in general nor the Hardeman County trust in particular because he did not supervise the internal operations of Caldwell and Company, and that Carter was the official who was responsible for the trusts.[18]

When Carter himself came to the stand it was an entirely different story. On direct examination he repeated his testimony given before the Legislative Investigating Committee earlier in the year, going into every detail which would paint Caldwell in as bad a light as possible. He tes-

---

[16] *Caldwell Brief*, pp. 132-33.

[17] *Ibid.*, p. 175.   [18] *Ibid.*, pp. 157-93.

tified that he knew of the trust violations as early as 1928 and had discussed the fact with Caldwell on numerous occasions prior to the failure of the company and that he had attempted to get Caldwell to provide adequate capital for the business so that trust violations could be stopped. Following this, Carter testified concerning his resignation on March 17, 1930, and introduced the letters he had written Caldwell as exhibits to his testimony. He averred that with these letters before him Rogers Caldwell necessarily knew the conditions that existed, and that he had consented to remain in the business only because Caldwell had agreed to clear up all violations of trusts. Carter stated he had constantly impressed upon Goodloe the necessity of getting the trusts in order and that when Goodloe began submitting monthly reports on the conditions of the trusts he took these matters up directly with Caldwell. He said further that Caldwell had stated in conversation concerning the condition of the business that, if necessary, his father, James E. Caldwell, would help out, and that if anything should happen to the business he, Rogers Caldwell, intended to assume full responsibility for all matters that had been irregularly handled.[19]

On cross-examination, Carter testified that he had received a salary of $37,700 annually from Caldwell and Company and subsidiary corporations, that he had not spoken to Caldwell nor offered one word of help or sympathy since the crash of the company, and that he furnished the State and the Legislative Investigating Committee all the letters offered by himself and Goodloe as exhibits. When asked, "And you did all that against the man that fed you for twelve years, didn't you?" Carter replied, "I have done a great deal for that man in those twelve years, too." The cross-examination tried unsuccessfully to draw out of Carter the idea that he, rather than Caldwell, was responsible for the condition of the trusts. Carter consistently maintained that he was merely an employee of the company and, while responsible for part of its operations, was not responsible for the conditions of the trusts.[20]

After Carter's testimony, the State rested and Rogers Caldwell took the stand as the only witness for the defense except a number of character witnesses. On direct examination Caldwell testified concerning the early operations of the business, the hiring of Carter as a bookkeeper at $175 a month and his advancement to vice president, the placing of Carter in charge of sales and then the adding of the accounting department, of which the trust department was a section, to his duties, and the reorganization of the accounting department at the suggestion of Carter. He stated that Carter had supervision of the trust department

[19] *Ibid.*, pp. 193-203.   [20] *Ibid.*, pp. 203-16.

and that he relied upon him to manage it properly for he had every confidence in him. Caldwell stated that he did not direct or permit any-one to remove the securities from the Hardeman County trust and did not know of its condition until October 24, 1930, and that he did not "directly or indirectly inaugurate, encourage, permit, or have any system of violating" any trusts of Caldwell and Company. On October 24, he testified, he assumed the responsibility for getting the trusts straightened out because he felt Carter had failed to make the proper efforts and that after he took charge he received very little co-operation from Carter. He averred that he had not seen any of the letters concerning trust violations Goodloe had written, except the one written on March 18. Upon the receipt of this letter he called in Carter, who told him the violations were merely temporary technical ones and would be immediately straightened out. He denied ever having read the letters which Carter wrote him on May 20 until they were published in the Nashville papers during the investigation by the legislative committee earlier in the year and stated that he had never discussed them with Carter. He admitted receiving them from Carter but alleged he was so busy with the BancoKentucky deal that he did not have time to read them, and, also, that there was no necessity for Carter to write him for their offices adjoined each other.[21]

On cross-examination the State attempted to get Caldwell to admit that as president of the company he was in charge of all of its operations and hence responsible for the condition of the trusts. He maintained, however, that the business was departmentalized with men in authority to do whatever they considered necessary and that he paid Carter "$120 every working day" to do the things necessary in his department. He stated that it was the greatest disappointment of his life to find that Carter was not maintaining the trusts in order.[22] Thus Caldwell based his defense largely upon the fact that Caldwell and Company had grown so large, and had such wide and diversified interests which he as president had to supervise, that he had had no time to look after details of the internal operations which had been left largely to Carter.

Carter's bitterness toward Caldwell came out more in the trial than at any other time and it was on Carter's evidence that the State largely rested its case. At one time during Carter's testimony, the tension between the two men became so great that Caldwell in open court challenged Carter to surrender his immunity so it could really be decided who was guilty. Carter replied that he was not on trial, which was technically cor-

---

[21] *Ibid.*, pp. 217-41. [22] *Ibid.*, pp. 242-51.

rect, yet the real issue was whether Carter or Caldwell, or both, or some-one else was criminally responsible for the condition of the trusts.

After arguments by counsel and the court's charge, the case was sub-mitted to the jury, which on July 6, over a month after the trial had be-gun, brought in a verdict of guilty on the first count of the indictment, namely, fraudulent breach of trust, and set the punishment at not more than three years in the state penitentiary. Verdicts of not guilty were rendered on the other counts. Hearings on a motion for a new trial were set for September and on September 3 Judge Hart denied this motion. Notice of appeal to the Tennessee Supreme Court was given and Cald-well was released on a bond of $10,000.

The decision of the Tennessee Supreme Court was handed down on April 30, 1932, and remitted Rogers Caldwell for retrial to the lower court. The bases given for the decision were: (1) that the trial court had ruled against a continuance and change of venue partly on the basis of evidence obtained from private investigation by the trial judge and, (2) because the verdict of the jury necessitated its giving full credence to Carter's testimony and rejecting that of Goodloe and Smith, the inference being that because the jury did this it was affected by the prejudice that ex-isted against Rogers Caldwell at the time of the trial.[23] After the decision was handed down, Judge Hart stated that the date for the new trial would be set immediately, but Attorney General Atkinson seemed to have been in no hurry to retry the case and took no action to do so. His inaction may well have been due partly to the fact that his principal wit-ness, Carter, had been somewhat discredited by the Supreme Court's de-cision. In any event a date was never set for the retrial and the court's decision, while remanding Caldwell for retrial, had the effect of acquit-ting him of the charges.

It was generally thought that Rogers Caldwell would be tried, as soon as his first case had been settled, on the grounds of receiving de-posits in the Bank of Tennessee while it was insolvent. In the early sum-mer, after some prodding by the press and the criminal judges, Atkinson reported to the Criminal Court that he could not prepare the case be-cause D. D. Robertson, who was receiver of the Bank of Tennessee, had refused to give him the necessary records. Robertson, on the other hand, maintained that T. G. Donovan had the records, but Donovan insisted that this was absurd since the receiver of a bankrupt institution natu-rally had its records. While it would have been an easy matter for the court to have taken action to locate the records, this was not done and on June 20, 1932, Atkinson was allowed to enter a nolle prosequi on the

[23] *State of Tennessee* v. *Rogers Caldwell*, 164 Tennessee 325 ff. (1932).

grounds that Robertson had refused to furnish him with competent and creditable testimony on which to base his case.[24] Thus, so far as the Nashville indictments were concerned, Caldwell became a free man.

The manner in which both of the Nashville indictments against Rogers Caldwell were handled raises serious questions of justice. As to the first case, it was an accepted fact that Rogers Caldwell did not physically remove the bonds from the Hardeman County trust or directly order anyone else to do so but that they were removed in the ordinary course of business. However, the view that the defendant was not thoroughly cognizant that his company had been violating trusts for many years seems almost impossible. Not only were Goodloe's memoranda and reports on the condition of the trusts available for him but also every audit report from 1926 to 1929 contained an account of violated trusts. Such evidence would, it seems, lend weight to the view that, while there may not have been a "general scheme or plan of corporate organization designed by the defendant" to violate trusts as the State charged, the frequency of trust violations was sufficient to result in some such condition. Further, while it is true there existed such a feeling against Rogers Caldwell in Nashville at the time of the trial that a fair and impartial trial was unlikely, feeling against him had subsided sufficiently after the Supreme Court ruling to enable a fair trial to be conducted. The failure of the Attorney General to conduct the trial a second time is rather strong presumptive evidence that, to say the least, he was not eager to prosecute Rogers Caldwell.

As to the second Nashville indictment, after this charge was dropped, the records of the Bank of Tennessee which were needed in the case have been used in preparing evidence in a civil suit, the Knox County case.[25] The Attorney General could have obtained them for his case by taking proper action against Robertson because, even if Robertson did not have them in his possession when they were needed, he was responsible for them and doubtless would have produced them had sufficient pressure been brought. The way this case was handled and the failure to retry the Hardeman County case leave little basis for any view other than that Atkinson was shielding Rogers Caldwell.

The only other indictments in Nashville connected with the Caldwell crash were the misdemeanor indictments against Luke Lea, Luke Lea, Jr., and several of their associates which Special Attorney General Seth Walker had returned. The Leas, in September, 1931, filed a plea asking that the indictments be set aside because they were not guilty of the charges made against them and because of the manner in which the in-

[24] Nashville Banner, June 20, 1932.   [25] See Chapter xix, infra.

dictments had been obtained.[26] This plea was denied and a hearing was set for October 26,[27] but at that time postponement was granted and the case dragged on without ever being tried and was finally dismissed. Those desiring to prosecute the Leas were probably not eager to try them on a misdemeanor charge, and also the fact that they had been convicted in Asheville prior to this time reduced the feeling that they must be convicted in Nashville.

THE KENTUCKY PROCEEDINGS

While he was being tried in Nashville, Rogers Caldwell was under indictments in Kentucky in both State and Federal courts. The Governor of Kentucky had issued requisition papers for the extradition of Rogers Caldwell to Kentucky before the Nashville trial actually began but Governor Horton was not willing to turn his very ardent supporter over to the authorities of another state unless absolutely necessary. Horton's first step to halt extradition was to refer the matter to State Attorney General L. D. Smith. In his opinion, rendered on June 1, 1931, Smith said that while the indictment was sufficient to grant the extradition, the Governor of Tennessee had a right to refuse it on the ground that the party demanded was under indictment in Tennessee and giving him up to the officials of Kentucky might result in Tennessee's losing its jurisdiction over him.[28] Armed with this statement, Horton, on June 6, announced that extradition of Rogers Caldwell had been temporarily denied because Caldwell was still under indictment in both State and Federal courts in Tennessee and Attorney General Atkinson had asked that the extradition be postponed until the courts in Tennessee had disposed of their indictments. Horton required Caldwell to post a bond of $25,-000 to assure his appearance at some later date when final action on the extradition would be taken.[29] After Caldwell's trial in Nashville had been completed and while the appeal was being made to the Supreme Court, Kentucky renewed its demand for Rogers Caldwell but Atkinson again came to his aid and filed a petition asking that Caldwell be kept in Tennessee pending the outcome of the appeal. Horton was still quite willing to accede to this request and again refused to grant extradition.[30] The United States District Court in Louisville initiated efforts to get Rogers Caldwell before it with a petition on July 31, 1931, in the District Court in Nashville, asking for his extradition. In answering the pe-

[26] *Nashville Banner*, September 9, 1931.   [27] *Ibid.*, September 16, 1931.
[28] "On the Requisition from the Governor of the Commonwealth of Kentucky for Extradition of Rogers Caldwell," *Opinions of Attorney General L. D. Smith*, October, 1930, to September, 1931, pp. 17-20.
[29] *Nashville Banner*, June 6, 1931.   [30] *Ibid.*, July 13, 1931.

tition, Caldwell denied guilt on any of the counts in the Federal indictments against him and stated that there was no probable cause to believe him guilty. Judge John J. Gore of the District Court of Nashville, on October 31, 1931, temporarily denied the demand that Caldwell be sent to Kentucky, pending settlement of Caldwell's case before the Tennessee Supreme Court. After that court remanded Caldwell for retrial, Judge Gore, on May 21, 1932, issued an order for Caldwell to appear and show cause why he should not be removed to Kentucky. After hearing the evidence, Judge Gore refused to order Rogers Caldwell's removal to Kentucky in an opinion which said in part:

The only question now before me is whether or not the proof establishes probable cause of guilt. . . . It is a serious thing to remove a man from his home for trial . . . and before the court could be justified in ordering the removal of a person, he must be judicially satisfied that probable cause of guilt exists. . . . It is conceded the loans were made. It is conceded the defendant was president and connected with other corporations which made the loans. But the facts are that every loan that was made was secured by what the defendant and the officers of the National Bank of Kentucky considered to be adequate. . . . Now the fact that the loans were made and the defendant or the institution with which he was connected was unable to pay them, of itself, does not show criminal intent. If we are going to hold a man guilty of conspiracy to defraud a bank simply because the value of the collateral pledged has shrunk and is destroyed I doubt if there is a business man in the United States but who would be guilty of the act. . . .[31]

The court failed to take into consideration that the National Bank of Kentucky had loaned Caldwell and Company and its affiliated companies $2,400,000 when the limit of loans to one party that the bank could legally make was $600,000. However, Judge Gore's position was soon upheld, for in July, 1932, when Brown and Jones were tried on the same charges made against Rogers Caldwell, they were given directed verdicts of not guilty by the court, an order which also applied to the Federal charges against Caldwell.[32]

Though the Federal charges were thus rendered null, the state indictments against Rogers Caldwell in Kentucky were still outstanding, but the Governor of Tennessee refused to order extradition. No further action was taken by Kentucky until March 2, 1935, when the Attorney General of Jefferson County moved to dismiss the charges against Caldwell contained in both state indictments. The bases given for this action were: first, that even should a conviction be possible, the State would be

---

[31] Decree in the case *United States of America*, ex rel. *Rogers Caldwell* v. *Lillard, United States Marshal for the Middle District of Tennessee, et al.*, No. 2236, United States District Court for the Middle District of Tennessee.   [32] *Nashville Banner*, October 10, 1932.

compelled to obtain its evidence by audit of numerous corporation records at a prohibitive expense, estimated by reliable accountants at from $25,000 to $35,000; and second, that "the false statement relied upon as to the net worth of Caldwell and Company as of a certain date is copied into the original indictment and shows it was a mere estimate subject to investigation and subsequent arbitration, hence the Commonwealth could not hope for a conviction even if we could disprove by proper audit that the various corporations' assets constituting the net worth of Caldwell and Company was so stated."[33] On this recommendation, the remaining charges against Rogers Caldwell in Kentucky were dropped without his facing trial on any of the indictments against him in that state.

THE ASHEVILLE BANK CASES

The first of the indictments growing out of the failure of the Central Bank and Trust Company to come to trial were those against Wallace B. Davis, president of the bank, and J. A. Sinclair and C. N. Brown, directors, for submitting a false report on the bank's condition to the North Carolina Corporation Commission and publishing this report in the papers. This case was tried in April, 1931, when the two directors were found not guilty of both charges and Davis found not guilty of submitting the false report to the Corporation Commission but guilty of publishing the same report and sentenced to a term in the state prison of from five to seven years. An appeal to the Supreme Court of North Carolina resulted in a divided opinion upholding the lower court and, after Davis's appeal to stay the execution of the sentence was disallowed, he went to prison.[34]

Meanwhile, Davis had faced trial on the other indictments arising out of the failure of the Central Bank and Trust Company in which he, Luke Lea, Luke Lea, Jr., and E. P. Charlet were charged with conspiracy to defraud the Central Bank and with actually having defrauded it of more than $1,000,000. The trial was set for July, 1931, a special session of the Superior Court of Buncombe County having been called to hear the case and Judge M. V. Barnhill appointed to preside by special dispensation. The trial of Lea on the Federal indictment arising out of the failure of the Holston-Union National Bank had been set in Knoxville for approximately the same date, and the Federal officials and the state of North Carolina had some disagreement over which would try Lea first with Lea trying to play each against the other and get both trials postponed. In this, however, he was not successful, the Federal authorities agreeing

---

[33] From original indictments against Rogers Caldwell, Jefferson County Circuit Court, Criminal Division, Louisville, Kentucky.   [34] *State* v. *Davis*, p. 49.

to postpone the Knoxville trial and allowing Lea to go on trial in Asheville as scheduled in July, 1931.

Taking of the State's evidence began on August 19. The State called numerous witnesses, including former employees and officers of the bank, several witnesses from Nashville, and several connected with the Corporation Commission of North Carolina. The defendants elected to go to trial on the State's evidence, none of them taking the stand and no defense witnesses being called. The jury's decision, rendered on August 25, found E. P. Charlet not guilty on all charges. The Leas and Davis were found guilty on the charges of conspiracy, the specific acts being the issuance of the $300,000 of certificates of deposit to the Bank of Tennessee on October 8, 1930, which were returned to the bank and cancelled without having been used, and the issuance of $100,000 of cashier's checks to Luke Lea and Luke Lea, Jr., on October 8, 1930, which Lea had used in his efforts to provide the bank with funds by depositing them in banks and then transferring by wire to the Central Bank the funds thus secured.[35] They were also found guilty of having actually misapplied more than $1,000,000 of the bank's funds. The court sentenced Luke Lea to prison for from six to ten years on the charges of conspiracy and a like amount for misapplication, the sentences to run concurrently; Davis, four to six years; and Luke Lea, Jr., two to six years.[36]

Notices of appeal to the North Carolina Supreme Court were made, appearance bonds were posted, and then began the long struggle of the Leas to prevent their actual imprisonment. The appeal of the Leas and Davis to the North Carolina Supreme Court was unsuccessful, its decision holding that while the transactions on which the men had been convicted did not actually result in loss to the bank, it was a permissible inference from the record "that the credit of the bank was unlawfully used and to its hurt, and that the defendants conspired to so use it."[37] After this opinion had been announced and before it had been certified down to the Superior Court in Buncombe County for execution, the Leas made a motion to the Supreme Court to review the record and to reconsider its opinion, which was denied.[38] The next step of the Leas to keep out of jail was to place a motion before the Superior Court of Buncombe County, in its July, 1932, session, to obtain a new trial on the grounds that the jurors were prejudiced and were not handled properly during the trial and that the defendants had obtained newly discovered evidence. The lower court refused to grant the new trial and for the third time the Leas appealed to the Supreme Court, this time on the refusal of the Buncombe

[35] See Chapter XIV, supra.
[36] Lea Record, passim.
[37] State v. Lea, pp. 13-34.
[38] Ibid., p. 35.

County Court to grant a new trial and again for the third time the Court refused relief.[39]

From the time of the decision of the trial court in August, 1931, the Leas had been free on bond and had gone to their home in Tennessee. When the North Carolina officials began to try to extradite them, the Leas appealed to the Supreme Court of the United States to review the case, claiming that substantial Federal questions were involved, including the jurisdiction of the courts of North Carolina over them.[40] The Supreme Court of the United States, however, on December 19, 1932, denied the petition and refused to review the case. In January, 1933, the Solicitor of the state of North Carolina presented the record of the case to the Superior Court of Buncombe County and obtained a judgment *nisi* on the appearance bonds of the Leas which they had forfeited. A short time later the Governor of North Carolina issued a requisition upon the Governor of Tennessee, the newly elected anti-Lea man, Hill McAllister, who on February 7 issued a warrant for the arrest of the Leas so they could be returned to North Carolina. The agents of North Carolina came to Tennessee to arrest the two men who, through flight, avoided arrest until March 14, 1933, when they were taken in Clarksville, Tennessee, a town north of Nashville near the Tennessee-Kentucky line. The Leas then sued out a writ of habeas corpus in the Criminal Court of Clarksville where, on a motion of the North Carolina agents to quash the writ, the case was heard and argued at length, and the court on April 11, 1933, rendered a decision, quashing the writ of habeas corpus and remanding the Leas to the custody of the agents of North Carolina. From this decision the Leas appealed to the Supreme Court of Tennessee, asking that the decision of the Clarksville court be reversed.[41] In its decision handed down on December 9, 1933, the Supreme Court of Tennessee unanimously held that the Leas were fugitives from justice in North Carolina and that they should be returned to that state.[42]

Thus the Leas reached the end of their fight. They had appealed three times to the Supreme Court of North Carolina, once to the Supreme Court of the United States, and once to the Supreme Court of Tennessee and all courts had ruled against them. There was some delay in getting

[39] *Ibid.*, pp. 317-24.

[40] *Petition for Writ of Certiorari to the Supreme Court of North Carolina* in the case *Wallace B. Davis, Luke Lea, and Luke Lea, Jr., Petitioners* v. *The State of North Carolina, Respondent*, in the Supreme Court of the United States, October Term, 1932, p. 4.

[41] *Reply Brief of Laurence E. Brown and Frank Lakey* in the case *State of Tennessee, ex rel. Luke Lea and Luke Lea, Jr.* v. *Laurence E. Brown and Frank Lakey*, in the Supreme Court of Tennessee, 1933, pp. 6-8.

[42] *State of Tennessee, ex rel. Lea* v. *Brown and Lakey*, 64 Southwestern (2d) 842-45 (1933).

the Leas back to North Carolina after this last decision but in May, 1934, Luke Lea, Sr., and Luke Lea, Jr., were incarcerated in the North Carolina State Prison in Raleigh. A few months later Luke Lea, Jr., was paroled, and in May, 1936, two years after his imprisonment, Luke Lea, Sr., was granted a similar favor. In 1937 both were granted full pardons.

THE TRIAL OF A. B. BANKS

A. B. Banks was brought to trial in Little Rock, Arkansas, about the same time Luke Lea went on trial in Asheville. The first indictment against Banks, found by a Mississippi County grand jury charging him with receiving deposits in the First State Bank of Osceola while it was insolvent, was quashed but he was brought to trial on a similar charge with respect to the American Exchange Trust Company. In the trial court Banks was convicted and sentenced to prison for one year and, although this conviction was upheld by the Arkansas Supreme Court, Governor Parnell of Arkansas granted Banks a pardon before he began serving his sentence.[43]

THE KNOXVILLE BANK CASES

J. Basil Ramsey, the president of the Holston-Union National Bank and Holston Trust Company at the time of their failures, was tried in Knoxville in January, 1932, on the charge of the State that Ramsey was guilty of fraudulent breach of trust inasmuch as he had treated state deposits in the Holston Trust Company as the general funds of the bank, the State's contention being that these deposits were trust funds and should have been treated as such. The State was unable to establish its position to the satisfaction of the court and Ramsey was given a directed verdict of not guilty.[44]

The Federal indictments in Knoxville were not disposed of as promptly. It will be recalled that there were two Federal indictments arising out of the failure of the Holston-Union National Bank: the first against Rogers Caldwell, Luke Lea, and J. Basil Ramsey; and the second against only Lea and Ramsey. The trial of the first was set for July, 1931, and was postponed in order to allow North Carolina to try Lea in Asheville. Before another date was set for the trial the second indictment was returned and, believing that a conviction on the second was more likely than on the first, the United States attorney for the Eastern District of Tennessee recommended that a nolle prosequi be entered on the first indictment,

---

[43] *State of Arkansas v. A. B. Banks*, 48 Southwestern (2d) 848-50 (1932). See also *Nashville Banner*, November 23, 1932.

[44] *Ibid.*, January 25, 29, 1932.

which resulted in dropping all charges against Rogers Caldwell in connection with the failure of the Knoxville banks.[45]

The trial of Ramsey and Lea on the second indictment was set for May, 1932, but a continuance was granted and nothing was done about the case while Lea was making his desperate effort to keep out of the North Carolina jail. But after Lea was finally imprisoned, the Federal authorities took action to try Ramsey. The case finally came to trial in January, 1935, almost four years after the original indictment had been returned against him. The prosecution charged Ramsey with lending funds of the Holston-Union National Bank to the Knoxville Journal Company and other Luke Lea enterprises when the credit standings of these firms did not warrant the advances, and that the loans to Lea institutions by the bank at the time of its failure amounting to $1,200,000 showed that Ramsey was misapplying the bank's funds. After a trial lasting six weeks, Ramsey was acquitted by the jury.[46]

After this acquittal Lea petitioned the Federal Court to render a not guilty decision so far as the indictment applied to him, claiming that since Ramsey, as the principal, was not guilty of misapplying the bank's funds, he, as aider and abettor, could not be guilty. The move was opposed by the District attorney but the court granted the petition and the final indictments against Luke Lea were dropped.[47]

The Ramsey trial in Knoxville was the last of the criminal cases arising out of the Caldwell collapse. Shortly after Ramsey was acquitted the state indictments against Rogers Caldwell in Kentucky were dropped, thereby settling by one way or another all the indictments against all the individuals against whom criminal action was taken.

Of all the indictments returned, only those in Asheville against Luke Lea, Luke Lea, Jr., and Wallace B. Davis resulted in prison sentences which were even partially served. The net result of all the criminal prosecutions appears little short of a travesty on justice. Although Nashville had been the base of all the transactions that were carried on, no conviction of any of the persons involved was secured there, nor in the whole of Tennessee. That this was the case no doubt can be laid partially to the Governor and the Attorney General of Davidson County, neither of whom evidently wanted any convictions. Had less favorable officials held the respective offices, it is likely that some justified convictions might have resulted from the rather numerous indictments in Tennessee.

[45] *Ibid.*, May 31, 1932. [46] *Ibid.*, March 2, 1935.
[47] From records in the case *United States* v. *Luke Lea*, No. 11672, United States District Court for the Eastern District of Tennessee, Northern Division.

Chapter XIX

CIVIL ACTIONS ARISING FROM THE CRASH

In addition to the criminal actions there arose directly from the collapse of Caldwell and Company numerous civil actions in which creditors attempted to recover a part of their losses from negligent corporation officials and also from the signers of personal surety bonds. Several of these cases, particularly those in which the state of Tennessee took action to recover on the surety bonds covering its deposits in the Bank of Tennessee, are of sufficient interest to warrant attention.

When the Bank of Tennessee failed, the state of Tennessee had on deposit with it $3,418,000 secured by five surety bonds totaling $6,500,000. Each of these bonds was signed by Rogers Caldwell and at least one of the five vice presidents of the company, each of the vice presidents having signed at least one bond. The bonds were made to insure the State against any loss that might arise from the failure of the bank and the signers of the bonds became liable when the bank failed without sufficient assets to meet the State's deposit. As soon as a liquidating agent had been appointed for the Bank of Tennessee, the State established its position as a preferred creditor so that its claim had to be satisfied before any other depositors could receive any liquidating dividends. This position as preferred creditor was based upon a 1923 decision of the Tennessee Supreme Court, which held in a similar case where the State had been a depositor in a closed bank that it was the right of the sovereign to assert its preferential position, a common law right which at that time in Tennessee had not been modified by statute.[1] In spite of its preferred position, it soon became evident that the State would not be able to recover anything like the amount of its deposit after the assets of the bank were liquidated. Hence the attorney general of the State, L. D. Smith, took action to recover the State's losses through three suits filed in the Chancery Court of Davidson County in December, 1930.

The first suit was filed against Rogers Caldwell and the Nashville Trust Company as trustee under a deed of trust made by James E. Caldwell. It will be recalled that Rogers Caldwell had built his fine home, Brentwood House, on land belonging to his father, James E. Caldwell; and that the funds for the construction of the house had been advanced

[1] *Maryland Casualty Company* v. *McConnell,* 148 Tennessee 656 (1923).

by the Bank of Tennessee, the house being carried as an asset of the bank until the summer of 1930 when it was charged to Rogers Caldwell's account and paid for with a part of the $1,200,000 dividend declared when Caldwell and Company and BancoKentucky Company merged.[2]   In September, 1930, a few weeks prior to the failure of the Bank of Tennessee, James E. Caldwell and his wife conveyed to the Nashville Trust Company, as trustee, the land on which Brentwood House was erected for the benefit of Rogers Caldwell during his life and for a period of twenty-one years after the death of the last of any children that should be born to him. The conveyance was not filed with the Registrar's Office until November 17, 1930, twelve days after the failure of the Bank of Tennessee.[3]   The State held that the date of the deed of trust was sufficient to show that Rogers Caldwell and his father had conspired to do this in order to prevent the State from obtaining its just claims. Hence the State, in its bill, asked that the deed of trust be set aside and that the property be turned over to it to settle in part its claims against Rogers Caldwell. The State's bill was answered by Rogers Caldwell and James E. Caldwell who claimed that no conspiracy existed and that the land on which the house was erected belonged to James E. Caldwell and hence the creditors of Rogers Caldwell could not take possession of it.[4]   A decision in the case was postponed under an agreed decree entered in October, 1931, concerning all three of the State's cases. Rogers Caldwell was, of course, permitted to occupy Brentwood House, which he has continued to do and where he maintains a fair stable, although neither estate nor stable is as brilliant as formerly.

The State's second suit was against the Bank of Tennessee and its officers, Rogers Caldwell, J. D. Carter, E. J. Heitzeberg, Frank D. Marr, and H. C. Alexander.[5]   The bill filed in this suit pointed out that the men had all signed surety bonds covering the deposits of the State·in the Bank of Tennessee and that the court should allow judgment against them for the amount due the State. In his answer to the bill, Rogers Caldwell pointed out that by a trust agreement he had assigned to the Nashville Trust Company for the benefit of the State all of his property, including a small bank balance, various stocks, among which were his ten thousand shares of the common stock of Caldwell and Company, a small amount of real estate held in his name, and the proceeds to be obtained from the sale of his horses, which were by far the most valuable part of the property he had assigned. Thus stripped by these assign-

---

[2] See Chapters XII and XIII, *supra*.   [3] *Original Bill of Knox County*, pp. 95-96.

[4] From records in the case *State of Tennessee* ex rel. *L. D. Smith* v. *Nashville Trust Company, et al.*, No. 42719 in Part II, Chancery Court of Davidson County, Tennessee.

[5] From records in the case *State of Tennessee* ex rel. *L. D. Smith* v. *Bank of Tennessee, et al.*, No. 42720 in Part II, Chancery Court of Davidson County, Tennessee.

ments, Caldwell claimed he could do no more. Carter answered the bill by pointing out that he had assigned all of his property to the American Trust Company for the benefit of the State to cover his liability on the surety bonds. In his assignment Carter turned over to the trust company various securities and notes and his home and ten acres of land on Franklin Pike. Under a provision in the assignment, Carter and his family have occupied the house free of rent pending final state action.

Heitzeberg and Alexander in their answers to the bill admitted signing the bonds and invited the State to take whatever steps were necessary to obtain possssion of their property. Neither had much property in his own name, however, the usual precaution of transferring it to their respective wives having been taken. Marr, in his answer to the bill, maintained that he was not responsible for the debt, that he had signed the bonds only as a favor to the executives superior to him, that he was really only a salesman for the company in spite of his title of vice president, and that he had statements signed by the chief officials of the company stating that he had nothing to do with the policies of the business. However, in spite of the claims, Marr, along with the others, had transferred his property to his wife.

In his answer to this second suit, Rogers Caldwell mentioned the fact that he had assigned the proceeds of the coming sale of his horses to the State. The actual sale of these horses gave rise to a third suit. The sale by auction of the horses of Brentwood Stables was arranged for December 5, 1930, and was widely advertised. The outstanding horse in the stables was Lady Broadcast which had total winnings of $76,033. The second most valuable horse was the sixteen-year-old stallion, Hourless, which had made a good record in his day and was sire to many exceptionally good racers. On the date of the sale, the State filed a bill against Rogers Caldwell and C. J. Fitzgerald, who had charge of the auction, asking that a receiver be appointed by the Court to take over the proceeds of the sale. The petition was allowed and the Court appointed as receiver Joseph R. West, clerk and master of the Chancery Court. The auction was held and the total amount received for the horses amounted to $62,400, of which Lady Broadcast contributed $25,500, Hourless, $9,000, and some thirty other horses of less repute the balance.[6]

A week or two after the sale, the State filed a second bill in the case asking that instead of the receiver having charge only of the proceeds of the sale of the horses that Rogers Caldwell be adjudged insolvent and that the receiver take over all of his property and distribute it to his

---

[6] From records in the case *State of Tennessee* ex rel. *L. D. Smith* v. *Rogers Caldwell*, et al., No. 42721 in Part 11, Chancery Court, Davidson County, Tennessee.

creditors. The Chancellor sustained a demurrer on the ground that the State was not a creditor of a class which, either by the general rules of equity practice or the statutes of the State, was permitted to file a general creditors' bill and impound all of the property of the defendant for the benefit of itself and such other creditors as might become parties thereto. The State appealed the case to the Tennessee Supreme Court where the opinion of the lower court was upheld. The Supreme Court pointed out that since the State was such a large preferred creditor, the settlement of whose claims would leave no property for the general creditors, there would be no advantage to other creditors in becoming parties to such an action.[7] Thus the State was not permitted to force Rogers Caldwell into involuntary bankruptcy.

On October 29, 1931, a short time after this decision was handed down, an agreed decree was entered by Rogers Caldwell and the State covering all three cases. Under this decree, the State consented to turn over to Rogers Caldwell approximately one third of the proceeds from the sale of the horses with the State retaining the balance, pending final liquidation of the Bank of Tennessee and the ascertainment of the exact amount of the claim of the State against Caldwell. It was also agreed between the litigants that the decision in the case involving the possession of Brentwood House and the hearing of the case against the officers of the Bank of Tennessee should be postponed until the same time. It is indeed difficult to see any justification of the action of the State in agreeing to return a part of the proceeds from the sale of the horses to Rogers Caldwell. The State certainly knew by October, 1931, that the Bank of Tennessee would not liquidate at anything like a figure that would cover its deposit and that if it were to recover its losses it must be from the personal sureties. Yet, in spite of this fact, it was willing to enter into an agreement with its principal surety to turn over to him approximately one third of the funds he had paid to meet his liability on the bonds, when actually his liability was many times greater than the total amount the State had received.

Not content with the receipt of this amount of the proceeds from the sale of the horses, Mrs. Rogers Caldwell, on December 9, 1932, filed an intervening petition in this case stating that Lady Broadcast was her horse and that she should be paid the $25,500 received from her sale. It may be significant that Mrs. Caldwell's petition came after her husband had been remanded for retrial by the Tennessee Supreme Court and the fact that he would not be retried on this or any other charges in Tennessee had been definitely established. Hence her action would not be detri-

---

[7] *State of Tennessee* ex rel. v. *Caldwell, et al.*, 163 Tennessee 77 (1931).

mental to Caldwell in facing a jury. The State answered her petition and the Davidson County Chancery Court upheld the State's contention that the horse was the property of Rogers Caldwell since it was not established that he had given or sold the horse to Mrs. Caldwell; and that, since at the time of the supposed gift Caldwell was insolvent, the gift, if made, was invalid. When the lower court dismissed her petition, Mrs. Caldwell appealed to the Tennessee Court of Appeals which sustained the lower court. Her appeal to have her case heard by the Tennessee Supreme Court was denied by that body on December 17, 1937.[8] Thus the State was allowed to keep the proceeds from the sale of Lady Broadcast in the only case in which the higher courts of Tennessee have ruled against Caldwell interests.

Some eight years after the original bills in these three cases had been filed, the State was able to obtain a judgment against Rogers Caldwell. Meanwhile the Bank of Tennessee had been liquidated, the State recovering approximately $490,000 of its $3,418,000 deposit, or 14.5 per cent.[9] After receiving this amount, in accordance with the agreed decree of 1931, the matter of Caldwell's personal liability as a signer of the State's surety bonds was reopened and on November 21, 1938, Chancellor James B. Newman of the Davidson County Chancery Court handed down a decree giving the State a judgment against Rogers Caldwell for $4,354,702, which amounted to the State's deposit in the Bank of Tennessee with interest less the payments received from the liquidation of the bank and sums received from Rogers Caldwell. Pending outcome of an appeal of this case to the Tennessee Supreme Court, on December 29, 1938, an agreed decree was entered in the case involving Brentwood House under which Rogers Caldwell agreed to pay the State a rental of $250 a month on the house. Under this agreement, fire insurance premiums and state and county taxes for 1938 are to be credited against the rental payments. These charges should practically exhaust the payments.

These latest gains which the State has made in its efforts to collect funds from Rogers Caldwell appear to be largely on paper. The Tennessee Supreme Court may well uphold the judgment of the lower court against Rogers Caldwell. But unless it goes further and allows the State to take possession of Brentwood House, on which right even the lower court has not yet (1939) passed, the chances of collecting even a small part of the judgment are woefully small. Even the possession of Brentwood House would cover only a relatively small part of the State's claim. Hence, it seems rather obvious that the State will never recover its loss

[8] *State of Tennessee* ex rel. v. *Caldwell, et al.*, 111 Southwestern (2d) 377 ff. (1937).
[9] Letter from R. T. Bugg, State Bank Examiner, to writer, February 10, 1937.

arising from its policy of allowing its funds on deposit in the Bank of Tennessee to be covered by personal surety bonds, a policy which happened to be desirable for the chief supporters of the state administration then in power.

THE GIBSON COUNTY CASE

Several depositors other than the state of Tennessee have taken action to recover their losses sustained in the failure of the Bank of Tennessee and Caldwell and Company. The action of Gibson County, Tennessee, is representative.

When Caldwell and Company failed, Gibson County had a deposit balance with it of $197,000, which was a part of the proceeds from the sale of a $300,000 issue of 4.5 per cent road bonds purchased by Caldwell and Company on August 6, 1930, under a depository agreement.[10] In the trust agreement securing this deposit, Fourth and First National Bank was appointed trustee and Caldwell and Company pledged the Gibson County bonds as security with the provision that these could be withdrawn and that other securities of the same market value acceptable to the trustee could be substituted. When Caldwell and Company failed, Gibson County found its deposit of $197,000 secured by 26,000 shares of Inter-Southern and 15,000 shares of BancoKentucky stock. The latter was valueless while the former was sold for only $39,000.[11]

Gibson County brought suit against the Fourth and First National Bank on the ground that the bank had violated the trust covering its deposit in accepting the stocks because they did not have a market value equal to the Gibson County bonds which were withdrawn from the trust. The plaintiff also charged that the trust officer of the bank, Randell Curell, had verbally promised Gibson County officials that he would allow only municipal bonds and certificates of deposit in sound banks to be used as collateral for the deposit. The bank in its defense claimed that the written trust agreement was the only legal basis governing substitutions even had a verbal agreement been made, the existence of which was denied. The bank also claimed that, while the collateral after the collapse of Caldwell and Company did not have a market value equal to the county's deposit, it did have such a value when accepted. The Chancellor held that the facts given in the bank's defense were correct and that it was not guilty of breach of trust and hence not liable.[12]

An appeal was taken to the Supreme Court of Tennessee where the decision of the lower court was sustained, the Supreme Court holding

[10] "Report of Receivers of Caldwell and Company," Part I, p. 643.
[11] Ibid.
[12] Gibson County v. Fourth and First National Bank, 96 Southwestern (2d) 184 (1936).

that the value of the collateral after the collapse of Caldwell and Company could not be used to show its value prior to the collapse. The court in its ruling, failed to take into consideration that on November 10, three days before Caldwell and Company failed, the value of Banco stock had fallen to $8.50 a share on the Chicago Stock Exchange with only 1,700 shares being bought at that price,[13] and that if the 15,000 shares the bank was holding for Gibson County had been offered for sale, the market would have dropped even further; and, also, that the market price of Inter-Southern several weeks before the Caldwell crash had been $1.50.[14] At this price for its Inter-Southern and $8.50 for its Banco, Gibson County would have received only $166,500 of its $197,000 deposit. Nevertheless, the Tennessee Supreme Court, in line with its two previous decisions concerning Caldwell interests,[15] held in their favor.[16]

THE KENTUCKY CASES

There have been two notable civil actions in Kentucky arising out of the Caldwell collapse that should be mentioned. The case more closely connected with the Caldwell collapse arose from the action taken by Joseph S. Laurent, receiver of BancoKentucky Company, against the directors of that company to recover some $61,500,000 which the company had lost. This loss arose, Laurent contended, largely because the directors of Banco, in complete neglect of their duty, had approved the merger with Caldwell and Company without seeing a statement of the financial condition of the company. This merger later resulted in runs on the banks controlled by BancoKentucky, the failure of some of them, and the loss of control of all of them by Banco. Through these repercussions, the merger with Caldwell and Company had resulted in a total loss to Banco of $45,166,920. The balance of the loss which Laurent sought to recover was due to transactions which did not involve Caldwell and Company but which did include the lending of $2,000,000 to Brown.[17] Part of the testimony in the case was heard before a special master in

[13] *Laurent Evidence.*

[14] *Material Pertaining to Caldwell and Company Loss,* in the case *Anderson* v. *Akers, et al.,* p. 58.

[15] *State of Tennessee* v. *Rogers Caldwell* and *State of Tennessee* ex rel. *L. D. Smith* v. *Rogers Caldwell, et al.*

[16] Knox County, Tennessee, instituted action against the Fourth and First National Bank on grounds similar to those in the Gibson County case, the amount of the Knox County deposit being $735,000 and the loss $560,531. This case is directed not only against the bank but against Caldwell and Company, its receivers, several of its officers, and several of the officers of the Fourth and First National Bank. The county in this way hopes to attach some of the property of the individuals concerned since the corporate property of the companies sued is practically non-existent. Among other property that the county hopes to obtain is Rogers Caldwell's Brentwood House. The case is still (1939) pending.

[17] *Original Bill of Laurent* and records in the case *Laurent* v. *Akers, et al.*

Louisville but before it was completed a compromise was reached under which each of the directors agreed to pay $5,000 and costs and the case was dismissed. In this way, Laurent received less than $250,000 of the $61,500,000 he sought in his action.

The other case in Kentucky was similar to the BancoKentucky case and involved action taken by Paul C. Keyes, receiver of the National Bank of Kentucky, against the directors of that bank. Keyes charged that through gross neglect the directors had caused the bank losses of approximately $12,500,000, of which approximately $1,500,000 was due to the loans to Caldwell and Company. The case was heard before a special master who found the officer directors of the bank liable for some $6,500,000 and the non-officer directors liable for some $500,000, including a part of the loss due to the Caldwell loans. The officer directors were all bankrupt by that time and hence did not appeal the case. The non-officer directors and the receiver of the bank, however, did appeal from the master's decision, and Judge Arthur J. Tuttle of the United States District Court of Detroit, who served in the case under special dispensation, reversed the master on substantially every point, holding that the non-officer directors were not liable for the Caldwell loss but were liable for other losses amounting to about $4,000,000. An appeal was taken from this decision to the Circuit Court of Appeals where the losses for which the District Court had held the non-officer directors liable were reviewed. This court overruled Judge Tuttle on substantially every point and in general upheld the master's decision. A. M. Anderson, who had succeeded Keyes as receiver of the National Bank of Kentucky, appealed the case to the Supreme Court of the United States which early in 1937 agreed to review it. Hearings were begun at the 1937 fall term of the Court but, before completed, the case was remanded by Chief Justice Hughes to the Circuit Court for rehearing because of an error in procedure. The case is still (1939) pending.

It is rather apparent that the actions taken to obtain monetary damages from individuals connected with the several institutions have been about as barren of results as those taken by several states to impose criminal remedies. In both groups of cases, the defendants seem to have benefited through the law's delay, through the tendency on the part of some courts to give the Caldwell interests more than the benefit of the doubt, and through the failure of plaintiffs rigorously to push their cases.

[18] *Anderson* v. *Akers, et al.*, 7 Federal Supplement 924 (1934); *Atherton, et al.* v. *Anderson*, 86 Federal (2d) 518 (1936). The non-officer directors appealed the case and, since Akers was an officer of the bank, the next director alphabetically, Atherton, was named in the title of the case.

CHAPTER XX

LIQUIDATION OF THE CALDWELL INTERESTS

THE APPOINTMENT of receivers for Caldwell and Company and the Bank of Tennessee and the failure of the numerous affiliated banks in November, 1930, were followed during the next several years by a decentralization of control of the institutions affiliated with Caldwell and Company and by financial difficulties in many of them. Many of these companies were themselves placed in receivership, actions which resulted in taking their control completely out of the hands of the receivers of Caldwell and Company and of the Bank of Tennessee. Similarly, as the real estate mortgage bonds underwritten by Caldwell and Company were defaulted by the issuing corporations, bondholders' protective committees were created. Thus, simultaneously, many of the former Caldwell interests were thrown into the courts and liquidated or reorganized.

LIQUIDATION OF CALDWELL AND COMPANY

Messrs. Lee Douglas and Rutledge Smith, who, in November, 1930, were appointed receivers of Caldwell and Company by Judge John J. Gore of the United States District Court in Nashville,[1] were faced with a very complex situation. Their task was to take over a collapsed and completely discredited institution, liquidate its affairs with the least possible ill effects upon the many industrial and financial institutions and governmental units with which it had done business, and pay its numerous creditors as much as possible. They were confronted with the fact that the collapse of Caldwell and Company had shaken the financial structure of the Mid-South and that many of the surviving institutions were unable to stand additional strain. It was evident also that public knowledge of an institution's connection with Caldwell and Company might well subject it to pressure sufficient to result in its crash. A case in point is the American National Bank of Nashville which had taken over the Fourth and First National Bank a few days before Caldwell and Company closed. Among the debts of Caldwell and Company was a demand loan of $350,000 payable to the American National Bank. When this fact was published, along with the other payables of Caldwell and Company, the American National, to check a possible run, made a public

---

[1] In the case *Dean* v. *Caldwell*, No. 434, in equity.

statement that the loan had been paid, when, as a matter of fact, the receivers of Caldwell and Company had at that time paid none of the company's obligations and about the only way the American National could have got the loan off its books was through selling it to its affiliated security company, American National Company, which it probably did. The receivers of Caldwell and Company avowedly sought to prevent similar situations from arising and in this were aided by Judge Gore who gave the receivership a great deal of time and thought.[2]

When Caldwell and Company failed, the book value of its assets amounted to $39,590,000 while liabilities amounted to $18,648,000, leaving a book net worth of well over $20,000,000. Of the company's total assets, $31,475,000, or 80 per cent, were securities and investments in controlled companies.[3] One of the most important of these holdings was the controlling interest of Inter-Southern Life Insurance Company, which in turn controlled Missouri State Life and the Home Companies of Arkansas. Of the approximately 1,800,000 of Inter-Southern stock owned by Caldwell and Company and the Bank of Tennessee, all except 20 shares were pledged. Shortly after the receivers of Caldwell and Company had been appointed, an offer was made by M. J. Dorsey, president of the Keystone Holding Company of Hammond, Indiana, to purchase a minimum of 1,200,000 and a maximum of 2,000,000 shares of Inter-Southern at a price of $1.50 a share, provided the stock would be turned over to an escrow agent by November 28, 1930. Caldwell and Company's receivers, as well as the receiver of the National Bank of Kentucky which held a large block of Inter-Southern which Caldwell and Company had pledged to it, favored the transaction, and on November 26 the court at Nashville approved the offer and appointed the American National Bank escrow agent, which received 1,461,333 shares of Inter-Southern, netting the sellers $2,192,000.[4] All of the other insurance holdings of Caldwell and Company were pledged at the time of its failure and were foreclosed on when the obligations they were used to secure were not met.

The value of Caldwell and Company's investments in banks, with the single exception of its one-fourth interest in Bank Securities Corporation, was wiped out through the failure of the various banks; and its stock of Bank Securities Corporation had been sold to the Bank of Tennessee. Hence, the receivers of Caldwell and Company received

[2] Information obtained from various persons connected with the receivership proceedings in Nashville. See also "Petition of Receivers for Fees," *Dean* v. *Caldwell,* which, even properly discounted, shows the importance of the job the receivers had to perform.

[3] Balance Sheet of Caldwell and Company, November 13, 1930. For the complete balance sheet of Caldwell and Company as of November 13, 1930, see Appendix F.

[4] Court records relating to this sale, *Dean* v. *Caldwell.*

nothing from its investment in banks. The company's 19,000 shares of Shares-in-the-South, Incorporated, as well as the Bank of Tennessee's 44,500, were all pledged, hence neither company received any of the liquidating dividend of $7 per share paid by a committee which took over the investment trust. Nor did Caldwell and Company's half-interest in Southern Publishers net its receivers any funds, since this stock was also held by the Bank of Tennessee, and Southern Publishers itself was placed in receivership.

With these principal holdings of Caldwell and Company all pledged, the receivers had unpledged securities with a book value of $202,550, which netted only $82,850 in cash. In addition to this amount the receivers obtained $61,000 from the company's bank balances, $50,360 as the cash surrender value of the life insurance carried on its officers by the company, $35,200 from the real estate held for investment, $17,210 from notes and accounts receivable which had been carried on the books at more than $1,000,000, and sufficient funds from other sources to bring the total amount of cash received from the assets to $405,600.[5] This amount was all that was available to meet the expenses of the receivership and to pay the debts of the company. The court approved claims against the company totaling $19,736,000, of which $68,260 were preferred claims consisting of taxes and amounts due to employees and the balance was common claims.[6] The largest single claim allowed was that of the Bank of Tennessee. At the time of its failure Caldwell and Company had sold the Bank of Tennessee $12,655,000 of securities subject to repurchase upon demand, an obligation which Caldwell and Company had defaulted when a demand for repurchase was made after the Bank of Tennessee closed and prior to the closing of Caldwell and Company. The receiver of the bank hence filed a claim for the full amount of the securities sold to the bank under the repurchase agreement but, through a compromise, the amount of the debt was set at $4,035,000.[7]

Of the $405,600 in cash obtained from the non-pledged assets of Caldwell and Company, $68,260 was used to pay the preferred creditors in full; approximately $85,000 to pay a liquidating dividend of 0.4129 of 1 per cent on the common claims, the largest single amount being $16,660 paid to the receiver of the Bank of Tennessee on his claim of over $4,000,000; and the balance, or approximately $252,300, to meet the expenses of the receivership.[8] Of this latter amount, the court allowed the

[5] "Report of Receivers of Caldwell and Company," Part III.
[6] Report of Special Master, in the case Dean v. Caldwell.
[7] "Report of Receivers of Caldwell and Company," Part I, pp. 632-33.
[8] Ibid., Part III.

receivers approximately $30,000 each, and the first attorneys for the receivers, Price, Schlater, and Price, who had served in this capacity only twenty-eight days before resigning because of the illness of the senior member of the firm, $25,000, or nearly $1,000 a day. Former Governor Albert H. Roberts and his son A. H. Roberts, Jr., composing the firm of Roberts and Roberts, were allowed $80,000 for services as attorneys from the time the first attorneys resigned until the case was closed in 1936, which fee may have meant more to the former Governor than merely so much money, since it was collected as a result of services performed in the demise of a company with which his old political enemy, Luke Lea, had been closely connected and from which Lea had received considerable financial aid. W. R. Denney, who served in the capacity as special master to hear the petitions for claims against the company, was allowed $16,000.[9] The remaining $81,000 of receivership expense was used to pay the employees of the receivers and to meet other expenses.

While the 0.4129 of 1 per cent was all that was received by the common unsecured claimants against Caldwell and Company, the principal common creditors had secured claims. In all, Caldwell and Company had pledged with its creditors securities with a book value of $19,400,000, exclusive of the 400,000 shares of BancoKentucky carried at $10,000,000 which were in escrow with the Louisville Trust Company when Caldwell and Company failed. These other pledged securities were all sold in time by the various pledgees for approximately $5,670,700, all of which was applied to Caldwell and Company's obligations and none turned over to the receivers.[10] Thus, in all, Caldwell and Company's common creditors, both secured and unsecured, received approximately $5,755,700 on claims totaling $19,736,000, or about 30 per cent.

An analysis of some of the individual liability items reveals how banks and governmental depositors sustained heavy losses. Among the Caldwell-controlled banks, the receiver of the American Exchange Trust Company of Little Rock obtained $92,500 from the sale of collateral securing a loan and repurchase agreement of $290,000; the receiver of the Holston-Union National, $50,000 on a loan and repurchase agreement totaling $350,000; and the receiver of the National Bank of Kentucky, $1,140,000 on debts of $2,715,000. Banks not affiliated with or controlled by Caldwell and Company suffered equally heavy losses. Thus, Chase National Bank received only $82,600 for loans totaling $375,000; the First National Bank of Dallas, $200,000 for $450,000; while perhaps the greatest percentage loss on any secured loans was sustained by the Third National

[9] Various court records in *Dean v. Caldwell.*
[10] "Report of Receivers of Caldwell and Company," Part III.

Bank of Scranton, Pennsylvania, which received only $202 from the collateral on a loan of $185,000.[11]   On the whole, banks recovered through the sale of collateral 48.8 per cent of their demand loans to Caldwell and Company, 31.2 per cent of their time loans, and 47.2 per cent on the company's repurchase obligations.[12]

Secured depositors on the whole fared worse than banks, recovering only 26.1 per cent of their deposits through the sale of their collateral. This smaller percentage recovered can perhaps be attributed at least partly to the illegal shifts of collateral pledged on these deposits.   At least two depositors, Anderson County and Clay County, Tennessee, received nothing from the collateral securing their deposits of $26,500 and $58,000, respectively; while Mead County, Kentucky, received only $400 on a $20,500 deposit and Mobile, Alabama, $1,250 on $100,000. Among the better-secured depositors were Owensboro, Kentucky, which received $81,370 for collateral securing a deposit of $603,000; Butler County, Kentucky, $11,050 on a $96,900 deposit; Clarke County, Alabama, $8,400 on $29,000; while Hardeman County, Tennessee, which had prosecuted Rogers Caldwell, received $40,000 on a $412,000 deposit.   There were, however, a few depositors who recovered the full amount of the deposits, among which were Columbia County, Arkansas, with a deposit of $10,900, and Weakly County, Tennessee, with a deposit of $40,200. Both of these deposits were secured with municipal bonds.[13]

It is interesting to note at this point that a few weeks after Caldwell and Company failed, Rogers Caldwell stated in an ill-advised interview that the debts of Caldwell and Company would all be paid in full and that very soon the company would be operating as it had in the past. The creditors who suffered the appalling losses just recounted—especially those unsecured who recovered less than one half of one per cent of their claims—perhaps got little satisfaction out of Caldwell's ridiculous statement.

The tremendous losses borne by Caldwell and Company's creditors reflect the intrinsically low quality of a large part of the securities the company had underwritten.   In most, but not all, cases the pledgees obtained the full pledged value of municipal bonds but there were less than $700,000 of these pledged.   The losses arose primarily from real estate mortgage and industrial bonds and stocks of banks and industrial corporations, the value of the bank stocks having been wiped out through failures, while the market for the other securities was extremely weak. In addition to these considerations was the fact that during the early

---

[11] *Ibid.*, Part I, *passim.*
[12] Compiled from *ibid.*, Part III.   [13] *Ibid.*, Part I, *passim.*

months of the receivership the political connections of Caldwell and Company were played upon by the press and politicians in such a way as to promote a psychological state conducive to sacrifice selling.

LIQUIDATION OF THE BANK OF TENNESSEE

When the Superintendent of Banks, D. D. Robertson, was appointed receiver of the Bank of Tennessee on November 5, 1930, an audit of the bank revealed assets with a book value of $13,969,532, of which $12,655,100 or 90 per cent were stocks and bonds. That this bank was a dumping ground for nonsalable Caldwell securities is shown by the fact that all national banks in 1930 had only 23.7 per cent of their assets invested in stocks and bonds.[14] The principal liabilities of the bank were deposits of approximately $9,880,000 and bills payable to banks of $2,888,000. Of the deposits, approximately $2,596,000 were of controlled companies, of which $1,487,000 were secured; and $3,418,000 were of the state of Tennessee secured only by the personal surety bonds of the officers of the bank. The remaining $3,866,000 of deposits, of which $2,775,000 were secured, were deposits of municipalities arising from the purchase of their bonds by Caldwell and Company under depository agreements. The more important municipal depositors were Knox County, Tennessee, with $735,000; and funds of Louisiana municipalities of approximately $1,350,000 which had been deposited first in Louisiana banks, and then in turn deposited by these banks in the Bank of Tennessee. The banks which had loaned the Bank of Tennessee funds were as widely scattered as those Caldwell and Company owed, some being Caldwell-controlled banks, but many were independent of the investment house. All their claims were secured.

As was pointed out above, the state of Tennessee established its position as preferred claimant on the unpledged assets of the bank. Since these assets yielded less than 14.5 per cent of the State's claim of $3,418,000, or approximately $490,000, the other unsecured creditors of the bank lost the full amounts of their claims,[15] while the secured creditors recovered on their claims the amounts received from the sale of collateral. Since the Bank of Tennessee had pledged approximately $1,700,000 of municipal bonds to its creditors, while Caldwell and Company had pledged only $700,000, it is likely that the secured creditors of the bank received a somewhat larger proportion of the pledged value of their collateral than did the secured creditors of the investment house. However, the other

---

[14] *Report of Comptroller of Currency,* 1931. The Balance Sheet of the Bank of Tennessee as of November 5, 1930, is found in Appendix F.

[15] Letter from R. T. Bugg, State Bank Examiner, to the writer, February 10, 1937.

collateral pledged on the Bank of Tennessee's obligations was of the same low quality as that pledged on the obligations of the parent organization.[16]

Among the assets of the Bank of Tennessee was the entire capital stock of Rogers Caldwell and Company, Incorporated, of New York, which had been turned over to the bank by Caldwell and Company after its examination by the State Banking Department in September, 1930.[17] The New York company had a very small volume of business during 1930 and the small amount of funds needed for its operations had been furnished by Caldwell and Company, these advances constituting its chief liabilities. Its assets were composed primarily of a small volume of stocks and bonds and notes and accounts receivable. The receiver of the Bank of Tennessee took over the assets of the company, settled its liabilities other than the amount due Caldwell and Company and obtained a small amount of cash to be added to the assets of the bank. The claim of Caldwell and Company against the New York company was cancelled in the compromise settlement of the Bank of Tennessee's claim against the investment house.

Another company, all of whose stock the receiver of the Bank of Tennessee fell heir to, was Southern Banks, Incorporated, this stock having been obtained by the Bank of Tennessee in the same transaction in which it obtained the stock of Rogers Caldwell and Company, Incorporated. The chief obligations of this company were $600,000 of notes payable to National Bank of Kentucky, which were charged against the receivers of Caldwell and Company since that company had used the funds; and a note of approximately $35,000, secured by stock of the defunct Holston-Union National Bank, payable to Caldwell and Company. Its only asset was the Holston-Union stock, the ownership of which resulted in an assessment it could not meet. Hence the ownership of this somewhat notorious holding company—Rogers Caldwell had been indicted in Kentucky for forming it—yielded the receiver of the Bank of Tennessee nothing.

LIQUIDATION OF BANKS AND DISPOSITION OF INSURANCE COMPANIES

All of the banks affiliated with Caldwell and Company except the Union Planters National and Manhattan Savings banks in Memphis closed in November, 1930. Caldwell control of these two banks was lost in the merger between the Fourth and First National and American National banks in November, 1930, the stock of the Memphis banks having been used as collateral by Fourth and First Banks, Incorporated,

---

[16] Data are not available as to the amount individual creditors or creditors as a whole of the Bank of Tennessee received from the sale of collateral pledged to them.

[17] See Chapter xiv, *supra*.

on a loan at the American National which was a part of the agreement under which the American National took over the Fourth and First National. The failure to pay this loan resulted in giving control of the Memphis banks to the American National.

At the time of the failure of Caldwell and Company, however, the West Tennessee Company, which had been formed to take over the assets of the old Union and Planters Bank and Trust Company that had been withdrawn from this bank at the time of reorganization, still had some $285,000 of these assets and no obligations. The entire stock of this company was owned by Bank Securities Corporation, and the Caldwell and Company stock in this latter company was owned by the Bank of Tennessee. The assets of the West Tennessee Company were all transferred to Luke Lea and Rogers Caldwell on April 9, 1931,[18] presumably because these two men had signed notes for Bank Securities Corporation amounting to $75,000. If the transference was then known to any state official, nothing was done to stop it, the general opinion being that all of these assets were worthless anyway, since they consisted of past due notes and real estate on which deferred payments and taxes were long overdue.

Among the notes turned over to the two men, however, were two totaling $21,385, signed by J. F. Mathis of Memphis and secured by 480 shares out of a total of 1,000 shares of the common stock of the Rodessa Land and Oil Company, which owned rather extensive blocks of mortgaged land in Louisiana. Late in 1935 oil was found on some of this land and the once worthless stock of the company became very valuable. The administrator of the estate of J. F. Mathis attempted to regain possession of the 480 shares of stock through the payment of the notes and accrued interest thereon only to find that the stock had been bought by Rogers Caldwell and Luke Lea at a foreclosure sale which they had conducted; that the former had transferred his 260 shares to James E. Caldwell and Company, a family holding company; and that Luke Lea had given 25 shares of his 220 shares as collateral on a loan and had sold the remaining 195 shares to his wife who had in turn sold them to Sam Cohn, a Nashville associate, all of the sales having been made at ridiculously low prices. When the Mathis estate took court action to obtain the stock, the state of Tennessee became a party to the suit on the grounds that the stock was an asset of the Bank of Tennessee, the line of ownership running through the Bank of Tennessee's stock of Bank Securities Corporation to the West Tennessee Company which had taken over the Mathis notes and collateral from the Union and Planters Bank. The

[18] Financial Statement of West Tennessee Company, April 9, 1931.

banks from which Bank Securities Corporation had borrowed funds prior to the crash, namely, the Chase National Bank of New York, the Chemical Bank and Trust Company of New York, the Shawmut National Bank of Boston, the American National Bank of Nashville, and the Nashville Trust Company, also entered petitions in the suit claiming ownership of the stock since they had sustained heavy losses on their loans to the holding company.

Under a compromise agreement reached in April, 1938, the state of Tennessee received approximately $30,000, representing the amount of the Mathis notes plus interest, and in exchange for this sum released all claims on the Rodessa stock. Of the 455 shares of the stock held by James E. Caldwell and Company and Sam Cohn, as representatives respectively of Rogers Caldwell and Luke Lea, the creditor banks of Bank Securities Corporation received 115 shares; the Mathis estate, 177 shares; James E. Caldwell and Company, 93 shares; and Sam Cohn, 70 shares. The value of the stock at the time of its distribution is indicated by the fact that the dividends declared during the two-year period of litigation and paid to the recipients of the stock on a prorata basis at the time of the settlement amounted to $670 per share.[19] The State again came out with a minimum return for its efforts and Rogers Caldwell and Luke Lea, indirectly, of course, received respectable fortunes.

The other Caldwell affiliated banks were liquidated by Federal and state receivers. Depositors have received liquidating dividends as follows: National Bank of Kentucky, 67 per cent; Holston-Union National Bank, 45 per cent; and American Exchange Trust Company, Little Rock, 45 per cent. Depositors in the Lea-controlled Liberty Bank and Trust Company of Nashville have received nothing on their deposits since the State, as in the case of the Bank of Tennessee, established its position as a preferred claimant on the assets of the bank. Even by doing this, the State was able to recover only $204,000 of its $354,000 on deposit, or approximately 57.5 per cent.[20] Depositors in the Central Bank and Trust Company of Asheville have received approximately 3.5 per cent.

Practically all of the stock of the Caldwell life insurance companies, except that of the Shenandoah Life Company of Roanoke, was in the portfolio of Inter-Southern when the collapse occurred. The stock of the Shenandoah was pledged to Lehman Brothers of New York who sold it back to the interests in Roanoke from whom Caldwell and Company first bought it. A second Caldwell life insurance company, the South-

---

[19] Court Records, *In the Matter of the Estate of Joel F. Mathis, Deceased,* Probate Court of Shelby County, Tennessee, No. 34,226-R. 38.

[20] Letter from R. T. Bugg, state bank examiner, to the writer, February 10, 1937.

eastern of Greenville, South Carolina, also found its way back to its original owners when Inter-Southern sold its stock in this company shortly after the Dorsey interests had purchased the Inter-Southern stock formerly held by Caldwell and Company.

Inter-Southern lost another of the Caldwell life companies in May, 1931, when the Home Life Insurance Company of Little Rock was placed in receivership[21] in spite of the efforts made by the Louisville company to prevent such action. Inter-Southern was weakened considerably by this event but not nearly so much as by the falling price of the stock of Missouri State Life Insurance Company which was by far its principal asset. Some 116,000 shares of this stock had been purchased by Inter-Southern at $88 a share in May, 1930, and during 1931 and 1932 had been carried by Inter-Southern at $60.40 a share, or $7,006,400. As the market price of this stock sank much below this level, the insolvency of Inter-Southern could no longer be overlooked by the Kentucky Department of Insurance and the company was placed in receivership. Its policyholders were reinsured by the Kentucky Home Life Insurance Company, which took over the Missouri State stock along with the other assets of Inter-Southern.[22]

The value of this Missouri State stock to Kentucky Home Life Company disappeared in 1933 when the Superintendent of Insurance of Missouri placed Missouri State Life in receivership, and the company's policyholders were reinsured by the General American Life Insurance Company of St. Louis which was established for this purpose. In taking over the assets of Missouri State, the General American obtained a controlling interest in the Southwestern Life Insurance Company of Dallas and a contract calling for the purchase of additional stock of this company. This contract was carried out and at the end of 1935 General American held 53 per cent of the stock of Southwestern. At that time David M. Milton, a son-in-law of John D. Rockefeller who had organized General American, arranged for the control of this company to be bought by a Dallas company, Southwestern Investors, set up for this purpose and financed by Southwestern Life, the transaction resulting in a profit of $425,000 to Milton interests.[23]

In addition to its life insurance companies, Caldwell and Company at the time of its failure had substantial interest in Southern Surety Com-

[21] The Home Fire and Home Accident companies had already been lost by Inter-Southern through receivership proceedings of the previous November.

[22] Best's Insurance News (Life Edition), xxxii (May 1, 1931), 43; xxxiii (May 2, 1932), 38.

[23] Ibid., xxxiv (September 1, 1933), 332; Time, xxviii (December 28, 1936), 40. For an account of other Milton profits see John T. Flynn in the New Republic, lxxxix, 299, 327, January 6 and 13, 1937, respectively.

pany, the controlling stock of which the Home Insurance Companies of New York had agreed to purchase from Caldwell and Company and Kidder-Peabody and Company. After the Caldwell collapse, repeated efforts, including a lawsuit, to get the Home Companies to carry out their agreement failed. Meanwhile, Southern Surety had suffered from the Caldwell collapse in that it had lost $124,000 deposited in the Bank of Tennessee; the securities it had purchased from Caldwell and Company had declined rapidly in value; and, even more important, it became liable on a number of surety bonds it had written covering deposits in the Bank of Tennessee and Caldwell and Company. The cumulative result of all of these events was to place the company in receivership at the end of 1931, at which time its entire casualty business was reinsured by Home Indemnity Company of New York.[24]

Thus all of the Caldwell insurance companies, except the Southeastern Life, the Shenandoah Life, and the Southwestern Life, all three of which were under Caldwell control for a relatively short time, were forced into receivership which resulted in wiping out the value of their stocks, a large part of which had been sold to the public, as well as in heavy losses to the policyholders.

SALE OF THE NEWSPAPERS

Caldwell and Company's investments in newspapers were wiped out through a series of three receiverships; namely, those of Southern Publishers, Incorporated, Memphis Commercial Appeal, Incorporated, and the Knoxville Journal Company. Southern Publishers defaulted its interest payments on its collateral trust bonds held by Minnesota and Ontario Paper Company and the latter company had its debtor placed in receivership and foreclosed on the common and preferred stock of Memphis Commercial Appeal which was the collateral behind Southern Publishers' bonds. Memphis Commercial Appeal went into receivership on December 12, 1930, the step having been taken to protect the assets of the paper, supposedly from Colonel Lea. This company paid interest on its own debentures while in receivership and, shortly after the stock of the company was turned over to the Minnesota and Ontario Paper Company, the receivership was terminated, the paper continuing to be published under the editorship of George Morris. In 1933 Minnesota and Ontario Paper Company sold its stock in the publishing company to James Hammond, who, after placing the paper on a sound financial basis, sold out to the Scripps-Howard chain in 1936.

The bonds and controlling stock of the Knoxville Journal Company which Southern Publishers had owned were pledged to the Canal Bank

[24] *Moody's Banks,* 1932.

and Trust Company on a $400,000 note of Caldwell and Company, the collateral being taken by the bank when the investment house failed. The publishing company was unable to continue to meet its liabilities and in December, 1930, was placed in receivership. In 1932 the Canal Bank failed, with the Knoxville company's securities still in its portfolio and with the paper still being published by its receivers. Efforts by the receiver of the Canal Bank to find a purchaser of these securities failed until the summer of 1936 when Roy N. Lotspeich, a Knoxville business man, bought control of the paper for $450,000.[25] By this sale the Canal Bank was able to recover the principal and part of the interest on Caldwell and Company's $400,000 note.

FINANCIAL DIFFICULTIES IN THE CALDWELL INDUSTRIAL CORPORATIONS

The period following the crash of Caldwell and Company proved extremely difficult for a large proportion of the industrial corporations it had financed. While some of these difficulties can be traced to the depression, even more important factors were the high overcapitalization relative to normal earnings of many of them and the losses of deposits suffered by some when the Bank of Tennessee and other Caldwell banks failed. A few of these enterprises had ceased operations prior to the collapse, two of which were Frank Silk Mills and Cadet Hosiery Company. However, most of the companies went into receivership after the Caldwell failure and were reorganized. Typical among this group were Alabama Mills, Kentucky Rock Asphalt Company, and Southern Department Stores.

Alabama Mills Company defaulted the interest payments on its $3,000,000 of bonds shortly after Caldwell and Company's failure and for a time thereafter it appeared as if the whole organization would fold up, bringing unemployment to several thousand workers and complete loss to the holders of the securities of the company. However, a plan of reorganization was agreed upon under which the mills could continue to operate. The common stockholders' equity was wiped out completely, thus rendering worthless most of Caldwell and Company's unpledged interest. Other security holders were given new securities of a lower grade, but the company has not paid interest on its income bonds which the old first mortgage bondholders received or dividends on its preferred since reorganization and its bonds have sold generally in the low 20's.

Kentucky Rock Asphalt Company managed to stay out of the courts much longer than Alabama Mills. Dividends on this company's preferred were paid until 1932 and interest on its bonds until June 1, 1934.

[25] Memphis *Commercial Appeal*, August 7, 1936.

At that time it became apparent that a reorganization accompanied by a decrease in fixed charges was absolutely necessary. The company accordingly was reorganized under Section 77B of the Bankruptcy Act, with the holders of the $613,000 of 6.5 per cent first mortgage bonds being given a like amount of new first mortgage bonds with 3.25 per cent fixed interest and 3.25 per cent contingent interest payable only if earned, but with any deficiencies in the contingent interest being cumulative. Old bondholders were also given two shares of new common stock for each $100 of bonds owned. The old preferred was exchanged share for share for new Class "A" stock with par value of $25, with noncumulative dividends of 4 per cent and participating with the common up to 6 per cent. The common stockholders received one share of new common for two shares of the old.[26] Since reorganization, the company has met fixed charges on its bonds but in spite of this they have usually sold in the low 30's.

The holders of Southern Department Stores' $1,000,000 of 6 per cent, three-year notes have fared very badly. These notes and the company's $895,000 of preferred stock, offered in January, 1930, were the last new industrial issues underwritten by Caldwell and Company. When the Bank of Tennessee failed, the company lost a deposit balance of $200,000. In spite of this blow it met its interest payments on January 1, 1931, but passed its preferred dividends. In the same month, in an effort to strengthen its financial condition, it sold its interest in one of its stores, Lebeck Brothers of Nashville, for $150,000. This, however, did not enable it to meet interest payments on July 1, 1931, when receivership proceedings were begun.[27] The noteholders' protective committee, with which $901,000 of the $1,000,000 of notes were deposited, bought the assets of the company for a sum which, after paying receivership costs, yielded the nondepositing noteholders the ridiculously small amount of $14.57 per $1,000 note. The common and preferred stockholders were completely eliminated and the depositing noteholders took common stock in a new company which has since become worthless. Fortunately enough, a relatively small amount of the notes was sold to the public, but the $898,500 of these notes held by Caldwell and Company and the Bank of Tennessee were all hypothecated on loans and deposits, thus leaving the creditors of these two institutions with the loss.[28]

Though a majority of the companies having bonds outstanding that

---

[26] *Plan of Reorganization of Kentucky Rock Asphalt Company,* United States District Court, Western District of Kentucky, June 29, 1935.

[27] Memorandum on Southern Department Stores by E. J. Heitzeberg, in files of Receivers of Caldwell and Company. Not dated.

[28] "Report of Receivers of Caldwell and Company," Part I, p. 451.

were underwritten by Caldwell and Company defaulted interest payments, there were some exceptions. Among these may be mentioned the Alligator Corporation of St. Louis which has paid its bond interest regularly and is operating profitably. Also, Apex Oil Company met interest payments regularly although its financial condition was at times very serious. In 1936 T. G. Donovan, former secretary of Caldwell and Company, was placed in charge of this company by the dominant stockholders and in 1937 the controlling stock of the company was bought by Rogers Caldwell and his father. Thus one of the less important industrial companies financed by Rogers Caldwell has become a vehicle by which he is attempting to stage a business and financial comeback.

Certain of the Caldwell-financed corporations which had no bonds outstanding have fared well indeed. Among these is the Mark Henderson Company, a shirt factory in Nashville, of whose total common stock of 1,000 shares Caldwell and Company owned 625 shares as well as all of its 600 shares of preferred. This stock was pledged to secure depositors, and when the pledgees offered it for sale it was bought by E. J. Heitzeberg, the former vice president of Caldwell and Company, who paid $2,232.25 for the controlling block of 625 shares of common and $1,099 for the 600 shares of preferred.[29] Since buying control Heitzeberg has taken active charge of its management and is operating it profitably.[30] Spur Distributing Company, another company which had only stock outstanding, was in the promotional stage in 1930 and very little of its stock had been sold to the public. Caldwell and Company's holdings of 28,796 shares, which represented control, had been sold to the Bank of Tennessee, which held it unpledged. The receiver of the bank sold the stock to J. M. Houghland for $30,000, which was $90,000 less than Caldwell and Company had paid for it.[31] Houghland increased the company's working capital and profitably extended its operations so that at present the controlling interest is valued at some $2,000,000, a fact which has been used by Rogers Caldwell in legal proceedings to maintain the preposterous claim that Caldwell and Company was indeed solvent in November, 1930.[32]

Of the other controlled companies, only the Nashville Baseball Asso-

---

[29] *Ibid.*, p. 466.

[30] Of the three executives of the company, only Carter has remained in the investment banking business, operating the Nashville Securities Company. Heitzeberg left the field immediately upon the purchase of the Mark Henderson Company. Caldwell attempted a comeback in the security business but was unsuccessful.

[31] "Report of Receivers of Caldwell and Company," Part I, p. 486.

[32] *State of Tenn.* ex. rel v. *Caldwell, et al.*, 111 Southwestern (2d) 377 (1937). This is the case in which Mrs. Caldwell attempted to obtain the $25,000 received from the sale of Lady Broadcast.

ciation will be mentioned. Caldwell and Company's controlling interest in this organization, at the time of its failure, was pledged to Hardeman County, Tennessee, which, obviously, was not desirous of operating a baseball club. The organization was greatly in debt and its stock, for which Caldwell and Company had paid $195,400, was rapidly losing its value. Various negotiations were held with interested parties and the club was sold to R. G. Allen, a former owner of the Little Rock Baseball Association, for $50,000. Under a compromise agreement the debts of the association were scaled down and paid and Hardeman County received a total of $250 for its stock, a sum which constituted a part of the $40,000 it received for its deposit of $412,000.[33]

REAL ESTATE MORTGAGE BONDS

The holders of real estate mortgage bonds underwritten by Caldwell and Company have suffered a proportionately greater number of defaults and reorganizations than the holders of industrial bonds. Although data are not available for some $3,505,000 of the total of $23,487,500 of first mortgage bonds outstanding at the date of Caldwell and Company's failure, of the approximately $20,000,000 for which data are available, only one issue, the $1,000,000 of 5.5 per cent bonds of the Baptist General Convention of Texas, has not been defaulted. Thus certainly no more than $4,505,000 of these bonds have not suffered defaults, while a more likely estimate, based upon the nature of the bonds for which data concerning interest payments are not available, would be $2,000,000. In some cases, after a reorganization was perfected, interest on the new bonds was paid regularly, and for at least one issue, that of the Andrew Jackson Hotel in Nashville, the entire issue was retired a few years after the interest rate on the bonds had been reduced through an agreement between the bondholders and the issuing corporation. Most issues have not fared so well, however. Thus, the holders of the first mortgage bonds on the Orndorff Hotel in El Paso, Texas, received after a reorganization the same amount of second mortgage income bonds on which no interest was ever paid and which the majority of the holders sold in 1935 at $20 per $100 bond to a Texas group which had obtained the first mortgage.

Bondholders' protective committees were formed to take care of the interests of the holders of the defaulting bonds. For some of the issues separate committees were set up, but, in addition to these, two general committees were organized which attempted to act for the holders of nearly all defaulting Caldwell bonds. One was made up entirely of Nashville men and had as members James B. Hill, president of the Nashville, Chattanooga, and St. Louis Railroad, and B. E. McCarthy and J. C. Bradford, investment bankers. The secretary of the committee and the one most active in its operations was L. B. Stevens, who had formerly been in charge of Caldwell and Company's real estate bond department. The other committee called itself the "Independent Protective Committee" and attempted to get distressed bondholders to allow it to protect their interests primarily by having, as its general counsel, Mrs. Mabel Walker Willebrant.

The two committees spent at least part of their time fighting each other. For instance, after a majority of the bonds on the Orndorff Hotel of El Paso had been deposited with the Nashville committee, the independent committeee addressed a letter to all bondholders under the heading: "Plain Talk Regarding the Orndorff Hotel." In this the committee stated that it was of the opinion that the hotel could pay interest if it wanted to and that if the bonds were deposited with them they would take steps to see that interest was paid.[34] The Nashville committee countered in a few days with a statement saying that it held the view "from the statement of 'opinion' made by the self-styled Committee that its members are not familiar with the facts."[35] In this particular issue as well as in others the Nashville committee won the support of the bondholders and has continued to operate, supposedly protecting the interests of the bondholders, but with little advantage to the bondholders in many instances.

It is thus seen that, with few major exceptions, all of the companies connected with Caldwell and Company, either through direct control or merely through financing carried on by the investment house, have become involved in financial difficulties which resulted in tremendous losses to investors, depositors, and policyholders, and that the infection due to Caldwell control continued to make itself felt in many instances long after the banking house closed in November, 1930. That these losses, which constitute the great tragedy in the failure of Caldwell and Company, brought about an impairment of resources in the South and certain sections of the Mid-West sufficient to cause an intensification of the depression in these regions cannot well be controverted.

[34] Circular letter to holders of first mortgage bonds on the Orndorff Hotel, from Independent Protective Committee, September 26, 1931.

[35] Circular letter to holders of first morgage bonds on the Orndorff Hotel, from James B. Hill, B. E. McCarthy, and J. C. Bradford, September 30, 1931.

CHAPTER XXI

CONCLUSION

THE STORY of the growth and collapse of Caldwell and Company has been traced but there were certain forces which shaped its history to such an extent and certain long-standing social problems of such importance involved that further observations are warranted.

Caldwell and Company was a product of both external and internal forces, the former probably being the more important. One important external condition was that the South experienced very rapid industrialization during most of the period of Caldwell and Company's operations and the investment house was in a position to profit greatly from this development. Increasing demands for all types of securities, epitomized by the runaway bull market in 1928 and 1929, was another powerful external force in the company's development. Closely coupled with this was the lack of critical analysis of the bases of business prosperity on the part of bankers, business men, and investors, which so far as Caldwell and Company was concerned enabled it to obtain a much larger amount of funds with which to expand its business than would have been the case if the soundness of the prosperity of the period, of which Caldwell and Company was largely a product, had been more carefully questioned.

The internal forces influencing the development of the company center in its management, which was aggressive in increasing its size and scope but which failed in any way to question the validity of its rapid growth, to give proper attention to its internal operations, and to exercise due restraint in the use of other people's money. The company was apparently willing to originate and underwrite all qualities of securities, a policy which naturally resulted in increasing the volume of business done as well as the volume of total assets under its control. But the executives lacked either the desire or ability to determine whether a security was sound and, in their mad rush to expand, offered securities to the public without proper scrutiny and bought control of companies without adequately considering whether the purchase price was justified or not. The company's management utterly failed to adopt and to put into practice sound policies which would have resulted both in a better functioning internal organization and in commitments which could have been more easily met.

The result of these forces can be seen first in the company's lack of permanent working capital which necessitated its reliance upon bank loans, deposits, and other outside sources of funds subject to withdrawal upon demand. This heavy dependence on such funds, coupled with the dominance of low-grade securities in its inventory, in turn resulted in the large number of violated trusts. A second result of the forces affecting the company was the speculative trend of its business. Starting operations solely as a municipal bond house, it expanded into the more speculative investment fields faster than the ability of the management to direct such activities increased and just as rapidly as the security-buying public would take the more speculative issues. While this trend was largely responsible for the remarkably rapid growth of the company, it was a movement which carried in it the seed of the company's ultimate destruction.

In the fall of 1929 Caldwell and Company found itself with commitments which it could meet only by selling a large part of its inventory or by obtaining an amount of funds from outside sources even greater than that obtained in the past. The collapse of the securities markets, coupled with the nature of its inventory, effectively did away with the first alternative and, hence, the company was forced to use the second. In getting funds from the outside it brought considerable pressure upon its affiliated institutions to deposit substantial parts of their cash balances with the Bank of Tennessee or directly with Caldwell and Company. This policy naturally weakened the financial condition of the affiliates and at the same time did not provide sufficient funds to enable the investment house to carry on. In order to get funds from nonaffiliated banks, Caldwell and Company was required to pledge higher grade collateral. As the amount of unpledged collateral of this type became smaller and smaller and was ultimately exhausted, Caldwell and Company could obtain no further advances with which to meet the increasing demands for payment of its liabilities. Thus, changes in the important external forces in the company's development accentuated its internal weaknesses to such a degree that failure became inevitable.

Turning to the important and still unsolved social problems which are raised again by the practices of Caldwell and Company, there are three of primary importance that should be noted; namely, the concentration of control of industrial and financial assets in the hands of investment bankers, the dominance of governmental processes by powerful private interests, and the standard of business ethics.

The total assets over which Caldwell and Company exerted substantial control after the merger with BancoKentucky Company well surpassed

$600,000,000. While this amount does not approach the $22,000,000,000 of assets which the Pujo Committee in 1912 estimated to be under the control of the Money Trust headed by J. P. Morgan and Company, nevertheless the assets which Caldwell and Company controlled were of sufficient size and suitable nature to enable it to engage in the same type of activities for which the Money Trust has been so roundly condemned: excessive promotional profits, unloading of securities on controlled insurance companies, and having control over and access to funds deposited by unsuspecting customers in affiliated banks.[1] And Caldwell and Company was able to get away with such transactions largely for the same reason that the Money Trust could; namely, that it had become so much larger and more powerful than any other similar firm in the section it was serving— or perhaps better, exploiting—that control through competition was nonexistent. Control of Caldwell and Company by state action, so far as the state of Tennessee was concerned, was equally lacking. About the only instances of the power of the company being curbed by governmental control were: first, the action on the part of the Comptroller of the Currency of the United States which effectively prevented Caldwell and Company from borrowing from the Union Planters National Bank of Memphis and resulted unquestionably in saving the bank; and, second, the occasional checks which the Missouri Department of Insurance placed on transactions Caldwell and Company attempted to carry on with the Missouri State Life Insurance Company but which checks were not sufficiently adequate to prevent the eventual collapse of the insurance company. In the absence of competition, effective governmental control is essential, and the more powerful the monopolistic enterprise becomes, the more necessary becomes such control. The practices of Caldwell and Company exhibit only too well the limits to which powerful businesses controlled neither by competition nor by government can and do go, and emphasize the need for drastic restrictions on such enterprises.

A second important problem of which the operations of Caldwell and Company provide a shining example is the dominance of governmental processes by powerful private interests. Private interests waxing fat at the public trough are found perhaps in all governmental units no matter how large or how small and result in unnecessary burdens which this country as a whole is becoming less and less able to carry. Caldwell and Company was obviously using to its own advantage the administration of the state of Tennessee when Kyrock was sold to the State, such sales partially enabling it to make a profit of $1,600,000 from the sale of the stock of Kentucky Rock Asphalt Company. It was using the state ad-

---

[1] See Louis D. Brandeis, *Other People's Money and How the Bankers Use It.*

ministration to an even greater extent when it was able to turn the stream of state funds into the Bank of Tennessee, which amounted in the course of sixteen months to approximately $9,000,0000, in addition to the deposits of the State placed in other affiliated banks such as the Holston-Union National and the Fourth and First National. That Caldwell and Company's influence was not limited to the administrative branch of the State can at least be inferred from the failure of the state of Tennessee to convict anyone for any of the violated trusts that existed at the time of the collapse and also from the return by the State to Rogers Caldwell of approximately one third of the proceeds from the sale of his horses on the absurd ground that it had not then been determined to what extent Rogers Caldwell was liable on the surety bonds he had signed covering the deposit of Tennessee funds in the Bank of Tennessee, when as a matter of fact, the State, even had it kept all of Rogers Caldwell's horse money, would have sustained losses of several million dollars.

Finally, the practices of Caldwell and Company involve the question of business ethics. Caldwell and Company can be justly charged with violating sound business ethics, assuming such to exist, in at least two respects: namely, first, actual violations of law; and second, carrying through those transactions which, while technically within the law, were of such a nature that they should clearly be outside the code of business morals.

The administration of the company's trust agreements provides the outstanding example of actual violation of law. At least from the year 1926 to the closing of the business, Caldwell and Company or the Bank of Tennessee, or both, were guilty of breaches of trusts. Some of these trusts were grossly violated, others not so seriously, but all were violations nevertheless. The responsible officials of a company which permitted, if not sanctioned, such practices would stand hopelessly guilty in the minds of most individuals for violation of both statutory law and business ethics, regardless of whether they were actually convicted in a court of law or not. The least that can be said is that Caldwell and Company was guilty of gross violation of law. The fact that the state of Tennessee did not break through the corporate shell of the company and attach the responsibility for these acts to some one or more individuals does not in the least signify that some individual or individuals was not personally responsible. It means rather that the doctrine of legal entity was stretched too far in order to protect individuals from suffering the consequences of their deeds.

The officials of Caldwell and Company completely failed to take into consideration the moral obligations business men should have to the institutions they control and to the customers with whom these institutions deal. It was the lack of good faith with respect to these obligations that led both to the transactions which were violations of law and to those which were violations only of sound business ethics. Transactions of this latter type are numerous and show clearly that Caldwell and Company, in carrying them on, was subordinating the interests of its controlled companies and clientele to its own interests with results that were tragic in most cases for all concerned.

Probably the first such transaction was the formation of the Bank of Tennessee. With such an institution, wholly owned and controlled, Caldwell and Company had taken the first step which was essential for it to violate trusts successfully. Also, with this institution, it was able to obtain certain large deposits, particularly those of the state of Tennessee, which Caldwell and Company, as an investment house, could not have had. It is no doubt true that a larger volume of questionable transactions was carried on between Caldwell and Company and the Bank of Tennessee than between Caldwell and Company and all of its other controlled companies.

A second outstanding transaction of this type concerned the controlled insurance companies. Without going into the questionable policy of loading its insurance companies with the securities it was underwriting, a policy which may have been an honest error in regard to the soundness of the securities, there could not possibly have been any such extenuating circumstances in the sale of the control of the Missouri State Life Company and the Home Insurance Companies of Arkansas to Inter-Southern Life Company in 1930, which resulted in the virtual looting of the portfolio of Inter-Southern, and to which may be directly charged the receivership of Inter-Southern and the accompanying losses to stockholders and policyholders.

A third group of transactions of this character were the loans Caldwell and Company obtained from the National Bank of Kentucky in 1930. By having some of its already existing subsidiary companies borrow funds, Caldwell and Company was able to obtain some $1,800,000 from the bank, which was three times the legal limit of loans the bank could make under the Federal law to one party. Not content with this amount, it chartered Southern Banks, Incorporated, with the sole purpose of obtaining $600,000 of additional funds from the bank, and was thus able still to remain within the letter of the law but clearly outside its spirit.[2]

---

[2] Other transactions of this type include the excessive loans from Fourth and First National Bank; the pressure on controlled companies to keep deposits in the Bank of Tennessee; the unloading of securities on Shares-in-the-South, Incorporated; and the ap-

Enough has been said to show that Caldwell and Company's operations were at least spotted with transactions that were illegal or questionable or both. All such transactions, no doubt, have not been brought to light and will probably never be. But those that have show unmistakably the loose ethical standards that prevailed in this business. It must be borne in mind, however, that Caldwell and Company was largely a product of its time, a period which was characterized by low standards of business ethics for a large number of business institutions in general and particularly for investment banking houses. It was a period of pronounced business prosperity and as Walter Lippmann has said in his *Method of Freedom:* "Prosperity covers a multitude of sins."[3] It would be indeed difficult to find a business which offers better support for this statement than does Caldwell and Company.

---

propriation by completely legal methods of the funds which Memphis Commercial Appeal, Incorporated, had on deposit with the Bank of Tennessee.

[3] P. 22.

APPENDICES

Appendix A

A Sample of Municipal Bonds Bought by Caldwell and Company. 1918-1930
(In Thousands of Dollars)

Year	Tenn.	Ala.	La.	Fla.	N. C.	S. C.	Va.	Ky.	Miss.	Ark.	Texas
1918	$ 200	$.....	$.....	$.....	$.....	$.....	$.....	$.....	$.....	$.....	$.....
1919	1,358		425						287		
1920	250		1,875								
1921	365	650	1,000	275							
1922	370		852	355	525						
1923	125	90	3,700					100			
1924	390	1,330		5,527	915				600		
1925	470	144		1,982	780	1,350			600		
1926	1,597	1,017	1,958	3,957	350			800	1,789		
1927	4,450	1,747	1,847	1,278	3,049	1,355	160	525	465		2,550
1928	4,364	175	55	225		1,276	185	2,975			2,314
1929	2,660	1,150	1,840	80	3,153	525	150	1,866	250	117	803
1930	384	10			87	25		235	236	131	558

Compiled from *Manufacturers Record* and "Report of Receivers of Caldwell and Company," Part i. The sample includes no state bonds.

Appendix B

First Mortgage Real Estate Bonds Originated and Underwritten by Caldwell and Company. 1922-1930

Property	Location	Date	Amount of Issue	Coupon Rate
Abilene Christian College	Texas	Sept. 1929	$ 200,000	6
Andrew Jackson Hotel	Nashville	July 1924	750,000	7
Andrew Jackson Hotel Addition	Nashville	Jan. 1925	200,000	7
Arkansas Baptist State Con.	Arkansas	Aug. 1927	900,000	6
Associated Motor Land Trust	St. Louis	May 1928	650,000	
Associated Motor Terminals	St. Louis	May 1928	400,000	6½
Bankhead Hotel	Birmingham	Nov. 1925	950,000	7
Baptist General Convention	Texas	June 1928	1,000,000	5½
Baylor University	Dallas	Jan. 1925	1,100,000	6
Beha Laundry	Louisville	Nov. 1925	75,000	6
Broadview Hotel	E. St. Louis, Ill.	May 1926	850,000	6½
Broad-Wal Garage	St. Louis		200,000	6½
Caddo Transfer & Warehouse	Shreveport, La.	Jan. 1925	140,000	7
Calvary Baptist Church	Dallas		30,000	
Carling Hotel	Jacksonville	Sept. 1925	1,000,000	7
Central Baptist Church	Johnson City, Tenn.	Nov. 1924	45,000	6
Citadel Square Baptist Church	Charleston, S. C.	Mar. 1926	160,000	
Citizens Bank Building	West Palm Beach	Sept. 1922	280,000	7
Cotton States Life Building	Memphis	1922	670,000	7
Cotton States Life Building	Nashville	Jan. 1925	350,000	7
Cumberland University	Lebanon, Tenn.	Oct. 1925	150,000	6½

APPENDIX B *(Cont.)*

FIRST MORTGAGE REAL ESTATE BONDS ORIGINATED AND UNDERWRITTEN BY
CALDWELL AND COMPANY. 1922-1930

Property	Location	Date	Amount of Issue	Coupon Rate
Dallas Sanitarium	Dallas	Nov. 1927	$ 400,000	6
Elks Lodge	Bristol, Tenn.	June 1927	55,000	6
First Baptist Church	Shreveport, La.	July 1924	125,000	6
First Methodist Church	Florence, Ala.	Oct. 1924	65,000	6
First Methodist Church	Johnson City, Tenn.	Oct. 1928	80,000	6
First Methodist Church	Fulton, Ky.	Oct. 1927	50,000	6
First Methodist Church	Sapula, Okla.	Mar. 1928	95,000	5½
First Presbyterian Church	Columbia, S. C.	Oct. 1925	175,000	6
First State Bank Building	Sarasota, Fla.	May 1924	250,000	
Florence Medical Clinic	Florence, Ala.	Feb. 1926	45,000	7
Glenn Court Apartment	Nashville	Nov. 1922	125,000	7
Grand Lodge of La., F.&A.M.	New Orleans	Mar. 1925	1,500,000	5½
Harry Nichol Building	Nashville	July 1922	400,000	7
Jefferson Davis Hotel	Montgomery, Ala.	June 1928	575,000	6½
John Wesley Hotel	Savannah, Ga.	Apr. 1923	225,000	7
Kentucky Children's Home	Lyndon, Ky.	May 1927	100,000	6
Kentucky Hotel	Louisville	Feb. 1924	1,750,000	7
Kings College	Bristol, Va.	Nov. 1928	100,000	6
Lambuth College	Jackson, Tenn.	Oct. 1924	100,000	6
Lander College	Greenwood, S. C.	Nov. 1925	90,000	6
LaSalle Apartments	Birmingham	Sept. 1926	180,000	7
Leontine C. Andrews	Atlanta	May 1928	250,000	6
Laurel Heights Apartment	Knoxville	Nov. 1923	152,500	7
Liles Building	Anniston, Ala.	June 1926	225,000	6
Lookout Mountain Hotel	Lookout Mt., Tenn.	July 1927	650,000	6
Markham Hotel	Gulfport, Miss.	Sept. 1926	600,000	6
Masonic Temple Association	Jackson, Miss.	Mar. 1925	190,000	5¾
McWilliams Building	Clarksdale, Miss.	Oct. 1926	275,000	6½
Merchants & Manuf. Terminal	Birmingham	Oct. 1926	275,000	6½
Midland & Atlantic Bridge	Ashland, Ky.	Aug. 1926	290,000	7
Montgomery Ward Building	Nashville	Apr. 1930	200,000	6½
Nashville Baseball Grandstand	Nashville	Jan. 1927	75,000	
National Birmingham Garage	Birmingham	Sept. 1927	380,000	6½
National Memphis Garage	Memphis	Apr. 1926	450,000	6½
Northern Garage	Nashville	Jan. 1925	65,000	7
Orndorff Hotel	El Paso	July 1925	825,000	6½
Rector Building	Little Rock		275,000	7
Riverside Baptist Church	Jacksonville	Oct. 1926	100,000	6
Seven-Wal Garage	St. Louis		275,000	6½
Seville Apartment	Tampa	Aug. 1925	150,000	7
Shepard Building	Montgomery, Ala.		250,000	7
Southern Bap. Mission Bldg.	Cuba	Jan. 1926	400,000	6
Southern Baptist Sanitarium	Texas		300,000	7
Tennessee Enterprises Theater	Chattanooga	July 1923	400,000	7
Tennessee Enterprises Theater	Knoxville	July 1929	450,000	6½
Prichard Hotel	Huntington, W.Va.	Sept. 1924	700,000	7
Wolford Hotel	Danville, Ill.	Mar. 1926	700,000	6½

SOURCE—Typewritten list of Bonds Originated and Underwritten by Caldwell and Company, in files of
Receivers of Caldwell and Company.
    NOTE—All those issues for which no date of issue is given were issued prior to 1926 and were retired prior
to the failure of Caldwell and Company.

Appendix C

Comparative Consolidated Balance Sheets of Caldwell and Company, Bank of Tennessee, and Rogers Caldwell and Company, Incorporated, 1918-1930*

Date†	1918	1920	1921	1922	1923	1925	1926	1927	1928	1929	Dec. 31, 1929	June 30, 1930	Sept. 30, 1930††
ASSETS													
Current Assets:													
Cash	$ 24,602	$ 300,910	$ 130,771	$ 472,223	$ 628,324	$ 538,651	$ 489,656	$ 668,217	$ 517,706	$ 982,090	$ 1,194,251	$ 602,191	$ 741,115
Receivables	359,211	1,086,076	2,018,677	1,886,854	2,233,491	2,194,708	1,615,983	2,367,463	2,161,175	1,948,907	3,843,038	2,987,639	2,584,830
Securities	1,702,879	6,355,996	6,474,269	6,476,966	6,175,836	12,661,994	9,197,464	9,884,542	13,688,038	15,236,859	15,986,717	19,425,247	17,169,025
Total Cur. Assets	$2,086,692	$7,742,982	$8,623,717	$8,836,043	$9,037,651	$15,395,353	$11,303,103	$12,920,222	$16,366,919	$18,167,856	$21,024,006	$23,015,077	$20,494,970
Investments in													
Controlled Cos.						$ 645,379	$ 3,694,497	$ 3,849,498	$ 5,937,577	$14,036,439	$15,263,548	$35,440,836	$35,353,411
Other Assets	49,745	222,315	118,547	557,228	2,121,710	1,137,098	761,668	1,100,418	1,722,614	2,317,559	1,223,028	511,050	904,488
Fixed Assets	1,483	7,924	9,731	101,502	490,037	522,026	523,730	520,730	534,122	546,370	564,509	548,921	541,926
Total Assets	$2,137,920	$7,973,221	$8,751,995	$9,494,773	$11,649,398	$17,699,856	$16,282,998	$18,390,868	$24,561,232	$35,068,224	$38,075,091	$59,515,884	$57,294,795
LIABILITIES													
Current Liabilities:													
Notes Payable	$ 161,061	$3,285,511	$ 910,516	$1,153,294	$ 3,289,262	$ 1,602,224	$ 3,428,040	$ 4,427,993	$ 8,488,137	$ 8,301,176	$ 7,320,824	$10,131,370	$ 8,009,050
Repurchase Agreem'ts			1,416,000				467,217	465,000	171,600	59,423	2,503,281	1,111,800	2,178,900
Deposits	1,463,855	4,457,902	4,475,339	5,591,265	5,883,655	12,470,842	8,226,864	7,305,954	11,338,190	9,733,985	12,192,141	14,420,638	12,189,239
Due to Controlled Cos.						40,000	1,697,912	3,199,960	1,365,930	6,913,294	7,526,149	3,724,161	4,990,544
Due to Broker	361,423		1,721,529	1,247,956	38,319	4,473		279,283	782,700	993,377	1,375,723	1,631,623	1,443,607
Other Cur. Liabilities	23,000	50,737	29,492	571,788	1,069,926	1,650,839	455,358	733,100	672,664	2,452,439	2,085,826	4,167,996	4,998,969
Total Cur. Liabilities	$2,009,339	$7,794,150	$8,552,876	$8,564,303	$10,281,162	$15,768,378	$14,275,391	$16,411,290	$22,819,221	$28,453,693	$33,003,944	$35,187,588	$33,810,309
Other Liabilities:													
Payables (not current)					240,653	168,888				3,030,000	2,020,000	1,411,182	1,325,825
First Mort. Bonds				400,000	400,000	380,000	370,000	360,000	345,000	330,000	322,500	315,000	311,250
Reserve for Sustained Security Losses											943,960		
Total Liabilities	$2,009,339	$7,794,150	$8,552,876	$8,964,303	$10,921,815	$16,317,266	$14,645,391	$16,771,290	$23,164,221	$31,813,693	$36,290,404	$36,913,770	$35,447,384
Net Worth:													
Capital Stock	$ 100,000	$ 100,000	$ 100,000	$ 100,000	$ 100,000	$ 100,000	$ 100,000	$ 100,000	$ 100,000	$ 1,000,000	$ 1,000,000	$ 2,000,000	$ 2,000,000
Reserve for Cont'g's				97,259	166,667	100,000	200,000	284,000	375,000	1,125,000	1,225,000		
Surplus	28,581	79,071	99,119	333,211	460,916	1,182,590	1,337,607	1,235,578	922,011	1,129,531*d*	440,313	20,602,114	19,847,411
Total Net Worth	$ 128,581	$ 179,071	$ 199,119	$ 530,470	$ 727,583	$1,382,590	$1,637,607	$1,619,578	$1,397,011	$ 3,254,531	$ 1,784,687	$22,602,114	$21,847,411
Total Liabilities and Net Worth	$2,137,920	$7,973,221	$8,751,995	$9,494,773	$11,649,398	$17,699,856	$16,282,998	$18,390,868	$24,561,232	$35,068,224	$38,075,091	$59,515,884	$57,294,795

*Bank of Tennessee included after 1918, Rogers Caldwell and Company, Inc., after 1925.

†Balance sheets from 1918 to 1923, inclusive, are as of December 31; others as of June 30, unless otherwise noted.

††This is the date of the last consolidated balance sheet of the companies prepared. "*d*" indicates deficit.

Source—Compiled from "Audit Report of Caldwell and Company" as of dates given.

APPENDIX D

ANNUAL EARNINGS OF CALDWELL AND COMPANY, BANK OF TENNESSEE, AND ROGERS
CALDWELL AND COMPANY, INC. 1918-1930*

Year ending December 31, 1918.................................$ 38,265
              December 31, 1919.................................   48,496
              December 31, 1920.................................   11,498
              December 31, 1921.................................   12,906
              December 31, 1922.................................   233,302
              December 31, 1923.................................   127,705
              December 31, 1924.................................   257,583
Six months ending June 30, 1925.................................   464,095
Year ending June 30, 1926.................................   28,281-loss
              June 30, 1927.................................   57,688
              June 30, 1928.................................   164,568-loss
              June 30, 1929................................. 1,907,522
              June 30, 1930................................. 2,511,000-loss

*Bank of Tennessee earnings are included after 1919 and Rogers Caldwell and Company, Incorporated, after 1925.

NOTE—The loss in 1930 does not take into account the arbitrary write-up of security values on the books of Caldwell and Company in connection with the merger of this company with BancoKentucky Company.

SOURCE—"Audit Report of Caldwell and Company," as of dates given.

APPENDIX E

INDUSTRIAL BONDS ORIGINATED AND UNDERWRITTEN BY CALDWELL AND COMPANY.

1924-1930

Corporation	Location of Home Office or Plant	Type of Bond	Date	Amount	Coupon Rate
Alabama Mills Company...........	Birmingham, Ala....	Mortgage .	Apr. 1928	$3,000,000	6½
Allen Corporation................	Franklin, Tenn......	Mortgage .	Nov. 1929	240,000	7
Alligator Company...............	St. Louis, Mo......	Debenture.	Aug. 1928	250,000	7
Apex Oil Company...............	Nashville, Tenn.....	Debenture.	May 1929	300,000	6½
Atlanta Laundries, Incorporated....	Atlanta, Ga........	Mortgage .	Jan. 1928	1,500,000	6½
Atlanta Laundries, Incorporated....	Atlanta, Ga........	Notes.....	Jan. 1928	500,000	7
Cadet Hosiery Company...........	Columbia, Tenn.....	Debenture	June 1929	1,000,000	6½
Chattanooga Implement and Manufacturing Company.......	Chattanooga, Tenn..	Mortgage .	Mar. 1929	150,000	7
Cloverland Dairy Products........	New Orleans, La.....	Mortgage .	Jan. 1928	725,000	6½
Cloverland Dairy Products........	New Orleans, La. ...	Debenture.	Jan. 1929	350,000	6½
Cumberland Portland Cement Co....	Cowan, Tenn........	Mortgage .	Aug. 1927	450,000	7
Estill Springs Sand and Gravel Co..	Estill Springs, Tenn..	Mortgage .	May 1929	87,000	7
Frank Silk Mills.................	Murfreesboro, Tenn..	Mortgage .	Apr. 1928	250,000	7
Gray-Knox Marble Company.......	Knoxville, Tenn.....	Mortgage .	Apr. 1926	350,000	7
Harlan-Wallins Coal Corporation....	Pineville, Ky.......	Mortgage .	Oct. 1924	600,000	7
Harlan-Wallins Coal Corporation....	Pineville, Ky.......	Debenture.	Apr. 1930	369,000	7
Kentucky Rock Asphalt Company ..	Louisville, Ky......	Mortgage .	June 1926	1,500,000	6½
Kentucky Rock Asphalt Company ..	Louisville, Ky......	Notes.....	June 1926	200,000	6
Layne & Bowler, Incorporated.....	Memphis, Tenn.....	Debenture.	Jan. 1927	850,000	6½
Memphis Commercial Appeal, Inc....	Memphis, Tenn......	Debenture.	May 1927	2,500,000	6½
Oak Manufacturing Company.......	Atlanta, Ga........	Mortgage .	Dec. 1927	350,000	7
Rock Hill Printing & Finishing Co...	Rock Hill, S. C......	Mortgage .	May 1929	1,100,000	6½
Saratoga Victory Mills............	Albertville, Ala......	Mortgage .	July 1928	825,000	6½
Southern Department Stores........	Louisville, Ky......	Notes.....	Jan. 1930	1,000,000	6
Tennessee Products Corporation....	Nashville, Tenn.....	Mortgage .	Jan. 1926	1,500,000	6½
Textile Realty Company..........	Decatur, Ala........	Mortgage .	Dec. 1926	380,000	7
Wakenva Coal Company...........	Kentucky..........	Mortgage·.	Jan. 1926	1,000,000	7
Wertham, Morgan, Hamilton Bag Company.....................	Nashville, Tenn.....	Notes	Mar. 1928	500,000	6½
Total volume of issues......				$21,826,000	

SOURCE—Compiled from typewritten list of bonds underwritten by Caldwell and Company in files of Receivers of Caldwell and Company.

APPENDIX F

BALANCE SHEET OF CALDWELL AND COMPANY, NOVEMBER 13, 1930

ASSETS		LIABILITIES	
Cash in banks and on hand .....$	67,552.43	Notes payable:	
Notes receivable, less reserve.....	381,942.44	Banks, demand.................$	3,581,882.94
Accounts receivable, less reserve..	444,829.21	Banks, time...................	1,588,822.93
Accrued interest, rentals and		Others.......................	792,565.20
concessions.............	185,198.67	Repurchase agreements.........	2,257,100.00
Due from officers and employees .	81,500.44	Deposits:	
Securities owned:		Demand......................	3,591,515.67
Certificates of deposit........	85,000.00	Time and trust funds...........	293,370.86
U. S. Government bonds.....	875.75	Bank overdraft...................	2,195.53
Foreign bonds..............	9,685.02	Due to Kidder, Peabody and Company	1,311,855.92
Corporation bonds...........	4,581,509.09	Customers balances................	237,990.56
Municipal bonds...........	710,056.93	Joint accounts and concessions payable	14,394.92
Stocks....................	4,071,678.57	Purchase commitments..............	3,064,356.21
Deposits on issues..........	1,295,368.64	Interim receipts...................	94,201.18
Bonds subject to repurchase.....	746,256.19	Accrued interest, taxes, etc..........	41,831.69
Investments in controlled		Dividend payable to Rogers Caldwell.	219,379.57
companies..............	20,720,997.36	Liability for securities borrowed......	697,875.00
Advances to controlled companies	1,951,920.02	Liability for securities sold short	299,859.12
Assets pledged with the Bank of		First mortgage bonds on office bldg...	310,000.00
Tennessee..............	2,036,752.73	First mortgages on other property....	247,084.89
Real estate, less depreciation....	381,237.78	Deferred credits to income..........	1,230.90
Drainage lands................	52,097.07		
Past due bonds and coupons.....	158,847.84	Total Liabilities........$18,647,513.09	
Certified checks...............	136,045.00		
Prepaid expenses, insurance, etc..	115,555.15		
Cash value corporation life ins....	74,210.00	**Net Worth**	
Bonds borrowed................	697,875.00		
Claims against Receiver of Bank			
of Tennessee.............	4,725.50	Reserve for Contingencies...........$	300,000.00
Office building, less depreciation..	489,191.66	Capital Stock.....................	2,000,000.00
Furniture, fixtures and		Surplus.........................	18,642,142.93
automobiles............	108,747.53	Total Net Worth.......$20,942,142.93	
		Total Net Worth and	
Total Assets......$39,589,656.02		Liabilities.........$39,589,656.02	

BALANCE SHEET OF THE BANK OF TENNESSEE, NOVEMBER 6, 1930

ASSETS		LIABILITIES	
Cash in banks and on hand......$	73,831.19	Notes payable:	
Notes receivable, less reserves....	734,574.17	Banks, demand.................$	1,844,100.00
Accounts receivable.............	34,502.99	Banks, time...................	1,043,000.00
Securities owned:		Deposit accounts:	
Certificates of deposit.......	257,295.60	Demand......................	3,568,382.60
Corporation bonds...........	1,890,652.26	Time deposits and trust funds....	3,935,469.57
Municipal bonds............	1,712,752.37	Due to Caldwell and Company....	201,540.18
Stocks....................	1,161,654.29	Due to controlled companies......	1,969,919.40
Investments in controlled		Outstanding drafts and bank over-	
companies..................	7,632,740.09	drafts.........................	32,359.12
Real Estate...................	211,418.34	Certified cheques..................	172,740.00
		Capital stock.....................	500,000.00
		Surplus...........................	441,910.43
Total Assets......$13,709,421.30		Total liabilities and net	
		worth.............$13,709,421.30	

SOURCE—Caldwell and Company: Balance sheet filed in *Dean* v. *Caldwell;* Bank of Tennessee: Balance sheet filed in *State of Tennessee* ex rel. *Robertson* v. *Bank of Tennessee.*

Contract and Supplemental Agreements Covering Merger of
Caldwell and Company and BancoKentucky Company

MEMORANDA OF AGREEMENT, made this 28th day of May, 1930, by
and between the BANCOKENTUCKY COMPANY, a Delaware Corporation, as first party, and CALDWELL & COMPANY, a Tennessee Corporation,
as second party.

WITNESSETH:

For and in consideration of the mutual promises and covenants of the
parties hereinafter contained, it is agreed:

1. The second party has increased its authorized capital from $1,000,000
divided into 10,000 shares of the par value of $100.00 each, to 20,000 shares
of the par value of $100.00 each.

2. The first party will issue and deliver to the second party 900,000 shares
of the par value of $10.00 each of its present authorized but unissued stock
for the additional 10,000 shares of stock of the second party, as provided in
Section 1 hereof, which said 10,000 shares the second party will issue and
deliver to the first party at the time of delivery to it of the aforesaid 900,000
shares of capital stock of the first party. Upon such mutual delivery of stock
the second party will deposit 200,000 shares of the said 900,000 shares of
capital stock of the first party with the Louisville Trust Company, Louisville,
Kentucky, to be held by said trust company for redelivery to the second
party upon the joint order of the respective presidents of the respective parties,
pending such examinations and investigations as the first party may desire
to make under Sections 7 and 8 of this agreement and as security of performance by the second party under Section 7 and 8.

3. At the time of such mutual delivery of stock, the first party will have
5,000,000 shares of stock of the par value of $10.00 each authorized, of which,
exclusive of the aforesaid 900,000 shares to be issued to the second party,
1,633,705 shares shall have been issued, and there is no option or sale of
stock of the first party outstanding (with the exception of options on an
aggregate amount of 250,000 shares of Common Capital Stock to H. M.
Byllesby & Company, Blythe & Company, and Wakefield & Company at
$26.50 per share, such option expires June 1, 1930).

4. At the time of said mutual delivery of stock, the second party will have
an authorized capital stock of 20,000 shares of the par value of $100.00
each, of which, exclusive of the 10,000 shares to be issued to the first party,
10,000 shares shall have been issued.

5. Neither party, pending consummation of this transaction by the mutual
delivery of said stocks, will make any disposition of any material portion of
its assets or take any unusual step or one other than in the due course of business except with the written consent of the other.

6. The first party covenants that it owns the following amounts of the total issued and outstanding stock of the following banks:

Name	Location	Total Capital Par Value	Amounts of Stock Owned
National Bank of Kentucky } Louisville Trust Company	Louisville	$5,750,000	$5,391,190
The Brighton Bank & Trust Company	Cincinnati	500,000	442,900
The Pearl-Market Bank & Trust Company	Cincinnati	600,000	472,160
Peoples Liberty Bank & Trust Company	Covington, Ky.	650,000	169,800
Central Savings Bank & Trust Company	Covington, Ky.	60,000	54,300
Ashland National Bank	Ashland, Ky.	800,000	626,300
First National Bank	Paducah, Ky.	150,000	136,500
Security Bank	Louisville, Ky.	300,000	209,000

The first party represents that on May 1, 1930, the combined or total capital, surplus and undivided profits of the aforesaid banks as shown by their books, were $17,192,870.76 and that the total assets of said banks, as shown by their books, were $124,129,966.95; that the first party had no liabilities and on said date it had cash to the amount of $1,297,893.47 and good and collectible notes in the principal amount of not less than $2,000,000.00.

7. The second party represents that as of May 28, 1930, its assets were of such fair aggregate value that, after deducting therefrom all of its liabilities, it had a net worth of not less than $9,000,000.00.

8. The first party shall have within twelve (12) months from date hereof, to satisfy itself as to the valuation of the assets of the second party in the computation of the net worth of the second party, as set forth in Section 7 of this agreement.

The President of the BancoKentucky Company and the President of Caldwell and Company will determine the valuation of such assets in the computation of the net worth of the second party with the right of either party to have competent assistants in reaching a determination. If the Presidents of the respective parties are unable to agree upon the valuation of any asset or assets, then and in that event, they will select a third party as arbitrator, who will then determine the said valuation. If the Presidents of the respective parties are unable to agree upon a third party to act as arbitrator as aforesaid, then and in that event they will select Mr. Whitefoord R. Cole who will, in turn, select an arbitrator.

If the net worth of the second party is ascertained to be less than $9,000,-000.00 based upon such valuation of its assets, then and in that event the second party at its option will deliver to the first party $2.22 in cash or stock of the first party (on basis of $25 per share) for each $1.00 of such deficit or the second party may forfeit any dividends on such part of its stock as is not now owned by the first party until an amount equivalent to such deficit is accumulated in the treasury of the second party (provided its stockholders other than the first party shall agree to such forfeiture of dividends). If the net worth of the second party is ascertained to be more than Ten Million ($10,000,000.00) Dollars, then and in that event the first party will deliver to the second party $1.00 of its capital stock (on basis of $25.00 per share) for each $1.00 of such excess.

9. The first party agrees that in the event it desires to sell or otherwise dispose of all or any part of its stock interest in the second party at any time subsequent to the consummation of this contract, that it will not sell or otherwise dispose of said stock without first offering same to Rogers Caldwell, his successors and assigns, for an amount not in excess of bona fide offers obtained for such stock from other parties.

10. The first party agrees to establish and maintain a cooperative working agreement between the security departments of its several banks and the second party in the distribution and underwriting of securities.

11. The second party will retain a substantial investment in the insurance business and may carry further its program to acquire, direct and develop insurance companies.

12. The general spirit and purpose of this agreement and the consolidation of the interests of the first and second parties is to further the development of each company and to create a vehicle for further extension and development in the commercial and investment banking and insurance fields.

In Witness Whereof, the parties hereto have executed this instrument in duplicate through their officers duly authorized to act by their respective boards of directors on the day and date first written above.

THE BANCOKENTUCKY COMPANY
(Signed) By James B. Brown, *President*
First Party
CALDWELL & COMPANY
(Signed) By Rogers Caldwell, *Pres.*
Second Party

Supplemental Agreements:

May 28, 1930
Louisville, Ky.

This supplemental agreement between BancoKentucky Company, a Delaware Corporation, party of the first part, and Caldwell and Company, a Tennessee Corporation, party of the second part.

WITNESSETH:

The parties have this day agreed that in consideration of mutual agreements in a contract of this date between the same parties, that first party has delivered to the second party 100,000 shares of its stock (being part of 900,000 shares referred to in said contract) in consideration of the second party agreeing to purchase from National Bank of Kentucky for 100,000 shares of BancoKentucky stock all of its rights, interests in or obligations owned by it of the Kentucky Manufacturing Company and National Motors Corporation.

The second party agrees to liquidate or otherwise dispose of said companies, their obligations and/or securities and to receive for services the necessary cost incurred and to repay the first party all net proceeds realized from any disposition that may be made of same.

(Signed) ROGERS CALDWELL

(Signed) JAMES B. BROWN

LOUISVILLE, KENTUCKY
May 28th, 1930

BancoKentucky Company
Louisville, Kentucky

GENTLEMEN:

For and in consideration of the mutual promises and covenants of Banco-Kentucky Company and Caldwell and Company, contained in contract of agreement dated the 28th day of May, 1930, I hereby agree that, in the event I desire to sell or otherwise dispose of all or any part of my interest in the capital stock of Caldwell & Company, at any time subsequent to the consummation of the aforesaid contract, that I will not sell or otherwise dispose of said stock without first offering same to you for an amount not in excess of bona fide offers obtained for purchase of such stock from other parties.

Very truly yours,

(Signed) ROGERS CALDWELL

APPENDIX H

Letter from J. DeWitt Carter to Rogers Caldwell

May 20, 1930

DEAR MR. CALDWELL:

You have asked me to give you in writing the thoughts expressed to you verbally the other day. In brief they are, that definite faults in the organization and financing of the business that have existed all along have led to a great many of the present problems, and that had they been corrected several years ago a great many of these present problems would not exist. In other words, that the most serious problems in the business today, poor loans, depressed morale and disorganization, are caused by a failure to properly organize and handle the business in the past, and that the financial problems and unsound methods used in some instances to secure funds are largely caused by a loose attitude in the past in the handling of such matters. It may be claimed by some that market conditions are the biggest cause of the present troubles but to my mind they are only secondary to the real cause. Market ups and downs are a part of the business risks assumed in entering the business and ought to be recognized as such and the business kept in shape so that it can weather such reverses without resorting to the means that have recently been used. The fact that many other houses have come to "grief" at this time may be used as a defense with outsiders but if we permit it to lull us into a feeling of not being wholly responsible for present conditions in this business we are only fooling ourselves and are on very dangerous ground. The present conditions in Caldwell and Company are the direct result of the way things have been handled in the past and unless something is done to correct these faults the business cannot continue as it is. Many efforts have been made by the writer and some of your associates to correct these conditions in the past, but have resulted in either nothing being done or only in temporary improvement. In my opinion you are largely responsible for this for reasons I shall mention later on. Let me state here that some of your associates have been seriously handicapped all along in their efforts along these lines by an impression on your part that their efforts to correct these conditions have been misinterpreted by you as being a desire on their part to advance their own personal interests thereby handicapping them in frankly discussing these matters with you. Furthermore many times when you have differed with them on important matters you have ascribed their position to some personal fault such as hardheadedness, prejudice, unfairness and so forth which is very wrong for it makes further discussion on the merits of a proposition impossible. I mention these matters only to try to get you to realize the handicaps I, for example, have had in whatever efforts I have put forth in the past to correct these situations in the business.

To my mind present conditions in Caldwell and Company are largely due to:

First: Failure to install and carry out sound policies and principles in building, managing, and handling the company and its affairs.

Second: Lack of adequate permanent capital (which probably would have been corrected in one way or another if the first had been handled properly).

It is very probable that there is no concern with the resources under its control and the ramifications that this one has that is managed as this one is. It has no clearly defined policies for the conduct of its business which are adhered to, nor definite lines of responsibility and authority fixed and recognized by its head. The greatest single factor contributing to this condition is a lack of appreciation on your part of the necessity for doing things in an organized way, and [of] a lasting desire on your part and willingness to work with people in your organization toward concerted thought, understanding, and action. The business has largely been conducted as the exigencies of the situation demanded, being in fact more of a trading vehicle for your activities than an institution. Commitments have been entered into in a more or less haphazard way, in many cases with only a part of the organization familiar with or sold on the deal, and with no very definite plans laid for getting out of them. Large deals have been gone into by you either without or against the judgment or advice of leading members of your organization. Likewise major undertakings as to new employees and departments of the business have been entered into by you without notice to your associates. Many times you have reversed your principal officers' decisions without even giving them a chance to voice their opinions or positions on the matters in question. While you probably have not considered it, the fact remains that you can not handle things in this manner in a large organization of people without seriously disturbing the peace of mind, enthusiasm, loyalty and effectiveness of them and particularly of your best men and closest associates in the business. Furthermore the handling of matters in this way results directly in lack of cooperation and serious questions as to responsibility and authority about which there should be no question. There are numerous instances where matters of paramount importance to the company and its customers have been handled in a similar offhand manner, your close associates in the business learning of them through outside sources or even in some instances through the newspapers; things in which we or our customers have large sums of money invested. Decisions are made on major changes in the structure of our assets without private and careful consideration between the heads of the business, but with outsiders present which makes free and frank discussion with Caldwell and Company's affairs in mind impossible. Your close associates in the business often find that their subordinates are much more in your confidence on this or that major problem than they are, thus diffusing responsibility and authority, creating friction and misunderstandings and dulling ambition. You sometimes criticize to their faces men far down in the organization, in some instances unfairly because you are not close enough to the details to know the true situation, which certainly doesn't build up their esteem for you. If they deserve correction or criticism it should be done by someone closer to them and their daily work than you are. Likewise when many of the men come to you with their problems in the business you are unsympathetic, often leaving the impression that you assume no part of the burdens for such problems, and therefore offering no hope of solution but at the same time you often make decisions on minor details which seriously affect these same men's problems and work. These are details which should be handled by your subordinates. You have so many interests and are so constantly interrupted by them and by people outside the business that it is hard for you to give connected thought to any one thing for any length of time or to allow one of your men which wishes to do so to talk to you long enough to finish to his satisfaction and understanding a conference with you. You are merely "hitting the high spots" on a great many things, not getting into the details of them as thoroughly as you should to make a proper decision, and not properly delegating the details or decisions to others.

Any desire or effort on the part of your associates to assume greater responsibilities in connection with organizing and handling the business and affairs of the company are largely frustrated by these conditions. Thus no efforts to organize the various units and individuals of the business into an effective whole are being made or will ever be effective unless you realize the necessity for it and conduct yourself accordingly. As a result you even more than ever are authority on all matters, no matter how inconsequential, thereby causing delays in decisions, temporizing with matters of vital importance, divergencies of opinion becoming apparent and general disorganization. You now as you have been all along are the only point of liaison between men and departments. In the past as now many honest differences of opinion exist between these men and departments and you are the only final word of authority for settlement of them. As it is you are often not available when they should be settled and as a result there are either costly delays in the settlement of the matter or they go unsettled. As a matter of fact many of them should never reach you as your time could be given to more important matters to better advantage.

Authority and responsibility in the organization flow in many different directions causing confusion and lack of proper control. They should flow downward through the organization in well defined boundaries. Like the waters of a river if kept in clearly defined channels authority and responsibility become a useful, powerful but controlled force, but if the channel is not well defined, they, like water, flow in many directions, forceless, useless and uncontrolled.

In my opinion a solution of the present situation lies largely in two things:

First. A full appreciation on your part of the great necessity in the business of proper organization and handling of matters in an organized way and at all times to give due regard to your associates in the business in all matters affecting them and the company or the operation of the business and the handling of matters important to it.

Second. That someone should be selected in whom you have the utmost confidence and who is well qualified to do the work and give full responsibility to do any and all things necessary to be done to properly organize the business so that its affairs can be handled in an efficient, economical, and concerted way and clothe him with sufficient authority and backing so that there can be no question in the minds of the people of the organization as to your confidence in him.

In selecting this man take your three or four senior officers into your confidence fully and let them see why you propose such a move, and give them in turn an opportunity to express themselves as to their opinions and ideas about such a move and the man selected. In fact let them act as an executive committee and have a voice not only in starting such a plan and selecting the man but in carrying on the work by meeting with you and the man from time to time and passing on major questions about the organization and its affairs. Make the utmost effort to have them fully satisfied as to the step and heartily in sympathy with the plan and the man and in turn let the man selected understand exactly their feelings and ideas about him and his work and make him realize the necessity for tact on his part toward them and their feelings. In other words arrange it so that the chance of a misunderstanding either now or later in such a move is reduced to a minimum. Let the appointment of such a man be announced to the entire organization so there can be no doubts in the minds of any as to his position and so that they can see visible signs of movement being made to correct past conditions and bring about a new order of things. Whoever undertook such a task in view of present conditions of the business would have a herculean task ahead of him, but notwithstanding this and the delicate situation involved in arranging for it, it is imperative that it be done, and it can be done.

It would be quite a task to enumerate the various things a man in this position should do, but one of the first things that needs to be done is to try to put the company on an earning basis which would necessitate not only a drastic cutting of expenses throughout the organization through eliminating of all unnecessary employees, unnecessary expenses of all kinds, but thought and effort should also be given means of increasing the company's revenues, not only through its present assets, but also through the purchase and sale of a larger number of securities suitable to present market conditions. One particular thing that should be done towards reduction of expenses would be for all the officers of the company to take sizeable reductions in their salaries. There is no use going into further detail as to the various things that should be done to create greater efficiency, economy and earning power and better morale. Many things which are needed and can be done are apparent to many who are in close touch with the day to day problems of the business.

If the proper principles of building an organization had been adopted in the past it is probable that the present financial situation would not exist for a better control would have been exercised over the affairs of the company resulting in a more orderly assumption of commitments and handling of them when they were assumed. A great deal of money could and would have been saved in operating the business had it been some one person's responsibility rather than anybody's and everybody's. Furthermore, proper principles of organization would probably have made everybody feel their [sic] responsibility to a greater degree than they have felt it under present conditions which breed the feeling that the business is privately owned and conducted.

Of course the most acute problem of the business today is adequate permanent capital with which to carry on the business. For that matter it has been a problem for a long time and without doubt has been the cause of serious problems in other directions. For example, it has been partly responsible for unwise buying of issues, which had it not been for the deposits involved we would probably have never bought. These issues have caused us great embarrassment, loss of prestige and thereby loss of sales power at a time when it is most needed. It has been the cause of abuses in our dealings with concerns in which the heads of Caldwell and Company have an interest, often causing wonder and doubt in the minds of the heads of these companies as to the financial stability of Caldwell and Company, thus to some extent undermining their respect and confidence in the organization. Likewise, because of our financial condition it has been necessary for the company to ask for abnormal accommodations at many banks and to carry loans in some of them almost continuously and without in many cases compensating balances causing questions as to our situation. Our financial position has caused us in many cases to pay abnormal rates of interest on deposits, and to secure unduly large deposits from the State of Tennessee which will probably some day be the source of damaging publicity. These and many things like them cause talk which adds to our general problem for there is much "discreet gossip" going on about our financial stringency which is apparent to many outside the business as well as in it. It is most apparent to some of the best men in the company who are no doubt in touch with that part of the business, and is no doubt causing them no little worry and uneasiness thus lowering their spirits and effectiveness. In this respect the situation is very serious and the danger that if it continues to go on it will become more and more apparent to an ever widening circle possibly causing precipitate withdrawals at some unexpected time. The financial standing of the company is being further impaired in the minds of those outside and inside the business by Colonel Lea's close connection with you and the company, and the handling of some of his obligations by the company and other concerns in which it is interested. The worst aspect of the financial situation are the practices which are being carried on in some instances at the present time to secure funds and the very bad situation in the Trust Department of the company with which you are familiar, but the effects of which I doubt whether you fully realize. These practices are not the result of present conditions in the business, but on the contrary present conditions are largely due to the same point of view in the past which would permit such conditions to develop. For several years I have made almost a lone and wholly unsuccessful effort to have these conditions corrected. It will never be possible as long as you countenance the giving of instructions to men to handle things in this way. It is a violation of the basic principles of sound business and has done untold harm in lowering the morale and enthusiasm of key men in the company. It is hard to picture to its fullest extent the very demoralizing and depressing effect that the long continued financial stringency has caused the principal executives and the organization as a whole. The situation is daily growing more serious, but without any concerted thought or action being given to it. We are financing from day to day hoping for something to turn up and resorting to more and more unsound methods. The situation should not be temporized with any longer as the company's asset situation is getting more and more involved and unwieldly and the organization is getting less and less effective.

A permanent solution of the company's financial problems will only come through drastic changes in policy and methods of handling the business and its affairs. In the meantime steps can be taken to at least temporarily improve the situation. Efforts should be made to collect all funds due us on notes and accounts receivable, and a more vigorous policy of enforcing our rights in the collection of all sums due the company should be inaugurated. Efforts should be made to sell all bonds and stocks that can be sold without letting whether they are sold at a loss or not be the determining factor. What we are facing is the saving of the business whatever the cost, and the most important element in doing this is money.

The company's quickest assets as of March 31, 1930, after full reserves are as follows:

Notes receivable	$1,304,088
Accounts receivable	702,942
Bonds and stocks originated by others or on which we had strong partners	1,613,128
Subject to repurchase by others	381,952
	$4,002,110

Not including cash as of that date.

To collect many of these notes and accounts will require a very firm attitude on the company's part which could be brought about by a thorough understanding among the executives of the company that each would be firm if appealed to by the maker of these obligations for further extensions. The policy of trying "to have our cake and eat it too" as you expressed it several weeks ago ought to be abandoned and an open policy should be adopted on the liquidation of some of the assets we are tied up with. To my mind our policy on the disposal of such assets has always been to adopt a trading attitude which might get us a few more dollars in the event of a sale but which makes a sale much harder to consummate. This has probably been done because of a feeling on our part that if it were known that an effort was being made to sell some of these properties that some people might take it as an evidence that we were in close finances. Conditions are such that much less talk would come from a frank attitude on the sale of these properties than from our present condition. Therefore, I feel that definite efforts should be made to sell the various parcels of real estate, banks and insurance companies, newspapers and industrial companies in which the company owns stock or control.

We have been unduly "easy" on the collection of funds due us or our customers from properties which we have financed often letting these situations get worse and worse simply because of lack of aggressiveness on our part. A much more aggressive situation ought to be adopted and carried out on these matters, and the collection of all kinds of past due bonds and coupons. A definite policy should be thought out and carried out with respect to future commitments. In my opinion no more commitments of any character should be made except of a character that can be sold promptly. Likewise no further loans or accounts receivable should be granted and in some manner further loans to Colonel Lea should be obviated.

Most important of all you as head of the house should go on record in no uncertain way with all parties in the organization concerned with the handling of finances as to a complete discontinuance at once of the abuses in the trust department.

I seriously doubt whether the company's house is in order enough for capital to be sought from outside sources except as a last resort. However, concerted thought ought to be given means of securing capital and if a plan can be devised which seems likely of success effort should be put behind it to secure execution.

The suggestions made in this letter with reference to means for a betterment of the financial situation and also for the adoption of sounder principles of organization and handling the business are made with the thought in mind that if adopted in the main and carried out they will lead to getting "the house in order," so that funds for capital can openly and successfully be sought at some later date.

The only other matter mentioned in our conversation was the suggestion made by me that you should have a long time ago rewarded some of your older associates in the business by providing some means for them to become interested in the business with you. This would not only have tied them closer to you but would have given them an interest different from the one they now have and in this way would have made them feel their responsibility all the more, and would have secured that last ounce of effort which is often the deciding factor between failure and success. These men have been quite instrumental in the development of the business, have shared its burdens and liabilities with you, have given some of the best years of their lives to your business, but are continuing from year to year as employees on salaries or bonuses with no means provided by which they can feel that they are building up a competency against their less productive periods. To my own knowledge two of your principal executives have expected for six or seven years that they would be provided a means by which they would become interested in the business and if they have felt this way it is probable that others have also. Being the type of men they are it is not a subject they would discuss among themselves. That they haven't been so recognized has no doubt been a discouragement to them and has probably caused an under the surface misunderstanding of you. Furthermore, ambitious and capable men throughout the company seeing no such recognition being given the men ahead of them are getting discouraged and are wondering what the future holds for them in their present connection. The high type of man power necessary in so many places in a business of this sort is not the type of man that will continue indefinitely merely as employees. Many examples exist in the business world of the soundness of the principle of having employees interested as owners in a business, and there are many evidences where failure to do so have proven the opposite. You know better than I do what your feelings are as to this idea. If you should decide to adopt such a plan the thoughts which were on your mind the other day about it could undoubtedly be worked out in accordance with your ideas.

I do not consider the present situation impossible of solution but under existing conditions in the business and a continuance of present policies and plan of operation the situation is serious and fraught with danger. Adversity and unpleasant experience can be valuable if we learn from them how to avoid them in the future. In fact they are the best teachers, but if we do not make every effort to profit by them in this way we are on dangerous ground and are slipping backward. Caldwell and Company is slipping backward at this time but the process can be reversed if we set ourselves to analyze the present situation and how we got into it and set up means to get out of it and keep out of it in the future. By doing so without further delay a new spirit can be brought about in the company by evidencing to the people in the organization that preparations are being made to benefit in the long run by the experience we have had and are now going through.

In giving you this picture of the business as I see it it is entirely possible that my views may be wrong and therefore my recommendations are unsound. Whether my views are wrong or not this is at least a very frank expression of the situation as I see it. You may feel that it is very poor diplomacy on my part to speak so frankly but if you will accept this letter in the spirit in which it was written you will not be offended for it is written only with a sincere desire on my part to be of service to you, the company and its customers.

In any event understand that I have only the best wishes for you and your success and that I shall always appreciate deeply my years of association with you because of your many sterling qualities and the many things you have done for me.

Yours very truly,

(Signed) DeWitt Carter

BIBLIOGRAPHY

NOTE: This bibliography contains a selected list of sources from which most of the primary data for this book have been obtained. Financial manuals, as well as governmental publications from which isolated facts or statistics have been taken, are omitted. Acknowledgment is made of all such sources in the footnotes.

FINANCIAL REPORTS AND OTHER DOCUMENTS CONCERNING
SPECIFIC COMPANIES

(Arranged according to company)

BancoKentucky Company
>Report to Stockholders for period ending December 31, 1929. March 10, 1930.
>Contracts covering merger with Caldwell and Company. May 28, 1930.

Bank of Tennessee
>Comparative monthly balance sheets. June 30, 1929, to November 6, 1930.
>Balance sheet and schedules of assets and liabilities. November 6, 1930.

Bank Securities Corporation
>Income tax return, supporting schedules, and correspondence concerning same. 1929.
>Correspondence files.

Bank Securities Corporation and West Tennessee Company
>Consolidated balance sheets and income accounts. March 31, June 30, July 31, August 31, December 31, 1929; December 31, 1930.

Caldwell and Company
>Audit Reports
>>Year ending December 31, 1918. Grannis-Blair Audit Company, Nashville, Tennessee. February 17, 1919.
>>Year ending December 31, 1921. Homer K. Jones and Company, Memphis, Tennessee. May 10, 1922.*
>>Year ending December 31, 1922. Ernst and Ernst, Cleveland, Ohio. May 28, 1923.
>>Year ending December 31, 1923. Ernst and Ernst, Cleveland, Ohio. February 27, 1924.
>>Fourteen-month period ending February 28, 1925. Ernst and Ernst, Cleveland, Ohio. June 13, 1925.
>>Four-month period ending June 30, 1925. Ernst and Ernst, Cleveland, Ohio. August 20, 1925.

* This and following audit reports cover Caldwell and Company and Bank of Tennessee.

Year ending June 30, 1926. Ernst and Ernst, Cleveland, Ohio. September 28, 1926.

Year ending June 30, 1927. Price, Waterhouse, and Company, St. Louis, Mo. September 17, 1927.*

Year ending June 30, 1928. Price, Waterhouse, and Company, St. Louis, Mo. August 20, 1928.

Year ending June 30, 1929. Price, Waterhouse, and Company, St. Louis, Mo. August 10, 1929.

Six-month period ending December 31, 1929. Accounting department of Caldwell and Company. February 13, 1930.

Eleven-month period ending May 31, 1930. Accounting department of Caldwell and Company.

Year ending June 30, 1930. Accounting department of Caldwell and Company. September 1, 1930.

Balance sheet, December 31, 1920.

Monthly financial statements. October, 1929-August, 1930. Prepared by accounting department of Caldwell and Company.

Schedule of pledged and unpledged securities, by months. June 30, 1929, to September 30, 1930.

Accountant's working papers. May 31, 1930.

Confidential report concerning financial condition of Caldwell and Company, from T. G. Donovan to J. DeWitt Carter. August 1, 1930.

Balance sheet and schedules of assets and liabilities. November 13, 1930.

Charter of Incorporation, State of Tennessee. October 1, 1917.

Amendment to Charter of Incorporation, State of Tennessee. June 30, 1922.

Amendment to Charter of Incorporation, State of Tennessee. April 15, 1930.

Minute Book of Stockholders' and Directors' Meetings. 1917-1930.

Contract covering sale of Missouri State Life Insurance Company stock to Inter-Southern Life Insurance Company. April, 1930.

Contract with North Carolina Bank and Trust Company covering loan to Caldwell and Company. May 7, 1930.

Letter to Lehman Brothers concerning purchase of Shenandoah Life Insurance Company. January 25, 1930.

Prospectuses of industrial and real estate bond issues.

Constitution Publishing Company

Contracts covering purchase of the company by Caldwell and Company and Luke Lea. 1927.

Fourth and First Banks, Incorporated

Financial statements. June 30, 1931.

---

*This and following audit reports cover Caldwell and Company, Bank of Tennessee, and Rogers Caldwell and Company, Incorporated.

Harlin-Wallins Coal Corporation
  Balance sheet. September 30, 1930.
  Voting trust agreement. November 10, 1924.
Home Insurance Companies
  Report on Examination as of June 30, 1929. Joseph Fraggett and Company, Incorporated. September 19, 1929.
  Contracts covering sale of these companies by A. B. Banks, *et al.,* to Caldwell and Company. May, 1929.
Insurance Securities Corporation
  Reports and Accounts, as of June 30, 1928. Price, Waterhouse, and Company. August 20, 1928.
  Reports and Accounts, as of June 30, 1929. Price, Waterhouse, and Company. August 10, 1929.
  Monthly balance sheets and income accounts. July 31, 1929, to May 31, 1930; also September 30, 1930.
  Charter of Incorporation, State of Delaware. January 5, 1927.
Kentucky Rock Asphalt Company
  Annual Report to Stockholders. December 31, 1930.
  Voting trust agreement. December 1, 1926.
Memphis Commercial Appeal, Incorporated
  Financial and operating statements. October, 1930.
Nashville Baseball Association
  Balance sheet and income account. December 15, 1930.
Shares-in-the-South, Incorporated
  Annual Report to Stockholders, as of January 31, 1929. February 11, 1929.
  Balance sheet and income account. December 31, 1929.
  Certified Balance Sheet and Relative Exhibits. January 31, 1930. Price, Waterhouse, and Company. February 3, 1930.
  Annual Report to Stockholders, as of January 31, 1930. February 5, 1930.
  Financial reports prepared by accounting department of Caldwell and Company. Submitted in letter of August 6, 1929.
  Resolution passed by Board of Directors. March 6, 1929.
Southern Banks, Incorporated
  Balance sheet. October 31, 1930.
  Charter of Incorporation, State of Tennessee. September 2, 1930.
  Minute Book of Stockholders' and Directors' Meetings. 1930-1931.
Southern Publishers, Incorporated
  Audit Report covering period from April 1, 1927, to February 25, 1931. W. L. McFarland and Company, Nashville, Tenn.
  Financial statements, February 28, 1929.
  Minute Book of Stockholders' and Directors' Meetings. 1927-1930.
West Tennessee Company
  Schedule of assets turned over to Rogers Caldwell and Luke Lea. April 9, 1931.

MEMORANDA PREPARED FOR RECEIVERS OF CALDWELL AND COMPANY
CONCERNING AFFILIATED COMPANIES

Apex Oil Company. Edward J. Heitzeberg. January 2, 1931.

Associated Life Companies, Incorporated. Thomas W. Goodloe. Not dated.

Atlanta Laundries, Incorporated. Edward J. Heitzeberg. January 2, 1931.

BancoKentucky Company. Thomas W. Goodloe. December 15, 1930.

Cooper, Wells and Company. Edward J. Heitzeberg. Not dated.

Cumberland Portland Cement Company. Edward J. Heitzeberg. January 3, 1931.

Fair Stores Company. J. DeWitt Carter. Not dated.

Inter-Southern Life Insurance Company. Thomas W. Goodloe. Not dated.

Kentucky Rock Asphalt Company. Edward J. Heitzeberg. Not dated.

Kentucky Rock Asphalt Company. Edward A. Goodloe. December 15, 1930.

Mark Henderson Company. R. L. Voss. December 19, 1930.

Nashville Baseball Association. R. L. Voss. December 16, 1930.

Nashville Properties, Incorporated. L. B. Stevens. December 6, 1930.

Nashville Suburban Development Company. L. B. Stevens. December 16, 1930.

Real estate bond issues in default. L. B. Stevens. March 28, 1931.

Rock Hill Printing and Finishing Company. Edward J. Heitzeberg. Not dated.

Southern Department Stores, Incorporated. Edward J. Heitzeberg. Not dated.

Southern Surety Company of New York. J. DeWitt Carter. December 22, 1930.

Spur Distributing Company. Thomas W. Goodloe. Not dated.

Tennessee Products Corporation. Edward J. Heitzeberg. Not dated.

LETTERS

Bugg, R. T., Tennessee Bank Examiner. Letter to writer concerning liquidation of Bank of Tennessee and Liberty Bank and Trust Company. February 10, 1937.

Caldwell, James E. Letters to Stockholders of Fourth and First Banks, Incorporated. November, 1933.

Crutcher, William H., Jr., Louisville attorney. Letter to writer concerning law suit against the directors of National Bank of Kentucky. March 30, 1937.

Davis, Paul M. Letter to Stockholders of Fourth and First Banks, Incorporated. November, 1933.

Donovan, Timothy G. Letter to Honorable J. M. Broughton, Raleigh, North Carolina, concerning pardon for Colonel Luke Lea. June 7, 1935.

Donovan, Timothy G. Letter to Governor J. C. B. Ehringhaus, Governor of North Carolina, Raleigh, North Carolina, concerning pardon for Colonel Luke Lea. June 1, 1935.

Hill, James B., Chairman Bondholders' Protective Committee. Form letters to bondholders concerning defaulted Caldwell bonds. 1931.

Independent Protective Committee. Form letters to bondholders concerning defaulted Caldwell bonds. 1931.

Maddin, Percy D. Letter to Stockholders of Fourth and First Banks, Incorporated. November, 1933.

Moore, J. Merrick, Little Rock attorney. Letter to writer concerning Caldwell purchase of Home Insurance Companies of Arkansas. September 3, 1935.

Wasson, Marion, Arkansas Bank commissioner. List of Arkansas state banks that were controlled by A. B. Banks' interests and letter to writer concerning same. July 23, 1935.

COURT DECISIONS

Anderson v. *Akers*, et al., 7 Federal Supplement, 924 (1934); 9 Federal Supplement, 151 (1934); 11 Federal Supplement, 9 (1935).

Atherton, et al. v. *Anderson*, 86 Federal (2d), 518 (1936).

Gibson County v. *Fourth and First National Bank*, 96 Southwestern (2d), 184 (1936).

Lea, et al. v. *Citizens and Southern National Bank*, et al., 27 Federal (2d), 385 (1928).

Maryland Casualty Company v. *McConnell*, 148 Tennessee, 656 (1923).

State of Arkansas v. *Banks*, 48 Southwestern (2d), 848 (1932).

State of North Carolina v. *Davis*, 203 North Carolina, 49 (1932).

State of North Carolina v. *Lea*, et al., 203 North Carolina, 13, 35, 317 (1932).

State of Tennessee v. *Rogers Caldwell*, 164 Tennessee, 325 (1932).

State of Tennessee, ex rel. v. *Caldwell*, et al., 163 Tennessee 77 (1931).

State of Tennessee, ex rel. v. *Caldwell*, et al., 111 Southwestern (2d), 377 (1937).

State of Tennessee, ex rel. *Lea* v. *Brown and Lakey*, 64 Southwestern (2d), 842 (1933).

COURT RECORDS

Anderson, Receiver of National Bank of Kentucky v. *Akers*, et al., No. 649 in Equity, United States District Court for the Western District of Kentucky, Louisville, 1931-1934. Original Bill, Transcript of Evidence, Briefs, and Special Master's Report.

Commonwealth of Kentucky v. *Rogers Caldwell*, Jefferson Circuit Court, Criminal Division, Louisville, Kentucky. Two indictments dated April 3, 1931, and May 2, 1931.

Dean, et al. v. *Caldwell and Company*, No. 434 in Equity, United States District Court for the Middle District of Tennessee, Nashville, 1930-1936. A vast number of petitions, answers, orders, and reports in this case, in which Caldwell and Company was placed in receivership, have been examined and used. While it has not been thought necessary to list all of these

records, among the more important were: Records concerning claim arising from purchase of Home Insurance Companies. Records covering sale
of controlling stock of Inter-Southern Life Insurance Company to the
Keystone Holding Company and various petitions filed by Inter-Southern
Life Insurance Company in the case. Petitions of Devonstreet and Company for the claim of Kidder-Peabody and Company. Petitions of Receiver
of Holston-Union National Bank. Petitions of Receivers and Attorneys-
for-Receivers for fees. Report of Special Master. Report of Receivers of
Caldwell and Company, Parts I and III.

Knox County, Tennessee v. *Fourth and First National Bank,* et al., No. 44871,
Part II, Chancery Court of Davidson County, Nashville, 1932. Original
Bill and Exhibits thereto.

Laurent, Receiver of BancoKentucky Company v. *Akers,* et al., No. 206688,
Jefferson Circuit Court, Chancery Division, Louisville, 1931. Original
and Supplemental Bills, Transcript of Evidence, Exhibits, and Orders.
Among the more important exhibits was the Minute Book of BancoKentucky Company.

Nashville Trust Company, Trustee, et al. v. *Southern Publishers, Incorporated,*
et al., No. 42737, Part II, Chancery Court of Davidson County, Nashville,
1930-1931. Petitions, Answers, and Orders.

State of North Carolina v. *Wallace B. Davis, Luke Lea, and Luke Lea, Jr.,* No.
585, Supreme Court of North Carolina, 1931-1932. Transcript of Proceedings and Briefs.

State of Tennessee v. *Rogers Caldwell,* Davidson Criminal Law, No. 14, Supreme Court of Tennessee, December Term, 1931. Bill of Exceptions and
Briefs.

State of Tennessee, ex rel. *Luke Lea and Luke Lea, Jr.,* v. *Laurence E. Brown
and Frank Lakey,* Supreme Court of Tennessee, 1933. Reply Brief of
Defendants.

State of Tennessee, ex rel. *D. D. Robertson* v. *Liberty Bank and Trust Company,* No. 42664, Part II, Chancery Court of Davidson County, Nashville,
1930-1935. Petitions, Answers, Reports, and Orders.

State of Tennessee, ex rel. *D. D. Robertson* v. *Bank of Tennessee,* No. 42644,
Part I, Chancery Court of Davidson County, Nashville, 1930-1935. Petitions, Answers, Reports, and Orders.

State of Tennessee, ex rel. *L. D. Smith* v. *Bank of Tennessee,* et al., No.
42720, Part I, Chancery Court of Davidson County, Nashville, 1930. Petitions and Answers.

State of Tennessee, ex rel. *L. D. Smith* v. *Rogers Caldwell,* et al., No. 42721,
Part II, Chancery Court of Davidson County, Nashville, 1930. Petitions
and Answers.

State of Tennessee, ex rel. *L. D. Smith* v. *Nashville Trust Company, Trustee,*
et al., No. 42719, Part II, Chancery Court of Davidson County, Nashville,
1930. Petitions and Answers.

United States of America v. *James B. Brown, Charles F. Jones, and Rogers Caldwell*, United States District Court for the Western District of Kentucky, Louisville, 1931-1932. Indictments and Orders.

United States of America v. *J. Basil Ramsey*, No. 11672, United States District Court for the Eastern District of Tennessee, Knoxville, 1931-1935. Indictments and Transcript of Evidence.

United States of America, ex rel. *Rogers Caldwell* v. *Lillard, United States Marshal for the Middle District of Tennessee*, et al., No. 2236, United States District Court for the Middle District of Tennessee, 1932. Petitions, Briefs, Exhibits, and Orders.

GOVERNMENTAL DOCUMENTS

Pole, J. W. (Comptroller of Currency of the United States), "National Bank of Kentucky, Louisville, Kentucky, Brief of Reports of Examinations and Actions Taken by Office of the Comptroller of the Currency," *Hearings on the Operations of the National and Federal Reserve Banking Systems*, Part v. Seventy-first Congress, Third Session.

State of Tennessee, *House Journal of the Sixty-seventh General Assembly*, 1931.

State of Tennessee, *Opinions of Attorney General L. D. Smith*, September, 1926-September, 1930.

State of Tennessee, *Opinions of Attorney General L. D. Smith*, October, 1930-September, 1931.

State of Tennessee, *Public Acts*, 1909, 1913, 1929.

State of Tennessee, *Senate Journal of the Sixty-seventh General Assembly*, 1931.

State of Tennessee, Special Legislative Investigating Committee, *Hearings*, January-May, 1931; *Interim Report*, March, 1931; *Second Report*, May, 1931; *Minority Report*, May, 1931. All of the *Hearings* were not available in spite of the provision that they be placed in the office of the Secretary of State for public inspection. That part of the *Hearings* that were on file were readily made available to the writer but the testimony of many witnesses, especially that of some of the former officials of Caldwell and Company, had not been placed on file.

NEWSPAPERS AND PERIODICALS

Best's Insurance News (Life Edition) (New York), 1927-1934.

Chattanooga Daily Times, 1928-1931.

Commercial and Financial Chronicle (New York), 1915-1930.

Knoxville Journal, 1928-1931.

Louisville *Courier-Journal*, 1930-1931.

Manufacturers Record (Baltimore), 1915-1930.

Memphis *Commercial Appeal*, 1928-1936.

Memphis *Press-Scimitar*, 1928-1931.

Nashville Banner, 1918-1935.

Nashville Tennessean, 1918-1935.

Raleigh *News and Observer,* 1930.

State and Municipal Compendium, supplement to *Commercial and Financial Chronicle* (New York), 1915-1930.

Time, the Weekly Newsmagazine, 1931-1937.

MISCELLANEOUS

Alexander, T. H. "A Rich Man's Son Earns His Own Success," *The New South,* I (March, 1927), 23 ff.

——, "Austin Peay: A Brief Biography," in *Austin Peay . . . A Collection of State Papers and Public Addresses.* Ed., Mrs. Austin Peay. Kingsport, Tenn.: Southern Publishers, Inc., 1929.

"Development of Caldwell and Company." A brief, mimeographed pamphlet prepared by Caldwell and Company for use in its salesmen's training courses. Not dated.

Proceedings of Sales Convention of Caldwell and Company, St. Louis, October 10, 11, 1927. Nashville: Caldwell and Company, 1927.

Proceedings of Sales Convention of Caldwell and Company, Louisville, December 10, 11, 1928. Nashville: Caldwell and Company, 1929.

GENERAL WORKS

Brandeis, Louis D. *Other People's Money and How the Bankers Use It.* Washington: National Home Library Foundation, 1933.

Caldwell, James E. *Recollections of a Life Time.* Nashville: Baird-Ward Press, 1923.

Cartinhour, Gaines T. *Branch, Group, and Chain Banking.* New York: Macmillan Co., 1931.

Coulter, Ellis M. *William G. Brownlow, Fighting Parson of the Southern Highlands.* Chapel Hill: University of North Carolina Press, 1937.

Flynn, John T. *Investment Trusts Gone Wrong.* New York: New Republic, Inc., 1930.

Graham, B. and Dodd, D. L. *Security Analysis.* New York: McGraw-Hill Book Company, 1934.

Hillhouse, Albert M. *Municipal Bonds: A Century of Experience.* New York: Prentice-Hall, Inc., 1936.

Lagerquist, W. E. *Investment Analysis.* New York: Macmillan Co., 1922.

Leven, M., *et al. America's Capacity to Consume.* Washington: The Brookings Institute, 1934.

Lippmann, Walter. *Method of Freedom.* New York: Macmillan Co., 1934.

INDEX